MONOGRAPH SERIES

UNITED STATES CATHOLIC HISTORICAL SOCIETY

Volume 37

ST. PATRICK'S CATHEDRAL
NEW YORK

A POPULAR HISTORY OF THE ARCHDIOCESE OF NEW YORK

By

REV. MSGR. FLORENCE D. COHALAN

Yonkers, New York
United States Catholic Historical Society
1983

Published by the United States Catholic Historical Society
c/o St. Joseph's Seminary, Dunwoodie, Yonkers, N.Y. 10704

©1983 by the U.S. Catholic Historical Society and
Rev. Msgr. Florence D. Cohalan

LC Card number: 82-084246
ISBN: 0-930060-17-2
ISSN: 0146-5651

Cover Illustrations by: John J. Mahoney
Book Design and Production: Bookmakers, Inc., Washington, D.C.

Foreword

What is essential to writing a book of local history? Certainly, an author needs to have an abundance of factual knowledge, enthusiasm for research, perseverance, and the ability to analyze as well as synthesize.

What is helpful to writing such a history? Certainly, an author needs to be endowed with a deep personal interest and commitment, a sense of humor, balance and selectivity in dealing with material, and a generosity of spirit—the desire to share all of this with others.

Monsignor Florence Cohalan, pastor of St. Paul's Parish, Staten Island, has demonstrated all of the above in compiling a history of the Archdiocese of New York, and in addition, he brings to the task a deep sense of faith and love acquired during a lifetime of priestly service as a dedicated professor and pastor.

In 1975, to mark the Centennial of the creation of the first American cardinal, Monsignor Cohalan wrote an interesting biographical sketch of John Cardinal McCloskey, Archbishop of New York. At that time, I asked that he expand his work into a book that would, in a popular way, trace our roots back to the founding of the Diocese in 1808. He graciously agreed to undertake this task, and this book is the result of his dedicated scholarship.

Monsignor Cohalan has chosen to sketch the history of the Archdiocese in chapters devoted to each of the eight Bishops and Archbishops of New York who served God's people and proclaimed the Good News of Jesus Christ.

Church history must always recognize that as Christians we live with an eye to eternity. However, we must also be concerned with the present and plan for the future, never overlooking the heritage of faith from the past.

I am grateful to Monsignor Cohalan for this fine work in which he gives us the insight into accomplishments achieved by all of our predecessors with the help of God.

I also wish to express my appreciation to the United States Catholic Historical Society, and to all who collaborated with Monsignor Cohalan in producing and publishing this volume.

It is my hope that those who read its pages will join me in thanking God for leading the people of the Archdiocese by His grace to a life of faith, hope and love.

†Terence Cardinal Cooke
Archbishop of New York

Preface

Interest in a complete and scholarly history of the Archdiocese of New York has been expressed in various quarters for many years. Father John Talbot Smith's two volumes appeared in 1905 and, though they are still useful, they are outdated and are practically unobtainable. Francis Cardinal Spellman's ambitious plans for a full-length history of the Archdiocese itself and a biography of each bishop and archbishop were blocked by circumstances beyond his control. He had to content himself with only one of the many volumes he had in mind and that was *The Cardinal Spellman Story* by Father Robert I. Gannon, S.J. The obstacles he encountered remain, for, as time passes, the Church in New York undergoes continuous and rapid change, new problems are added to old, and the material accumulates at an alarming rate. It is clear that when the full-length history appears, it must be a multivolume work produced by many hands. Such a work is not even in the planning stage now and is unlikely to appear in the foreseeable future.

That being so, it seemed to those most competent to judge that there is room for a much less ambitious project. They thought of an interim report in the form of a single volume covering the fortunes of the Catholics in the New York area from the arrival of the Dutch on Manhattan Island in 1626 to the death of Cardinal Spellman in 1967. For almost half of that time, from 1626 to 1783, or from the coming of the Dutch to the departure of the British, there were few traces of a Catholic presence in what is now New York State. Things changed in 1784 when it became possible for the Catholics to practice their religion openly. The formation in that year of the first Catholic congregation in the State (St. Peter's on Barclay Street in Manhattan), the erection of the Diocese of New York in 1808, and the coming of the first resident bishop in 1815 were events of lasting significance. They marked the initial stages of a growth that though slow at first, and always unevenly spread, has continued to the present day.

That growth recalls the gospel parable of the mustard seed. The twenty active members of St. Peter's congregation in 1784 have grown into ten dioceses—eight in New York State plus Newark and Paterson in New Jersey—that made up the original Diocese of New York. Those dioceses now have a combined Catholic population more than twice as numerous as the total population of the United States in 1790. Remarkable as their story is, it is only a small part of the greater story of the growth of the Church in the English-speaking world since 1815. That is one of the major surprises in the entire history of the Universal Church.

In this country alone while the total population has multiplied by about fifty-five since 1790, the known Catholic population has multiplied by about sixteen-hundred and has grown from less than 1% to about 23% of the total. The Catholic community in the United States is now the fourth largest in the world, outranked only by Brazil, Mexico, and Italy. Its growth, like that of the entire country, was due chiefly to immigration. The available figures indicate that about 42 million immigrants, millions of them Catholics, came to this country between 1820 and 1960 and about 34 million came from Europe. It was the largest peaceful migration ever known and it is still in progress. An unknown number but surely many millions have come since 1960, the greater part from Latin America and thus linked in some way with the Church.

The Church organization grew to match the growth in America's area and population. The one diocese of 1789 and the six of 1808 have grown to over 170. Some are among the largest and most important in the world. They include the Military Ordinariate with about 1,850,000 Catholics, and seven dioceses for Catholics in the Oriental Rites. Only two dioceses, Fairbanks and Juneau in Alaska, have fewer Catholics than the Diocese of New York had in 1815.

Growth in area and population were not the only unexpected major developments that affected both the Church and the Republic. When the Diocese of New York was erected, Thomas Jefferson was President of the United States. Though he had practically doubled the area of the country by the Louisiana Purchase, America was a poor and unimportant country. It hardly entered the calculations of the Great Powers, whose attention was focused on Napoleon, then at the height of his power. He was the master of France, and France, already the master of Europe, was striving to dominate the civilized world. Napoleon also threatened the Holy See, which had reached its lowest point in centuries when Pius VI died in a French prison in August 1799. Pius VII had reason to fear a similar fate when the French occupied Rome in February 1808. There were some who thought of him as they had thought of Pius VI, and as others were to think of Pius IX, as the last of his line. Today, no one thinks that of John Paul II.

Since 1808 the circumstances of daily life in the western world have changed more than in all preceding ages. If we consider only such basic items as food, clothing, housing, utilities, education, transportation, communication, medical services, and sanitation, it is fair to say that a man who lived in New York when Jefferson was president had less in common with a late 20th century American than with a man who lived in Rome under Julius Caesar.

The key to most of these changes was industrialization, which was made possible by, and in turn fostered, the invention of machinery and the utilization of new sources of power. The Industrial Revolution created the huge urban proletariat that is characteristic of modern society and the source of many of our most serious social problems. At the same time, it created the wealth that made our present social programs possible. It was linked closely with the Scientific Revolution.

Though New York's part in the overall picture of the Church in America is small, it is far from unimportant. One of the oldest and largest dioceses, it has held its position in an increasingly cosmopolitan city that has long been the cultural and financial center of the country and has been the gateway for millions of immigrants. Each ethnic group that entered it left a colony here, and a major part of the history of the Archdiocese has been its continuous, and of course never-wholly-successful, attempt to cope with successive waves of immigrants.

That effort has always been made with insufficient personnel and money and with an ample supply of grumblers like those who greeted Father Whelan in 1784. While ethnic diversity has complicated the work of the Church in New York, it has enriched its spiritual life and added to the number and variety of educational and charitable works in which it takes legitimate pride.

The vast majority of immigrants were poor but the practicing Catholics in their ranks were willing and often eager to share their modest resources with the Church. They found in her the guardian not only of their faith but of the cultural traditions they clung to in the new, often hostile, environment in which they found themselves. As their situation improved they provided vocations to the priesthood and religious life. Though many and perhaps most of them had much to suffer during the transition, the ultimate rewards were great, and they found the freedom they sought. It gave them an opportunity for economic, cultural, social, and political advancement. They found too that the Church was free to carry out her mission and had both the leadership and the inner strength needed to survive the inevitable and formidable opposition encountered.

Until recently, most of her critics were outside her ranks, and her teaching on faith and morals was given clearly, firmly, and with conviction and authority.

The deep self-inflicted wounds the Church has suffered since 1963 have obscured her teaching for many, and have weakened her hold on millions of Catholics in this country alone. The internal conflicts came at a time when much of the anti-Catholic bigotry of old had died down or taken different forms. How much of the change in non-Catholic attitudes is due to a general loss of interest in organized religion and the consequent shift to political instead of religious bigotry is disputed. So is the amount of credit due to a genuine growth of religious tolerance or to the Ecumenical Movement.

What is not disputed is that anti-Catholic feeling is still very strong. The far-reaching claims the Church can never renounce must always inspire opposition in those who resent them on conscientious grounds, and that opposition will vary according to the ever-changing circumstances of time and place. Today, it is directed more at Catholic moral teaching than at the Church as an institution or at the Holy See itself.

In spite of external opposition and widely publicized internal confusion, in spite of laxity and disaffection, the Church has become and will remain a vital and powerful force in American life, to which, as many of her critics admit, she has made a major contribution. She has latent resources of inner strength and of goodwill outside her ranks, of which friend and foe are sometimes unaware. They surfaced during the triumphal visit of Pope John Paul II in 1979. The heartening demonstrations of respect and affection he evoked on all sides were due not only to his quite exceptional personality but to a changed perception of his Office by millions of non-Catholics—that would have astonished their ancestors and ours.

The growth of the New York Archdiocese and the richness and diversity of its life and works make it difficult to compress its story within a reasonable compass, but both principle and practicality suggest a solution. In its Dogmatic Constitution on the Church (*Lumen Gentium,* November 21, 1964) Vatican II reminds us that the individual bishop is the visible principle and foundation of unity in his particular diocese. Attention was focused, therefore, on each of the successive bishops and archbishops who have exercised jurisdiction in New York. After the necessary sketch of the conditions that existed in North America before the establishment of the American Hierarchy in 1789, a section is devoted to each episcopal administration, with an account of each incumbent's background; his early life and career; the circumstances in which his appointment was made; his talents, resources, problems, programs, successes, and failures; and with some attention to his relations with the community at large and his role, if any, in the national and international affairs of the Church.

Other interesting and valuable material has been omitted. There is no mention of the many priests, religious and lay people who rendered special service in their day. Separate volumes could be devoted to, among other things, the Catholic publishers and periodicals, the growth of the Catholic schools on every level, the charitable institutions and works of every kind, the various groups of national parishes, the lay societies, and the rise of the Catholics in the professions. There is a story behind each of the institutions. Few of them owe much to the rich and powerful, and most of them were made possible chiefly by a faith, industry, and capacity for sacrifice that would seem incredible if the records were not so clear.

The record of the Catholic Church in New York would be immeasurably poorer if it were not for the contribution made by the religious communities, most of which have still to tell their story. They came from many countries, and all of them, including those founded here, had a hard struggle.

Except for the section on the Corrigan administration, which makes use of material on Dr. Edward McGlynn which is in the possession of the Archdiocese, and the diary of Monsignor Richard L. Burtsell which, with a few gaps, covers the years from 1865 to January 1912, this history is based entirely on secondary sources. Unless described as estimates, population figures are taken from official sources.

I am grateful to the present Archbishop of New York, His Eminence Terence Cardinal Cooke, for having entrusted this project to me and for having offered me all the assistance available, for having waited patiently as its completion went considerably beyond the estimated time, contributing a foreword, and facilitating its publication.

Thanks are due also to Monsignor Gustav J. Schultheiss, who shared his knowledge of the Spellman administration with me, and to Monsignor Eugene V. Clark, who read the entire manuscript with his customary painstaking care and critical acumen. Both of them made many helpful suggestions. With them I associate in memory Monsignor Joseph M. Egan (1893–1959), a dear personal friend, a fine scholar, and one of the best professors Dunwoodie ever had. More than forty years ago, outside class, he directed my attention to the subject with which this volume deals. Then and later, he often shared his knowledge of it and especially of the Corrigan years in which he took a deep interest. Of course all the opinions and judgments expressed and the mistakes made are my own.

Others have helped, too. Sister Marguerita Smith, O.P., the Archdiocesan Archivist, has been unfailingly helpful in checking many details. Only those who know my handwriting can estimate my debt to Mrs. Eileen Denora who (after the initial shock) mastered it and most patiently typed and retyped the manuscript, which has been revised several times.

For almost a century the United States Catholic Historical Society has rendered an important and often underestimated service by publishing studies of various aspects of the history of Catholic New York. In its own field it has labored to fulfill Our Lord's command to "gather up the fragments that remain lest they be lost" (John 6:12). I am grateful to it for publishing a popular study that owes so much to the learned works it has already produced.

Florence D. Cohalan
St. Paul's Rectory
Staten Island
New York, N.Y.
1981

Contents

List of Illustrations

*Courtesy of the Library of Congress.
**Courtesy of the New York Historical Society.
† Courtesy of the National Portrait Gallery, Smithsonian Institution.
 All others are from the archives of the Archdiocese.

xvii

CHAPTER 1

The Position of Catholics in the Colonies

If we are to have any adequate realization of how much the Catholics in America have to be thankful for as the Republic enters its third century, we must recall, however briefly, their position and prospects when it was founded, and the obstacles the first generations of American Catholics had to face before and after the Revolution.

It is a simple statement of fact that anti-Catholicism is the oldest and strongest prejudice in America and has deep roots in the history of the thirteen colonies and the England from which it sprang. The long struggle between the Catholics and Protestants for supremacy in England from the time of Henry VIII to that of James II ended in the total victory of the Protestants in 1689. They were understandably anxious to consolidate their victory, and their attitude toward the Catholics was determined by that goal. Moreover, England was engaged from 1689 to 1763 in a great political and military struggle with France which was then the leading Catholic country in Europe. England's rise to imperial power depended on the successful outcome of that struggle, which was carried on in Europe, on the high seas, in India, and in North America, and was not settled definitively in England's favor until 1815. It was easy to fuse patriotism with religion and to portray

1

English and Irish Catholics as allies of the hereditary foe. The same thing had been done under Elizabeth I when Spain was the national enemy.

The four great European wars between 1689 and 1763 had their counterparts in America. Although the English colonists greatly outnumbered the French, it was easy to stir up fear of the French and their Indian allies. The age of religious toleration and indifference had not yet dawned. Religion was a powerful force in the national life, and the idea of religious unity within the state was widely accepted in all camps. It was generally believed that one who rejected the state religion could not be a fully loyal subject. In England itself, even the dissenting Protestants were denied equality with members of the established Church.

The English government was convinced that in order to safeguard the settlement of 1689 and Protestant supremacy, it must exclude Catholics from the political, religious, and cultural life of the country. This involved, among other things, barring them from public office, voting, the armed forces, the universities, and teaching positions of any kind. Since land was the chief source of wealth, they often had to pay a double land tax. The government believed correctly that steady, heavy, legal, social, and economic pressure would substantially reduce the Catholic body in England. After 1689, it avoided bloodshed, and so St. Oliver Plunket (1625–1681), Archbishop of Armagh, Ireland, was the last person put to death for religion in the British Isles. By 1776 the English Catholics were thought to be down to about one percent of the population, and their fortunes were at their lowest point since St. Augustine of Canterbury landed in Kent in 597.

The government had a more difficult problem in Ireland, where a substantial majority of the people were Catholics and there was no hope of converting, conciliating, or eliminating them. This was so clear that there was no serious effort to convert or conciliate them. The alternative was to keep them poor, ignorant, and disarmed, so as to deprive them of all chance to influence the political life of their country. This was done through the Penal Laws, many of which were copied from those in force in England. These laws were described by Edmund Burke as "a complete system, full of coherence and consistency, well digested and composed in all its parts. It was a machine of wise and elaborate contrivance, and as well fitted for the oppression, impoverishment and degradation of a people and the debasement in them of human nature itself as ever proceeded from the perverted ingenuity of man." It resulted in a Government in Ireland that was unique in Christian Europe. It was summed up by Burke as one in which "the rats are not tolerated for the sake of the ship, but the ship is kept up for the sake of the rats."

The deliberate mismanagement of Ireland had long-range consequences for the American colonies as well as for England and Ireland. Many of the Irish who came to America in the 18th century were dissenters, mainly Presbyterians from Ulster, who resented the religious, political, and economic discrimination they suffered under the English, and were sympathetic to the

Revolution in the colonies. They were also intensely anti-Catholic. The Penal Laws widened the already deep gap between England and the Irish Catholics, which long antedated the Reformation, with consequences felt by both sides in the 19th and 20th centuries. The two nations were separated so widely by race, religion, culture, and economic interest that political harmony was impossible.

One significant difference in the English government's attitude toward the Catholics in England and those in Ireland was in its treatment of the clergy. In England all bishops and priests were barred legally, though some were tacitly tolerated. An informer who secured a conviction was paid a hundred pounds. In the latter part of the 18th century, the courts began to demand proof that the accused had actually been ordained. This the informers could not produce, so their interest slackened. Still, as late as 1767, Father John Maloney was sentenced to life imprisonment "for unlawfully exercising the functions of a Popish priest." He was released and banished in 1771. In Ireland, bishops and diocesan priests who registered with the government were allowed to exercise their ministry, but religious order priests were barred. In both countries, all external signs of Catholic worship were forbidden, as were all Catholic schools and seminaries. In Ireland the Catholic hierarchy did not die out as it did in England. Though the Penal Laws could not be fully enforced, they imposed a very heavy burden on their victims.

The situation in England and Ireland explains why the government had no serious problem with Catholics in the American colonies. Ultimately all thirteen of the colonies dutifully adopted all or part of the anti-Catholic legislation of the mother country. These laws affected relatively few people and were designed more to keep Catholics out than to subdue them. Most of the Colonies were founded by people who thought that England was, if anything, insufficiently anti-Catholic.

In 1763, the Holy See asked Bishop Richard Challoner, the Vicar Apostolic of London (whose jurisdiction included the colonies) for a report on the Catholics here. He replied that in only two colonies, Maryland and Pennsylvania, could the Catholic religion be practiced openly and that even in these it was severely curtailed. There were twelve priests and about sixteen thousand Catholics in Maryland, and about half as many of each in Pennsylvania. There was neither priest nor church in the remaining eleven colonies where only scattered handfuls of Catholics were known. On the eve of the Revolution, John Adams could say correctly that in Massachusetts a Catholic was as rare as a comet or a Jacobite. This was a condition that Bishop Challoner thought would endure indefinitely in New York and New England because the people there were so bitterly anti-Catholic.

The anti-Catholic restrictions in Maryland and Pennsylvania were tightened after the beginning of the Seven Years War (1756–1763). Maryland had been founded in 1634 as a refuge for Catholics, but freedom for them did not survive beyond 1654. As the 18th century advanced, their position grew worse, although in England anti-Catholic pressure was being slowly relaxed. In Maryland, Catholics had to pay the double land tax, and in Pennsylvania, they were barred from citizenship, armsbearing, and other civil rights. In Maryland, Mass could still be said in private homes; in Pennsylvania, churches were allowed with the first built in 1732. In Maryland, only half the Catholics were practicing. In 1765, when the Holy See thought of erecting a Vicariate Apostolic in the American Colonies, Charles Carroll of Annapolis opposed the idea strongly, fearing it would intensify the persecution, and even contemplated moving to Louisiana to escape living under the British Crown.

The status of Catholics in pre-revolutionary New York was hardly better than in Massachusetts where in a Thanksgiving Day sermon in Boston in 1759, the Pope was described quite seriously as "the successor of the Apostle Judas and the Grand Vicar of Satan." There were very few Catholics in Dutch New Amsterdam. The first priest known to have visited the settlement was the Jesuit, St. Isaac Jogues (d. 1646), who passed through in 1643 on his way to France after he escaped from the Indians. He was treated very kindly by the Dutch, who had tried to rescue him. He found only two Catholics, one a transient young Irishman from Maryland, the other an old Portuguese woman. The Governor told him that eighteen languages were spoken in or near New Amsterdam, and Jogues replied that it had already acquired "the arrogance of Babel." He and his confreres, René Goupil (d. 1642) and John Lalande (d. 1646), who were later proclaimed saints also, were the first and so far the only martyrs who died in what is now New York State. The French mission to the Iroquois began in 1642 and ended in 1709, leaving few visible remains apart from the example of the Jesuit martyrs and of Kateri Tekakwitha (d. 1676), an Indian girl whose cause for canonization has been introduced in Rome.

When King Charles II of England acquired New Amsterdam in 1664, he renamed it New York and gave it to his brother and heir James, Duke of York. James, who became King James II in 1685, had embraced Catholicism in 1670, precipitating the long political struggle that drove him from the throne in 1688. The Catholics saw favorable prospects when James granted religious liberty in New York in July 1674 and later when he made an Irish Catholic, Thomas Dongan, Earl of Limerick, Governor of New York (1683–1688). Under Dongan, who granted the shortlived Charter of Liberties, there were plans for a Catholic school to be run by the three English Jesuits who came with him. The English Jesuits also planned mission work among the Indians to counteract the activities of the French Jesuits. The first Mass known to have been said in New York City took place on October 30, 1683, in Fort James, on Bowling Green where the former United States Custom House now stands.

From the fall of James II until the eve of the American Revolution (almost a century later), the handful of Catholics in New York endured a subterranean existence. Traces of their existence are few and far between. There were only nine known Catholics in the city in 1696. In 1700, a law against priests was passed. It provided that any priest remaining here after November 1, 1700 should be "deemed and accounted an incendiary and disturber of the public peace and safety and an enemy to the true Christian religion." He was to suffer life imprisonment and, if he escaped and was recaptured, was liable to the death penalty. Anyone harboring a priest was to be fined two hundred pounds and stand in the pillory for three days. Catholics were forbidden to vote, hold office, bear arms, or serve on juries. Except in one case of mistaken identity, there is no record of these penalties having been applied or of any occasion for enforcing them having arisen.

The Catholics were not the only ones whom the authorities feared or against whom they discriminated. Blacks, too, were the target of repressive laws. By 1750, New York had the largest percentage of Blacks of any city north of the future Mason and Dixon line. In 1741, there were about 2,000 slaves in a population of approximately 10,000. In that year, a white woman falsely accused some Blacks of incendiarism and set off a panic. Before it ended 154 slaves were arrested. Of that group, fourteen were burned to death and eighteen hanged. Twenty-four whites were jailed, four of whom were executed. In the midst of the panic, a letter arrived from General James Oglethorpe of Georgia. He warned against some Spanish priests who were, he thought, spies about to burn the chief cities in the north. This resulted in the hanging of John Ury, an Anglican clergyman, who was falsely accused of being a Catholic priest and a leader in the alleged plot. The fact that he was patently not Spanish made no impression on the authorities in New York. Some of the Blacks who were hanged with him were Catholics from the Spanish colonies who had been seized and sold as slaves. In 1745, it was reported to London that there was in New York "not the least trace of Popery."

In the very year in which Bishop Challoner made his somber forecast of the prospects of the Church in New York and New England, an event occurred which was to transform the situation and prove him wrong. This was the French cession of Canada to England. A few astute observers foretold that it would lead to the loss of the thirteen Colonies. It surely was a very important preliminary to the American Revolution. By eliminating the French threat, it made the Colonies much less dependent on England, more self-confident and assertive, and less willing to accept direction and supervision from London. At the same time, it presented England with another group of Catholic subjects and one that could not be treated like those in England, Ireland and the American colonies to the south.

The terms of the French capitulation at Quebec required the British to allow the Canadians freedom to practice their religion, security in the possession of their property, and the continued use of French Civil Law.

These provisions were carried out in the Quebec Act, which had been under discussion in Parliament since 1772 and became law in June 1774. The Quebec Act also extended the boundaries of Canada to the Ohio in the south and the Mississippi in the west. It was difficult to justify giving the French Canadians a privileged position in the Empire, but the English, well aware of the growing dissatisfaction of the Americans, thought it necessary if they were to hold Canada.

The Quebec Act immediately became one of the "Intolerable Acts" the Colonists used to justify the Revolution. It caused an astonishing outburst of anti-Catholic feeling, especially, but not only, in New England. In New York the first flag flown by the Sons of Liberty, March, 1775, was inscribed "No Popery." Later historians, in a more secular age, have tended to concentrate on the territorial provisions of the Act as an explanation of the excitement it caused, but it is clear from the records of the time that most of the popular indignation among the colonists was due to its religious clauses and that this indignation was exploited skillfully by the leaders of the patriotic cause.

In retrospect, it is hard to see what the excitement was all about. The Catholics of that time must have been astonished at the attention being paid to their insignificant group. In 1776 the total population of the colonies was about 2.5 million of whom 80% were white. Two-thirds of the whites had been born in the British Isles and about 10% were Germans, a third of whom lived in Pennsylvania. Most of the non-whites were blacks, and most of the blacks were slaves. At 20% of the total, they constituted a higher percentage of the population than today—about 13.2%. About 95% of the people lived in rural areas as against 27% today. Their per capita income (figured in 1976 dollars) was $400. The average personal net worth was $3,510 in 1976 dollars, in contrast to $21,475 now. There were, of course, gross disparities in the actual distribution of wealth. The regional disparities were striking too. Thus it is estimated that in 1774 the per capita net worth of free colonists was $1,540 in New England, $2,460 in the Middle Colonies, and $6,275 in the South. In 1790 the South led the distribution of the population with 48.5%, while New England had 25.7% and the Middle Colonies 25.8%. Massachusetts, including Maine with a population of 475,199, was three times the size of Quebec (population 150,000—of whom only 360 were Protestants). It is easy to see which was more likely to attack the other. Few claim that the Catholics were more than 25,000 strong. They were about the same percentage of the population here as in England and were concentrated almost entirely in Maryland and Pennsylvania.

When the Revolution came, the small Catholic body had little reason to be enthusiastic about either side. Neutrality was impossible and so was unanimity, but most Catholics supported the patriots. Owing to their small numbers and resources they could not play a major role, but several served with distinction. Among them were Commodore John Barry, the "Father of the American Navy," General Stephen Moylan, and Colonel John Fitzgerald, who was an aide to Washington. In February 1776, in a surprising step, the Continental Congress enlisted the aid of two Catholic civilians in what must rank as one of the most hopeless missions ever entrusted to envoys of the United States. They were Charles Carroll of Carrollton (1737–1832) and his cousin, Father John Carroll (1735–1815). They belonged to an old Irish family that had come to Maryland in 1688. Charles Carroll was reputed to be the richest man in the colonies. He was to become the only Catholic signer of the Declaration of Independence and later, a United States Senator. John Carroll was to become the first American bishop, the Father of the American Hierarchy. Both had been educated in Europe and spoke fluent French.

Their mission was to induce the Canadians to throw in their lot with the Americans. Congress decided to send a committee of three, two of whom were to be chosen from its ranks. They were Benjamin Franklin and Samuel Chase. The third was Charles Carroll, who was asked to prevail on Father John Carroll to accompany them. The desirability of gaining Canada seemed clear to all, but the Americans had already destroyed their own case. In its Address to the People of Great Britain, issued on October 21, 1774, Congress had protested against Parliament establishing, by the Quebec Act, "a religion fraught with sanguinary and impious tenets," adding "nor can we express our astonishment that a British Parliament would ever consent to establish in that country a religion that has deluged your island in blood and disbursed impiety, bigotry, persecution, murder and rebellion through every part of the world." Five days later, in its Address to the Canadians, it reminded them that liberty of conscience in their religion was a God-given right for which they were not beholden to Parliament, and added, "We are too well acquainted with the liberality of sentiment distinguishing your nation to imagine that a difference of religion will prejudice you against a hearty amity with us." It appealed to Switzerland as an example of Catholic and Protestant states living in harmony. Finally on October 26, 1774, in its petition to George III, Congress protested against the religious and territorial clauses of the Quebec Act.

The contradictions in these documents could not be covered over and the Canadians were well aware of them, as the American envoys learned on their arrival. They were, of course, equally aware of the two unsuccessful American expeditions against Canada in August and December 1775, under Generals Schuyler, Montgomery, and Benedict Arnold. The Canadian clergy reminded Father Carroll plainly that the Catholic faith had been proscribed in the thirteen English Colonies since the beginning of the colonial era, that priests were not free to exercise their ministry publicly, and that the conversion of Congress could not be taken seriously. The mission, which lasted from April 2nd to June 11th, was a total failure. Their chief opponent, the man who saved Canada for England, was Jean Briand (1715–1794) who became Bishop of Quebec in 1766. He threatened to bar from the

Sacraments any Catholic who helped the Americans, and to suspend any priest who let Father Carroll say Mass.

The real impact of the Catholics on the Revolution was made by the French Alliance of February 6, 1778, a consequence of the Battle of Saratoga, on October 1, 1777. The Alliance made victory possible and also made it necessary for the Americans to moderate the expression of their anti-Catholic feeling. This they were quite prepared to do in return for the substantial help the French had begun to supply as early as May 1, 1776. The French Alliance was as unpopular with the Tories as the Quebec Act had been with the Patriots. The latter now found themselves accused of selling out Protestant interests to the Catholics and the alliance itself was described by the Tories as a "horror and infamy worse than the Declaration of Independence." That much of the frenzy over the Quebec Act was contrived, though it appealed to genuine feelings, may be seen from the ease with which it was toned down when major practical considerations made that desirable. For a long time Guy Fawkes Day, November 5th, had been kept in New England to commemorate the Gunpowder Plot of 1605, but in the years just before the Revolution it had become the occasion for factional fights in Boston. It was revived with great enthusiasm in 1774, but in November 1775, George Washington forbade his troops to take part in "the observance of that ridiculous and childish custom of burning the effigy of the Pope."

Congress itself took part in various acts of civility to Catholics. Thus on July 4, 1779, many of its members attended a *Te Deum* at St. Joseph's Church in Philadelphia which had been arranged by the French Minister to mark the anniversary of the Declaration of Independence. Going even further, many members attended the funeral for the Spanish Agent in the same church on May 8, 1780. Among those present was Benedict Arnold, who was bitterly anti-Catholic. Later he was to give as a partial explanation of his treason: "The sight of your profligate congress at Mass for the repose of the soul of a Roman Catholic in purgatory and participating in the rites of a church against whose anti-Christian corruption your pious ancestors would bear witness with their blood." There was another *Te Deum* to celebrate the news of Yorktown. Note was taken of the $6 million gift in 1780 from the Assembly of the French Clergy, of the aid given by Spain, which entered the war on June 21, 1779, and of the helpful role of the French clergy in the Ohio Valley and Maine.

CHAPTER 2

Bishop John Carroll

The success of the Revolution made it possible and necessary to provide a stable form of organization and government for the Catholics in America. The Vicar Apostolic of London no longer wished to have anything to do with the former colonies, and the Catholics in the new republic were unwilling to remain under English control in any way.

The situation was difficult since no Vicar Apostolic of London had ever attempted to come to America. They had been content to do little more than grant faculties to the priests working in the American colonies and were quite willing to be relieved of a responsibility they found a heavy and unnecessary burden, given the difficult circumstances in which they themselves lived. From 1634 all the priests working in the colonies had been Jesuits, under the control of their local superior, but in 1773 the order was suppressed by Rome for political reasons. Confronted by the Revolution, the outcome of which was uncertain for several years, cut off from Rome, and hoping for a speedy restoration of their Society, most of the former Jesuits adopted a low profile, carried on much as before, and awaited the development of events. By 1783 it was clear that something more was needed. Their numbers were dwindling, for they had no replacements; peace would bring immigrants and probably foreign priests and other religious communities, and some local authority was essential. Accordingly, in November 1783 the American priests petitioned Rome to make their former superior, Father John Lewis, superior of the Catholic Church in America and to grant him certain episcopal powers such as the right to confirm, to bless the holy oils, to consecrate chalices, and to give newly arrived priests faculties to exercise their ministry.

The petition was received favorably, partly on its merits and partly because the Roman authorities were already giving active consideration to the situation in America. In January 1783, they had alerted the Nuncio to Paris to the opportunities opening here and had instructed him to urge the French Government to obtain guarantees of religious freedom for the American Catholics. In September the Nuncio reported that Benjamin Franklin assured him that the way was clear for the appointment of a Bishop or Vicar Apostolic, whichever Rome should decide. Unsure of the local situation and having been warned of the danger of appointing a bishop, Rome decided to move cautiously but firmly. Hence, on June 9, 1784, it erected a Prefecture Apostolic which was to be immediately subject to the Holy See, and appointed Father John Carroll as Prefect Apostolic. Father Lewis, who was English, was passed over on the grounds of age and health. It is probable that his friendship with Franklin and his being a native American influenced the selection of Father Carroll.

John Carroll's background, training, experience, and personal qualities clearly made him the most suitable available candidate for the difficult post to which he was now assigned, and which, under different titles, he was to fill with distinction for thirty years. He came from the leading Catholic family in the country, and had been educated mainly at home, first by his mother, who had been educated in Europe, and then by private tutors. In 1748 he had been sent to Europe with his cousin Charles to study at the English College of St. Omer in French Flanders. Beginning in the reign of Elizabeth I (1558–1603), the English and Irish Catholics had maintained separately (with funds supplied mainly from the continent) a chain of schools on the continent to which candidates for the priesthood and the children of their small number of wealthy members could be sent.

In 1753, after finishing his studies, John Carroll became a Jesuit. He was ordained in Liège, Belgium, on February 14, 1761, and taught in Liège, Bruges and St. Omer. From 1771 to 1773, he accompanied a young English Catholic nobleman on a grand tour of Europe, during which he spent some months in Rome. There he found hostility to the Jesuits so strong in official circles that he made as few clerical contacts as possible and never had any desire to see Rome again. He was imprisoned briefly in Bruges in October 1773 by the Austrian authorities who were responsible for carrying out in Belgium the terms of the suppression of the Jesuits, and then spent some months in England as chaplain to old friends. After twenty-six years' absence, he returned to America in 1774 and lived quietly at his mother's home in Maryland from which he exercised his ministry in the surrounding area. He was there when the news of his appointment as Prefect Apostolic arrived.

John Carroll had returned from Europe a well educated, experienced, and a widely traveled man. He had seen, and for several years was still to see, the Penal Laws in operation in Maryland and the other Colonies. He had seen and felt their force in his own life in America and in England. He had seen, too, the tight control of the Church by the nominally Catholic governments in Europe, and had himself experienced its most odious effect in the suppression of the Jesuits. When the Revolutions came in America and France, he had no reason to lament the fall of the regimes they overthrew. He saw clearly from the beginning the wholly unexpected opening the American Revolution offered the Church, and the basic harmony between Catholic teaching and the principles on which the American Republic was founded.

Personally he was patient, prudent, industrious, well balanced, and a good administrator. He did not expect perfect results and knew how to work well with sometimes very imperfect instruments. His dignity, serenity, and quiet courtesy were marked by many. There was nothing ostentatious about him. He had, as one of his contemporaries tells us, a "precious gift" most useful in a bishop anywhere at any time "of gaining hearts without failing to inspire respect."

Since the interminable delays in getting mail from Europe were a serious inconvenience after the great wars of 1792–1815 had begun, it is interesting to see how relatively rapid the mail traveled between the end of the American Revolution and 1792. John Carroll learned of his appointment from four sources: a private letter from Rome, dated June 9, 1784, reached him on August 20th; a letter from England dated July 3rd, came on September 18th; a letter from the French Minister, dated from New York on October 22nd, came on November 8th; and the official letter from Rome dated June 9th, came on November 26th.

In his letter of appointment, the new Prefect Apostolic was told that Rome intended to establish "soon" a Vicariate Apostolic headed by a bishop, but that nothing would be done until it received more accurate information and his opinion on the situation in America. He was asked to send as soon as possible a correct report on conditions in each of the thirteen states, giving the good and bad points in each, and including as much information as possible on the clergy. He was to be under the authority of the Sacred Congregation for the Propagation of the Faith (usually called Propaganda), the Roman department charged with the supervision of all the mission territories of the universal Church. His jurisdiction was coterminous with the boundaries of the United States of America.

The reluctance to appoint a bishop at once was due largely to the fear of precipitating another anti-Catholic outburst, against which Rome had been warned. As late as 1773, the proposal to send the Bishop of Quebec here to confirm had been resisted strongly on that ground by Father Ferdinand Farmer, one of the most zealous and trustworthy of the missionaries in the Colonies. In fact, the hatred of bishops and prelates of every kind was so strong among the Protestants that none of them dared to introduce their own bishops here until 1784 when the Anglicans and Methodists did so (this was true even though the Anglicans were the Established Church in several colonies). If Franklin's assurance that the way was clear was well founded, America was one of the very few places in the world outside the Papal States where the Holy See could appoint a bishop without some preliminary agreement with the government. Rome was confirmed in its belief in the wisdom of delay when the American priests, on hearing of the proposed bishop, protested in October 1784.

The new Prefect formally accepted his appointment on February 27, 1785, and shortly thereafter sent in his report. His first official act had been to publish the Jubilee of 1775–1776 which was, by special privilege, extended to the United States from November 26, 1784, to November 26, 1785. He had made a visitation of Maryland, Pennsylvania, and New York City but had not gone to New England because the small numbers of Catholics there did not warrant the expenditure of time. The statistics, which were soon to change rapidly, were much the same as Bishop Challoner's in 1763. There were, he reported, about 25,000 Catholics, most of whom lived in Maryland and Pennsylvania. Virginia had about 200, who were visited occasionally by a priest. New York State had about 1,500. He gave no estimate for the other states or for the Mississippi and Ohio Valleys. That these figures were just estimates may be seen from the fact that the French Minister, writing at the same time, estimated that there were 44,500 Catholics in the entire country. The figures on the clergy were easier to find. There were twenty-four in Maryland and Pennsylvania: eleven were American, five German, four English, one Irish, one Belgian, one from Luxembourg, and Father Carroll did not know the background of the twenty-fourth. He had never met and could not name some of the former Jesuits in Pennsylvania. There was also one Irish Franciscan in New York. Two of the priests were over seventy, three were very near it, and others were in poor health. There were two churches in Philadelphia, one in Baltimore, none in the other states. There were no religious communities, no Catholic schools, and no Catholic charitable institutions or works of any kind.

The statistical part of Father Carroll's report was less important than the change in the legal position of the Catholics since 1776, which was even more surprising than the Revolution itself. The war had not been fought for religious liberty, which is not mentioned in the Declaration of Independence, but it was unquestionably one of its most important and enduring consequences. Suddenly and beyond all expectation, most of the legal barriers against Catholics and other religious minorities crumbled.

No single reason or event explains the change. The aversion of the "founding fathers" from the prevailing European system, the indifference of many of them to organized religion and even to Christianity itself, the difficulty of deciding which if any group should be favored over another, and the fact that a very substantial proportion of the people were unchurched, all had a share in the shaping of the new situation. Certainly sympathy for Catholicism did not. It was a time when organized Protestantism was in a state of considerable disarray, and Deism and infidelity had spread widely among members of the small educated class.

Nowhere was the change more apparent than in New York. The Revolution made it necessary to replace the Royal Charters and to establish new State Constitutions. The New York Constitution of 1777 had a provision barring from naturalization all who failed to repudiate allegiance in spiritual matters to any foreign prince or potentate. This provision, inserted under pressure from John Jay, was clearly aimed at the Catholics. It lasted only until the Federal Government took charge of naturalization in 1790. In 1784 the New York law against priests was repealed. Exactly 150 years after the first English-speaking Catholics arrived in Maryland in 1634, and almost exactly a century after the fall of James II, the Catholics in New York found themselves assured for the first time of legal protection in the free exercise of their religion, a protection that did not depend on the good will of a particular prince or official.

The first priest to take advantage of the law of 1784 was Father Charles Whelan (1740–1806), an Irish Capuchin who had served as a chaplain in the French fleet during the Revolution and who arrived in New York in October 1784. After Yorktown, his ship had been captured in the West Indies by the British, and he had spent thirteen months as a prisoner of war in Jamaica. As the only chaplain available to the sick prisoners, he estimated that he had given the sacraments to almost 4,400 of them in that period.

Father Whelan arrived just as the population of New York City was undergoing a substantial change. It had grown from about 20,000 in 1776 to about 33,000 in 1783. When the British left, on November 25, 1783, it fell to about 10,000 people mainly of English and Dutch background. Most of the well-to-do had left. By 1786 it had risen to 24,000 out of a total population in the State of about 340,000. Of the latter, about two-thirds were English, Scotch and Welsh. The Dutch comprised 17%, the Germans 8%, the Irish 8%, and smaller numbers of French and Swedes. As was to be the case so often in the future, a new people had arrived, this time mainly from New England and some from Ireland.

By 1790 New York was the second largest city in the country. It was outranked only by Philadelphia at a time when half of the ten largest cities had populations of under 10,000. One major reason for its rapid recovery was that it had become the national capital, as of December 1784, and remained so until 1790. It was also the State capital from 1785 to 1797. The coming of the national government brought not only Congress but the diplomatic and consular corps, among whom the French and Spanish were outstanding. It also brought merchants from many foreign countries.

The coming of the diplomats and foreign merchants, coinciding with the repeal of the law against priests, brought the Church into the open. Under the British occupation the Penal Laws had been enforced, and any priest entering New York did so at his own risk. In 1781–1782, and even early in 1784, Mass was said secretly in a loft over a carpenter's shop in Barclay Street and in a private house on Water Street by Father Farmer (1720–1786), whose real name was Steinmeyer. Born in Germany he entered the Jesuits in 1743, volunteered for the missions in China, but was assigned instead to work among the German Catholics in Pennsylvania. He lived in Philadelphia, and made occasional trips to New York and New Jersey, from 1758 until his death. In 1778 the chaplain of a captured French ship that had been brought to New York was given permission to move about the town. Some Catholics asked him to say Mass for them but warned him of the law against it. He asked permission to say Mass, was refused, misunderstood the refusal, and went ahead, and was imprisoned at once and kept in jail until he was exchanged.

Father Whelan's first task in 1784 was to form a congregation and then to build a church. He found perhaps 200 Catholics, among whom were "many grumblers," and about twenty who practiced their religion. The Catholics included Spanish, French, Portuguese, and Germans, but the largest group was Irish. Many of the immigrants were poor, and in 1784 both the Friendly Sons of St. Patrick and the German Society were founded to assist them. The law of April 16, 1784 allowed each religious group to incorporate. Male persons of adult age could meet and elect nine trustees to administer the property of the church and would have sole control of payments of the church money, as well as of the renting of pews, but they were not to have authority to fix the salary of the clergyman or to alter in any way the doctrine, discipline, or worship of the church.

The French Consul, Hector St. John de Crèvecoeur, accepted the chairmanship of the Catholic body and on February 23rd, 1785, they appealed to him for help in obtaining a site for a church. He asked the Common Council for help and they in turn referred him to the Trustees of Trinity Church, who on October 7th, 1785, made available the lots on the corner of Church and Barclay Streets where St. Peter's Church now stands. Meantime, on June 10th, 1785, "the Roman Catholic Church in the City of New York" was incorporated. The congregation selected St. Peter as the patron of the first Catholic church in New York. Anticipating the closing of the deal for the property, the Spanish Minister, Don Diego de Gardoqui, laid the cornerstone on October 5, 1785.

In the very beginning Father Whelan had gathered his flock in the home of a Portuguese merchant, José Roiz Silva. Later, he used the Spanish and French legations while the church was being built. An attempt to obtain from the Common Council the use of the old Exchange on Broad Street, which was unoccupied, failed on the ground that the building might be unsafe. It had previously been used as a drilling ground for troops and shortly afterward was used as a meeting place for the Law Society and the Tammany Society.

The building of the church went on slowly because of lack of funds. Appeals were made to the Kings of France and Spain and to the Warden of Galway, Ireland. The Spanish King sent $1,000 and gave permission for an appeal to be made in Mexico and Cuba. While the work was proceeding, a problem arose that was to trouble St. Peter's parish for more than half a century. This was the attempt of the trustees, ignoring the provisions of the Law of 1784, to interfere in the internal discipline of the Church and to control the appointment of the clergy. It started, as was so often the case, with a conflict of personalities. Father Whelan was a zealous man, but he was a poor speaker and was more fluent in Gaelic and French than in English. This was a serious drawback in the opinion of many of his parishioners who tended to rate him on his merits as a preacher, as so many Protestant congregations rated their pastors. Moreover, he seems to have been a tactless man, with little skill in managing or soothing difficult people. In the fall of 1785 another priest appeared, a fellow Capuchin from Ireland, an eloquent preacher, fluent in English, an experienced missionary, a man with an ingratiating manner, but also a born troublemaker. The stage was set for conflict.

Father Andrew Nugent (1740–1795) soon established a following of his own. One Sunday in December 1785, his adherents seized the collection, and as Monsignor Peter Guilday, the historian, tells us: "With money as the cause, the first schism in the American Church became a reality." Father Carroll, alerted by a French priest living in New York, warned all the parties to the dispute. He told the trustees that if they took legal action against Father Whelan, as they threatened, he would give no priest faculties in New York. Father Whelan offered to resign for the sake of peace. He left in February 1786, and died in Maryland in 1806, believing rightly that he had been treated shabbily in New York.

Father Nugent remained on the scene and Father Carroll had no choice but to recognize him as pastor. Things were quiet enough for awhile and the building of the church proceeded. It was dedicated, though unfinished, on November 4th, 1786, the feast of St. Charles Borromeo who was the patron saint of King Charles III of Spain and of his heir, the future Charles IV. This was done to acknowledge the generosity of the Spanish Royal House. There was a Solemn High Mass celebrated by Father Nugent and the chaplains of the Spanish and French legations. Later, the Spanish Minister gave a banquet for the attending notables, including the President of Congress, many members of Congress and the Cabinet, and the Governor of New York. Father Carroll was not present as his invitation came too late. Very shortly after the dedication, the trustees quarrelled with Father Nugent and petitioned for his removal. He denied their right to do so and Father Carroll's authority to do so and challenged the Prefect publicly in St. Peter's, causing such a scene that

Mass had to be moved to the Spanish Legation and he himself was suspended. He returned to France in 1790, and died there in 1795. He was succeeded at St. Peter's in October 1787 by a Dominican, Father William V. O'Brien (1740–1816), who remained as pastor for twenty fruitful years. Father O'Brien had been educated in Bologna and Rome and was ordained in Rome about 1769. He had returned to Ireland in 1770 and worked in Dublin before coming to Philadelphia in 1786.

The disturbances in New York and other cities, including those in Philadelphia which resulted in the erection there of Holy Trinity, a German parish (the first national parish in America), melted most of the local opposition to the appointment of a bishop, which was now seen by most to be desirable. Accordingly, the American priests petitioned Rome in March 1788 to proceed with the appointment. By special privilege, which they requested, they were allowed to nominate the first bishop and select the site of his see. Out of twenty-nine qualified voters, twenty-four cast their ballots for Father Carroll. Two other candidates received one vote each, and three neglected or refused to vote. Baltimore was selected as the site and this was approved by Rome, and on November 6, 1789, John Carroll was formally appointed Bishop of Baltimore.

The erection of the diocese of Baltimore was the third event which for quite different reasons made the year 1789 forever memorable in the annals of the United States, the Western World, and the Universal Church. They were, in chronological order: (1) on April 30th, the inauguration of George Washington as the first President of the United States; (2) on May 1st, the beginning of the French Revolution; (3) on November 6th, the establishment of the Hierarchy of the United States.

When John Carroll was appointed bishop of Baltimore, the only prelate in North America above the Rio Grande was the bishop of Quebec. The new bishop could have gone there or to Dublin, to which he was invited in January 1790, but he had already accepted an invitation (should he ever be appointed a bishop) to be consecrated in the home of very dear English friends whom he had known since his student days. He did not hear of his appointment until April 1790. He left for Europe in June, and was consecrated in Lulworth Castle, the home of the Weld family, on August 15, 1790. The chapel was new, being the first one built by an English Catholic since the beginning of the repeal of the Penal Laws. The ceremony was carried out as splendidly as circumstances permitted, that is, by one bishop instead of three, but privately lest unnecessary provocation be given to the non-Catholics in the area.

Before leaving for England, the new bishop had the pleasure of signing, on behalf of the clergy, the Address from the Roman Catholics to George Washington, congratulating him on his election to the Presidency. It was signed on behalf of the laity by Charles Carroll of Carrollton, Daniel Carroll of Maryland, Thomas Fitz Simons of Philadelphia, and Thomas Lynch of New York. Daniel Carroll, the bishop's brother, and Fitz Simons were the only Catholic signers of the Constitution. The address was received and answered courteously by Washington who received similar documents from all the religious groups in the country.

One of the first tasks undertaken by Bishop Carroll on his return from England was the holding of a National Synod, which took place in Baltimore in November 1790 and was attended by twenty-two priests. In it he laid down rules for uniformity in the administration of the sacraments, the celebration of the liturgy, religious instruction, the holding of church property, and other matters. The gospel was to be read in the vernacular. If possible every church was to have Vespers and Benediction every Sunday afternoon. The clergy were all to wear black.

In 1791 two of his most cherished dreams became realities. One was the founding of Georgetown College which he had been planning for years. It opened in October 1791 and was made possible in part by the gifts of money the Bishop had received in England. The other, also in October 1791, was the opening of St. Mary's Seminary, Baltimore. It was the first seminary in the United States, and was staffed and supported at their own expense (otherwise it could not have been opened) by the Sulpician Fathers who were seeking a refuge from the French Revolution. Though neither Georgetown nor St. Mary's bore fruit quickly, both bore it abundantly later and continue to do so.

The first priest ordained in the United States, Stephen Badin (1768–1853), was a Frenchman who came with the Sulpicians and was ordained on May 25, 1793. The first native-born priest, William Matthews (1770–1854), was born in Maryland and ordained in 1800. In its first twenty-four years, the seminary produced only twenty-six priests, while from 1784 to 1789 thirty priests came from Europe and Canada. Many more Sulpicians came than were needed in the Seminary, and they were extremely useful to the Bishop in meeting the growing demand for priests.

While in England for his consecration, Bishop Carroll had been contemplating the division of his immense diocese or the appointment of a coadjutor. He foresaw that communication with Rome would become very difficult, and feared that in the event of his own death the appointment and consecration of his successor might take a long time. Rome wanted uniformity of discipline and custom here, and preferred a coadjutor to a division. In September 1792 it asked Bishop Carroll to consult the older priests and propose a candidate for the coadjutorship. The choice fell on Father Lawrence Graessel (1753–1793) of Philadelphia. He was born in Bavaria, entered the Jesuits, became a diocesan priest after their suppression, and came to America in 1787. He was a zealous, gifted, and much loved man who heard confessions in German, English, French, Italian, Dutch, and Spanish. He was appointed bishop on December 8, 1793, two months after his death from yellow fever.

The soundness of Bishop Carroll's presentiment about communication with Rome was shown in the appointment of Graessel's successor. Father Leonard Neale (1746–1817) was born in Maryland, educated at St. Omer, entered the Jesuits in 1767, and was ordained on June 5th, 1773, just before their suppression. He worked in England and British Guiana from 1779 to 1783, and then returned home. He was president of Georgetown College from 1799 to 1806. In 1795 he was appointed coadjutor of Baltimore, but it took five years for the news to reach this country. His consecration, on December 7, 1800, in Baltimore was the first ever held in the United States.

With all the problems that pressed on him from every side, Bishop Carroll could give very little time to any part of his diocese that did not clamor for attention. New York was one of them. The departure of the diplomatic corps when the national capital was moved to Washington diminished the social standing of the Catholics. Those who remained were very poor, but for the most part things were peaceful. St. Peter's Church was completed and the pews offered for sale in 1794. That was made possible largely by Father O'Brien's begging trip to Cuba and Mexico in 1792. He had been a classmate at Bologna of the Archbishop of Mexico City who received him kindly, and he returned to New York with some paintings and about $6,000 which helped but did not solve the financial problem which remained a burden for almost a century. How heavy a burden it was is seen in the report for 1800 which listed receipts at $1,500, expenses at $1,400 and the debt, all but $2,000 of which was held by the Trustees, at $6,500. Father O'Brien's devotion to duty during the yellow fever epidemics of 1795, 1798, and 1805 made a very favorable impression on the general public.

The Catholics began to take part in public life and in 1802 Andrew Morris, a trustee of St. Peter's, was elected assistant alderman. He was the first Catholic office holder in New York City. In 1806 Francis Cooper was elected to the State legislature. When he refused to take the anti-Catholic oath inserted in the Constitution of 1777 by John Jay, it was repealed. In 1800 a Free School, which lasted until 1935, was opened at St. Peter's. The Dutch Reformed, Episcopal, and Presbyterian churches already had charity schools. The first public school was opened in May 1806. In the same year, the Catholics were proud to be able to install a bell at St. Peter's.

The most important event in Father William O'Brien's pastorate, though no one realized it at the time, was the conversion of Elizabeth Ann Seton (1774–1821), the future saint, who was received into the Church on March 14th, 1805, by Father Matthew O'Brien, an assistant at St. Peter's. She was one of the most important converts in the history of this country. She was brought up as an Episcopalian. Her father, Dr. Richard Bayley, was a professor at Columbia and a leader in the medical world. Her husband, William Seton, was a businessman who had died in Italy in 1803 on a trip for his health and left her with five children and no money. Her conversion caused quite a stir. Evidently one of the arguments urged against it was the inferior social position of Catholics here, because she was warned they were "the offscourings of the people" and their congregation "a public nuisance." She left New York forever in June 1808 and went to Emmitsburg, Maryland, where in 1809 she founded the American Sisters of Charity, who exist today in six separate religious communities and who made possible the start of the parochial school system.

Before her departure, there was a change in the pastorate of St. Peter's. Father William O'Brien resigned in August 1807 because of ill health. In January 1810, "out of regard and respect to the Rev. Mr. O'Brien," the trustees voted him a pension of $500 a year, equivalent to his salary. He remained in New York until his death on May 14th, 1816, and was buried at St. Peter's, where his monument may still be seen.

Father O'Brien was succeeded as pastor by Father Louis Sibourd, a Frenchman who had assisted him from time to time in caring for St. Peter's French parishioners. On March 9th, 1807, the trustees had asked for Father Sibourd's removal as assistant because of his poor English, and he lasted as pastor only until November 1808. He was for awhile the confessor of Mrs. Seton and introduced her to Bishop Dubourg who urged her to leave New York for Baltimore. Later Father Sibourd was Bishop Dubourg's Vicar General in New Orleans and returned with him to France. In the month in which Father O'Brien retired, Robert Fulton made the first trip to Albany in his steamboat *Clermont,* beginning a new age in transportation. He astonished everyone by making the 150-mile trip in thirty hours. Passengers paid seven dollars for the entire trip and those who went part way paid five cents a mile. Soon a steam ferry to Paulus Hook, New Jersey, covered the mile-and-a-half trip (which often took three hours by sailboat) in twenty minutes. The increased speed played a major role in promoting commuting from New Jersey to New York City.

Only one other religious community of women preceded Elizabeth Seton's community in the former colonies. They were Discalced Carmelites who came from Belgium in 1790 and settled in Baltimore. They were English, with several American members. The Visitandines of Georgetown were in process of formation. After 1803 the Ursulines of New Orleans, founded in 1727, came under Bishop Carroll's jurisdiction. The orders of men beside the Sulpicians were the Augustinians in Philadelphia (1796) and the Dominicans in Kentucky (1805).

In 1803 the Louisiana Purchase, probably the most important event in the United States between the Revolution and the Civil War, practically doubled the area of the country. It was coterminous with the diocese of New Orleans, erected in 1795, which was vacant in 1803 because the first bishop had been promoted to Guatemala. As a stopgap measure, Rome made Bishop Carroll administrator of New Orleans (1803–1812), thus doubling his jurisdiction. This made more urgent than ever the division of the diocese of Baltimore which Bishop Carroll had been recommending since 1790, and had asked for again in 1802. The most obvious reason for it was the impossibility, admitted by all, of one person supervising so large an area.

Had it been only a question of the size of the Catholic body, a division could have waited for years even though there had been a substantial increase in numbers. By 1810, when the division took effect, the Catholics numbered about 100,000, the number of priests had grown from about twenty-five to seventy, and the number of churches from three to eighty. The priests, like the people, were unevenly distributed. There were six in Kentucky, seven or eight farther west (where for awhile Father Badin was alone in several states), and the rest were east of the Alleghenies. Among the new churches was the Cathedral in Baltimore which the Bishop had in mind in 1790 but was unable to start until 1806. It was opened in 1821. It was designed by Benjamin Latrobe, one of the architects of the National Capitol.

The practical reasons for the delay in dividing Baltimore, beside Rome's already stated desire to see uniformity of discipline and custom established in America, were the disturbed conditions in Europe which interfered with communication with Rome, a division of opinion on how many dioceses to erect and where to put them, the question of finding suitable candidates, and doubt of the economic viability of some of the sees suggested. All this involved the Bishop, who had no secretary, in a long, tedious and taxing correspondence. Finally, in 1806, he proposed the erection of new dioceses at Bardstown, Kentucky (now at Louisville), Boston, New York, and Philadelphia. His candidates for Bardstown, Boston, and Philadelphia were, respectively, Fathers Benedict J. Flaget (c. 1763–1850), a French Sulpician; John Cheverus (1768–1836), a Frenchman; and Michael Egan, O.F.M. (1761–1814), an Irishman. He felt unable to decide on a suitable candidate for New York, so he proposed no one, and suggested for the time being that it be left under the jurisdiction of the Bishop of Boston.

CHAPTER 3

Bishop Richard Luke Concanen, O.P.

It took five months for Bishop Carroll to hear that the long-planned division of his diocese was an accomplished fact, that his candidates for the new sees were accepted by Rome, and that he himself had been made Archbishop of Baltimore on April 8, 1808. The official documents did not arrive until August 1810, and it was not until October and November 1810 that he was able to consecrate his suffragans. Only one point in his plan had been changed. Rome decided to fill all the new sees at once and, as no candidate had been suggested for New York, the Pope appointed a man he knew personally and judged to be suitable for that onerous post.

When Richard Luke Concanen was born in Kilbegnet, County Roscommon, on December 27, 1747, the fortunes of the Irish Catholics had reached their lowest point. They had been subdued so thoroughly that when the last Jacobite Rising occurred in England and Scotland in 1745 it evoked no response in Ireland. He left Ireland forever in 1764 and went to Louvain, Belgium, where, on September 14th, he entered the Irish Dominicans. In 1765 he was sent to Rome, to the Minerva, the Dominican Generalate, and was ordained to the priesthood in the Lateran Basilica, on December 22, 1770. He was a uniformly good student and became fluent in Italian and was an excellent preacher serving for years as a confessor at St. Mary Major.

The Irish Dominicans have their own headquarters in Rome at San Clemente, where they have been established since 1677. Father Concanen lived there from 1769 to 1792, serving as novice master from 1773 to 1780 and prior from 1781 to 1787. From 1792 to 1808 he lived at the Minerva, teaching theology and serving as assistant to the Dominican Master General. He served also, from 1792 to 1808, as Roman agent for several of the Irish bishops and for the Bishop of Baltimore, meantime keeping up his preaching, teaching and confessional work. From 1805 to 1808 he was also the Roman agent of Bishop Milner of England.

Father Concanen's years as assistant to the Dominican Master General coincided with a disastrous period in the history of all the religious communities in the Church. The great wars of the French Revolution and Napoleon began in 1792 and continued almost without intermission until 1815. Everywhere the French armies went, which was everywhere in Europe except Scandinavia, the British Isles, and part of the Balkans, the robbery and suppression of the religious houses rated high on their list of priorities. The resultant losses were immense. They were even greater than those inflicted by the Reformation, which left much of Europe untouched. His work included correspondence with the Dominicans in the Holy Roman Empire and Eastern Europe, where the losses were very heavy. The preliminary to all this had been the suppression of the Jesuits in 1773, which he had witnessed as a young priest. He lived in Rome through the calamitous pontificate of Clement XIV (1769–1774), and was in Rome when Pius VI died a prisoner in France in 1799. When he himself died, Pius VII was a prisoner in France.

The only ray of hope came from the British Isles, where the success of the American Revolution and fear of the French made the English government relax the Penal Laws, and from the United States, where Father Concanen saw hope for a foundation that would offset Dominican losses in Europe. He entered enthusiastically into the plan of Father Edward Fenwick, O.P. (1768–1832) for an American foundation, which was realized in 1805 in Kentucky. He himself thought at one time of coming to America as a missionary.

His interest in the United States was not confined to the Dominicans. He sympathized with John Carroll's plans for the division of the See of Baltimore, and as early as 1803 was urging Rome to proceed with the division it decreed in 1808.

Naturally enough, a man in his position and with his experience was considered for a diocese in Ireland, but he was determined to refuse all offers and to remain just a Dominican friar. He had resolved, he said, "to live and die in the obscure and retired way of life I have chosen from my youth." In 1798 he refused the diocese of Kilmacduagh, from which he escaped by a personal appeal to the new pope, Pius VII, in Venice in 1800 and in 1802 he refused Raphoe. His nomination to these sees gave offense to the English

Government, ostensibly because it opposed the choice of friars for the episcopate. A stronger reason, probably, was his opposition to English intrigue in Rome. After the Irish Rising of 1798, the English determined on a political union of England and Ireland. To weaken Irish opposition, they held out to the Catholics the prospect of Catholic Emancipation—the right to sit in Parliament—to which they intended to add safeguards for the Protestants. These were to include a veto by the Crown on episcopal appointments in Ireland and the State payment of salaries to the bishops and priests. Father Concanen's firm and persistent opposition to this scheme led the unofficial British agent in Rome to describe him to London as "a very smooth and wily friar."

In the midst of his troubles with Napoleon, whose troops occupied Rome in February 1808, and the chronic wars in Europe, the Pope appointed a committee of Cardinals to consider the erection of new sees in the United States. Father Concanen urged on them the acceptance of Bishop Carroll's proposal. When asked who should go to New York if the Pope should decide to fill that post, he recommended his assistant, Father John Connolly, O.P. The Pope received and accepted the report of the cardinals on March 4, 1808, and ordered the official documents to be prepared. They were signed and promulgated on April 8th, 1808. At that time, Father Concanen was so seriously ill he expected to die and he was astounded by a visit from Cardinal di Pietro, the Prefect of Propaganda, who came to tell him he had been appointed to New York by the Pope himself and was commanded to accept. Having no alternative, he accepted and was consecrated on April 24, 1808, by Cardinal di Pietro in the Dominican Church of St. Catherine in Rome. New York was fortunate in the man chosen to be her first bishop. He was mature, experienced and very well informed, and he combined very attractively the quite separate gifts of sound judgment, self-effacement and a pleasing personality. He had excellent connections in Rome and all through the English-speaking Catholic world.

Appointment to New York was one thing, getting there was another. England and France, with their rival embargoes, had cut off almost all contact with America in 1808. The port of Leghorn seemed to be the best bet for departure and the new bishop went there early in June. He had with him all the official documents for the new sees and bishops, and for Archbishop Carroll, the pallium, the symbol of his authority as Archbishop. He also had faculties from the Dominican Master General empowering him to deal with any Dominicans in the Western Hemisphere who could not get in touch with Rome directly. He remained in Leghorn until October. Then, despairing of a sailing for New York, he returned to Rome to the Minerva.

In Rome he occupied himself with his old interests and performed episcopal functions, which were in demand during the captivity of the Pope and the cardinals. Meantime, on July 23rd, he had written to Archbishop Carroll asking him and authorizing him to appoint a Vicar General for New

York. From Rome, by way of Paris, he managed to send to Archbishop Carroll authentic copies of all the official documents relating to the new sees. In September 1809, he was suggested for the Archdiocese of Tuam, in Ireland, but declined. In June 1810 there was a chance to leave for New York from Naples. He hurried there, only to be barred from the boat by the French. He died suddenly on June 19th and was buried the following day in the local Dominican church. His tomb remained unmarked until Cardinal Cooke dedicated a commemorative tablet over it on July 9, 1978.

CHAPTER 4

The Kohlmann Years: 1808–1815

When Archbishop Carroll received Bishop Concanen's request to appoint a Vicar-General for New York, his mind turned at once to Father Anthony Kohlmann, S.J. (1771–1836) who had come to America in 1804 and had been working on the missions in Pennsylvania and Maryland. Born in Alsace and educated in Switzerland, he had worked as a diocesan priest in Italy, Austria and Holland, and had joined the Jesuits in Russia in 1803. He spoke excellent English, German and French and was a farsighted, industrious and prudent man who made a notable contribution to the Church in New York. It is probable that one reason for his appointment was a desire to please the Germans, who had been pressing the Archbishop for a priest and parish of their own.

When he came to New York in October 1808, he found the city had grown to about 60,000 inhabitants and had reached Canal Street on the north. The French and German Catholics numbered a few hundred each; the rest were Irish. A new street map, then in preparation, provided for the layout of streets in squares and for numbering streets and avenues. When the finished map was presented to the Legislature in 1813 it was noted that "it is improbable that for centuries to come the ground north of Harlem Flats will be covered with houses." It was believed too that the new plan "provided for a greater population than is collected in any spot this side of China."

More fortunate than most of his predecessors at St. Peter's, who were usually short-handed, Father Kohlmann had the aid of Father Benedict Fenwick, S.J., and of four Jesuit scholastics. He was able to give more service and got better results. There were sermons every Sunday in English, French and German, and the catechism classes were increased in number. The consequent revival of piety was notable and was reflected in the great increase in confessions. Many who had been away for years returned to the Church and during this time some converts entered the Church. In 1809, Fathers Kohlmann and Fenwick visited Thomas Paine on his deathbed at his invitation, but he rejected their services and died rejecting Christianity. A sign of the improved spirit was the willingness of the trustees, for the first time, to provide a residence for the clergy.

There was a pressing need for another church, and to mark the erection of the diocese it was decided to build a cathedral, which, at the suggestion of Archbishop Carroll, was dedicated to St. Patrick. It was the second church under that title in America. The site selected, at Prince and Mott Streets, was bought in 1801 as a graveyard. The cornerstone was laid by Father Kohlmann on June 8, 1809, in the presence of about 3,000 people. It was hoped that the work could be finished in a year, but it dragged on to 1815. The Embargo and Non-Intercourse Acts and the War of 1812 had severely adverse effects on the commerce of New York and money was scarce. Like Archbishop Hughes in a later year, he was blamed for building a cathedral so far out of town. St. Patrick's was the largest church in the city and designed by Joseph F. Mangin, the architect of the New York City Hall (1811).

Father Kohlmann had other plans that were not as successful. He foresaw a great future for New York, a much greater one, in his opinion, than Washington or Maryland could ever have. He regarded Maryland as the worst and poorest State in the Union, "a State from which even seculars retire to the wilderness of Kentucky, a State in which the Society [the Jesuits] will eternally be buried as in a tomb." He wanted a Jesuit school in New York City that would ultimately develop into a college. Very soon after his arrival his school opened, as "The New York Literary Institute," in small quarters on Mulberry Street. In March 1810 it moved to the site of New York's present Cathedral "at a distance of four small miles from the city." By 1813 it had seventy-four boarding students, including many non-Catholics. It was closed then by the Jesuit superiors in Maryland who, fearing to spread their men too thin, decided to concentrate on Georgetown. When the school closed, its premises were occupied by a group of exiled French Trappists who were awaiting the fall of Napoleon.

He was less fortunate in his plans for the education of girls. In 1812 he induced the Ursuline nuns to come from Cork, Ireland, to open an academy and a poor school. They came on condition that if in three years they had not received a certain number of novices they would leave and close their school at Third Avenue and 50th Street. The scarcity of pupils, the lack of novices, and above all, the inability to get to Mass frequently, led them to return to Ireland in 1815. His plans to bring over the Presentation Sisters to work among the poor had to wait almost sixty years.

Although the old Cathedral is his monument, Father Kohlmann's most important contribution to the welfare of the Church in New York was his role in the lawsuit that brought legal protection to the seal of the confessional in New York and later throughout the country. In March 1813, acting on information received in the confessional, he became the intermediary by whom stolen goods were returned to their owner. When he refused to tell the police or the grand jury or the courts who had given him the goods, his case was put off for further consideration and was settled finally by a friendly lawsuit. The case was argued on June 8, 1813, before the Court of General Sessions presided over by Mayor DeWitt Clinton. The full court decided unanimously in Father Kohlmann's favor. Later, in 1828, when Clinton was Governor of New York, he persuaded the Legislature to pass a law not only allowing but requiring priests and ministers of religion to withhold confidential information. It is worth noting that Father Kohlmann was represented by William Sampson, one of the more prominent lawyers of the day, who was an Irish Presbyterian, and a refugee from the unsuccessful Irish Rising of 1798.

When the Jesuits were restored on a permanent worldwide basis in 1814, their superiors here were free to make long-range plans. These involved, among others, Father Kohlmann who was recalled to Georgetown to act as Master of Novices, leaving New York in January 1815. Later, he went to Rome where he had among his pupils the future Pope Leo XIII. Father Fenwick remained to attend to the completion of the cathedral and await the arrival of Bishop Connolly. The cathedral was dedicated on May 4, 1815, Ascension Thursday, by Bishop John Cheverus of Boston, in the presence of a large congregation that included most of the public officials and prominent citizens of the city. It had taken thirty years for the Catholics of New York to build a second church. It cost $90,000 and in 1815 the debt was $53,000. In that year, the Bishop of Quebec described the interior as magnificent but lamented the lack of a steeple and proper sacristies.

CHAPTER 5

Bishop John Connolly, O.P.

The long delay in appointing a successor to Bishop Concanen was due primarily to Napoleon's imprisonment of Pope Pius VII, which lasted from June 10, 1809 to January 24, 1814. The Pope refused to appoint any bishop while he himself was in prison because he was cut off from his advisors and the necessary information. By the time he returned to Rome, dozens of sees, including some of the largest in Europe, were vacant and filling them involved protracted dealings with the post-Napoleonic governments. He also had to face the formidable task of re-establishing the papal government in Rome. Another important item, perhaps the major event of his pontificate, was the re-establishment of the Jesuits on a worldwide basis, which he decreed on August 7, 1814. Another reason for not dealing sooner with New York was that the Anglo-American War of 1812, which was still going on, had cut off communication with the United States. In those circumstances, the Pope finally selected a man he knew personally, a priest who had lived in Rome for thirty-seven years and who had been suggested for New York by Bishop Concanen when he had no knowledge that his own appointment to that post was being considered.

Father John Connolly, O.P., was born in County Meath, Ireland, in 1747. He was educated at Louvain and ordained at Malines, Belgium, on

September 24, 1774; shortly afterwards, he was sent to Rome where he remained until his departure for New York. His career paralleled closely that of Bishop Concanen. He, too, had been Prior of San Clemente, librarian at the Minerva, Roman agent of the Irish bishops, and had refused an Irish diocese, Raphoe.

He had remained in Rome during the French occupation and three times had refused to swear allegiance to Napoleon. He and Father Concanen were the only two who escaped the French expulsion of all British subjects from Rome. He tried hard to protect the Irish Dominican foundations from spoliation by the French. Appointed to New York on October 4, 1814, he was consecrated in Rome by Cardinal Brancadaro on November 6th. Since he was a British subject, he remained in Rome until the War of 1812 ended, and then, in the spring of 1815, started for Ireland to seek help for his new mission. En route, he stopped at Liège for Holy Week to consecrate the holy oils for that large diocese which the French had kept vacant for fourteen years. He reached New York on November 25, 1815, after a sixty-seven day voyage from Dublin in the *Sally,* a ship that displaced 350 tons. His voyage took so long that he had been given up as lost at sea.

When he landed in New York, Bishop Connolly found himself literally and figuratively in a new world. The city was growing rapidly, and it was clear that even greater growth was coming soon. The population, which had almost tripled since 1790, was about 96,000. New York had surpassed Philadelphia and had already become the most populous city in the country. Its growth was spurred by the restoration of peace. From 1810 to 1816 the population grew by only 4,200, but from 1817 to 1820 the increase was 23,000 and brought the city to 123,000.

The winter of 1815–1816 was an exceptionally hard one for the very poor. On February 1st a soup kitchen was opened and in its first twenty-four hours had 1,200 applicants. By March 1st some 6,600 people were being fed daily. At the same time, there were 1,700 licensed grog shops, in addition to which 1,600 groceries were licensed to sell liquor in small quantities and 600 other places could sell rum in small quantities. Efforts were being made to cope with what were seen as long-term problems. In 1816, Bloomingdale, the first local insane asylum, was opened and in 1817 the Society for the Prevention of Pauperism was founded. In 1816 the American Bible Society was founded and the city already had seven daily papers.

Bishop Connolly's diocese, half the size of Italy, had four priests on active duty and three churches to serve about 15,000 Catholics. A fifth priest, Father William O'Brien, former pastor of St. Peter's, was a hopeless invalid who would die in 1816. The two churches in the city, the Cathedral and St. Peter's, were heavily in debt. The third, St. Mary's, in Albany, built in 1798, was the only Catholic church between New York and Detroit. There was not one Catholic religious house or charitable institution. There was one school, taught by lay teachers, which had been attached to St. Peter's since 1800.

Three of the four priests, Fathers Peter Malou, a Belgian, Maximilian Rantzau, a German, and Benedict Fenwick, a Marylander, were Jesuits. The fourth, Father Thomas Carbry, an Irish Dominican who arrived in December 1815, was an old friend of the bishop. All but Father Malou were soon to leave New York.

Before he left New York in 1817, Father Fenwick was involved in one of the most remarkable conversions in the history of the Church in New York. This was the story of Virgil Barber, an Episcopal minister, who was president of an academy at Fairfield (Herkimer Co.), New York. He, his wife, and their five children were received into the Church at St. Peter's in February 1817. The Barbers separated and entered the religious life, he as a Jesuit and she as a Visitation nun. Their example was followed in due season by their children, all of whom without exception entered and persevered in the priesthood or the religious life. Moreover, Virgil Barber's father, also an Episcopal minister, and his mother, his sister, Mrs. Tyler, and her husband entered the Church. The Tylers had eight children, all converts, four of whom became Sisters of Charity, and one, William, the first Bishop of Hartford. The first step toward Virgil Barber's conversion was the reading of a novena to St. Francis Xavier borrowed out of curiosity from an Irish servant in his household.

With the departure of the three priests, Bishop Connolly was confronted by three basic problems that were to plague him and his successors for a century or more: an acute shortage of personnel, a shortage of money, and a rapidly increasing Catholic population that outstripped all efforts to provide adequate service. A fourth problem, trusteeism, was a major problem for Bishop Connolly and his immediate successor, Bishop John Dubois.

All of this was in sharp contrast to Bishop Connolly's life in Rome. At 68, he found himself promoted against his own will and judgment to an immense, unwieldy, poverty-stricken diocese that was almost wholly devoid of the tools necessary for the task in hand. Monsignor Guilday, the biographer of Archbishop Carroll, says of Bishop Connolly: "It may well be doubted if, in the entire history of the Catholic Church in the United States, any other bishop began his episcopal life under such disheartening conditions." Nonetheless, he accepted his situation and did his best. He gave no sign of suffering from self-pity.

He turned first to the shortage of priests. Rome had urged him to find them in Ireland. He found a few students, but in almost ten years was able to ordain only six priests, all of whom were born, and four of whom were trained, in Ireland. He had to depend on priests who volunteered or were recommended by others, and on a few priests with whom he had personal contact and whom he invited. By the time he died, he had about eighteen priests in his diocese and all were Irish.

Every bishop in the country had the same problem. Native vocations were scarce and took years to train. The demand for priests and churches came from all sides and was insatiable. What could be done? Unable to supply priests himself, the bishop often had no choice but to ratify the selection made by the trustees of the various parishes, who often went hunting on their own, not always with satisfactory results. Many priests certainly came at the invitation of a bishop, others came as volunteers. Many of those were suitable and some were not. One of the volunteers, John Nepomucene Neumann (1811–1860), of whom we shall see more later, was a saint.

There are many examples of the strength and weakness of the trustees' involvement in selecting the clergy. Two of them involve outstanding priests of the Connolly era. Peter A Malou (1753–1827), a banker in private life, took part as a General in the Belgian uprising against Austria in 1789. After pleading the cause of Belgian independence before the French Revolutionary Convention, he had to flee for his life. He came to America in 1795, and on his return to Belgium in 1797 found that his wife had died. In 1806, having provided for his children, he entered the Jesuits in Russia as a lay brother, but was recognized by a chance visitor to the novitiate and was transferred to theology. He returned to America in 1812 at his own request and remained in New York until his death. His personality probably explains why the Jesuit superiors, who were desperately short of men, left him in New York when his fellow Jesuits were recalled to Maryland.

Father Malou was an able, angular, contentious man and a tireless letter writer who bombarded Rome with complaints, usually wholly unfounded, against his superiors and the bishop. Ordered out of New York in 1820 by the bishop of Quebec, who had been commissioned by Rome to make an on-site investigation of his complaints, he refused to go. The following year he was suspended by the long-suffering Bishop Connolly and was expelled from the Society of Jesus. The trustees of St. Peter's sustained him and, since he had independent means, he was able to live privately near St. Peter's and continue his work. Father Malou's faculties were restored when Bishop Connolly died, and he continued at St. Peter's until he died. He very willingly used and was used by the trustees in their campaign against the bishop, but the same was true of several others. The other side of this singular man, who kept all his anger for his superiors, was his care of the sick and afflicted and his interest in catechetics. He prepared John McCloskey, the future Cardinal, for First Communion and his devoted care of John's father, whom he visited daily for six weeks before Mr. McCloskey's death in 1820, made an indelible impression on the McCloskey family.

Father John Power (1792–1849) was a different type of man. Born in County Cork, Ireland, and ordained at Maynooth, he came to America in 1819 at the invitation of the trustees of St. Peter's and was pastor of St. Peter's from 1822 until his death. He had the misfortune to see the church sold at public auction in September 1844, because of mismanagement by the trustees, whom he could not control. He was a richly gifted man, well described by Archbishop Corrigan as "a man of great learning, piety and talent, a ready extemporaneous speaker and a good writer. Evidently he was much thought of by the Catholics of New York as he was called upon on all prominent occasions to be their spokesman. He was a man of great benevolence of character and universally esteemed." He was a friend of Alexis de Tocqueville, who said he spoke perfect French, a friend and protégé of Bishop England of Charleston who tried hard to have him appointed bishop of New York in 1826 and again in 1838, and was Vicar General of New York under three bishops.

Father John Shanahan (1792–1870) is one example of the many priests who came here on their own and studied for the priesthood in this country. He arrived from Ireland in 1818 and offered himself to Bishop Connolly as a candidate for the priesthood only to be rejected because the bishop was too poor to help him pay for his seminary course. He went to Baltimore where he found work as a teacher. Having crossed the path of Father Simon Bruté, he was invited to enter Mount St. Mary's Seminary at Emmitsburg where he was a contemporary of the future Archbishops Hughes and McCloskey, and a student of Bishop Dubois. After his ordination in 1823 he began the life of a roving missionary, which he found very congenial, serving in many churches in the present dioceses of New York, Newark, Paterson, Albany, Brooklyn and Syracuse. From 1850 to 1854 he was in California and Nevada helping the gold miners and covering very large areas on foot. He returned to New York when his health failed and lived at St. Peter's. In spite of going blind in 1863, he carried on an active apostolate in the confessional until his death. He was popular as a confessor to the clergy, whom he used to ask as part of their penance to read to him for fifteen minutes. He assisted Bishop Connolly on his deathbed.

If Bishop Connolly's first task was to recruit more priests, his second was to deploy them properly. Except in the city, and even there in part, the priests had of necessity to be roving missionaries. When Father Michael O'Gorman was sent to Albany in 1817, he was given charge of the area from Albany to the St. Lawrence. Father Philip Lariscy, O.S.A., attended in 1822 "Staten Island and the Hudson Valley towns." He was much in demand because he heard confessions in Gaelic.

By the end of his life, Bishop Connolly had established churches in Brooklyn, Paterson, N.J., Auburn, Utica, Carthage, Rochester, Syracuse, and other places. St. James in Brooklyn, established in 1823, was the third church within the present limits of New York City. Not one of the churches Bishop Connolly built is now in the Archdiocese of New York.

The church buildings themselves were usually small, of the plainest possible construction, and poorly furnished. The first church of St. John in Paterson, New Jersey, was only 20 × 30 feet. The liturgy was celebrated with the utmost simplicity even on the greatest feast days. But, however simple, a church building was at least a start and a rallying point. Sometimes a church would be built as an inducement to the Bishop to send a priest. Sometimes the inducement was needed to get a priest to agree to come. If he agreed, he would then be presented to the Bishop for appointment. Usually, a visiting priest would have to bring everything needed for Mass. Naturally, in these circumstances most Catholics could not hope to hear Mass regularly or frequently. Baptisms and marriages were performed whenever the priest came on his rounds, for many could not afford the time needed to go to him. Mass was often said in private homes, in public buildings, in borrowed halls, and even sometimes in Protestant churches. Even at the Cathedral, where Bishop Connolly was pastor, there was little opportunity for more elaborate ritual since the Bishop was often alone while the priest or priests who lived with him went to Brooklyn or Paterson to say Mass on Sundays.

And for the Bishop there was continuing trouble with the trustees of the Cathedral and St. Peter's. The trustees of both churches were a single body until 1817, when the Bishop succeeded in dividing them, believing that he could count on better cooperation at the Cathedral. To the end of his days he had trouble at St. Peter's. In March 1818 the trustees "ordered" him to suspend a priest there, which he refused to do. The New York State law of 1813 regulating church property restricted the vote for the trustees to the pewholders. At the Cathedral this meant those who gave not less than four dollars annually in quarterly installments and were not more than six months in arrears. There were nine trustees, three of whom were replaced each Easter Monday, with notice of the coming election being given on the three preceding Sundays.

From the time of his arrival in New York, Bishop Connolly had hoped to open the orphan asylum that Father Kohlmann had planned. He succeeded in doing so in 1817 when his most important work in New York, the bringing in of the Sisters of Charity, was accomplished. In June three Sisters of Charity arrived from Emmitsburg to open the asylum in a small frame building on Prince Street near the Cathedral. (The building was previously known as Dead House, having been a military hospital during the Revolution.) The asylum opened in August with five orphans. It was the first charitable institution opened by the Church in New York State, and the Sisters of Charity were the first religious community to make a permanent foundation in the State. It gave Mother Elizabeth Seton much pleasure to see a foundation of her community in New York in her lifetime. The Sisters were paid $36 a year each, plus their keep. The whole project was made possible by the Catholic Benevolent Society, founded in 1817, and leaned heavily on the Ladies Auxiliary which was started immediately. When the asylum opened, there was only one other orphan asylum in New York City.

The only other things Bishop Connolly was able to achieve in the City were the opening in 1817 of a Free School, in the basement of the Cathedral, a substantial reduction in the Cathedral debt, and the enlargement of the Cathedral cemetery. At the dedication of the cemetery, Father O'Gorman preached in Gaelic. The school is still in existence and is the oldest in the Archdiocese.

Like Archbishop Carroll before him, Bishop Connolly found communication with Rome slow and uncertain and must often have felt very much on his own. In February 1818 he wrote to the Cardinal Prefect of Propaganda to acknowledge the receipt, on the same day, of letters from Rome dated February 5, April 19, and September 20, 1817, from which he learned that none of his letters of 1816 and 1817 had reached the Holy See.

The rapid growth of the Catholic population was caused mainly by the end of the Napoleonic Wars which ushered in a long period of relative peace in Europe, where there was no general war between 1815 and 1914. It was helped too by the building of the Erie Canal (1817–1825) which did much to make New York City the commercial and financial center of the United States. New York became the country's leading port and the main gateway for immigration. The canal brought New York State the preeminence in population it was to enjoy until 1963 and greatly accelerated its growth. New York State had already moved from fifth to first place by 1820, having been previously outranked in 1790 by Massachusetts, North Carolina, Pennsylvania, and Virginia. From 1830 to 1860 New York State had one-seventh of the national population. From 1790 to 1850 the national population increased by a third every ten years, and during much of that time the population of New York City increased at five times the national rate. In the same period, over two million square miles were added to the national territory.

The Erie Canal could not have been built without immigrant laborers, chiefly Irish, who came after 1815. When it was started, the population of New York State was only 1.3 million and much of the canal was built through open country. Agents were sent to Ireland to recruit workers and speed their passage. The need for workers was so great that many New York employers took down their "No Irish Need Apply" signs. Many Irishmen in jail in New York City for minor offenses were pardoned by Governor Clinton, the "Father of the Erie Canal," on condition they serve the rest of their term working on it. An ordinary workman made from 37.5 to 50 cents a day, plus a quart of whiskey, as the standard wage, compared with a skilled mechanic's daily wage of $1.25 in the city. If a released prisoner left work on the canal, he was to return to jail. The greatest hazards of the job were pneumonia, malaria, typhoid, and ague, but the canal workers seem to have escaped yellow fever, which hit New York City hard for the last time in 1822–1823, when about 1,200 died and there was widespread panic.

The canal itself was the marvel of the pre-railroad era. It was the largest in the world (363 miles), was built in the shortest time (1817–1825), cost $7 million or about $20,000 a mile, and was an outstanding financial success. (Its cost may be compared with the recent estimate for the Second Avenue subway in New York City of $26,000 a foot or the Alaskan Pipe Line's $7 million a mile.) In 1821 the State advertised for 1,200 men to work on the Lockport section of the canal, a particularly difficult one, offering $12 a month and food. (On the Alaskan Pipe Line in 1975, some skilled workers could earn $60,000 a year.)

The dividends from the canal were immense and immediate. It cut the time and cost of moving a ton of freight from New York City to Buffalo from three weeks and $120 to eight days and six dollars. In the city at least 500 new businesses opened in 1825, the year in which gas lighting was introduced, and 3,000 new houses were built. In that same year, as one of the city's historians has noted, "a seven-story tenement was erected at 65 Mott Street, the Society for the Reformation of Youthful Delinquents opened the House of Refuge, and the first organized gang appeared." Washington Square was laid out in 1827.

The canal had a great influence on the Church, too. It opened new settlements which clamored for priests and churches and soon had substantial Catholic populations, and it greatly improved the conditions under which the available priests could visit their flocks. In pre-canal days it took at least three weeks to go from Albany to Buffalo, and there was no regular passenger service west of Geneva. It took about ten days on the canal. It took thirty hours to Albany by steamboat and two to five days by sailboat. The faster canal boats made four miles an hour, and St. John Neumann has left us a pleasant description of his voyage from Schenectady to the stop nearest Rochester in four days.

With the canal, as with so many other things, Bishop Connolly was not to see the harvest. His health held up in spite of unremitting labor. He was described by Bishop Edward Fenwick, O.P., of Cincinnati in December 1824, as "drudging by night and day," but age, work, and disappointment began to take their toll. He made two visitations of the diocese, in 1817 and 1820. In the latter year, he traveled over one thousand miles alone, giving special attention to the canal workers. In December 1824 the trustees of the Cathedral, taking note of his health, voted that, "because of his age and infirmities and his zealous discharge of his duties in all sorts of weather," they would hire a horse and a one-horse carriage for his own use and would provide a servant to act as his coachman. He did not enjoy them long.

In his last two years, he had at the Cathedral two young priests in whom he placed confidence. Father Michael O'Gorman (whom he had asked for as coadjutor) and Father Richard Bulger were respectively the first priests ordained for and in New York. Both of them died unexpectedly, presumably of pneumonia, within a few days in November 1824. The shock, and a heavy cold contracted at the second funeral, were too much for the Bishop who died at his residence, 512 Broadway, on February 6, 1825. He was buried in the Cathedral after being waked at St. Peter's for the convenience of the people. The local papers spoke of him as "the pious, worthy and venerable Bishop Connolly," and about thirty thousand people attended the wake. By a strange oversight, the location of his grave was forgotten, and was discovered only in February 1976. His body had been removed from its tomb to make way for a prominent layman whose family had influence with the Cathedral trustees, and had been placed in a vault in which several other bodies were or would be buried, and which remained unmarked.

Bishop Connolly was described by contemporaries as a kind, industrious, hospitable, and cultivated man. He was short, very neat in appearance, simple in his manners and positive in his opinions. Bishop John England of Charleston (1786–1842), his outstanding contemporary in the American hierarchy, said of him: "Everybody admitted his virtue, his humility, and his exertions in discharging his duties in the confessional and attending the sick; but he was not generally considered to be a prelate acquainted with missions and fitted to form a new and extensive diocese." Bishop Cheverus of Boston said he possessed piety, knowledge, amiability, everything in fact but physical strength. His absorption in his work in New York was such that he left the diocese only once, to act as co-consecrator for Archbishop Ambrose Maréchal of Baltimore in that city in December 1817. He rarely commented on events outside his own diocese, but did urge the Holy See very strongly to erect a diocese in every state as a matter of policy.

CHAPTER 6

Bishop John Dubois

Before his death Bishop Connolly chose his Vicar General, Father John Power, to serve as administrator of the diocese during the impending vacancy. During the short period in which he held that office, Father Power founded New York's first Catholic newspaper, *The Truth Teller,* opened the third church in Manhattan, St. Mary's, now on Grand Street, and built a brick building for the orphan asylum, in which he took the deepest interest. The Sisters regarded him as their first great friend in New York. Part of the money for the asylum came from a benefit concert given in the Cathedral on June 22, 1826 by the Garcia troupe, which introduced Italian opera to the United States in 1825. The concert netted $2,500. Father Power also received into the diocese Father Felix Varela (1788–1853), the Cuban patriot and exile, who was the first Spanish-speaking priest to serve in New York. Father Varela founded Transfiguration Parish, was Vicar General under Bishop John Dubois, and was a prominent and valuable member of the Catholic community.

The three episcopal candidates recommended to Rome by the American Bishops for New York were Father John Power, Father Benedict Fenwick, S.J., and Father John Dubois. The first was recommended enthusiastically by Bishop England of Charleston and by the trustees of St. Patrick's

Cathedral. The choice was narrowed to two, when, on May 10, 1825, Father Fenwick was appointed bishop of Boston, ending a vacancy there that had existed since January 15, 1823. When he arrived in Boston, Father Fenwick found three priests and eight churches in all of New England.

Father Dubois was appointed bishop of New York on May 23rd, 1826. Once again, Rome had chosen a man with a wide experience of priestly life and an exceptional background. John Dubois was born in Paris on August 24, 1764, and educated at the College of Louis le Grand, the Oratorian Seminary of St. Magloire, and the Sorbonne. At first it was assumed that he would go into the army, but he chose the Church instead. At college he had two classmates who became infamous in the Reign of Terror, Maximilian Robespierre and Camille Desmoulins. A junior fellow pupil in all three schools was John Cheverus (1768–1836), who was ordained in 1790, was the first bishop of Boston (1808–1823), and died as Cardinal Archbishop of Bordeaux.

John Dubois was ordained on September 22nd, 1787, by the Archbishop of Paris, and assigned as curate to St. Sulpice and as chaplain to an insane asylum run by the French Sisters of Charity. He remained there until the fury of the Revolution drove him into exile in May 1791. General Lafayette gave him letters to a number of eminent Virginians, including Patrick Henry and James Monroe, who welcomed him warmly after his arrival at Norfolk in August 1791. He was a houseguest of Monroe for some time and was taught English by Patrick Henry. He supported himself by teaching French. Meanwhile, he did what he could for the few Catholics in Norfolk and Richmond. Through the favor of his non-Catholic friends, he was allowed to say Mass in Richmond in the State House.

By 1794, Father Dubois had made enough progress in English to be assigned as pastor of Frederick, Maryland, which included Emmitsburg, to which he moved in 1808. The congregation was small and scattered, the area quite extensive. The only church was located in Emmitsburg. He and Father Stephen Badin of Kentucky were then the only priests between Baltimore and St. Louis. While in Frederick, he came into close contact with the Sulpician Fathers in Baltimore, and it was at the suggestion of one of them that he decided to open a preparatory seminary at Emmitsburg, which he named Mount St. Mary's. He did this in 1808, the year in which he joined the Sulpicians. There were not enough students to support a school exclusively for seminarians—there were then only about 100,000 Catholics in the entire country—so Dubois accepted lay students who were interested in a strictly classical course.

The school opened with seven pupils but grew to sixty by 1812. In that year, Father Simon Bruté (1779–1839), later the first Bishop of Vincennes (Indiana), joined the staff and was very helpful to the hard-pressed president. He had been ordained in Paris in 1808, after finishing his medical studies, and came to America in 1810 when Napoleon was about to suppress the

Sulpicians. He remained at Mount St. Mary's, except for the years 1815–1818, until his consecration as bishop in 1834. On his arrival, he had found wooden buildings and very primitive accommodations, but Father Dubois soon started collecting for a stone building and (with immense exertions) began construction in 1823. The new building was destroyed by fire just as it was finished on June 6th, 1824, but was rebuilt by June 1826, shortly before Father Dubois' unexpected departure for New York.

When Mount St. Mary's was founded, only three other Catholic colleges existed in the United States. Georgetown, in Washington, D.C., was run by the Jesuits, St. Mary's in Baltimore by the Sulpicians, and St. Thomas in Kentucky by the Dominicans. All three were very small, as were all American colleges at that time. Mount St. Mary's had a seminary and a college department. The latter was really a preparatory school. Some of the seminarians taught and prefected in the college. Among those who did so were Father Dubois' two immediate successors in New York, John Hughes and John McCloskey. The course of studies was strictly classical, with heavy emphasis on Latin, French, and English. Life was rugged, the schedule was full, and discipline was strict. The students were absorbed in the busy routine of institutional life. They got to know one another very well and formed lifelong friendships. They were practically the first generation of American Catholic college students, and many were destined for prominent roles in the rapidly expanding American Church.

Besides his work at Mount St. Mary's, where he was something of a one-man band, and his continued interest in Emmitsburg, Father Dubois found time to play an important role in the early history of the American Sisters of Charity. He welcomed Mrs. Elizabeth Seton and her companions when they arrived in Emmitsburg in June 1809. He became their ecclesiastical superior on May 12, 1811 and was superior when their rule was approved in September 1815. He retained that post until his departure for New York. As superior he conducted the negotiations with Bishop Connolly that led to the Sisters' foundation in New York, and he attended Mother Seton on her deathbed in January 1821.

John Dubois' appointment as bishop of New York came as a surprise to him and many others, and he did not accept at once and therefore delayed his consecration. It took place in Baltimore on October 29th, 1826, at the hands of Archbishop Maréchal, Bishop Conwell of Philadelphia, and Father John Power. His episcopal ring was a gift from Charles Carroll of Carrollton. His installation took place on November 4th.

Although the preacher at his consecration, Father William Taylor, an eccentric, talented, and ambitious convert from the Church of Ireland who was soon to leave New York, had warned plainly of stormy days ahead, the Bishop was gratified by the friendly reception he received on his arrival. He wrote to Archbishop Maréchal on November 24, 1826: "I have had nothing but consolation since my arrival here. The frightful prognostications of the good Mr. Taylor have vanished like smoke and I see around me only good will and union, but it will take time to form a decided opinion."

Events soon changed this sanguine estimate of the situation. The Bishop found that his reception was courteous and cool and the reasons for that were made quite clear. He dealt with them in his first pastoral letter in July 1827. They boiled down to three points: first, he had been appointed to New York by the scheming of Archbishop Maréchal of Baltimore and the Sulpicians; second, he was a Frenchman; third, he was not taken from the clergy of New York. In his pastoral, he said that the Archbishop had opposed his appointment to New York, and the Sulpicians, like himself, knew nothing of it until it had taken place. The second and third charges were undeniable but, he felt, irrelevant. He had been in this country thirty-four years. This was in fact longer than many, if not most, of his critics had been here.

The Archbishop had opposed his appointment because he feared it would affect Mount St. Mary's adversely. The opposition to a bishop of French nationality was due to the current rivalry between some of the French and some of the Irish. The Irish, who were much more numerous, felt the French tended to despise them, and were over-represented in the hierarchy. Actually, suitable candidates for the episcopate were scarce, and many of the French refugees were well qualified and had been in America for years. Between 1789 and 1829, twenty bishops were appointed in this country. Four of them were born here, seven in France, six in Ireland, and one each in England, Italy, and Belgium. Three were Dominicans, one was a Jesuit, one a Franciscan, two were formerly Jesuits, three were Sulpicians, one a former Sulpician, and two were Vincentians. One, Archbishop James Whitfield of Baltimore, was a convert. Rome had cast her net wide. His being French should not have made a difference in Bishop Dubois' acceptance in New York, but in fact it did. This was partly because he, like so many well-educated Frenchmen, had trouble speaking English correctly, though he understood it perfectly and wrote it well.

The complaint that he was not from New York was based on the disappointment that Father Power, whom he made Vicar General, had been passed over. It was also an excuse for the trustees to give the Bishop trouble. In fact, they were able and willing to give Father Power trouble too. Bishop Dubois soon found out that, even before his arrival, the trustees had debated whether or not to receive him. They finally decided to do so, but "to give him trouble as one intruded on them by undue influence." He was to have trouble with the trustees at the Cathedral and at St. Peter's, also in Rochester, in Buffalo, and in other places until his death.

When Bishop Dubois arrived, he found three churches in the city, with six priests and, he estimated, about 35,000 Catholics. There were seventy Protestant churches. The population of the city in 1825 was 166,086. It would grow to 312,710 by 1840. Outside the city there were, he thought, about 120,000 Catholics in New York State and about 20,000 in the half of

New Jersey belonging to the diocese of New York. They were served by twelve priests and had about nine real churches. With one addition his problems were the same as Bishop Connolly's, but the increased Catholic population made it a lot easier to add more, though not enough, parishes. He was unable to induce any religious community to come to New York and was able to add only two orphan asylums, in Brooklyn and Utica, and half a dozen parochial schools. He did see the beginning of secondary education for girls in St. Joseph's Select School for Girls (1833), which later became, in 1847, Mount St. Vincent's Academy, and in the founding of St. Mary's Academy (1835). He added a wing to the Orphan Asylum, opened the Half Orphan Asylum, and enlarged the Cathedral. In 1831 the Sisters of Charity took charge of St. Peter's Girls School. In 1837 and 1838, respectively, the Cathedral and St. Peter's put up the first school buildings erected by the Church in New York. Bishop Dubois founded the Confraternity of the Blessed Sacrament in the Cathedral parish and held special devotions every Wednesday and Friday of Lent at which he often preached.

From the time he came to New York, the Bishop's chief ambition was to found a seminary. He did not share Bishop Connolly's gloomy view that American youth had "an invincible repugnance" to the ecclesiastical state. His experience at Mount St. Mary's convinced him that its success could be repeated in New York. His failure to achieve this goal was the major disappointment of his episcopate.

His first duty was to inspect his diocese and then, like many American bishops of his time and the next generation, sail for Europe in search of personnel and money. In 1828 and 1829 he covered much of New York State alone. In 1829 he traveled 3,000 miles and heard over a thousand confessions. In Buffalo, where he expected to find fifty or sixty Catholics, he found between seven and eight hundred. They included Frenchmen, Canadians, Swiss, Germans, and Irish. He heard the confessions of over two hundred Germans through an interpreter and was able to celebrate High Mass in the courthouse. Later, he went to the Indian missions in the St. Lawrence Valley.

On September 20, 1829 he sailed for Rome, which he reached in thirty-eight days. He did not return to New York until November 20, 1831. During his absence in Europe, he missed the First Provincial Council of Baltimore in 1829, which he had advocated for a long time, and at which he was represented by Father Varela. The Council attempted to establish a uniform system of discipline for the entire country. It strongly urged parochial schools and warned against trusteeism. It forbade the custom of having co-pastors in any parish as bound to lead to dissension. From Rome and from the Society for the Propagation of the Faith (hereafter called S.P.F.) which had been founded in France in 1822, he received funds for the seminary, but he found no priest willing to join him in New York. His contact with the S.P.F. was a fortunate one for New York. From 1827 to 1866 it gave the diocese

$112,160. New York received grants for a longer time than any of the first five dioceses except Louisville, which was cut out in 1867. From 1822 to 1839 the total contribution to the S.P.F. from this country was six dollars. In 1828 Propaganda told the S.P.F. it considered New York to have the most pressing needs of any mission diocese in the world.

The one problem Bishop Dubois faced that Bishop Connolly had been spared was a large-scale, well-organized, anti-Catholic movement. It started while he was in Europe. The only surprising thing about it was that it did not start sooner. The bitterly anti-Catholic spirit that had dominated the thirteen colonies had not been eliminated by the Revolution and the wave of toleration that followed it. It was there just below, and in many cases hardly below, the surface. It did not take much to bring it to the top. It only awaited leadership and the occasion that would set it ablaze. The principal occasion was the relatively large increase in Catholic numbers, due chiefly to immigration from Ireland. It became evident that far from dying out (as some had thought of the handful of Catholics here in 1790), they were going from strength to strength and no one could foresee the end. Between 1820 and 1830 the Catholic population grew by sixty percent. In 1830 there were about 600,000 Catholics in the United States.

The Nativist fears were stimulated by both the fact and the quality of this large-scale immigration. Public opinion was impressed and alarmed by the passage of the Catholic Emancipation Act in England and Ireland in 1829, which admitted Catholics to membership in Parliament. It was the culmination of years of agitation by Daniel O'Connell (1775–1847), the first great modern popular orator who knew how to mobilize the masses for political purposes, and was extorted from the British Government under the threat of revolution or civil war in Ireland. The Act was intensely unpopular with the Evangelical Protestants in England, who were told it would undo the Revolution of 1688, and with their counterparts in the United States.

The opposition to the immigrants was not based solely on zeal for the purity of the Gospel, though that influenced some. It was also based on an understandable alarm at the arrival of large numbers of people who differed from the average American in race, culture, religion, and economic standing. There would have been some opposition no matter whence such people came. When they belonged to a group the average American had been brought up to fear and despise, an outbreak was inevitable. It is important for the heirs of its victims to remember that the Nativists never succeeded in barring immigrants. They impeded, but could not prevent, their entry into full citizenship here. Moreover, although the anti-Catholic agitation was widespread, it was always limited. In the very year in which it started, 1831, the first Catholic ever to serve in the Federal Cabinet, Roger B. Taney of Maryland (1777–1864), was made Attorney General by Andrew Jackson; he also tried to make him Secretary of the Treasury in 1833 and did make him Chief Justice in 1836. None of these appointments was attacked on religious grounds. Unquestionably, much of the anti-Catholic feeling was due to the belief that the Church was the church of foreigners, and of poor foreigners, servants and laborers at that. In 1837 Harriet Martineau, the English writer, thought the hostility to the Irish Catholics in New York was equalled only by the general dislike of Blacks.

Since New York was the chief port of entry for the immigrants, it is understandable that the opposition to them was organized here, and then spread rapidly to other places where the same problem existed, e.g., Pennsylvania and Massachusetts. In January 1831, the New York Protestant Association, which provided the leadership for the anti-Catholic drive, was formed. Its sole object was "to promote the principles of the Reformation by public discussion groups which shall illustrate the history and character of Popery." It organized monthly meetings at which anti-Catholic lectures were given, and produced a torrent of anti-Catholic propaganda in the columns of the religious and secular press. It declared, "Popery, to be hated needs but to be seen in its true character," and "if the American people can be induced to look that monster in the face and observe his hideous features, they would turn from it in horror and disgust." The name of one of the publishing companies, "The Downfall of Babylon Press," is an indication of the spirit of the movement.

Part of the press campaign dealt with the well-known theological disputes between Catholics and Protestants, but much more of it took the form of lurid and even salacious accounts of alleged moral disorders in the Church, past and present, with special attention to the evils of the confessional and of convent life. Pornography did not then enjoy its present position in American life, and many readers accepted it eagerly in the only form available to them: the defense of home and hearth against the machinations of Rome. All this agitation culminated in August 1834 when a mob burned the Ursuline Convent in Charleston, Massachusetts, an outrage connived at by the public authorities before and after the fact, and heartily approved by public opinion. In 1835 the anti-Catholic movement entered local politics in New York with the formation of the Native American Democratic Association. The spirit of the nativists and their genuine fears are well expressed in a resolution adopted on June 10, 1835 at a meeting of the Association. It said: "Resolved: that the American independence is in danger of being annihilated by the machinations of the Pope, the Jesuits, and the Romish priesthood, and the advent of foreigners who yield a blind obedience to the Pope, and that all Catholics are in a conspiracy to subvert the government." Its platform pledged opposition to foreigners in office, to pauper and criminal immigration, and to the Catholic Church. It ran its first candidate for mayor, unsuccessfully, in 1836. He was Samuel F. B. Morse, the inventor of the telegraph, who was a fanatical anti-Catholic. They were more fortunate in 1837 when their candidate, Aaron Clark, was elected mayor and they also carried the City Council.

The Nativist Movement produced its masterpiece, the best-known work of anti-Catholic propaganda ever published in America, in *The Awful Disclosures of Maria Monk,* which appeared in 1836. This was a scurrilous and wholly fictitious account by a bogus ex-nun of life in a Montreal convent. It created an immense sensation, was given absolute credence by nearly all the non-Catholic religious press, and is still reprinted occasionally. Its success led inevitably to imitation, and soon the lecture circuit was crowded with "ex-nuns" describing their astonishing adventures to enthusiastic audiences whose avid credulity they exploited for years. Such publications had the twofold effect of revealing and intensifying the anti-Catholic spirit that was so strong in every part of the country.

While all this excitement was going on, Bishop Dubois went ahead with his plan to build a seminary. With the money he had obtained in Rome and France, he bought a farm in Nyack (Rockland County, N.Y.), and started to build in 1833. The clergy and many of the people thought it was too far from the city—about thirty miles—and the necessary funds came in slowly. Meantime, on January 12, 1834, nearly fifty years after the organization of St. Peter's congregation, he had the pleasure of ordaining the first native New Yorker who joined the diocesan priesthood. This was Father John McCloskey (1810–1885), his former pupil at Mount St. Mary's and his second successor in New York. The first native New Yorker to become a priest, James A. Neill (1798–1838), was ordained a Jesuit in 1828, left the Society for reasons of health in 1833, and died an assistant at St. Peter's in 1838. The first native New Yorker to enter the convent after Mother Elizabeth Seton was Susan Clossy of St. Peter's parish, who entered the Sisters of Charity in May 1809 and died on May 6, 1821.

Bishop Dubois also ordained the only priest ever attached to the diocese of New York who has been canonized. John Nepomucene Neumann (1811–1860) was already a deacon when he arrived from his native Bohemia on June 2, 1836. He was welcomed warmly by the Bishop who ordained him on June 25, and three days later assigned him to a mission area near Buffalo. On his arrival there, he found a parish with four unfinished churches in an area of 900 square miles. He joined the Redemptorists in 1840 and was their first American recruit. His appointment as Bishop of Philadelphia in 1852 was a heavy burden for him. His exceptionally short stature, unpolished English and manners, and his talent for self-effacement caused many, even among the clergy, to feel he was unsuited to Philadelphia but he made a lasting mark there and, by example, on the country. He began the first diocesan program of the Forty Hours Devotion in America and also the first diocesan school system. In addition, he opened the first Italian national parish in this country. He was an apostle of the confessional and knew six languages besides English. He learned enough Gaelic to hear the confessions of the itinerant Irish laborers he met on his pastoral rounds. New York profited from his labors because the Franciscan Sisters of Hastings, New York, who work at

Mount Loretto and several other areas in the Archdiocese, are an offshoot of a Pennsylvania community he founded. He fell dead in the street in Philadelphia on January 5, 1860, and was canonized by Pope Paul VI on June 19, 1977.

In February 1834 Father John McCloskey was assigned to St. Joseph's seminary, Nyack, N.Y., as vice president and professor of philosophy. The building was unfinished, but work continued, and the chapel was dedicated on August 10, 1834, in a ceremony at which he preached. There were five pupils. Shortly afterwards the entire plant was destroyed by a fire of suspicious origin. There was no insurance and the entire investment was lost. The Bishop, undaunted, began at once to plan another seminary, but nothing could be done for some time. In September 1838 a new seminary was opened at Lafargeville, New York, near the Canadian border, but was so remote— over three hundred miles from the city, requiring a journey of eight to ten days by steamer, canal barge, and coach— that it was moved to Fordham (Bronx, N.Y.) in the autumn of 1840 by Bishop Hughes.

Unable to do much for the institutional side of the diocese, Bishop Dubois concentrated on the parochial structure. In New York City, he rebuilt St. Peter's and St. Mary's and opened five new parishes. St. Paul's in Harlem was the first city parish north of Fourteenth Street. Although Dubois was a firm believer in dignified and even imposing churches wherever possible, more than half the congregation of St. Paul's had to stand outside the Church during Mass. In 1833 the Bishop also founded the Ladies of Charity, a lay organization to help the poor that still flourishes.

An important chapter in the history of the Church in New York was the opening of the first national parish in 1833. This was the German parish of St. Nicholas. The pastor, Father John Raffeiner (1785–1861), was an Austrian who arrived in New York in 1833 and was, until his death, the apostle to the Germans, first in the diocese of New York and, later in the divided dioceses of New York and Brooklyn. He was Vicar General for the Germans under Bishop Hughes and was responsible for founding thirty parishes. The German parishes were as prone to trouble with the trustees as the Irish parishes, and the parish of St. Nicholas was no exception.

Pressing as were the demands of the Catholics in New York City for more parishes, the Bishop did not let them absorb all his resources. Within the present limits of the Archdiocese, he founded the first parish in the following counties: Ulster, at Saugerties, 1833; Putnam, at Cold Spring, 1834; Dutchess, at Poughkeepsie, 1836; Orange, at Newburgh, 1837; and Richmond at New Brighton, in 1839. He could not do as well upstate, where the Catholics were often more widely scattered. Thus, in 1837, Father William Beecham was made pastor of seven counties in the future diocese of Albany, with permission to live chiefly at Rome, Carthage, or Utica, as he chose. He chose Rome because there he would be more likely to meet another priest and be able to go to confession.

One of the parishes in which trusteeism was most troublesome was St. Joseph's in Greenwich Village. The parish was started in 1830 to care for the Catholics of what was then a self-contained community, about an hour's journey from the city by horse car, and used by many New Yorkers as a summer resort. It was also a refuge from the outbreaks of yellow fever that afflicted the city so often. In 1824, on July 12th, Orangemen's Day, anti-Catholic rioters in Greenwich Village had wrecked the homes of some Irish laborers. In 1830 it was difficult to buy a suitable site there for a Catholic Church. A large hall on Grove Street was rented for $800 a year, and in 1833 the present site of St. Joseph's Church was acquired. The Church was dedicated on March 16, 1834 by Bishop Dubois, who celebrated a Pontifical Mass. The deacon was Father William Quarter, later the first Bishop of Chicago, the subdeacon was Father John McCloskey, and the sermon was preached by Father Constantine Pise. Father John Hughes of Philadelphia was present, making one of his first appearances in New York. All these men had been closely associated at Mount St. Mary's. The parish boundaries went from Canal Street to Twentieth Street and from Broadway to the Hudson River. The collection at the dedication amounted to $1,500, a substantial sum in those days.

The trustees of St. Joseph's became a problem almost at once, and in three years there were four pastors. The Bishop moved one, Father James Quinn, to Troy against the wishes of the trustees, who proceeded to make life miserable for Father Pise, who replaced him.

Constantine Pise (1801–1866) was born in Maryland of an Italian father and an American mother. He was educated at Georgetown, in Washington, D.C., and in Rome, was a Jesuit for awhile, and was ordained at Mount St. Mary's for the Archdiocese of Baltimore in 1825. He taught at Mount St. Mary's and then did parochial work in Washington and Annapolis, Maryland. He was the first, and to date the only, Catholic priest to serve as chaplain to the United States Senate. He came to New York in 1834 at the request of Bishop Dubois, and lived at St. Joseph's until 1837. Later, he was pastor of St. Peter's, Barclay Street, and then of St. Charles' parish in Brooklyn, where he died. He was a close friend of Father John McCloskey, who presided and preached at his funeral. He was an excellent scholar, writer, and preacher, a man of polished manners, and of an exceptionally meek and gentle character. He was not the man to manage the trustees, from whom he was glad to escape by resignation in August 1837. They liked and esteemed him but resented his appointment, and most of them were determined not to accept him. He was succeeded by Father McCloskey.

When the new pastor arrived, he found the trustees and their supporters up in arms. His own opinion of trusteeism was quite definite. He described it in a letter to Bishop Dubois from Rome on July 28, 1835 as being "at the bottom of all the most serious evils that have yet arisen in the Church in America." Many wondered if he, who seemed so much like Father Pise, was the man to tame the trustees of St. Joseph's. For six months they refused to pay his salary and stayed away from any Mass he said. On his first Sunday, the pews in the middle aisle were empty and there were not a dozen people between him and the door. The trustees refused to furnish the rectory, pleading that his mother could well afford the expense and would spend the money if she really wanted him to have furniture. That, of course, he would not let her do. They even stooped to sending false sick calls at night. His reaction to all this was characteristic and showed the iron self-control which was hidden from many by his mild and courteous manners. He ignored it all, and never complained of it then or later. He prepared his sermons carefully and read them as if the church was crowded. The trustees said he was incapable of writing such sermons, which must have been prepared for him by Father Pise, with whom he dined weekly. He was uniformly gracious to all he met, kept to himself, criticized no one, did the work that came his way, and gradually won them over. Many of the trustees became lifelong friends and supporters. His only comment on it all, made years later, was that they were good and well intentioned but very obstinate people. They were led by Patrick Sarsfield Casserly who ran a successful classical school and personally had wanted Father Pise kept on. Casserly insisted later that his son Eugene be prepared for First Communion by Father McCloskey and no one else. Eugene Casserly became the first Catholic senator from California and was always a devoted friend of Father McCloskey. A friend who was watching the struggle said confidently of the pastor: "He will not fight but he will win."

While the Catholic community was giving an undue amount of time to these intramural disputes, the city itself was changing. By 1827 the last vestiges of slavery vanished when the slaves, emancipated in 1797 and indentured for 30 years, fulfilled their terms of service. In 1832 the first outbreak of cholera terrified the general public. There were about 6,000 victims, half of whom died. In the same year, the first railroad in New York opened. It ran from 14th Street to Prince Street and by 1838 was extended to Harlem. In 1831 New York University was founded to offset the influence and break the monopoly of Columbia (founded as Kings College, 1754), which was thought by many to be too conservative. N.Y.U. was more liberal, and really nonsectarian, though under Presbyterian influence. In 1834, the Mayor, who had once been appointed by the Governor, and later elected by the Common Council, came to be elected by the people, though some property qualifications as a restriction on voting lasted until 1842. Two things that astonished Bishop Dubois when he came to New York did not change. These were the high cost of dying and the mobility of the inhabitants, half of whom, he said, changed their residence every year on the first of May. The Great Fire of 1835 destroyed almost every building south of Wall Street and east of Broadway. The Panic of 1837, which lasted until 1843, brought widespread unemployment and distress. In 1837 an observer wrote that "the cost of living had so increased that it was next to impossible for a man with a moderate income to support a wife and child." The modest scale on which State public assistance was given to the needy can be seen from the figures for 1834. In that year the State spent $300,000 on relief, and New York City spent $90,000, to assist 19,000 paupers. After the Panic of 1837, one-third of the working population was unemployed and wages fell thirty to fifty percent from 1839 to 1843. During the next seven years, wages were frozen and the cost of living rose by nearly fifty percent.

By 1834 there was already much discussion of a coadjutor bishop for New York. The size of the diocese, the difficulty of traveling, the increase in population, and the growing infirmity of Bishop Dubois who often had to use crutches because of rheumatism, made help advisable if not imperative. Father Kohlmann, who was teaching in Rome and was often consulted on American affairs, favored Father John Power. So did Bishop John England of Charleston, South Carolina. Rome knew there was friction between Bishop Dubois and Father Power, his Vicar General, who regarded the Bishop as a notably incompetent administrator. This was well known to the Bishop who in turn had doubts about Father Power's judgment and loyalty. While Rome would have granted a request from the Bishop for Father Power as coadjutor, it was unwilling to force matters, so nothing was done for a while. In April 1837 the American bishops, having been appealed to by Bishop Dubois, approved his list of three names, all from outside the diocese, which he then forwarded to Rome. On the list were Bishop Francis Kenrick, coadjutor of Philadelphia and later Archbishop of Baltimore, Father John Hughes of Philadelphia, and Father Samuel Mulledy, S.J., a former president of Georgetown College. The choice of the Holy See was Father Hughes, who was notified on November 3, 1837, of his appointment on August 8th, as coadjutor Bishop of New York, with the right of succession. His titular see was Basileopolis.

The consecration of the coadjutor was the first episcopal consecration ever held in New York, and the ceremony made a great impression. It was performed on January 7, 1838, in St.Patrick's Cathedral by Bishop Dubois, assisted by Bishops Francis Kenrick and Benedict Fenwick. It was boycotted by some New York priests who resented the failure of the Holy See to appoint Father Power. The sermon was preached by Father Mulledy, S.J. Though there were then eight churches in the city, all the vestments and everything else needed for the ceremony had to be borrowed from Philadelphia, except for two copes provided by the New York Cathedral. The Cathedral was crowded for the occasion and, in spite of wintry weather, the windows were left open and stands erected on every part of the surrounding cemetery from which a view of the sanctuary could be had.

Few who attended his consecration could have guessed that the new bishop would prove to be unquestionably the outstanding Catholic in 19th century New York. John Joseph Hughes was born on June 24, 1797, in Annaloghan, County Tyrone, Ireland, in the Archdiocese of Armagh. His parents were small farmers. John's early schooling was interrupted by poverty, and he worked as a gardener until he came to America in 1817. His family settled in Chambersburg, Pennsylvania, about thirty miles from Emmitsburg, Maryland. He himself had shown early signs of a vocation and tried hard to enter Mount St. Mary's when he came to America, only to be told there was no vacancy. He worked as a stonemason and gardener until, in November 1819, he was employed as a gardener at the college, pending a vacancy that came in September 1820, when he enrolled as a full-time student. At that time the buildings were all log cabins.

When he was ordained for the diocese of Philadelphia on October 15, 1826, it was arranged that he live for awhile with Father Michael Hurley, O.S.A., a prominent pastor in that city, who would direct him in further study and guide his first steps in the priesthood. Father Hurley was much impressed by his pupil and predicted a glorious future for him. He saw in him "a discretion beyond his years, an indomitable will, a courage nothing could shake, and a zeal that never tired." Others must have seen the same qualities, for John Hughes was recommended for coadjutor of Philadelphia in 1829, for Cincinnati in 1833, for Pittsburgh or Philadelphia in 1836, and finally for New York in 1837.

Largely because of the administrative weakness of Bishop Henry Conwell, the diocese of Philadelphia was in a state approaching chaos when Father Hughes arrived. He had ample opportunity to learn at first hand the trouble trusteeism could cause. He saw, as well, the bad effect on the morale of ordinary Catholics caused by the failure of their leaders to reply to the anti-Catholic propaganda and agitation rampant at the time. He was the first priest in Philadelphia to take up the cudgels for his flock and the response was notable. In 1831 he built a new church in Philadelphia, St. John's, that had no lay trustees. When he had trouble with finances, he learned Spanish in six months, in preparation for a begging tour in Mexico. When his parishioners learned of his plan, they increased their contributions and the trip was cancelled. He had a good schooling in trusteeism, controversy, and anti-Catholic agitation before he reached New York.

It did not take long for people to realize that with the arrival of Bishop Hughes a new and brighter day had dawned for the Church in New York. His firm hand was soon felt as more and more of the work of the diocese was entrusted to him by Bishop Dubois who was failing, the victim of a series of strokes that began in January 1838 and left him disoriented at times. It was part of his malady that he did not recognize how sick he was, so he was upset and at first rebellious when, in August 1839, Archbishop Samuel Eccleston of Baltimore arrived to tell him personally that Rome had made Bishop Hughes administrator of the diocese. Describing his own reaction, Bishop Dubois said that he obeyed the bit but not until he had covered it with foam. He took no further part in the administration of the diocese, though he was kept informed of events by Bishop Hughes. He continued to live at the

Cathedral and died there on December 20th, 1842. He was buried, at his request, under the pavement in front of its entrance. He left the memory of a high-minded, devout, industrious, learned, and courteous man who lacked the capacity to deal with the administrative problems he met in New York.

Even before becoming administrator, Bishop Hughes had fought and won his first big battle in New York. It was with the Cathedral trustees whom he confronted and routed. In 1834 Bishop Dubois had suspended a priest at the Cathedral for insubordination. The trustees made the man director of the school, voted him a salary, refused to accept or pay the priest appointed by the Bishop, and threatened to cut off the Bishop's salary. He, who was poor all his life, replied, "Well, gentlemen, you may vote the salary or not just as seems good to you. I am an old man and do not need much. I can live in a basement or a garret. But whether I come up from the basement or down from the garret, I shall still be your Bishop." The matter dragged on until a year after Bishop Hughes arrived.

The trustees then went further. They authorized their candidate to invoke the aid of the police and eject the catechist assigned to the Sunday School by the Bishop. When this was done on February 10, 1839, the issue was joined. On February 24th, time having been given for an apology that did not come, a strong letter written by Bishop Hughes and signed by Bishop Dubois was read at all the Masses in the Cathedral. It called on the parishioners to repudiate the trustees and accept the law of the Church. At a crowded meeting that afternoon, Bishop Hughes spoke firmly and persuasively and received an ovation. The trustees were repudiated and the battle was won. The effects were felt all through the diocese. While trusteeism was not eliminated instantly or completely, it had suffered a fatal defeat. By a single stroke, the coadjutor had done what none of his predecessors had been able to do since 1784; he had established episcopal authority firmly in New York. Bishops Carroll and Concanen had been nonresident, and Bishops Connolly and Dubois had lacked the strength of will and forceful personality needed for the task.

CHAPTER 7

Archbishop John Joseph Hughes

When Bishop Hughes became administrator of New York in 1839, he found that the entire diocese had twenty-two churches, ten of which had been built in 1837 and four of which were in New Jersey. Not one of them owned a rectory. By 1850 there would be 176 churches in New York State alone and by 1860 the number would reach 360. In 1839 there were forty priests and about 200,000 Catholics in New York State in a population of about 2.7 million. Catholics were thought to constitute at least a fifth of the population of New York City. City churches owed about $300,000 on which the interest was seven percent. Seven of the eight parishes were below 14th Street. The Sisters of Charity were still the only religious community in the diocese. There were eight parochial schools, all in the city, with 5,000 pupils. It was estimated that only about half the Catholic children went to schools of any kind. In 1839 there were 17,000 children in the public schools, but more than 12,000 children between the ages of 4 and 14 went to no school at all. There were two Catholic orphan asylums in New York City, and one each in Utica and Brooklyn.

New York City itself was on the verge of great growth. The population would grow between 1840 and 1865 from 312,710 to 726,386 and would expand at five times the national rate. In 1840 the city's northern boundary line was Fourteenth Street. It would reach Thirty-Fourth Street by 1850 and Forty-Second Street, above which there was then no paving, by 1860. In 1840 one-third of the population still lived below Canal Street. The city had 150 churches of which the Presbyterians had thirty-nine and the Episcopalians twenty-nine. The rest were divided among seventeen groups.

Once Bishop Hughes had familiarized himself with the needs of the diocese, he went to Europe. His journey lasted from October 1839 to July 1840. Characteristically, he enjoyed a great storm at sea on his way to Europe, where he visited Rome, Vienna, Munich, Paris, London, and Dublin. He spent three months in Rome, which he was reluctant to leave. In Vienna he met Prince von Metternich, the famous Austrian diplomat who was considered the outstanding statesman of the age. In Paris he was presented to King Louis Philippe by the American Minister. He was agreeably surprised to find that he could go from Paris to London in only thirty-six hours. In London he met Daniel O'Connell whom, we are told, "he admired with an ardor almost amounting to enthusiasm." Everywhere but London, he was looking for personnel and funds to help the necessary expansion in New York.

THE SCHOOL CONTROVERSY

On his return, Bishop Hughes found the stage set for his most famous controversy, the attempt to get State aid for the Catholic schools. From the foundation of the colonies, education in America had been religious and no real problem arose until a substantial amount of religious diversity appeared. In 1806 New York State established a fund which, when it reached $50,000, was to be apportioned to the various towns and cities. The Common Schools Acts of 1812 and 1813 established regulations for the distribution of those funds. Outside New York City they were to be administered by commissioners, inspectors, and trustees elected by popular vote. In New York City they were vested in a commission of five members appointed by the Mayor and Common Council. The Legislature named the New York City institutions to which a share was to be allotted: the Free School Society and such incorporated religious societies as then supported or might establish charity schools. The allotments were to be based on enrollment. Actually, after 1825 no public funds were given to any Church-affiliated schools, including the parochial schools.

In 1805 the Free School Society was established in the city to educate children not cared for by the denominational schools. Its name was changed to the Public School Society in 1826, but despite its title it was always a private organization. It soon became the dominant educational organization in the city. It was consistently hostile to the claims of the denominational schools to a share in public funds and was supported in this attitude by many Protestant groups who were prepared to go without public help themselves rather than see the Catholics get any support.

The controversy of 1840 was started inadvertently by William H. Seward (1801–1872), who was Governor of New York from 1839 to 1843. In his annual message to the Legislature in 1840, he recommended aid for the denominational schools. This encouraged the Catholics, led by Father Power, to organize to press their claims. All of this happened during the absence of the Bishop and without his knowledge, but he approved of it and took charge on his return. The Catholic strategy was to appeal first to the New York City Council, where they anticipated defeat, and then to the Legislature. The Catholic appeal touched a neuralgic nerve and the resultant uproar lasted for years. Almost the entire secular and Protestant press denounced the Catholic claims, and for months many of the Protestant pulpits were used to denounce both the petition and the Catholic religion. The Catholics were defeated both in the city and the Legislature. Late in October 1841, both major parties in the city pledged themselves not to support any candidate for the Legislature who favored the Catholic claims. This forced the Catholics, at the last minute, to run a slate of their own even though it was certain to be beaten. Their candidates, who ran on four-days notice, received 2,200 votes. The Whigs beat the Democrats by 290 votes. This was a lesson the Democrats remembered.

The main objection of the Catholics to the public schools was their anti-Catholic atmosphere. Professedly nonsectarian, they were in fact strongly Protestant but of a non-denominational kind. The Catholics wondered why their children could not read the Catholic Bible, rather than the Protestant one, and why they had to use textbooks that were often patently offensive. They had no desire to deprive the Protestants of their own version, but were consistently and unfairly portrayed as anti-Bible and as wishing to exclude the Protestant Bible and religion from the school system. They were acutely aware of being excluded from any active role in the management of a school system they helped pay for and in which their religion was consistently derided.

The final solution, the Maclay Bill, adopted on April 9, 1842, was a defeat for both sides. By barring all religious instruction from the public schools, it led ultimately to the secularization of all public education in the United States and turned out to be a major factor, perhaps the major factor, in the decline of organized Protestantism in this country. It also forced the Catholics, despairing of obtaining justice from the State, to put their hopes in the parochial school system, and to assume an ever-growing financial burden that amounted to substantial double taxation. Their system, the largest private school system in history, has never been able to accommodate even half their children and has been maintained by immense sacrifices. On the night the Maclay Bill was passed, a Nativist mob attacked Bishop Hughes' residence and the militia had to be called out to protect the Catholic churches in the city.

Recognizing at last the depth and intensity of the anti-Catholic feeling, which he had underestimated, Bishop Hughes made no further attempt to reopen the school controversy. He turned his attention instead to the growth and development of the parochial schools and, in a pastoral letter issued on November 15, 1850, he told the people "the time has almost come when we shall have to build the schoolhouse first and the church afterward." In 1857 he said, "In our age the question of education is the question of the Church." By the end of his administration, New York alone had 15,000 children in the parochial schools. It had twelve Select Schools and thirty-one free schools. In the rest of New York State, the three dioceses carved out of New York— Albany, Buffalo, and Brooklyn—had 26, 28, and 13 schools respectively, so a substantial effort had been made. By the end of the century, the parochial schools on the national level had nearly a million students.

One of the unexpected results of the school controversy was the winning over to the Nativist camp of many middle class Protestants who accepted the charge that the Catholic Church was anti-Bible. This gave the Nativists, for a time, greater respectability than they previously had. In June 1843, the American Republican Party was organized in New York City, where it did very well in the fall elections. The movement then spread to upper New York and to Pennsylvania. Its basic aims were: (1) to change the naturalization laws in such a way that foreigners would have to wait twenty-one years for naturalization, because native Americans had to wait that long to vote; (2) to restrict control of naturalization to the Federal Courts; (3) to reform the gross abuses arising from party corruption. Since the Party was openly anti-Catholic as well as anti-foreign, there was great danger of violence when it became active in places where Catholics and foreigners were concentrated, as they were in New York and Philadelphia.

Understandably, the Catholics were divided about the best way to meet the problem. Some, like Bishop Francis P. Kenrick of Philadelphia, thought the best way was to endure it patiently, make no response, and offer no defense or resistance. Others, like Bishop Hughes, urged militant vigilance. The Catholics should demand protection from the public authorities and be prepared to meet force with force if the authorities failed to protect them or sided with their enemies. Experience showed the latter course to be correct. In April and May 1844, Philadelphia was swept by riots in which two Catholic churches were burned and looted, several people were killed, and many Catholic homes were destroyed. Not for many years was even partial compensation paid, and then only in the face of bitter opposition.

Things were different in New York, thanks mainly to Bishop Hughes, who blamed the Catholics of Philadelphia for not defending their churches, and warned Mayor James Harper bluntly that if a single Catholic church were burned in New York the city would become a second Moscow. When urged by some worried public officials to "restrain the Irish," he said, "I have not the power, you must take care that they are not provoked." He exhorted the Catholics to stand up for their rights calmly, and to be sure not to strike the first blow. Having been told the State was not obliged to pay compensation for damaged property, he placed a guard of armed men, over a thousand strong, around each Catholic church, and notified the Mayor he had done so. A plaque in the original St. Patrick's Cathedral commemorates those stirring times. It says: "Erected to the memory of the members of the Ancient Order of Hibernians of the City of New York—who in April 1844 at the call of the Most Reverend John Hughes—rallied to the defense of the Cathedral when it was threatened with destruction by the forces of bigotry and intolerance." Mayor Harper, himself a Nativist, belonged to the publishing house that had arranged the printing of Maria Monk's fables. The excesses of the Nativists caused a reaction against them, and shortly afterwards the Mexican War and its aftermath diverted attention from the Catholics and foreigners for a few years.

Though his struggles with the trustees, the Public School Society, and the Nativists were truly important, they took a very small part of Bishop Hughes' time and energy, and the attention given to them has tended to overshadow many other important and constructive activities. They gave him the lasting image of the fighting bishop, and made him for many years one of the most bitterly criticized men in the country and a favorite target for most of the press. Not all his critics were outside the fold. Some of the more prosperous Catholics in New York were terrified by the storm, especially during the Nativist days. He described them as "generally good, cautious souls who believe in stealing through the world more submissively than suits a freeman." One of his most bitter and persistent critics was James Gordon Bennett (1795–1872), the founder and long-time publisher of *The New York Herald.* Bennett, born in Scotland, was a former Catholic seminarian who fell away from the Church, to which he returned on his death bed. He was one of the pioneers in sensational journalism, which developed when improved printing methods made the penny paper and mass circulation possible.

From his earliest days in New York, Bishop Hughes was keenly interested in starting a seminary and college that would fulfill the plans of Bishop Dubois and Father Kohlmann. Even before leaving for Europe, he had paid $30,000, of which the diocese raised $13,000, for Rose Hill Manor, Fordham (Bronx County), about ten miles from the city, where he intended to establish both. He was able to open St. Joseph's Seminary there in September 1840 and St. John's College (now Fordham University) on June 24, 1841. Father John McCloskey was the first president of the college but served only for a year because of his poor health. It was hard enough to raise the money in America or in Europe, but it was harder still to find a faculty for either the seminary or the college. There were so few priests in the diocese, which was growing rapidly, that it was impossible to supply the necessary manpower. Hence, the Bishop was delighted when the Italian Vincentians agreed to staff the seminary, which they did until their departure for Missouri in 1846. The French Jesuits then agreed to take over both schools. This arrangement, while permanent for the college, was not mutually satisfactory for the seminary, which reverted to the diocesan clergy in 1856. In 1861 St. Joseph's Seminary was forced to close because of the Civil War, but was reopened in 1864 in Troy, New York, where it remained until September 1896. In its relatively short life, the Fordham Seminary gave New York 107 priests.

St. John's College was more successful. The Catholic population was growing, and, as many of its members moved up the economic and social ladder, they wanted and could afford a solid education for their sons. Starting a college in 1841 was easier than it would be now. All the colleges had small student bodies and the necessary equipment was not elaborate. In 1846 when the College of the City of New York was founded (to provide a completely secular education), Columbia and New York University, the only other non-Catholic colleges in the city, had a combined enrollment of 245. By 1845 Fordham had 145.

Bishop Hughes was well aware of how indispensable the religious communities are to the proper, long-term functioning of the charitable and educational works of the Church, and he did his best to bring them here. He started the process by which eventually almost all the major and many of the minor communities with an international apostolate came to New York. In the educational field alone he was able to found, or help to found, not only Fordham, but Manhattan College, Manhattanville, and Mount St. Vincent, all of which were chiefly boarding schools, and Xavier College (1850–1918), a successful Jesuit day school which initially charged fifty dollars a year for tuition. By 1863 Xavier, which had been chartered in 1861, had 450 students and Fordham had 250. Among the religious communities introduced in the Hughes administration were the Redemptorists (1841), the Jesuits (1846), the De la Salle Christian Brothers (1848), the Fathers of Mercy (1841), the Religious of the Sacred Heart Sisters (1841), the Ursuline Nuns (1855), the Sisters of Mercy (1846), and the Good Shepherd Sisters (1855). He also encouraged Father Isaac Hecker to found the Paulist Fathers.

Bishop Hughes' work among the religious communities included the establishment of an independent community of the Sisters of Charity in New York. In 1845 he had been notified by the superiors at Emmitsburg, Maryland, that the Sisters planned to withdraw from the care of boys over three years of age. Since he had no hope of replacing the Sisters and at the same time was compelled to enlarge the Boys Orphan Asylum, he felt it necessary to start a new community which would be confined to New York and would have its mother house and novitiate in the city. It was a decision that, given his temperament, he would almost certainly have come to anyway. Each of the Sisters then working in New York was given the choice of remaining in New York or returning to Maryland. Thirty-three out of sixty-two remained, and the new community, the Sisters of Charity of Mount St. Vincent, came into existence on December 8, 1846. Their novitiate opened on February 16th, 1847. The new community was a success from the beginning and has continued to be the largest in New York. In 1849 and 1859 respectively, two independent communities, the Sisters of Charity of Halifax, Nova Scotia, and of Convent Station, New Jersey, branched off from it. The founder of the latter community, Mother Mary Xavier Mehegan, was born in Ireland in 1825. She was one of the first novices of the New York Community, and was Superior in New Jersey until her death in 1915. She saw her community grow from six members in 1859 to 1,400 in ninety institutions at the time of her death.

The New York Sisters of Charity chose their first Superior wisely. Mother Elizabeth Boyle (1788–1861) was born near Baltimore and was received into the Church in April 1808 just before Mother Seton reached Baltimore. She was one of the original American Sisters of Charity and served as mistress of novices and then as assistant superior in Mother Seton's time. She was the first Sister of Charity that John Hughes met when he applied for work at Emmitsburg. Later, she was superior of St. Joseph's asylum in Philadelphia, the first Catholic child-caring institution in the country, and then of the Asylum in New York. After her term as superior of the community (1846–1849), she was local superior of the Orphan Asylum for most of her remaining life. Her personal influence over the orphans became legendary.

The rapid growth of the Sisters of Charity made possible the expansion and rearrangement of the orphan asylums and the establishment of St. Vincent's Hospital, the first Catholic hospital in New York State. A large building was erected for the Boys Asylum at Fifth Avenue and Fifty-First Street; the Prince Street Asylum was given entirely to the girls; and the Half Orphan Asylum was closed. The hospital was the first new work undertaken by the Sisters after their separation from Emmitsburg, and was the first New York hospital supported entirely by private funds. It opened on November 1, 1849, in a small rented building on East Thirteenth Street with four Sisters and room for thirty patients. The superior was Sister Angela Hughes (1806–1861), a sister of Bishop Hughes and a future superior of the community. She had previously been superior of the Mullanphy Hospital in St. Louis which had been opened in 1828. It was the first hospital opened in this country by the Sisters of Charity.

The story of St. Vincent's Hospital is another story of modest beginnings. When it opened, the existing hospitals in New York City were the New York Hospital (which admitted its first patient in 1791), and Bellevue which, opened as an Alms House in 1807 and moved to its present site in 1816. St. Luke's Hospital was to be opened by the Episcopal Church in 1853, but was being planned by 1845. In its temporary quarters, St. Vincent's had no running water, no light except oil lamps, no heat but a small stove in the cellar. The patients who could afford it paid three dollars weekly for board, laundry, medical attendance, nursing, and medicine. The rest paid what they could, if anything, so the hospital ran at a loss. In April 1856 the hospital moved to its present site on West Twelfth Street and Seventh Avenue. Formerly St. Joseph's Half Orphan Asylum, the building, which had been renovated, possessed the latest conveniences, such as running water on every floor, gaslight and steam heat.

St. Vincent's Hospital opened five years before Florence Nightingale began her great work. Preventive medicine was practically unknown. Anesthesia had been discovered in 1846, but bacteriology was yet to come (1875–1885). The hospitals of that day have been described as "a last refuge for the homeless poor, in which they could die with a minimum of inconvenience to those around them." It was not until 1873 that Bellevue opened its School of Nursing—the first in this country—and it was another nineteen years before St. Vincent's followed suit in 1892. The mortality rate was especially high in those early years because most of the patients came in with acute infectious diseases which are now practically unheard of in New York. The chief ones were typhoid, typhus, yellow fever, cholera, and pulmonary tuberculosis. Many patients were brought to the hospital to die, which helps explain the dread of hospitals found among so many of the poor until fairly recent years. Despite its humble start, the opening of St. Vincent's was rightly seen as an important development. It was the first and is the largest of the more than fifty Catholic general hospitals now within the original limits of the diocese of New York. It fulfilled another of Bishop Dubois' hopes since he had wanted a Catholic hospital in the city partly for its own sake, but especially because of the discrimination against Catholics in the public institutions.

Typhus, often called ship fever, was a disease that took a heavy toll among the immigrant poor and also affected the clergy who attended them. On February 11, 1848, Father Patrick Murphy, pastor of St. Peter's parish on Staten Island, died of fever contracted from a patient in the Quarantine Hospital in Tompkinsville, Staten Island. Father John Smith, pastor of St. James Church in Manhattan, went to anoint Father Murphy, caught the fever from him, and died a few days later. Father Murphy was described by the New York *Freeman's Journal* as having the hardest post in the diocese because his parish, which contained all of Staten Island, included the Quarantine Hospital which contained 850 to 900 patients, the greater number of whom were Catholics. Bishop Hughes presided and preached at the Murphy funeral, and his appearance in the procession in his episcopal robes was criticized by some of the press as an outrage on the Protestant community. In April 1852 the *Freeman's Journal* reported the death of the third young Redemptorist priest in seven months to die of ship fever caught in the Quarantine Hospital.

The Immigrants

Bishop Hughes' principal task was to cope with the influx of immigrants that lasted throughout his episcopate. Few seem to have guessed in 1842 the dimensions immigration would reach by 1860, although from 1790 to 1860 the population increased by about a third in every decade.

Between 1840 and 1860 about four million people came to the United States, and 70% of them came through New York. The largest groups were from Ireland and Germany. The German influx peaked between 1846 and 1855, when over one million arrived. Most of them came because of the economic conditions in Germany and because of the political unrest that preceded and followed the Revolution of 1848. Some came because of the Gold Rush in California in 1849. There were approximately 18,000 Germans in New York in 1840 and 120,000 in 1860. About forty percent of all the German immigrants were Catholics. In one generation they founded in New York City eight parishes, an orphan asylum, a hospital (St. Francis in 1865), several parochial schools, a high school for boys and one for girls. They became, as the Irish were in the 1830s, a largely self-contained community. There was, on the whole, little friction between the Germans and the Irish. There was a long-term scarcity of priests among them that reflected the same condition in the German-speaking areas of Europe.

The Irish who came between 1840 and 1860 numbered officially 1,694,838, exclusive of those who migrated to the United States by way of Canada and Newfoundland. The peak year was 1851, when 221,213 Irish Catholics landed in New York City. To understand the condition in which the Irish arrived and the problem they presented to the community at large and to the Church here, we must look at the conditions from which they fled. Many were fugitives from the Great Famine of 1845–1849. That famine was the worst of its kind in the history of Western Europe and brought about in Ireland the greatest social collapse seen in Europe since the Thirty Years War in Germany (1618–1648). Ireland had long been recognized as the worst governed country in the civilized world. The Duke of Wellington said "there never was a country in which poverty existed to the extent it exists in Ireland." Benjamin Disraeli said Ireland was the most densely populated country in Europe; on arable land, he said, the population was denser than that of China.

The famine had major consequences for Ireland, England, the United States, and for the Catholic Church in the whole of the English-speaking world. Much has been written truly of the horrors of the famine, of "the coffin ships" that carried so many of its victims to North America, and of the shameless way in which many of them were exploited on arrival. Against this must be set the very large sums collected all over this country for relief in Ireland, even though such relief was only a drop in the bucket.

Though no other group of immigrants fled to this country from such terrible conditions or arrived in such a state of destitution, the Irish made an immense contribution to both Church and State. Christopher Dawson, a distinguished English historian who became a Catholic, said of them in 1935: "If there ever has been a class entirely deprived of the necessary economic foundations of a good life, it was the refugees from the Great Irish Famine who were forced to escape from the physical death of starvation into the living death of the awful slums of Northern England and Eastern America. They were forced to live as even animals are not allowed to live nowadays. Yet it is to these men that the Catholic Church in England and America owes its strength today. They, even more than the survivors of the age of persecution and the converts of the Oxford Movement, are the true heroes of the faith and the creators of modern English and American Catholicism."

In New York, Bishop Hughes encouraged the formation of the Irish Emigrant Society, the Emigrant Industrial Savings Bank, and an Immigration Commission of the State Legislature which would protect the immigrants. The vast majority of the Irish immigrants, about 80%, were from rural areas, but in America they remained in the cities. Although the Bishop was very well aware of the moral dangers of city life, he had no sympathy with the various schemes to move the new arrivals to the land. He feared for their loss of faith because of the shortage of priests and churches. He knew, too, how very different farm life was in the United States—especially in the Middle West—from what they had known in Ireland. Not only was the pioneer's life desperately hard and poor, it was also very lonely. It often required capital (about one thousand dollars to start a farm) and that was far beyond the average immigrant's reach. Only about 6% of the Irish immigrants settled on the land. The Church in America was never to have more than 15% of its membership live in rural areas.

The immigrants not only made more churches, schools, and charitable works necessary, they supplied much of the personnel and money that made them possible. The very great majority of them merely passed through the city, but many settled in the metropolitan area, and a substantial number in New York State where the population rose from 1,724,033 in 1840 to 2,311,786 in 1850.

THE COADJUTOR

The growth in population and in the number of parishes and institutions made proper supervision more difficult, and the first step Bishop Hughes took to meet that problem was to ask for a coadjutor. He discussed the matter at the Fifth Provincial Council of Baltimore in May 1843. The bishops recommended Father John McCloskey. Their choice was ratified in Rome, and on November 21, 1843, the Papal Bull appointing him titular Bishop of Axierne and Coadjutor Bishop of New York with the right of succession was signed by Cardinal Lambruschini. The choice was an important one. The coadjutor was to be closely linked with the administration of the diocese as a bishop for over forty years, and he was Bishop Hughes' closest associate. He was the first New Yorker to undergo the training he received; and as he saw New York grow from a diocese with two churches to one of the major sees in the Universal Church, it is worthwhile to go into some detail about his early career.

John McCloskey was born in Brooklyn, N.Y., on March 10th, 1810, and was baptized on May 6th, 1810, by Father Benedict Fenwick, S.J. His parents, Patrick McCloskey and Elizabeth Harron, were natives of County Derry, Ireland, and came from the adjacent parishes of Dungiven and Banagher. There is a tradition in the family that their marriage was opposed by the bride's pastor because they were closely related. It took place in the Cathedral of Derry in the spring of 1808, and shortly thereafter the young couple came to America. They settled first in Brooklyn which had only about 4,500 inhabitants in 1808, and was not incorporated as a village until 1816.

Patrick McCloskey went into business and prospered and became the manager of a large distillery. He took an interest in public affairs and was one of the volunteers who helped erect barricades at Fort Greene and Fort Fisher to prepare for an expected British landing in the War of 1812.

No Catholic church was erected in Brooklyn until 1823, so John and his mother rowed from Brooklyn to New York on Sundays to attend Mass in whichever of the two churches was open that day. (For awhile the Cathedral and St. Peter's were closed on alternate Sundays to be sure the entire congregation helped with both debts.) There had been grumbling among the parishioners of St. Peter's at what some considered the extravagance of building St. Patrick's on Mott Street on so large a scale and so far out of town.

When John approached school age, his parents began to think of moving to Manhattan. In the meantime, he was enrolled as a weekly boarder at a school for small boys which was run in Brooklyn by Mrs. Charlotte Milmoth, a retired English actress who was a convert to the Church. She took such pains to make her pupils enunciate distinctly that John never forgot it and even in old age used to attribute to her the singular excellence of his own enunciation. When he was about seven, the McCloskeys did move to Manhattan and settled on Murray Street near St. Peter's. John was enrolled in Thomas Brady's Latin School, where he finished his elementary studies. While there, and as a parishioner of St. Peter's, he came under the lasting influence of Father Malou and Father Power, with whom his parents were very friendly. Many years later he said: "From my boyhood upward, Father Power was ever to me a kind and affectionate father, and in my mature years a trusty counsellor and friend."

When John McCloskey finished the courses available at Brady's Latin School, he was eleven years old, too young to know what he wanted to do, and without a preference of any kind. His widowed mother sought the advice of Mr. Brady, whose own sons later had brilliant legal careers; of Mr. Richard

Riker, a well known lawyer; and of Mr. Cornelius Heeney, John's guardian, who was a partner of John Jacob Astor in the fur business and one of the most generous benefactors of the Church in New York and Brooklyn. Mr. Brady was all for studies leading to law; Riker was strongly opposed; and Heeney settled the matter for the time being by arranging for John's enrollment in Mount St. Mary's College at Emmitsburg. In June 1821 John was introduced to Father Dubois, who was in New York looking for pupils, and it was arranged that John enter Mount St. Mary's in September 1821. As things turned out, he stayed there, except for one year, until his ordination in 1834.

At Mount St. Mary's, John McCloskey met three men who were to have a great influence on his career: Father John Dubois, Father Simon Bruté, and Father John Hughes. The school was small and the students received individual attention in a way that is impossible today. He was a good student and was noted for his application, talent for languages and mathematics, and his excellent manners. He graduated in July 1825 in a class of four. The others were Richard Whelan, later Bishop of Wheeling, Francis Gartland, later Bishop of Savannah, and Edward Sourin, later a Jesuit.

Though each of his classmates had decided on his vocation before graduation, John McCloskey had not, and he spent the academic year 1825–1826 at Mount St. Mary's studying philosophy. He returned home in July 1826 still undecided about his future. His mother had left the city and moved to Bedford, N.Y., where she bought a farm near the property of John Jay (1745–1829), the first Chief Justice of the United States, a former Governor of New York, and a notorious anti-Catholic. Once again, Mrs. McCloskey sought the advice of her friends: Mr. Brady again urged law and others suggested a business career. An effort was made to get him a position in a New York countinghouse and another year passed without any decision being reached.

During the summer of 1827, McCloskey suffered a serious accident that settled his vocation and changed the whole course of his life. A farmhand who was drawing logs near the house left an ox team and wagon unattended and in the wrong place. John passed by and attempted to drive them to their goal. His lack of skill frightened the oxen so they upset the wagon and he was buried under the logs. He was unconscious for several days and ill for a long time, suffering blindness and having to spend weeks in darkness. On the day after the accident, his mother received word that the place in the counting-house was open to him, but when he recovered, he decided to study for the priesthood and returned to Mount St. Mary's for that purpose in September 1827. Though his illness left no external mark, it aggravated a congenital weakness of constitution. All his life he lacked energy. He had to conserve his strength, measure his capacity, and not undertake more than he could do. He led, of necessity, an exceptionally disciplined life.

John McCloskey's seminary days were uneventful and laborious. The training was as much as possible like that given in the French seminaries in which his teachers had been formed. Formation and study, in that order, were the goals aimed at. He was one of the seminarians chosen to teach Latin in the college and to be prefect of the study hall. He liked that so much he asked for an *exeat* or release, from New York, so that he could continue teaching. This was refused by Father Power, the Vicar General, in the name of Bishop Dubois who was then in Europe. In due time, on December 3, 1832, he received tonsure, minor orders, and subdiaconate from Bishop Kenrick of Philadelphia at St. Francis Xavier Church in Gettysburg, Pennsylvania. Although he had completed his seminary course, he was still almost two years below the canonical age for ordination, so he spent the intervening time studying and teaching at Mount St. Mary's. When and where he received the diaconate is unknown, but he was ordained a priest by Bishop Dubois on January 12, 1834. As was to be the case on many of his great days, the weather was vile, and the only two priests who were able to attend, Fathers Power and Pise, came very late. For most of the ceremony, he, Bishop Dubois, and a handful of people were alone in the Cathedral. Few noted the significance of the occasion.

Father McCloskey's first assignment was a brief one at the Cathedral in New York. He took his turn in the regular work and was assigned to attend Bellevue Hospital and the Eleventh Street Cemetery. The hospital was to be visited twice a week and whenever sick calls came. The journey both ways was made on foot. In February 1834 he was made vice president and professor of philosophy of the new seminary at Nyack, a position for which the Bishop had considered him for some time. The president was Father John McGerry, former president of Mount St. Mary's, who came to New York to help his old friend, Bishop Dubois.

The short life of the seminary, February to August 1834, left Father McCloskey at loose ends and gave his devoted friend and former guardian, Cornelius Heeney, an opening he seized. He called on Bishop Dubois to suggest that the young man be allowed to go to Europe to study and recover his health at the expense of his family. At that time it was widely believed that anyone in delicate health was in danger of tuberculosis and that anyone with tuberculosis could best be helped by a long sea voyage. The Bishop accepted the proposal hesitantly because he was desperately short of priests, but on the other hand he thought the young man's present state of health would prevent him from being very useful and might be improved by a visit to Italy. He spoke of his having "an already broken constitution." John's health was one reason why Father Power refused him permission to leave Nyack to help in the cholera epidemic in New York in the summer of 1834.

His departure for Rome was a new and exciting experience for Father McCloskey, though a sad one for his relatives and friends. He was the first in the long line of New York priests sent to Rome for higher studies. He sailed from New York—there was no steamship service until 1838—on November

3, 1834, and reached LeHavre, France, on December 3rd after a stormy passage on which there was no chance to say Mass. There were seven passengers, all men, most of whom were French or Spanish. John McCloskey was a poor sailor but had plenty of time for reading and for practicing his French which was already excellent. He enjoyed the trip in other respects. One of his fellow passengers, a young non-Catholic doctor from New York, was also traveling for his health, and they teamed up for the trip to Rome, which took a month. They went by carriage, for the railroad had not yet been built, and on several occasions drove all night. They saw Paris, Rouen, Lyons, Marseilles, and other points of interest before reaching Villefranche where they were detained two weeks in quarantine. There was an outbreak of cholera and the precautions taken were very strict. At quarantine their passports were taken from them with tongs and during their stay there, which was at their own expense, any coins that changed hands were first placed in a dish of vinegar. They went through Nice, Genoa, Pisa, and Siena before reaching Rome on February 8, 1835.

Rome's population at that time was about 140,000. This figure had hardly changed in two centuries and was already matched by New York. The Papal Government was entering its last phase as the movement for a united Italy grew, but the resistance was not yet overt. Father McCloskey had meant to live at the Urban College of the Sacred Congregation for the Propagation of the Faith (popularly called "Propaganda"), the seminary maintained for students from all the mission fields of the world, but when he went there he met the rector, Father Karl Reisach, who changed his plans. The Rector suggested that, since he could afford to do so and was in poor health, he should board in one of the large religious houses and study at the Roman College, now the Gregorian University. It would be better for his health than living in the confined quarters of the mission seminary and he would be freer to visit the treasures of the Eternal City. He arranged, therefore, to stay at San Andrea della Valle, the Theatine Church, and to say Mass daily at the Gesú, the famous Jesuit church which, with the Roman College, was very near San Andrea.

The advantages of a stay in Rome were not solely spiritual and academic. It provided an opportunity to see and be seen by the Roman authorities, thus making useful contacts, to see how the affairs of the local church were viewed at central headquarters, and to make friends from other areas. Father McCloskey brought with him letters from Father Power which opened many doors in Rome. Father Power was an old friend of Father Paul Cullen, the rector of the Irish College, who acted as Roman agent for many American bishops. He welcomed the young American cordially, encouraged his visits, kept a place for him at table, and introduced him to the small English-speaking colony in ecclesiastical Rome. John McCloskey had a knack of winning and keeping friends, even among those who did not get on with one another. His friendship with Father Cullen was important and life-long. The latter also introduced him to Nicholas Wiseman, the rector of the English

College. Bishop Bruté, who was in Rome, introduced him to Cardinal Joseph Fesch, the uncle of Napoleon, by whom he was presented to the fallen Emperor's mother, then an exile in Rome. He also met Monsignor Angelo Mai, the Secretary of the Sacred Congregation Propaganda Fide, who was one of the outstanding scholars of the age. Fathers Cullen, Wiseman, and Reisach were all very young men to be in the positions they held. All went on to brilliant careers, becoming respectively the Archbishops of Dublin, Westminster, and Munich. All three entered the Sacred College of Cardinals.

Paul Cullen was the first person of Irish birth to become a cardinal and the first alumnus of "Propaganda" College to do so. Wiseman was the first cardinal resident in England since the death of Cardinal Reginald Pole of Canterbury in 1558. McCloskey himself was to be the first cardinal of the Western Hemisphere. Among the other interesting personages with whom he became friendly in Rome were Père Henri Lacordaire, O.P., the famous French pulpit orator who at one time thought of coming to New York, where Bishop Dubois offered to make him Vicar General; and also Cardinal Weld, an Englishman living in Rome who had taken a great interest in American affairs ever since attending the consecration of Archbishop Carroll. John McCloskey also renewed a family friendship with Father Anthony Kohlmann, whom his parents had known and esteemed during his years at St. Peter's in New York.

Student days in Rome were very different from anything then available to a seminarian or priest in the United States, and John McCloskey was very pleased with his courses at the Roman College. He attended two lectures daily in dogmatic and moral theology. He also attended weekly lectures in Canon Law at the Sapienza Academy and studied Scripture and Church History privately. His time was his own except that he could not stay out late. He had easy access to many fine libraries and time for a methodical visitation of the chief Roman churches and galleries. At the Roman College he had Father Perrone, S.J., as professor of dogmatic theology. He was deeply impressed by that famous scholar's mastery of the matter, clarity in exposition, fluency in Latin, and his deep and wide knowledge of all the objection to Catholic teaching then current in the European learned world. He was all the more pleased with his own living arrangements when he found out on his visits there how much sickness there was at the Propaganda College, even among the young American students, many of whom were threatened by tuberculosis.

The time in Rome passed all too quickly, and as the time for departure approached he was urged by his friends to take the examination for the degree of doctor of divinity. A close friend, Father Edward O'Reilly of the Irish College, later provincial of the Irish Jesuits, urged him on and even offered to coach him if he felt he needed it. He refused, saying he did not want to take the trouble. More probably his refusal was due to an almost total lack of competitive spirit. Later, he was to encourage the New York students to take degrees. The highlight of his Roman visit was the audience at which he was presented to Pope Gregory XVI by Father Reisach. He was in a small group of Americans that included a daughter and granddaughter of Charles Carroll of Carrollton, Mr. and Mrs. Pierce Connelly of Philadelphia, and Catherine Seton. The Connellys were recent converts destined for very different careers. Cornelia Connelly became the foundress of the Holy Child sisters, and the cause of her canonization has been introduced in Rome. He, an Episcopal clergyman, became a Catholic priest, defected, and died outside the Church. Catherine Seton, a daughter of Mother Elizabeth Seton, entered the Sisters of Mercy as their first New York novice, and for many years was one of the best known nuns in New York.

John McCloskey left Rome on February 10th, 1837, and, after a leisurely tour of Germany, Belgium, France, England, and Ireland, reached New York in the summer of that year. When he returned, his family felt free to tell him they had not expected to see him again. He found the city suffering from the Panic of 1837 and the Nativist Movement going strong. Shortly after his return, he was appointed pastor of St. Joseph's Parish in Greenwich Village.

In 1843, only a few days after his appointment as coadjutor of New York, two other New York pastors, Father Andrew Byrne and Father William Quarter, became respectively the first bishops of Little Rock, Arkansas, and Chicago, Illinois. It was a sign of the growing influence of New York in the Church in America. Byrne, Quarter, and McCloskey were the first priests of the diocese to become bishops, and John McCloskey was the first native of New York to do so. The consecration, the only triple consecration of New York priests (until June 1977) took place on March 10, 1844, which happened to be John McCloskey's thirty-fourth birthday. The ceremony was performed by Bishop Hughes, assisted by Bishop Benedict J. Fenwick of Boston, who had baptized McCloskey, and by Bishop Richard V. Whelan of Richmond, Virginia. The sermon was given by Father John Power. A contemporary description of the coadjutor tells us he was tall and slender in appearance, graceful in bearing, serene and cheerful in disposition, and had a beautiful voice and perfect enunciation. He was an excellent pulpit orator but rarely spoke outside it. He also had an impenetrable reserve and extraordinary self-control.

His appointment as coadjutor brought John McCloskey into a close association with Bishop Hughes that ripened and grew stronger while both of them lived. They had complementary characters and personalities. Between them, they governed the Church in New York for almost half a century. John Hughes was a born leader. Fearless, eloquent, an able controversialist, a man of vision and endurance, firm and decisive in action, he was wonderfully suited to the stormy times in which he lived. In defending the Church from critics within and without the fold, he neither gave nor sought quarter. He was vilified in the press as few men of his time were and, while he did not enjoy it, he did not let it deflect him from his goal. He understood his people well and had the capacity to inspire and retain their enthusiastic devotion. Many of them loved him for the enemies he made in their defense. He was neither elated nor overawed by the honors that came his way, and he neither sought nor shrank from them. He told Bishop Kenrick he "had studied the inside as well as the outside of a mitre and regarded the person obliged to wear it as entitled to pity, not envy." He added: "I had, if not humility, at least sense enough to be satisfied that the man who is qualified and willing to be a bishop in the United States deserves a recompense which he may not expect from this ungrateful world." Partly, no doubt, because he had seen at close range the evils flowing from episcopal weakness, he believed firmly that bishops are obliged to use their authority.

If John Hughes was born great, John McCloskey had greatness thrust upon him. He shrank from controversy and conflict, never aspired to leadership or pretended to be a leader, sought none of the honors that came his way, avoided the limelight as much as possible, made few enemies and many friends, kept the press at bay, and freely acknowledged his debt to others. At the same time, he succeeded in every post he filled. He never shirked an issue. He seemed to be incapable of envy or jealousy and he was wholly devoted to Bishop Hughes. Though he had chronic poor health and a retiring disposition, he was an able as well as a fortunate man.

The Nativist attacks on the Church were not without their compensations. They practically forced a strong sense of solidarity on the Catholics. The passionate public interest in the Church, even if largely ill informed, led many to inquire into her teachings, and the Oxford Movement in England had its counterpart on a minor scale here. Bishop McCloskey himself was instrumental in the conversion of three New Yorkers, each of whom played a prominent role in the Church for many years. One was James Roosevelt Bayley (1814–1877), a young Episcopal clergyman who was a nephew of Mother Seton. The Bishop, while president of St. John's College (Fordham), had many conversations with him. Bayley was received into the Church in Rome on April 22, 1844, studied briefly in Paris and at Fordham Seminary, and was ordained by Bishop Hughes in 1844. In 1853 he became the first Bishop of Newark, and later the Archbishop of Baltimore.

The second convert was Isaac Hecker (1819–1888), a Lutheran, whom Bishop McCloskey received into the Church at the Cathedral on August 21, 1844, and baptized conditionally. Hecker joined the Redemptorists, who were then taken up largely with missionary work among the German immigrants. He left them in 1858 to found the Paulist Fathers, remaining superior until his death. Their apostolate was to English-speaking non-Catholics. They were the first religious community of men founded in America and the first one of any kind that originated in New York.

The third convert was James McMaster (1820–1886), a Presbyterian, who entered the Church in 1845. Under the influence of Hecker, he tried his vocation with the Redemptorists. Having finally decided his vocation was to journalism, he bought the *Freeman's Journal and Catholic Register* from Bishop Hughes in 1847 and edited it until his death. He was a bitter and acute controversialist who spared neither friend nor foe. He was also a devout, honorable, courageous, and angular man "who tried desperately to be humble," but his Scottish Calvinist background kept breaking through. His paper had a wide circulation outside New York and was particularly popular among the priests. He was one of the most important Catholic journalists in this country. He was on better terms with Archbishops Hughes and Corrigan than with Cardinal McCloskey.

Bishop McCloskey's attitude toward converts was sound. He thought they should never be received quickly and should be very well instructed. He had the born Catholic's fear of the reforming spirit often found in converts and was opposed to lionizing them. He felt, too, that in this country, conversion often exacted a price socially and financially of which converts should be aware, and that they should realize that they were sure to find imperfections in the Church and her members. James R. Bayley was a case in point. He was disinherited by his maternal grandfather, James Roosevelt, because of his conversion and lost a legacy of $70,000.

The second step Bishop Hughes took to meet the problem of the over rapid expansion of the diocese was to divide it, a step he envisioned from the beginning of his administration when priests from the most distant parts of the diocese had to travel 500 difficult miles to see him. It was a necessary step in spite of the striking improvements in transportation and communication that came in a few years. Oddly enough, New York City did not profit from the railroad as quickly as many smaller places in New York State. The first railroad in New York State, the Mohawk and Albany, linked Albany and Schenectady in 1831. In 1842 it became possible to go from Albany to Buffalo by through train, and later in the same year from Buffalo to Boston. When the New York-Albany run opened in 1851, it cut that journey to five hours. The railroad made a great difference in travel as it was fast, cheap, and constant. It took only fifteen hours from Albany to Buffalo and cost only ten dollars, whereas the Canal took ten to fourteen days. Moreover, the Hudson was usually frozen for about one hundred days a year and the Canal for four months.

The opening of the New York-Albany railroad coincided with two other important developments that strengthened New York's position as a commercial center. In 1851 a clipper ship made the trip from New York to San Francisco in 89 days, and a ship went from New York to England in ten days. The most striking improvement in communication was the telegraph, which was introduced in 1844, but even greater in its impact on the general public was the improvement in the Postal Service. "Cheap postage" was introduced in 1845 and postage stamps in 1847. This led to the general use of envelopes. In 1851 the three-cent stamp was introduced. New York City used to charge two cents for the delivery of each letter, but that stopped in 1863.

In May 1846 Bishop Hughes appealed to the bishops at the Sixth Provincial Council of Baltimore, the Council which selected the Blessed Virgin, under her title of the Immaculate Conception, as the patroness of the United States. They agreed readily, and recommended to the Holy See that New York be divided in three. This was accepted by Rome, and on April 23, 1847, Pope Pius IX erected the dioceses of Albany and Buffalo. Bishop McCloskey was transferred to Albany, and Father John Timon, C.M. (1787–1867), then Prefect Apostolic of Texas, was sent to Buffalo. The division was uneven but was not intended to be final. Albany, from which Ogdensburg (1872) and Syracuse (1886) were cut off later, covered twenty-three counties in about 28,000 square miles. It had thirty-eight priests, forty-seven churches, some which were very primitive, five Catholic schools, no religious communities, about 60,000 Catholics, and a rapidly expanding population. Buffalo, from which Rochester (1868) was cut off later, had about 13,500 square miles, with sixteen counties, sixteen priests, sixteen churches, about 16,000 Catholics, four schools with lay teachers, one religious order of men, the Redemptorists, and one convent of the Sisters of Charity, who ran an orphan asylum. After the division, the remaining Diocese of New York was larger in population than it had been in 1838.

New York Becomes An Archdiocese

The expansion of the country following the Mexican War and the continued growth of the Catholic population, which more than doubled between 1840 and 1850, increasing from about 663,000 to 1,600,000, led to the creation of more dioceses and ecclesiastical provinces. The Seventh Council of Baltimore, May 1849, asked the Holy See to make Cincinnati, New Orleans, and New York archdioceses. Until then, only Baltimore, Oregon City, and St. Louis had that rank. This was approved, but because of the political troubles in Italy, the documents were delayed. It was not until October 3, 1850, that Bishop Hughes received the official documents, signed July 19, 1850, making New York an archdiocese and him an Archbishop. He was given as suffragans the Bishops of Albany, Boston, Buffalo, and Hartford. The Province of New York contained New York State, half of New Jersey, and all of New England. It remained unchanged until February 12, 1875, when the Province of New England was cut out of New York and Boston became an archdiocese. The new Archbishop went to Rome to receive the pallium, the symbol of his jurisdiction. As a special mark of favor, he received it from Pope Pius IX in person on April 3, 1851.

The success of the first division of the diocese led Archbishop Hughes to a second one. In 1853 ten new dioceses were erected in this country, the largest number ever created here in a single year. Four were in the province of New York. Brooklyn, New York, and Newark, New Jersey, were cut out of New

York, and Burlington, Vermont, and Portland, Maine, from Boston. Three of the new dioceses, Brooklyn, Burlington, and Newark, were filled at once by, respectively, Father John Loughlin (1817–1891), Vicar General of New York; Father Louis de Goesbriand (1816–1899), a French priest ordained for Cleveland; and Father James R. Bayley, secretary to Archbishop Hughes. Portland was filled in 1855 by Father David Bacon (1813–1874), a New York priest. Brooklyn, from which Rockville Centre was cut off in 1957, contained all of Long Island, and had twelve churches. Estimates of the Catholic population there in 1853 vary from 15,000 to 50,000. Newark included all of New Jersey and had about 40,000 Catholics and thirty-three priests, drawn about evenly from New York and Philadelphia. It has since been divided into Newark, Trenton (1881), Camden (1937), Paterson (1937) and Metuchen (1981). The Archdiocese of New York was reduced to its present boundaries, except for a minor modification of the Albany line in 1861. One sign of the rapid growth in those years was the increase in the number of priests. The forty of 1838 had grown to 124 in 1847 and 113 after the division in 1853.

THE BEDINI VISIT

The appointment of the new bishops coincided with the arrival of Archbishop Gaetano Bedini, the first papal envoy ever to visit the United States. He arrived in June 1853, and as a gesture of courtesy was invited to consecrate the new bishops. He did so in New York on October 30, 1853, assisted by Bishop John B. Fitzpatrick of Boston and Bishop Amadeus Rappe of Cleveland. The Archbishop of New York preached. It was the second triple consecration here. It was also one of the few wholly pleasant events in what developed into the stormiest visit ever paid to this country by a foreign envoy.

Archbishop Gaetano Bedini (1806–1864), Nuncio to Brazil, had been commissioned by Rome to stop here on his way to Rio. He was to investigate the possibility of establishing full diplomatic relations between the Holy See and America, to settle some local disputes that had been referred to Rome, and to make a general survey of the condition of the Church here. He discovered that the government in Washington, while agreeable in principle to the establishment of diplomatic relations, would not accept a papal envoy who was not a layman.

He discovered too that while Nativism had died down, it had not died out. Wherever he went in his attempt to survey the Catholic position, his footsteps were dogged by native anti-Catholics and by radical political exiles from Germany, Hungary, and Italy. Though he was received courteously by President Franklin Pierce, he was not protected properly by the local authorities. He was hanged in effigy in several cities including Boston and

Pittsburgh, and his life was threatened or attempted in New York and Cincinnati. He was denounced as "an ecclesiastical hyena" and the "Butcher of Bologna." The excitement reached such a pitch that Rome recalled him. On February 4, 1854, at the suggestion of the Mayor and the Police Department in New York, he left secretly from Staten Island. He never reached Rio. He remained in Rome, where he became Secretary of the Congregation of Propaganda Fide in 1854 and a cardinal in 1861. He strongly urged the founding of the North American College in Rome. Archbishop Hughes was absent in Cuba, and was indignant when he heard of the Nuncio's undignified departure. The way the visit turned out made many in both camps wish devoutly he would be the last, as well as the first papal envoy, to come here. Not long after his departure, a stone sent by the Pope for inclusion in the unfinished Washington Monument was smashed by vandals.

Though the reason given for the onslaught on the Nuncio was the allegedly repressive character of the Papal Government in the States of the Church, the real reason was, undoubtedly, anti-Catholicism. The traditional American sympathy for revolutionary movements professing to favor republicanism and democracy was genuine and present, but it was much enhanced in the case of Italy by the fond hope and blessed expectation that the unification and liberation of Italy, which would destroy the temporal power of the Pope, would deal the Church a mortal blow. There was also a strong anti-Catholic flavor in the tumultuous reception given Louis Kossuth (1802–1894), the radical Hungarian nationalist, who preceded Archbishop Bedini to America. Kossuth arrived in New York in December 1851. To many he was a symbol of Protestant opposition to the Hapsburgs as well as of liberty. The *New York Times* hailed him as "the Peter the Hermit of a new crusade." The enthusiasm for him died down when it was seen to involve the danger of bad relations with Austria and Russia. As in 1956, the Hungarians were given sympathy and verbal support but nothing more. Archbishop Hughes, who regarded him as a humbug and an enemy of the Church, urged the Catholics of New York not to get involved in the welcome to Kossuth or in opposing it.

It was noted in the Bedini affair that most of the foreign-born protesters were German. The Italians provided Alessandro Gavazzi (1809–1889), the dynamic speaker such movements require. Gavazzi was an apostate priest whose anti-Catholic lectures were so popular in England that he was invited here by the American and Foreign Christian Union. After 1849 he devoted his life to advocating the destruction of the Church.

The prominence of the Germans in these movements was due in part to the lesser role taken by the Italians. There were, in 1850, only 3,679 foreign-born Italians in a national population of about twenty-three million. By 1860 there were only 11,677. In 1855 there were only 968 Italians in New York City, but their number grew to about 5,000 by 1860. They were too few, too scattered, too poor, and too indifferent to form a congregation, and there was no Italian priest. When Lorenzo DaPonte, Mozart's librettist (who became the first Professor of Italian at Columbia), settled in New York in 1807, he lamented that the Italian language and its literature were as little known here as Turkish or Chinese.

The first Italian priest to work in New York, apart from the Vincentians in the seminary, had died a decade earlier. He was Father Alessandro Muppiatti (1803–1846), a Carthusian monk who left Italy for reasons of health and politics. He went first to Turkey, then to France, and came to America intending to go to the South. Father Felix Varela persuaded him to remain in New York, and he was an assistant at Transfiguration Church from 1842 until his death. Archbishop Corrigan said he was popularly regarded as a saint and had an amazing influence on the people. He had learned English quickly and, though he had serious heart trouble and was never without pain, he carried on a zealous and fruitful apostolate in the confessional and in the visitation of the sick.

The sudden flare-up of Nativism, which was to blossom again as the Know Nothing Movement from 1854 to 1856, disturbed the Catholics less than the earlier Nativist movements. The Catholics were now more numerous, much better organized and led. They were more at home on the American scene, and confident that they would ride out the storm. They also saw, and were more patient with, the sincerity of so much of the anti-Catholic movements from 1800 to 1860. Dr. Billington—a non-Catholic who is the outstanding historian of the Nativist Movement—tells us "the average Protestant American of the 1850s had been trained from birth to hate Catholicism."

How much many decent people took anti-Catholicism for granted may be seen from an incident that occurred in New York City in that period, and would be unthinkable now. On Sunday, May 28, 1851, a group of twenty-one Catholic soldiers on Governors Island were ordered to march to the Protestant service, refused, and were imprisoned. Their leader, Private James Duggan, was singled out for special treatment. He was fined five dollars a day for six months (a very substantial sum at that time), given two months in solitary confinement on bread and water, and four months at hard labor with a ball and chain on his leg. This savage sentence was confirmed by the Commander in the East, but ultimately overruled by the Secretary of War after a public protest. It was explained that he and his companions were punished not for refusing to attend the Protestant service but for not having asked permission not to do so.

The Know Nothing victory in the election of 1854, in which they sent seventy-five members to Congress, had very little effect on national politics. Their sweep in New York resulted in an attempt to perpetuate trusteeism through the Church Property Bill of 1855 which was never enforced. That bill was repealed in 1863 in favor of the present very satisfactory law on church property, which was drafted by Charles O'Conor at the request of Archbishop Hughes, providing that each parish be incorporated separately and have five trustees. Three of them, the Archbishop, the Vicar General, and the Pastor, serve *ex officio*. The others are appointed by the Archbishop on nomination by the Pastor.

The progress made by the Catholics since 1785 was summed up by Archbishop Hughes in 1856 in a lecture he gave in Baltimore. It was this that gave them confidence and alarmed their opponents. From 1785 to 1855 the Catholic population increased from about 25,000 to 2.4 million, the number of priests rose from 23 to 1,761, the number of bishops from zero to forty-one, the number of churches from four to 1,910, the number of colleges from zero to twenty-four, the number of seminaries from zero to thirty-five, and the number of female academies from one to 130.

During the same years, the national population rose from under four million to twenty-seven million. By 1860 the Catholics were the largest religious body in the country, numbering 3,103,000 in a population of 31,443,321. The hunger of the immigrants for education can be seen from a few figures. By 1866 there were sixty Catholic institutions for the higher education of young men, and between 1840 and 1849 Catholic secondary schools for girls increased by fifty-six.

Though he had reduced the Archdiocese of New York to about one-eleventh of its original area, the Archbishop found that within the new boundaries his problems remained much the same. The basic one was how to provide the people with a chance to hear Mass, to receive the sacraments and proper religious instruction, and how to foster their devotional life. In spite of all that was done, there was a substantial leakage from the Church. The number of parishes and priests failed to keep pace with the increase in population, so that in 1864 the ratio of Catholics for each parish and priest was higher than it had been in 1840. There was truth in Bishop Bayley's remark in 1853 that the two hundred Catholics in 1784 were better cared for than the 200,000 in 1853.

By 1850 New York City had nineteen churches, and the rest of the diocese forty-seven. There were then 220 non-Catholic churches, including six synagogues, in the City. Between 1840 and 1864 there were sixty-one parishes opened within the present limits of the archdiocese. Of these, twenty-four were in the city proper (Manhattan) and thirty-seven in the other counties. Only ten were opened after 1858, and five of those were established during the Civil War. The sixty-one included the first parish in what is now Bronx County, St. Raymond's (1842), and the first one in what is now Westchester County, St. Patrick's at Verplanck (1843). In every new parish the Archbishop opened, the property was vested in his name, thus avoiding the problem of trusteeism. He made no attempt to eliminate the trustees where they were already established, but, when some of those churches (St. Peter's, St. Paul's, Transfiguration, and St. James) went bankrupt, he bought them at a sheriff's auction and put the property in his name as archbishop.

From the time he came to New York, John Hughes wanted uniformity in discipline and a closer supervision of the parishes. The New York Synod of

1842 laid down basic rules, such as forbidding baptism in the home except where there was danger of death, urging that funerals be held in church and with a Mass if possible, discouraging eulogies of the laity, requiring the banns of marriage, and requiring every church to have everything needed for Benediction. He was the first bishop in New York to have a secretary (1846). The establishment of the Chancery Office in December 1853 was a major development in the organization of the archdiocese. Besides the Synod, the Archbishop held three Provincial Councils, in 1854, 1860, and 1861. The one in 1854 urged the provision of a rectory in every parish and the erection of a branch of the Society for the Propagation of the Faith in each diocese. Membership was to cost a penny a week. In 1853 New York contributed $42.72, which rose in a year to $389.16. In 1854 America gave $11,357.32.

In the average city parish, there were three, four, or at most five Masses on Sunday starting at 5:30 or 6:00 A.M. The last one, at 10:00 A.M., was usually a High Mass. A substantial number of the faithful could not be accommodated in the churches at Mass and had to stand outside. Most parishes had sung vespers on Sunday afternoon, and devotions, often with Benediction and always with a sermon, in the evening. Many had some form of instruction and devotion each evening or several times a week, usually assigning each to a different society. It was the age of long sermons for Catholics as well as Protestants. A twenty-minute sermon was considered short. At Sunday Mass, when time allowed, on special occasions, and often at the devotions, an hour was considered the suitable length for a sermon. In all the parishes, the confessional was well attended. Many churches had confessions on Friday as well as on Saturday. Some had them on Sunday for the benefit of those whose occupations prevented them from coming at other times. In the average city parish, a session of four to five hours was considered light duty by the confessor. In Father Raffeiner's church in Brooklyn, confessions on Sunday began at 5:00 A.M. and the first Mass was at 8:00 A.M.

In a report to Rome in September 1853, Archbishop Hughes said that many received Holy Communion monthly, and even weekly. A great many received once or twice a year. At that period, it was not usual to begin receiving Communion before the age of twelve or fourteen. In Father Raffeiner's Brooklyn parish the age was often after eighteen. Baptisms and weddings were performed every day. In spite of the Synod of 1842 and the Provincial Council of 1861, most funerals, because of the shortage of priests, took place from the home without a Mass. In addition to Mass, the sacraments, instructions, and Benediction, the devotional life of the people was fostered in various ways. May Devotions were introduced at St. Mary's Church (Grand Street, Manhattan) by Father William Starrs in 1854. In 1859 the Archbishop, while praising them, urged that Benediction be given at these devotions only on Thursday, and then only if a choir was present to sing the hymns properly. He urged that the devotions always be ended by early twilight. These recommendations were renewed by Archbishop Corrigan in 1892.

The Redemptorists were the first religious community of men to make a permanent foundation in New York. They brought with them their own special devotions, such as the novena to Our Lady of Perpetual Help, the Purgatorial Society, the Archconfraternity of the Holy Family, and the general Blessing of the Sick. This blessing consisted of a weekly gathering at which, after a sermon and an act of contrition, the sick were blessed with a relic. The Redemptorists also introduced the Parish Mission, which was first given in New York City at St. Joseph's Church in April 1855. The Fathers of Mercy at the French Church of St. Vincent de Paul in Manhattan introduced the Christmas crib, the Holy Thursday Repository, and the first Rosary Society in New York. Lent was taken very seriously. All the weekdays from Ash Wednesday to Easter were fast days of precept, allowing one full meal and a collation. Meat was allowed once daily on Monday, Tuesday, and Thursday from the First Sunday of Lent to Palm Sunday. Fish and meat were forbidden at the same meal.

One of the basic facts the Archbishop had to keep in mind was the poverty in which so many people lived. In the 1850s a common laborer earned less than five dollars a week. A skilled craftsman earned $1.25 to $1.50 daily. The *New York Times* said in 1853 that a family of four needed $12.00 weekly. Observers lamented that even the fortunate few who made $15.00 weekly saved very little. Many of the Irish immigrant women found work in the needle trades, where conditions were notably bad. In 1845 seamstresses in the ready-made clothing industry worked fourteen to sixteen hours a day for $1.25 to $1.50 a week. Apprentices among them had to pay for their training and work for six months for nothing. The Irish immigrated more frequently as individuals than the Germans who tended to arrive as family units. Many of the Irish women entered domestic service, where they received board and lodging and six dollars a month, which left them better off than their sisters in the needle trades. In 1856 eighty percent of the 35,000 foreign born domestics and waiters were Irish, and fifteen percent were German. Servants formed a quarter of the Irish working population and a tenth of the German. The Irish domestic often encountered strong prejudice. An ad in the *Daily Sun,* May 11, 1853, read: "Woman wanted: To do general housework. English, Scotch, Welsh, German or any country or color except Irish." The men had a hard time too. In 1855, 52.3% of the population of the city was foreign-born. Of that number, 28.2% were Irish and 15.7% were German. In that year 75% of all the artisans and laborers were foreign-born, and 87% of the foreign-born in this group were Irish. Laborers constituted 20% of all the gainfully employed Irish and 5% of the Germans. In the winter of 1854–1855 it was estimated that 195,000 out of 629,820 people in New York City were in absolute want. The long working day and the lack of adequate rapid transit facilities made it necessary for people to live as near their work as possible, so the housing situation was very bad. In 1850, in a population of 515,547 there were 29,000 living in cellars, four times as many as in 1843. In 1853 the first Tenement House Report said: "a decent and healthy home is an impossible luxury for multitudes." In 1854 it was revealed that in one tenement on the lower East Side—the Gotham Court— the infant mortality for a period of thirty-two months was 44%, and the adult mortality was 22% of all who had lived there at any time during that period. In 1857, two-thirds of all the people who died in the city were children under five, the majority of whom were surely of foreign parentage. Rackrenting was common, as was the custom of merchants in the very poor areas charging customers twenty to sixty percent more than stores in other areas charged for the same goods.

In social and economic conditions such as these, few were surprised that excessive drinking was a major problem. In 1846 a Total Abstinence Society was founded in St. James Parish, and in 1849 Father Theobald Mathew, the famous Irish Capuchin "Apostle of Temperance," gave the pledge individually to 20,000 people in New York. It was not surprising either that many could not afford the tuition which some of the parochial schools had to charge. In the Redemptorist Parish of the Most Holy Redeemer, even twenty-five cents a month was too much for many.

Visitors found the city a strange mixture of extreme wealth and poverty, of refinement and crudity. In 1842 the New York Philharmonic Orchestra was organized, and in 1854 the Public Library was established. The Police Department was established in 1844. But in 1847 there were said to be 10,000 pigs called "as dangerous as hyenas" in the streets, and cattle were still seen there. Municipal dog killers were employed in the summer to beat out the brains of dogs found on the streets without muzzles. In 1847, between June 15th and August 15th, 1,510 dogs were clubbed to death. One area in which lasting progress was made was in the provision of a proper water supply. The Croton Reservoir, still in use, was opened in 1842. Yet, in 1857 three-quarters of the city had no sewers, and the Association for Improving the Condition of the Poor (A.I.C.P.) described the streets as "probably the dirtiest in Christendom." The A.I.C.P. (1843) was one of about thirty private organizations founded to fill the gap left by the absence of adequate State programs. Among the most valuable and durable of these was the Children's Aid Society, founded in 1853. In 1854 it opened a lodging house for boys. The boys were regarded as self-supporting (many of them sold newspapers when they could) and nothing was given without payment. They got a clean bed for six cents and supper for four cents more. The Legislature granted money from the Liquor Excise Fund for a new building "for the legitimate reason that those who do most to form drunkards should be compelled to aid in the expense and care of the children of drunkards." In 1854 half of all those aided by the A.I.C.P. were Irish and 75% were Catholic.

Those who wonder now why all of this was tolerated must remember that at that time no one expected the government, on any level, to handle such problems. The economic base needed for large-scale government intervention, had that been judged desirable, did not exist. Neither did the necessary technology. The health and sanitary services, for example, were quite rudimentary but were thought to be the very best available. Moreover, these conditions were not the whole story, and were in fact better than conditions in Europe. The Archbishop said that, "in proportion to the population, the aggregate of misery in the European cities was greater than here." In the first half of the nineteenth century, wage scales for skilled and unskilled labor in the United States were generally a third to a half higher than in Western Europe. In Ireland, on the eve of the Famine, life expectancy in the rural areas was 19 years, and only 20% of the people passed 40. In the United States, the life expectancy of those who survived the first ten years was fifty-eight, an age reached by less than 5% of the Irish at home. It is thought that one-third of all the Irish who came to America during the Famine died within three years. Their great enemy was tuberculosis, which the Archbishop himself called "the natural death of the Irish immigrant." He called the poor Irish here "the poorest and most wretched population in the world, the scattered debris of the Irish nation." Here at least there was hope, a hope that became reality for great numbers. There was a steady improvement in the social and economic position of many Catholics, an upward mobility that carried many into the middle class, and a few into the upper class. At the same time, the disproportionate number of Catholics among those needing aid was an added incentive to Nativism in its various forms. There were widespread complaints that there were too many undeserving recipients of public and private assistance.

One of the most important achievements of the Hughes administration, and a major step in its efforts to alleviate the social evils of the day, was the introduction and firm establishment in New York of the Society of St. Vincent de Paul. The Society was founded in Paris in May 1833 by Frederic Ozanam (1813–1853) as a society of laymen interested in the personal service of the poor. It was started in the United States in St. Louis in November 1845 by Father John Timon. The second American branch was opened in New York's Cathedral parish in April 1846 by Father John Loughlin. The Society spread rapidly, and in fifteen years opened fifteen branches. It took part in practically every major work of the Church in New York and helped greatly with the Catholic Protectory and the Mission of the Immaculate Virgin. From the beginning, its members were active in visiting all the welfare institutions and, even more importantly, in youth work. The Sisters of Mercy, beginning in 1847, also made systematic visitations of all the public charitable institutions. Their Home for Immigrant Girls sheltered over 2,000 girls between 1846 and 1851, and found jobs for 8,000.

THE CATHEDRAL

Archbishop Hughes' most conspicuous monument is the new St. Patrick's Cathedral. He first spoke of it publicly when announcing his appointment as Archbishop, but it is probable that he had it in mind for some time and had already chosen the site. The property on which the Cathedral stands was acquired by Father Kohlmann in 1810 for his New York Literary Institute. It returned to private hands in 1821, and in 1829 was bought by the trustees of the Cathedral and St. Peter's, acting jointly. They intended to use it for a cemetery and did not discover until later that it was entirely unsuitable for such a purpose. In 1852 the Cathedral bought out St. Peter's share, and the property on the northeast corner of Fiftieth Street and Fifth Avenue, which had been given to St. John's Church in 1842, was returned to the Cathedral by the Archbishop.

The architect chosen for the new Cathedral was James Renwick (1818–1895), a non-Catholic New Yorker who had already designed Grace Church for the Episcopalians. The planning began in 1853 and continued until 1858 when the final plan was accepted. The contract was signed on March 5, 1859. The architect was to receive $2,500 a year for eight years. The building was to be of white marble above the foundation. The original plan was to finish it in eight years at a cost of $850,000, excluding the foundations, altars, and furnishings, but including the spires. Many doubted it could be built at the estimated cost in spite of the depressed conditions in the building industry. The Archbishop reserved the right to call off work at any time and did so in 1861 because of the Civil War. The contractor undertook to forbid the possession or consumption of liquor on the premises, to dismiss instantly anyone violating that rule, and not to employ knowingly any workman living or boarding at any place where liquor was sold, within a specified distance from the Cathedral site.

The announcement of the plans evoked a mixed response. Some thought there were more pressing needs that had a prior claim on the limited resources of the Catholics of New York and others thought the site ill chosen. They thought it too far out in the country and called it "Hughes' Folly." No one, they said, would travel to so remote a location. Others were prepared to help. In June 1858 the Archbishop asked for one hundred gifts of a thousand dollars, payable within a year, with which to start the work. He received one hundred and three, including two from non-Catholics. The cornerstone was laid on August 15, 1859, in the presence of seven bishops of the Province of New York, 130 priests, and about 100,000 people. The Archbishop preached. He did not expect to live to see the Cathedral finished, but he had a vision of New York becoming one of the great cities of the world, and he wished to begin on such a scale that his successors would be compelled to finish the work as planned. In the same year the Atlantic Cable was opened and so was the Fifth Avenue Hotel in Madison Square. Many wondered if the hotel also was too far from the center of the city to succeed.

Public Affairs

Archbishop Hughes was the first occupant of the see of New York to take an active interest in public affairs, civil and ecclesiastical, at home and abroad, apart from the public controversies that directly concerned his office. He was a firm supporter of the temporal power of the Pope and followed the misfortunes of Pius IX with deep sympathy. He helped found the North American College in Rome in 1859 and supported the plan for a Catholic university in Ireland. He wanted Baltimore recognized as the Primatial See in the United States. He was strongly opposed to the Young Ireland movement because he thought it could not succeed and would result only in further repression of Ireland by England.

In this country his talent for public affairs was recognized by several prominent officials. In 1846 James Buchanan, the future President, who was then Secretary of State under President James Polk, offered him a special mission to Mexico during the Mexican War, which had just begun. On the advice of the other bishops of the country, he turned it down because the government felt unable to give him an official rank and title. Buchanan's estimate of the Archbishop follows: "Independent of his exalted character as a dignitary of the Church, I believed him to be one of the ablest and most accomplished and energetic men I had ever known, and that he possessed all the prudence and firmness necessary to render such a mission successful." In December 1847, at the invitation of John Quincy Adams, he preached before Congress.

Archbishop Hughes took a keen interest in the Civil War. He was wholeheartedly for the preservation of the Union, but had no sympathy with the Abolitionists whom he rightly regarded as deeply anti-Catholic, and as having even less use for the Irish than they had for Blacks. He was convinced that immediate and unconditional emancipation would be bad for the slaves and their owners. He was anxious not to have the Union and Abolition linked in the minds of the Irish Catholics. At least through 1861 the majority of the New York City population supported the war, and it is estimated that 15% of the New York State troops in the Union Army were Irish. The Archbishop was aware, too, of the friction in New York between the Irish and the Blacks, which had its origin in economic rivalry. In 1855 there were only 11,840 Blacks in New York City. About 2,000 were active church members and only a handful were Catholics. Over half the gainfully employed Blacks, about 2,000, were in domestic service. There were 15 Black ministers. The public schools and transit system were segregated until after the Civil War.

The small community of Black Catholics produced one prominent member, Pierre Toussaint (c. 1766–1853), who was for many years one of the leading hairdressers in the city. He was born in Santo Domingo and brought to New York as a slave by his masters, the John Berards. When Mr. Berard died, his widow was left in straitened circumstances and was supported by Toussaint, whom she freed on her deathbed. He gave much of his time and money to charity, especially to the Orphan Asylum, and for nearly sixty years attended Mass daily at St. Peter's. The cause of his canonization was introduced in Rome in 1968.

Two events in the Civil War clearly show the Archbishop's attitude to it. In October 1861, his old friend, William H. Seward, then Secretary of State, invited him in President Lincoln's name to undertake a diplomatic mission to France to induce the French Emperor not to recognize the Confederacy. He was received courteously by Napoleon III and the Empress Eugénie, on December 24, 1861. He also visited Ireland and Rome. At the suggestion of the Pope, he remained in Rome for the canonization of the Japanese Martyrs on June 10, 1862, and did not return to New York until August 12, 1862. He went almost at once to Washington where the authorities professed themselves much pleased by the success of his mission. The Archbishop's enthusiasm for the Union Cause was not shared by the publisher, James McMaster, who opposed every move of the administration, and was finally interned by Lincoln for opposing the war effort.

The second event, and the Archbishop's last public appearance, was his intervention in the Draft Riot in New York City in July 1863. A draft had been ordered to fill New York State's quota in the Union Army. At the same time, any one subject to the draft who could find a substitute by paying him $300 was free to do so. Most of the first 12,000 drawn were poor laborers who could not afford to pay a substitute. A large proportion were Irish. There was widespread resentment of this grossly inequitable arrangement. The Republican papers and especially Horace Greeley's *Tribune* were blaming the Catholics, and especially the Irish Catholics, for bringing on the Civil War by supporting the Democratic Party, and for prolonging it by the refusal of the priests to preach abolition and anti-slavery doctrines from the pulpit. The Draft began on July 11th, a week after the Battle of Gettysburg, and on Monday, July 13th, the riots began and the Draft offices were burned. On July 14th martial law was proclaimed, and two days later the Archbishop printed an appeal to the rioters to visit him on July 17th. A crowd of about 5,000 did so, and he made an earnest appeal for peace in the city. He was too ill to stand while speaking to them. The Draft was suspended until the fall of the year. It was probably the reason why Lincoln did not carry New York in 1864. In spite of his interest in public affairs, the Archbishop was not an active participant. To avoid the charge of partisan politics, he voted only once. That was for Henry Clay in 1832.

DEATH OF ARCHBISHOP HUGHES

Those close to Archbishop Hughes noted with concern the extent to which his health deteriorated during his trip to Europe in 1862. It had begun to fail as early as 1848 because of the way he drove himself. Later, he suffered greatly from arthritis and finally from Bright's disease. In spite of the divisions of the diocese, it was substantially larger in population when he died than when he was appointed and, as he had no coadjutor after Bishop McCloskey left for Albany in 1847, the burden grew steadily heavier. He spoke from time to time of another coadjutor but never got around to asking for one. When he was very ill, he even spoke of resigning, but Rome indicated that would be unacceptable.

Following the last ecclesiastical function he attended—the dedication of St. Teresa's Church, on Rutgers Street, on June 21, 1863—he declined rapidly and was unable to say Mass for months. He was visited regularly by Bishop McCloskey, who was with him on December 29, 1863, when the doctors told him he was dying. The end came on January 3, 1864, while Bishop McCloskey was reciting the prayers for the dying. The funeral, held on January 7th, the twenty-sixth anniversary of his episcopal consecration, attracted a great multitude and was a fitting tribute to the man and his work. The Mass was said by Bishop John Timon. Bishop Bayley said it was the most impressive episcopal funeral in this country up to that time. The three hundred policemen on duty were given no trouble by the crowd.

Everyone recognized the passing of an outstanding leader, and many sought to identify the cause of his undeniable preeminence. He was not the best educated or the most eloquent or, some would say, the most intelligent of the bishops. He was not a systematic worker or a gifted administrator. He had very few close friends and, in his latter years, he moved of necessity in a small circle, rarely giving or receiving hospitality or meeting new people. With age and illness and success, he grew more impatient of opposition and sometimes reacted to it more strongly than necessary. He stood very much on his dignity, in part because of the fate of his predecessors in New York.

The clergy in general found him a hard taskmaster, but he could be kind and even merciful. One gifted New York priest who gave him trouble described him as "a tyrant with a heart." In another case, a priest arrived from Europe with high testimonials that were followed swiftly by private warnings that he was subject to periodic attacks of insanity. He came here to finish a massive work of scholarship that would reconcile the Church with the spirit of the age, and remove all grounds for a conflict between religion and science. After a number of months during which the Archbishop provided for him, and the visitor became involved in a short-lived local schism, the book was finished. It turned out to be a way to square the circle. The Archbishop paid the author's way home.

In spite of the reservations different critics made, all acknowledged the singular force of his personality, his courage, and his iron will. His achievements were admitted by all. He made an indelible mark on the Archdiocese and marked out the lines on which it has developed ever since. His friends and admirers accepted the explanation of his influence given in the just and eloquent eulogy by Bishop McCloskey, the closest associate the

Archbishop ever had. He said: "If ever there was a man who in the whole history and character of his life impressed upon us that he had been raised up by God, was chosen as His instrument to do an appointed work, and was strengthened by His grace and supported by His wisdom for the accomplishment of the work for which he was chosen and appointed, that man was Archbishop Hughes."

The Archbishop was buried in the Cathedral. Everyone recognized that his death had ended an era in New York. As things turned out, it did the same in Albany.

CHAPTER 8

John Cardinal McCloskey

When the question of the succession to the Archbishopric of New York arose, all eyes turned to the Bishop of Albany. It was widely believed that he was the obvious and inevitable choice. A dissenting opinion came from two sources. The first was a group of New York priests who felt that after twenty-five years of Archbishop Hughes it was time for a change of pace, policy, and personnel. Some of them felt Bishop McCloskey had always hoped and expected to return and had cultivated Archbishop Hughes with that end in mind. The second source was the Bishop himself, who knew because he was present, that the bishops of the Province had put his name first on the list of candidates they had forwarded to Rome. On the first ballot he had tied with Bishop Timon of Buffalo, for whom he voted, while Bishop Timon voted for Bishop Loughlin of Brooklyn. On the second ballot, by a switch of one vote, Bishop McCloskey came first and was first, too, on the list sent in by the priests of New York.

At a moment which was for him, in his own words, "one of deepest anxiety and fear," he decided to write to Rome to block his own promotion. Accordingly, on January 26, 1864, he wrote in confidence to his old friend Cardinal Reisach, who was living in Rome, an exile from Germany, and was one of the Commission of Cardinals whose duty it was to submit to the Pope names for the vacant sees of Baltimore and New York. His letter said in part: "I write to implore your Eminence in case there should be any danger of my appointment, or of my being transferred from Albany to New York, to aid me in preventing it and to save me from the humiliation and misery of being placed in a position for the duties and responsibilities of which I feel myself both physically and morally wholly unfit and unequal." He continued: "I speak from the deepest sincerity of heart and from the strongest conviction of conscience when I say I possess neither the learning nor prudence nor energy nor firmness nor bodily health and strength which are requisite for such an arduous and highly responsible office as that of Archbishop of New York. I recoil from the very thought of it with shuddering, and I do most humbly trust that such a crushing load will not be placed upon my weak and most unworthy shoulders. Either the Bishop of Louisville, Dr. Spalding, or the Bishop of Buffalo, Dr. Timon, would fill the post with dignity, efficiency and honor." This remarkable letter was evaluated correctly in Rome and its recommendations were set aside. Early in May, its author received official notice of his appointment to New York, and Bishop Spalding of Louisville was appointed to Baltimore.

The new Archbishop did not hurry to New York but spent three months winding up his affairs in Albany. As he looked back on his seventeen years there, he saw much for which to be grateful. The Catholic population had increased by almost five hundred percent. The number of priests had grown from thirty-eight to ninety-five, churches from forty-seven to one hundred and twenty, schools from five to twenty-seven. He had added several religious communities and charitable institutions. His major achievement and his first big project in Albany had been the Cathedral of the Immaculate Conception which he started almost at once. He laid the cornerstone on July 2, 1848, and the building was dedicated on November 21, 1852.

Archbishop Hughes, who preached on both occasions, encouraged him to look for help in New York. In doing so, he did not confine himself to the more prosperous Catholics. Shortly before the laying of the cornerstone, the following letter was read at St. Joseph's, in Greenwich Village: "Will you please to notify your people that we will commence the work of excavation at the Cathedral on Monday morning, that we hope to have it done by gratuitous labor, and that there will not be wanting those among the congregation of St. Joseph's who will cheerfully donate two or three days to the work. Those who can bring horse and cart will confer a great favor by doing so."

Bishop McCloskey's life in Albany had been much the same as that he had led in New York so all the problems were familiar ones. He had to appeal for help abroad, as Bishops Connolly, Dubois, and Hughes had done. He had written to Rome, to the Austrian Emperor, Francis Joseph, and to the Society for the Propagation of the Faith in France. All had responded generously. In October 1851, having made a thorough study of his diocese, he had gone to Europe to plead in person for help and had reached Paris on the eve of the *coup d'etat* that made Louis Napoleon Emperor of the French. He had visited Rome, where he first met Pius IX, and stopped in Vienna and Ireland before returning to New York on April 27, 1852. In Rome he had met the recently converted Anglican Archdeacon, Henry Edward Manning, later the Cardinal Archbishop of Westminster, who was then studying theology. They were to enter the Sacred College of Cardinals together in later years.

Among the problems he had encountered in Albany was trusteeism which had started long before the erection of the diocese. He had had to deal with it in Troy, Oswego, and especially in Carthage, where the situation had been so serious he placed the parish under interdict in 1861. Most of his time was passed in routine hard work of which fund raising was only a part. His methodical visitation of the diocese was not without minor annoyances and even danger, and several times he had had trouble getting into a hotel because he was recognized as a priest. In July 1859 he had been in an accident in which the conductor urged him to jump for his life. He did so and suffered a badly broken ankle. The railroad had given him $5,000 in compensation which he turned over at once to the Cathedral Building Fund. It was an experienced man with a thorough knowledge of every aspect of parish life and of the religious climate of the time who stole away on the Albany night boat on August 6, 1864, accompanied only by his secretary and successor in Albany, Father John Conroy. They were met only by Archbishop Hughes' secretary, Father Francis McNeirny, who later became the third Bishop of Albany.

Archbishop McCloskey's first day in New York saw a striking manifestation of his imperturbability. When he came downstairs after Mass, he was told a woman who claimed to be his mother (who had died March 26, 1845) had arrived and intended to stay. The police were called and the Archbishop himself had to go to the station house to make a complaint against the woman. The official in charge told him, "She tells a very straight story," and appeared to believe her. The Archbishop repeated his story calmly and turned to go. As he did so she begged him not to abandon her to the police, who would surely mistreat her. As they became indignant and rebuked her, the Archbishop said, "She tells a very straight story" and left.

The solemn installation of the new Archbishop took place on August 21st in the Cathedral. There was no procession because of the rain. The new Archbishop of Baltimore presided and conferred the pallium. In his sermon, Archbishop McCloskey chose as his text "Peace be with you." It expressed the spirit that was to guide his administration. He kept all the archdiocesan officials appointed by his predecessor, whom he knew well, and resolved to carry out the Hughes program, which he also knew very well. The approaching end of the Civil War was going to open a new era of expansion, and plans must be ready when the proper time came. He was well aware of the problems he faced. Most of them were old ones made more acute in some ways by the growth of the Catholic population. He would have to give special attention to the need for more parishes and to the problem of orphaned or abandoned children.

He found it easier to escape celebrations in his honor when leaving Albany than when arriving in New York. There, on November 8, 1864, he was given a dinner at Delmonico's by eighty prominent figures in New York public life. The chairman and chief speaker was Charles O'Conor (1804–1884), a leading lawyer of the day and the first Catholic to be nominated for President of the United States. O'Conor refused the nomination made by the "Straight out Democratic" ticket in 1872 and supported Grant against Greeley. Years later, he described Archbishop McCloskey as the most prudent man he had ever met.

The Archbishop's first important task was the opening of the new seminary building in Troy. When Archbishop Hughes had closed St. Joseph's Seminary at Fordham in 1861, he did so with the intention of reviving it as a provincial seminary as soon as possible. He had hoped it would be used and supported by all the dioceses in the Province. He was anxious to have the Sulpician Fathers take charge, but they were short of men and were fearful of weakening their other seminaries. Archbishop Hughes thought it important that every diocesan priest in New York know French, and the Bishops of Albany and Boston went to Europe and arranged for a faculty of diocesan priests from Ghent, Belgium. The seminary was to be housed in a former Methodist university in Troy, N.Y., which had been bought, with the consent of Bishop McCloskey, in December 1862. It was the third seminary, after Nyack and Fordham, with which the McCloskey administration was connected. It was dedicated by him on December 1, 1864.

Accurate figures on the Catholic population at that time are impossible to find and the estimates vary widely. The most probable figure for the Archdiocese is about 360,000 practicing Catholics. The population of Manhattan itself had more than doubled between 1840 and 1860, increasing from 312,710 to 805,358. Oddly enough, and for the first time, it fell between 1860 and 1865, dropping from 805,358 to 726,386. In 1860 the present Bronx, with a population of 23,593, had fewer inhabitants than Staten Island, which had 35,492.

All observers agreed that there were too few Catholic churches in the city, and that things were worse in the country areas. In 1860 there were thirty-one churches on Manhattan Island. Of these, twenty-two were Irish parishes, eight German, and one French. By 1868 there were thirty-eight churches, but even that was not enough. It was calculated in 1868 that if each church held 1,500 people, which was a generous allowance, 57,000 could attend High Mass on Sunday. If every church had four Masses on Sunday, which they did not, the total seating capacity would be 228,000. The estimated number of nominal Catholics was given by some as 450,000, while others put it higher. By any estimate, there was a grave shortage of churches.

In 1867 Immaculate Conception Parish on East 14th Street, which

averaged ten sick calls a day, had a very successful mission after which the
pastor and the missionaries estimated the Catholic population at "not less
than 25,000." Because of an influx of visitors, the missioners heard 28,000
confessions in three weeks. The parish had only five Masses on Sunday
because of the shortage of priests. Things were better by December 1880,
when the same parish was described as "not one of the larger parishes, it had
only 17,000 parishioners." Its school had fourteen sisters and twenty-two lay
teachers. If we accept the conservative estimate of 350,000 practicing
Catholics in 1865, there were 4,861 Catholics for each priest, whereas in
1840 there had been 4,454. The average parish in 1865 had 10,937
Catholics, against 8,500 in 1840. So, under Archbishop Hughes as under
Bishop Connolly, a great deal was done but it was insufficient. In 1865
fourteen of the city parishes were below 14th Street, fourteen were between
14th and 59th Streets, and three were above 59th Street in "suburban
Yorkville, Harlem, and Manhattanville." The opening of new parishes
continued all during the McCloskey administration, adding twenty-five in
Manhattan, four in the Bronx, one on Staten Island, and fifty-eight outside
the city. This compares favorably with the sixty-one parishes that had been
started by Archbishop Hughes, and the ninety-nine to be started by
Archbishop Corrigan in the next generation.

The rapid growth in population, which multiplied by eight hundred percent
between 1820 and 1870, was a mixed blessing to the city and brought the
usual predictable social and economic problems in its wake. There is a
familiar ring to the complaints that in the 1870s New York was becoming
increasingly a two-class city, the rich and the poor. The middle class was
moving to the suburbs, driven there by the cost of living in the city, the
housing shortage, taxes, and the transit problem. There were twenty-two
streetcar companies, all using horses. They charged five cents a fare south of
65th Street and six or eight cents above it. All the companies made a profit. It
was estimated that the average New Yorker spent an hour-and-a-half daily
going to and from work. The trolley drivers and conductors worked fifteen
hours a day for seven days a week for $2.50 a day. A factory girl earned four
dollars weekly for a ten-hour day and a six-day week. Men got twice as much.

One of the most pressing social problems was housing. The first Tenement
House Laws were passed in 1867. The Commissioner found that "most of
the dwellings of the poor are wretched hotbeds of disease which are unfit for
human habitation." It was estimated that 501,244 of the 726,382 inhabitants
of the city lived in tenements and cellars. Though these conditions could be
matched in London, Boston and many other European and American cities,
in 1863 New York had the highest recorded death rate of any large city in the
world. It was not until 1867, after the last epidemic of cholera, that the
Sanitary Commission was established.

Among the social evils brought on or greatly aggravated by the rapid,
unregulated growth of the city, none was more obvious than the neglect of the

children of the poor. Here the McCloskey administration made a major contribution. Among the many good works it developed or founded were three that merit special attention. They were the Catholic Protectory, the New York Foundling Asylum, and the Mission of the Immaculate Virgin. The Archbishop often said that he had been very fortunate. In no area was that more true than in the personnel he found to help him in the apostolate to children.

The Catholic Protectory, the last great work of Archbishop Hughes, opened on May 29, 1863, in small rented quarters on East 36th Street. At first it was restricted to boys committed by the courts or transferred by the Commissioner of Charities, but it was always intended to serve a much larger group. Because of overcrowding and the need to help as many children as possible, the Catholic orphanages did not keep boys over twelve or girls over fourteen. Archbishop Hughes, who was responsible for that rule, knew something had to be done for those who were ineligible for the orphanages, who were not under the care of the State, who were unable to find suitable employment, or who had relatives who would not or could not help them.

The urgency of the problems the Protectory dealt with was shown not only by its rapid growth but by some official figures on the situation in New York. In 1867 the Commission on Charity reported that the city had "about 30,000 (some said 40,000) children between the ages of five and twelve who receive no education, and whose days are passed in poverty and idleness. Utterly desolate and without parents and without the actual effective sympathy of those who could raise them above want, how can it be that as they grow up they should be other than dissolute and criminal." In 1870 the population of the City was 942,292.

The problems were not restricted to New York. The Pastoral Letter issued by the Fathers of the Second Plenary Council of Baltimore in 1866 said: "It is a melancholy fact and a humiliating avowal for us to make that a very large proportion of the idle and vicious youths of our principal cities are the children of Catholic parents." After lamenting that the children were often taken from the sectarian reformatories to which the courts had sent them and sent to distant locations where they were brought up in ignorance of and often in hostility to the Church, the Bishops appealed for Catholic protectories. This situation was relieved in New York State by the 1875 law recognizing the parents' right to have their children brought up in their own faith aided by the State.

The Protectory was assisted from the beginning by the St. Vincent de Paul Society and directed until his death by Levi Silliman Ives (1797–1867), a distinguished convert who had been the Protestant Episcopal Bishop of North Carolina. He was received into the Church in Rome by Pope Pius IX on Christmas Day 1852. It was believed that more than half the Catholic orphans or half orphans were without protection of any kind. Mr. Ives saw the Protectory as an instrument for "saving them from ruin in a way consistent with parental claims and social welfare in a way to insure the preservation and inovulation of their faith as Catholics." Ives was succeeded by Henry J. Anderson (1799–1875), also a convert and a president of the St. Vincent de Paul Society, who was a former professor of astronomy at Columbia University.

It was Archbishop McCloskey's task to see that the Protectory got the necessary staff and support. The De La Salle Christian Brothers had already agreed to take the boys department and the Sisters of Charity the girls department, which opened on October 1, 1863. It was moved to the present site of Parkchester, which is now in the Bronx but was then in Westchester, where 114 acres of farmland was bought for $40,000 in 1865. The State provided a $50,000 grant for the boys department to be matched by a similar sum from private donors. The entire cost of the girls department was raised by the Archbishop. A favorite fund-raising device at the time was a fair, and in May and June 1867 a fair held in Union Square netted $100,000. The new plant was dedicated in 1870, destroyed by fire in 1872, and rebuilt by 1874. In that year it had 1,700 children, and by the end of the century the capacity was 3,170. It was closed on November 1, 1938, because changing times and changing styles in child care made its methods seem outmoded. It had done great work and had sheltered more than 100,000 children.

The number of children who were not enrolled in school was less startling a century ago than it would be now. In 1870, 57% of the children between five and seventeen were enrolled in the public schools. The average pupil attended for 78.4 days a year. Their per capita cost was $1.64 for the entire population or $9.23 per pupil. By 1930 the percentage enrolled had risen to 81.3. In 1874 the New York State Compulsory Education Law, amended in 1876, required all children aged eight to fourteen to attend school for at least fourteen weeks a year, of which at least eight weeks a year must be consecutive. The employment of children under fourteen during school hours was forbidden unless the child could prove attendance at school for fourteen preceding weeks. This law was a dead letter for years. In the 1880s there were 200,000 children working full time in New York State. In 1875 all prayers, bible reading, and hymn singing were forbidden in the public schools of New York State. In 1880 the New York City public schools numbered 305, with 263,000 pupils, and cost $3,250,000.

Long before the New York Foundling Asylum was opened, there was widespread recognition that it was needed. Infanticide was very common and the public officials were slow to do anything about it, probably because they could not decide what to do. Abandoned infants were sent to women's prisons and left in the care of the prisoners. Very few of them lived long enough to qualify for transfer to institutions for older children. In 1857 work was started on a public hospital, but when the building was almost ready the Civil War came and it was taken over as a military hospital. In 1869 Archbishop McCloskey asked the Sisters of Charity to undertake the work, and they agreed. The Foundling Asylum was opened on October 11, 1869, the Feast of the Maternity of Our Lady, in rented quarters on East 12th Street, under the direction of Sister Irene (Catherine) Fitzgibbon (1823–1896). She had already shown administrative talent of a higher order and was keenly interested in the work, so she was the logical choice to head it. From the very beginning the new asylum was swamped, and this led quickly to the establishment of a boarding department. Another problem was proper nourishment. Scientific formulas for feeding infants were unknown at the time, so in some cases a mother was persuaded to remain for a few months to care for her child and sometimes for another child at the same time.

The public authorities were pleased by the opening of the Foundling Asylum, and noticed quickly the 50% drop in mortality. In 1870 the Legislature authorized the city to grant a site for an adequate building, and voted $100,000 toward its erection on condition that the grant be matched by private contributions. At the same time, it granted an allowance of a dollar weekly for each child. Once again the Archbishop organized a fair. It was held in the Twenty-second Regiment Armory in November 1870 and realized $71,000. Private donors made up the rest. The Foundling Hospital soon became and has remained a model of its kind, one of the most successful works of charity ever undertaken in New York. The first permanent building was occupied on November 1, 1873. It occupied the block between 68th and 69th Streets and between Lexington and Third Avenues. In the same year, the Legislature raised the allowance to .38 cents daily per child. In its first five years, the Asylum received 2,500 babies. As the work grew, new needs arose and were met. Sister Irene opened St. Ann's Hospital for unmarried mothers in 1880, St. John's Hospital for Sick Children in 1881, Nazareth Hospital for Convalescent Children in 1881, and Seton Hospital for tuberculosis cases in 1892. She remained superior until her death in August 1896. On that occasion, the *New York Times* described her as "the most remarkable woman of her age in her sphere of philanthropy." In 1894, in a report to the New York State Constitutional Convention, Elbridge Gerry stated that "child murder has been practically stamped out in the City of New York from the time the New York Foundling Hospital commenced."

If the Protectory and the Foundling Hospital were the projection of the personalities of Levi Ives and Sister Irene, the Mission of the Immaculate Virgin was the projection of the personality of Father John C. Drumgoole (1816–1888). Born in Ireland, he came here in 1824 and lived with his mother in St. Peter's parish, where, as a child, he was greatly impressed by Father Malou. His studies for the priesthood were delayed for years by poverty, and he was not ordained until 1869. Meanwhile, he worked as a cobbler and as sexton of St. Mary's Church on Grand Street, where he had plenty of chances to see the homeless boys who were later to provide the field for his labors. He was ordained a few months before Father Isaac Hecker, C.S.P., printed in *The Catholic World* an article on the vagrant children in New York among whom alcoholism was already a scourge.

The Society of St. Vincent de Paul opened a refuge, St. Vincent's Home for Homeless Boys of All Occupations. In July 1870, Father Drumgoole volunteered to be chaplain and within a year was director, with the approval of all parties. The boys, many of whom were newsboys, paid their way— twenty cents a day for board and lodging. This was paid only on working days. Expansion was inevitable, in spite of the Panic of 1873, but it was very hard. It was impossible to restrict the Home to working boys because so many other children were in need and no other place could help. With Archbishop McCloskey's aid, the founding of St. Joseph's Union as a fund-raising auxiliary, and the inevitable fair, the funds came in. St. Joseph's Union, which charged its members twenty-five cents a year, kept in touch with them through its publication *The Homeless Child*. It came to have a circulation of over 300,000, and among its subscribers were men as far apart in rank and residence as Lucido Cardinal Parocchi, the Vicar of Rome, and Father Damien of Molokai. Father Drumgoole worked closely, too, with the Society for the Prevention of Cruelty to Children. By 1881 a new building on Great Jones and Lafayette Streets, with a new name, the Mission of the Immaculate Virgin, was ready. It became one of the largest and best known child-caring institutions in the country and the Universal Church. In June 1882 Father Drumgoole bought the site for the country house, Mount Loretto, on Staten Island, where the entire institution is now located. In 1886 he was able to open the long needed girls department. Many prominent visitors from different walks of life and quite varied backgrounds visited the Mission, partly to see the work and partly to see the Director. One of the many tributes paid to him and the Mission was from Lord Rosebery (1847– 1929), the future (1894–1895) Prime Minister of England. He wrote: "I have never left your house without feeling better for it, and without feeling that I had got an insight into a higher and holier life than men are generally privileged to lead or indeed are capable of leading. God bless you, if that may be said to you without presumption." Father Drumgoole died on March 28, 1888, a victim of the Great Blizzard of '88, in which he attempted to go from Mount Loretto to the City home, to see if all was well. The death certificate said he died of exhaustion and pneumonia.

The children were not the only ones for whom the McCloskey administration attempted to provide. It began on a small scale what has become one of the major works of the Archdiocese—the care of the elderly. Just before and after the Civil War, Mother Frances Schervier (1819–1876), the foundress of the Sisters of the Poor of Saint Francis, came from Germany to visit convents of her congregation in Cincinnati and New York. Her community opened St. Francis Hospital in 1865, and three years later opened the Archdiocese's first home for the aged in conjunction with the hospital.

Mother Schervier, later proclaimed Blessed by the Church, was surprised to find that many sisters either rode in closed carriages if they wore a habit, or wore secular clothes if they went on foot, for fear of being insulted or injured if recognized as sisters. Her community were the first wearing a religious habit to solicit funds openly for their work with the sick and the elderly. In 1870, the Little Sisters of the Poor joined the apostolate to New York's aged.

Important as welfare work and new parishes were, they did not absorb all of the Archbishop's time and attention. Though the great push for parochial schools followed the Third Council of Baltimore in 1884, he did what he could from 1864 to 1884, and he doubled the number and capacity of the schools he found on his arrival. When he died, the Archdiocese had 33,000 children in its elementary schools. He brought in sixteen religious communities, including the Dominican and Franciscan Fathers, and increased the number of hospitals. One of these was St. Vincent's, in Harrison, Westchester County, which opened in 1876 as the first Catholic hospital for mental patients in New York State. He also paid special attention to the new immigrants. In his time, the first church for black Catholics, St. Benedict the Moor, was opened (1883), and both the Poles and the Italians, who were soon to arrive in great numbers, received their first churches in the City: St. Stanislaus, East 7th Street (1872) and St. Anthony (1866), on Sullivan Street.

In September 1868, the Archbishop held the Third Synod of New York, in which the Decrees of the Second Council of Baltimore (1866) were published. We get a glimpse of the customs of the time in the Synodal decrees forbidding Mass on Christmas before 4:00 A.M., and allowing Holy Communion at funerals. It strongly recommended the Forty Hours Devotion, and commended the existing custom of hearing confessions on Friday as well as Saturday. The Archbishop played a prominent role in the Baltimore Council of 1866, at which he was the keynote speaker, though the youngest Archbishop present. He was regarded by his peers as eloquent and wise in counsel. As he was entering the pulpit to deliver his sermon on October 6, 1866, he was handed a telegram which he read and put aside without comment then or later. The next day's papers reported the destruction of the New York Cathedral by fire. The Archbishop said the damage was already done, no one in Baltimore could do anything about it, and he did not wish to put a damper on the Council's proceedings. The Cathedral was rebuilt promptly and he rededicated it on March 17, 1868. Since work on the new Cathedral was then underway, he had the unusual task of building two Cathedrals in the same city at the same time.

At the Council, the Archbishop was a strong proponent of parochial schools, industrial schools, and ultimately a Catholic university. Another topic that concerned him was the possible condemnation of Fenianism. The Fenian Brotherhood was founded in this country in 1858 to work for the liberation of Ireland, which it was convinced could be achieved only by force. It attracted widespread support here. Archbishop McCloskey was strongly sympathetic to the cause of Irish nationalism, but was convinced that force would be ineffective and counterproductive. His attitude was that of his good friend Cardinal Cullen. In a pastoral letter dated March 2, 1866, the

Catholics of New York were warned against joining or supporting the Fenians, and on the following day he preached on that topic in the Cathedral. The failure of the Fenian Rising of 1867 confirmed his fears. The pro-Fenians incurred sharp and justifiable criticism by their attacks on the Orangemen's Parade in New York on July 12, 1870, and July 12, 1871. In the latter case, at least thirty-three people were killed. Once again, Archbishop McCloskey had warned Catholics in advance against supporting such tactics. He was also opposed to recruiting American Catholics for the defense of the Papal States.

Archbishop McCloskey shared that great devotion to the Sacred Heart and the Immaculate Conception which was so strong and widespread in the Church in the last century. He rejoiced in the establishment of December 8th as a holyday of obligation in the United States, which came about in 1868 as a result of Baltimore II. In 1873 he led the Bishops of the Province of New York in dedicating their dioceses to the Sacred Heart. In 1874 he encouraged the first American Catholic pilgrimage to Rome and Lourdes, and said Mass for the pilgrims before departure. The fare, on the French Line, was $125 payable in gold, with a 25% reduction for a round trip, while second class cost $75.

He attended the First Vatican Council, 1869–1870, where he was an Inopportunist. That is, while accepting fully the doctrine of Papal Infallibility, he was opposed to its definition by the Council, foreseeing correctly that it would provoke a worldwide wave of anti-Catholic agitation. The non-Catholic reaction to the Syllabus of Errors in 1864 was a fair indication of what he felt might be expected to follow the definition of Infallibility, and he was correct. It was used by Bismarck of Germany and Gladstone of England to justify their attacks on the Church. He voted for the definition on July 18, 1870, because he believed in the doctrine and saw that the vast majority of the bishops wanted it passed and settled. His attitude provoked a storm of criticism from the publisher of the New York *Freeman's Journal,* James McMaster, who took a much more severe view of the Inopportunists than the Pope did.

Because Archbishop McCloskey took no part in public controversies, the secular press was kinder to him than it had been to Archbishop Hughes or would be to Archbishop Corrigan. It was not less critical of the Church but was more restrained in expressing its abiding ill will. The Archbishop took both it and McMaster in stride.

The Red Hat

As early as 1850, when New York had become an archdiocese, there were rumors of the impending creation of an American Cardinal, and public opinion judged Archbishop Hughes to be the most likely candidate for that honor. Later, President Lincoln conveyed to Pope Pius IX his hope that it would be so. Nothing was done then, partly because Cardinal Antonelli, the Papal Secretary of State, regarded the proposal as premature and even ridiculous, and partly because the Archbishop had many critics inside as well as outside the Church. Pius IX, himself the first future pope ever to visit the Western Hemisphere, thought well of the idea but put it aside for the time being.

The new Archbishops of Baltimore and New York were barely installed in 1864 when rumors of the red hat revived, and the press was busy trying to decide on which of them the papal choice would fall. It is interesting to find Archbishop McCloskey writing to his close friend the Archbishop of Baltimore in August 1864: "Is it not provoking to have to endure such ridiculous reports as the one you extracted from the *Express* and sent me? I hope we shall have no cardinal's hat in this country. We are better off without one. I will not answer, however, for what may be in store for you. For myself, I have no fear." He and many others thought such an event would stimulate anti-Catholic feeling and bring more trouble than it was worth.

The official notification of the long-rumored promotion came on March 15, 1875. Archbishop McCloskey was notified by cable that he had that day been created and proclaimed a cardinal priest of the Holy Roman Church. He and Cardinal Gibbons of Baltimore, who succeeded him in the Sacred College in 1886, are the only American Cardinals to date who were not summoned to the consistory in Rome in which their elevation was announced. In both cases, this was due to the time element. The first American Cardinal was also the first in the Western Hemisphere. The first Canadian Cardinal was created in 1887, and the first Latin American, a Brazilian, in 1911. Rome was fully aware of the significance of giving a hat to the United States and wanted all the formalities carried out with great precision. Archbishop McCloskey received detailed instructions on the ceremonies that were to take place in New York and was informed that all the external signs of his new rank, except the hat itself, were being sent by special papal messenger. He was to go to Rome later to receive the red hat. His own first spontaneous comment on the news, made to his secretary and second successor, Father John Farley, was: "Oh, Cardinal Cullen got me into this box."

The news was received with general satisfaction and taken as an honor to the country. It was also seen as recognition of the growth of the Church in this country. In New York and New Jersey alone, the number of Catholics had grown from about 15,000 in 1815 to over 1,200,000 in 1875. They had become the largest single religious denomination by 1865. The anticipated anti-Catholic storm did not appear. President Ulysses S. Grant even sent the Pope a letter of thanks. The press took a lively and generally friendly interest in the proceedings and every detail of that splendid and complicated ceremony was reported at length. On April 7, 1875, Count Marefoschi, of the Pope's Noble Guard, was received by the Archbishop, who was surrounded by a group of friends, clerical and lay. The Count brought him a box containing the scarlet skull cap and a letter from Cardinal Antonelli. He made a speech in Latin to which the new cardinal replied in the same tongue. Father Edward McGlynn then read the official letter notifying the cardinal of his appointment. Monsignor Roncetti, the special papal envoy, then entered and made a formal speech of congratulations in French, to which the cardinal replied in French, and the ceremony was over.

The formal conferring of the scarlet biretta took place on August 27th in the Cathedral. Seven archbishops, twenty bishops, three hundred priests, and a distinguished congregation drawn from every sector of New York life were present. Bishop Loughlin of Brooklyn, an intimate friend of both Archbishops McCloskey and Hughes, sang the Pontifical Mass, and Archbishop Bayley of Baltimore was designated by the Pope to confer the biretta. It was a most splendid and widely reported ceremony and the last notable event held in the old Cathedral.

The Cardinal's tact and good sense showed in his handling of a minor episode in the festivities. A group of his friends presented him with a magnificent carriage, all scarlet, gold and glass like those used in Rome for great state occasions. He took a short ride in it so that he could thank them properly, and banished it forever. He ignored an outcry in a segment of the news against introducing monarchy into America.

The actual reception of the red hat was delayed until the next Pontificate, chiefly because the precarious health of Pius IX made it difficult to fix a precise date for the ceremony. The cardinal was in Rome in October 1875, and was given his ring and titular church but not the hat. On his journey he stopped in Paris, where he sat for a portrait by G. P. A. Healy, and in Ireland, where he was given a very warm welcome. When Pius IX died in February 1878, he left for Rome at once but arrived too late to take part in the conclave for the election of the new Pope. He received his hat in March 1878 in the first consistory held by Leo XIII. He had asked for and received as his titular church Santa Maria Sopra Minerva because of its links with his two Dominican predecessors in New York. He remembered having seen and being blessed by Bishop John Connolly.

In the midst of his work for churches, schools, and charitable institutions, the Cardinal never lost sight of the major task he set for himself on his return to New York, the completion of the new Cathedral. He was present when Archbishop Hughes laid the cornerstone on August 15, 1858, and fully shared his enthusiasm for it. The suspension of work in 1861 was a wartime measure. When work was resumed after the Civil War, the foundation and a few feet of the walls had already been finished. The work went along steadily, as did the collection of funds. Archbishop McCloskey took a keen interest in every detail, and on his trips to Europe in 1874, 1875, and 1878, he carefully inspected the furnishings and altars being made in France. A great fair, held in the unfinished building in October and November 1878, was opened by the

Mayor, and each parish in the city had a booth. It netted $172,625.48. In addition, each parish in the Archdiocese had been assessed annually in the ten years before the opening.

Finally, in 1879, all was ready for the dedication. The main altar, a gift from the priests of New York, was consecrated on May 24th, and on the following day the Cathedral was dedicated by the Cardinal. It was the Feast of St. Gregory VII. Six archbishops, twenty-five bishops, several hundred priests and a huge overflow congregation attended the long and imposing ceremonies. Among those present at the dedication was the architect, James Renwick. The Cardinal sang the Pontifical Mass and Archbishop Ryan, coadjutor of St. Louis and the future Archbishop of Philadelphia, preached. He was regarded as the outstanding orator in the hierarchy. At vespers that evening, Archbishop Gibbons of Baltimore presided and Bishop Keane of Richmond preached to a crowded house. The Cardinal and his friends considered the completion of the Cathedral to be the crowning achievement of his life. Still, he had Archbishop Hughes' coat of arms, not his own, set over the main door. The Cathedral, without the spires and the Lady Chapel, which were added by Archbishop Corrigan, cost $1,900,000. The Archbishop's house and the rectory were added in 1882–1884. The parochial school was opened in September 1882. These were paid for by the sale of the block between Madison and Park Avenues and Fiftieth and Fifty-First Streets for $440,000. At that time, about half the lots along Fifth Avenue between the Cathedral and Central Park were empty. There were only about a hundred houses on Madison Avenue between the Cathedral and the Harlem River. It was estimated in 1865 that there were 25,000 empty lots below 86th Street.

As the time for the dedication approached, the Cardinal had to appoint a pastor for the new Cathedral, and few were surprised when he chose his senior Vicar General, William Quinn, his closest adviser. Father Quinn (1821–1887) was born in Ireland, came to New York in 1841, and was one of the first students to register in St. John's College, Fordham, on its opening day. He was ordained by Bishop McCloskey in December 1845, and after a four-year curacy at St. Joseph's in Greenwich Village, and a few weeks as pastor in Rondout, Kingston, Ulster County, N.Y., succeeded Father Power as pastor of St. Peter's, Barclay Street, in November 1849.

His assignment at St. Peter's was one of the most difficult in the Archdiocese because, while the trustees had finally been eliminated, their mismanagement had left a monumental debt. As a result of its legal bankruptcy, the parish was obligated to pay only a third of the total debt (about $50,000), but Father Quinn was determined to pay it all. He was within a few thousand dollars of his goal when he was transferred. His success at St. Peter's led to his appointment as pastor of Old St. Patrick's Cathedral and Vicar General in 1873. He shared the latter position with Father Thomas Preston, and the two worked in great harmony. They were made domestic prelates (monsignors), the first in New York, in 1881.

Monsignor Quinn was a stern, aloof, competent, methodical, and dedicated man with a strong authoritarian streak and a flair for financial matters. He was also brusque in manner, abrupt and laconic in speech, and seemed incapable of giving a compliment or even a soft answer, not to speak of flattery. He was devoted to the Cardinal, for whose sake he refused the coadjutorship of Cincinnati, from whose shoulders he lifted as many burdens as possible, and whose orders, stated or presumed, he carried out to the letter. He was unquestionably the strong man of the McCloskey administration.

The opening of the new Cathedral was welcomed by the general public, which regarded it as an ornament of the city. Its erection coincided with the planning or building of several other landmarks that enriched the cultural life of the city and enhanced its fame. Thus, in 1880 the Metropolitan Opera Company was incorporated. In 1877 the Museum of Natural History occupied its present quarters. It had been incorporated in 1869 and moved into the Arsenal in Central Park. Lovers of sports and public meetings were not neglected, and in 1879 the original Madison Square Garden opened. Two major improvements which were not taken very seriously in the beginning were the telephone, which was introduced on a commercial basis in 1878, with 252 subscribers, and electric lights, which were inaugurated on September 4, 1882, on a very modest scale. The improvement that made the greatest impact on the popular imagination was the Brooklyn Bridge, which opened on May 23, 1883, after thirteen years of hard work.

The improvements were not all cultural. Serious efforts were made by private groups to cope with the ever more evident moral and social problems. In 1865 the first professional Fire Department, equipped with steam engines, replaced the unsatisfactory Volunteer Fire Department that had been a source of controversy and complaint for years. In April 1866 the Society for the Prevention of Cruelty to Animals was founded, eight years before the Society for the Prevention of Cruelty to Children. The latter was the first of its kind in the world. The Society for the Suppression of Vice was founded in 1873. The Presbyterian Hospital opened in 1872, a year after the Roosevelt Hospital. There were important changes in housing, too. In 1870 the first large apartment house opened. It was made possible by the introduction of the elevator in 1865. Previously, most buildings were limited to four or six stories. The city made spasmodic efforts to cope with the transit situation, which was so bad by 1865 that many considered it insoluble. In 1875 the newly established Transit Commission chose elevated railways as the most practical solution. They decided to build them on Second, Third, Sixth and Ninth Avenues. Service on the Third and Sixth Avenue lines began in 1878. The fare was ten cents, except during rush hours when it was five. The new trains helped open up new residential areas. In 1874 it took ninety minutes by horse car to go from 129th Street to City Hall. The new elevated railway cut that time to forty-five minutes, even to the Battery.

After the dedication of the Cathedral and the completion of its furnishings, the Cardinal felt he still had one more act of piety to perform in memory of

Archbishop Hughes. That was to transfer his body to a permanent resting place in the new cathedral. Accordingly, when the Archbishop's crypt under the High Altar was ready, the transfer took place. On January 30, 1883, the body was moved privately to the cathedral where it was met at the door by Cardinal McCloskey and Archbishop Corrigan. The latter gave the absolution, and on the following day celebrated a Pontifical Mass. Then, after five solemn absolutions by the Cardinal, the Archbishop, and Bishops Loughlin, McNeirny and McQuaid, the remains of Archbishop Hughes were entombed in the crypt. All the officiating prelates except Archbishop Corrigan had known him well.

A Coadjutor

Archbishop McCloskey's schedule was heavier than it had been in Albany, so he confined himself almost entirely to ecclesiastical affairs. An exception was the funeral in New York for Abraham Lincoln, during which he walked in the procession as Lincoln's body was carried through Union Square, and on Easter Sunday (1865) preached on the assassination. By a careful allotment of his time, he was able to perform all the episcopal functions needed in New York. This had the advantage of bringing him into direct contact with most of the priests, and of allowing him to obtain first-hand knowledge of every parish and institution in his care. He knew every diocesan priest and most of the religious order priests personally. He was careful to have the latter represented on his council.

He was accessible to all, uniformly courteous, a good listener, and a respecter of initiative. He was the first occupant of the See to obtain papal honors for priests who did not become bishops, and for deserving laymen. He first mentioned a coadjutor in 1873, but the bishops of the Province urged him to wait. In 1880, when his awareness of waning strength made him suggest it again, they agreed with him. At a meeting held on April 7, 1880, the six suffragans of the Province voted with him to send three names to Rome. They put Bishop Lynch of Charleston, South Carolina, first, unanimously. Bishops Loughlin of Brooklyn and Corrigan of Newark were put second and third, respectively. Bishop Lynch was thought to be the Cardinal's choice, but there was opposition to him in Rome because of his advocacy of the Confederacy during the Civil War, which, it was feared, might hamper his work in New York. On October 1, 1880, Rome selected Bishop Corrigan, the youngest of the three. From the time of his arrival in New York on November 8, 1880, he fulfilled most of the routine assignments and took a heavy load off the Cardinal's shoulders.

A Golden Jubilee

On January 12, 1884, the Cardinal reached the Golden Jubilee of his ordination. Both Bishops Connolly and Dubois had reached the same anniversary in less happy times. The former ignored his, and the latter had a modest celebration, appropriate for its time. The Cardinal was the first native New Yorker to reach it. Life expectancy among priests was lower than among the laity, partly because their work brought them in closer contact with the victims of many contagious diseases prevalent at that time. Around 1890 it was estimated that the average lifespan of a diocesan priest was thirty-seven. When the Cardinal celebrated his thirtieth anniversary as a bishop in 1874, it was noted that only three of the priests present at his consecration were still alive. When Father John Breen, pastor of Annunciation parish, Manhattan, died in 1873 at the age of fifty, he was described by John Gilmary Shea, the great historian of the Church in the United States, as "one of the most venerable workers in the vineyard of the Lord in New York."

The Golden Jubilee was celebrated on a large scale, and the Cathedral was packed for the Pontifical Mass, celebrated by Bishop Loughlin of Brooklyn. The Cardinal did not appear until after the Post Communion. He gave the Pontifical Blessing, listened to congratulatory addresses from the bishops, priests, religious and laity, and then made a speech in reply. The cathedral pulpit was a gift for the occasion from his priests. Naturally, the Jubilee led to comparisons of the state of the church in New York in 1834 and 1884. When the Cardinal was ordained, there were fifteen churches and about twenty priests in the entire diocese, covering all of New York State and half of New Jersey. In 1884 the same area had eight dioceses, twelve hundred priests, nine hundred and fifty churches and chapels, one hundred asylums and charitable institutions, and a Catholic population of over 1,400,000. The Archdiocese itself had 600,000 Catholics, over forty religious orders, 285 diocesan priests, and about 230 churches and chapels. New York City had passed the million mark in population before the census of 1880.

New York Catholics found relations with their non-Catholic neighbors better, too. Much of the old bigotry, which was often very sincere, had been dissipated by closer contact with Catholics. Naturally, not all anti-Catholic feeling did or could disappear, but it was more moderate in expression and action. The growing number and improved social and economic position of the Catholics were reflected in the political world. "Honest John" Kelly (1822–1886), who married the Cardinal's niece, was elected to Congress in 1854, and was the first Catholic New Yorker to attain that rank. Years later, after the fall of the Tweed Ring, he became leader of Tammany Hall (1873–1882), which would have been unthinkable in 1854.

In 1872 the Democrats nominated Francis Kernan (1816–1892) of Utica, N.Y., for Governor. His opponent, John A. Dix (1798–1879) of New York City, had had a distinguished career, having been, among other things, Secretary of State of New York State, United States Senator from New York, United States Secretary of the Treasury, and Minister to France. What made Dix's nomination for governor by the Republicans exceptional was that he was a very active member of the Democratic Party. According to Samuel Tilden, Kernan was nominated because of his "honesty, integrity and ability," and not because of his nationality and creed.

The first nomination of a Catholic for high public office in the State caused quite a stir. It was impossible to keep the religious issue out of the campaign. The *New York Times* professed to be eager to do so, but said the Liberal Republicans and the Democrats kept bringing it up. It asked them if they believed Protestantism to be dead. A few days before the election, *The Times* revived the old slander, which it could so easily have checked, that the site of the new Cathedral had been given to the Church by the Democrats in return for cooperation with Tammany Hall. It added that government support of Catholic charities was out of all proportion to the trifling sums granted Protestant institutions, and warned that a Catholic governor would endanger the public school system. It continued in this vein until the election. It had already, on February 2, 1871, carried an editorial entitled "How Long Will Protestants Endure?"

The *Times* was not alone in its attitude. *Harpers Weekly,* always bitterly anti-Catholic and anti-Irish, printed a Thomas Nast cartoon showing Kernan kneeling before the Pope. Kernan was pictured as saying, "I will do your bidding as you are infallible." A priest in the background was holding pamphlets labeled "Down with the Public Schools." *Harpers* had previously denounced Kernan as a bigot and a copperhead. It was a presidential election year, and the Republicans carried the State decisively. Grant beat Greeley, and Dix beat Kernan. Nearly 11,000 more people voted for Governor than for President. Both gubernatorial candidates ran ahead of the presidential candidates in the city. In 1874, Dix ran again but lost to Samuel Tilden. In 1875, Kernan was elected to the United States Senate by the Legislature. No other Catholic was nominated for governor until 1918, when Alfred E. Smith was nominated and elected. Though a Catholic could more easily be elected Mayor of New York City, the first one to be elected was William R. Grace (1832–1904), the Irish-born founder of the well known shipping and banking firm, who was elected in 1880, and served from 1881 to 1882 and again from 1885 to 1886. His first nomination led the Republican papers to warn of the danger to the public schools. The *New York Herald* said, "This is a Protestant country and Americans are a Protestant people."

That the anti-Catholic spirit was still powerful, and that Catholics could sometimes show their resentment effectively were shown dramatically in the presidential election of 1884. Dr. Burchard, a prominent Presbyterian minister in New York City, speaking for a delegation of Protestant clergymen to James G. Blaine, denounced the Democratic Party as the Party of "Rum, Romanism and Rebellion." Blaine failed to repudiate this charge immediately and thereby lost New York State and with it the Presidency. Henry Ward Beecher (1815–1887), the most prominent Protestant minister of his day in New York, whose father was one of the chief instigators of the burning of the Charleston Convent in 1834, said: "The Cardinal winked at the bishops, the bishops winked at the clergy, the clergy winked at the voters and a Republican majority of 200,000 vanished before Cleveland's majority in New York State of 1,200."

THE END

Soon after his Jubilee, the Cardinal's health failed rapidly, as signs of Parkinson's disease appeared, and his condition was aggravated by a recurrence of malaria. He offered his last Mass on Ascension Thursday, May 22, 1884. The Pope sent him permission to say Mass seated, but he was too weak to use it, was practically helpless for months at the end, and spent much time at Mount St. Vincent's. He was anointed on October 4, 1885, by Monsignor Preston, the Vicar General, and died peacefully in the presence of his household staff on Saturday, October 10, 1885. His body was removed to the Cathedral in a torrential rain storm, and the funeral was on October 15th. The Mass was sung by his successor, Archbishop Corrigan, in the presence of twenty-five bishops. Archbishop Gibbons of Baltimore, who preached, said: "The Catholic Protectory and the Cathedral are two great monuments of his zeal, just as, in his unsullied life and the person of his gifted successor, New York has inherited two precious legacies of his love. After spending upward of half a century in the exercise of his ministry, he goes down to his honored grave without a stain upon his moral character." The Cardinal was buried beside Archbishop Hughes.

CHAPTER 9

Archbishop Michael Augustine Corrigan

When Cardinal McCloskey died, he was succeeded instantly by his coadjutor, Archbishop Corrigan, who received the pallium on March 4, 1886, from Archbishop Gibbons of Baltimore in a ceremony at which Archbishop Ryan preached. The new regime began smoothly with no major changes in policy or personnel and with gratifying indications of general good will. Few foresaw that in some ways it was to be the most difficult in the history of the Archdiocese. After his initial encounter with the trustees of the Cathedral, most of Archbishop Hughes' difficulties had come from outside the fold, but most of Archbishop Corrigan's were to come from within. His relatively short administration was so filled with controversies and major developments that it seemed to many much longer than it was, and its story takes longer to tell. Since conflicts of personality played a major role in these disputes, we must pay attention to the men involved as well as to the important issues over which they fought.

Michael Augustine Corrigan was born of Irish-born parents in Newark, N.J., on August 13, 1839, when it was still part of the New York diocese. He was one of nine children, of whom four entered the priesthood or the religious life. His father prospered in the food and liquor business, and in real estate; his family lived in very comfortable circumstances. According to the custom of the time, Michael was baptized at home. After preliminary studies with a private tutor, he was sent first to St. Mary's College, Wilmington, where he was confirmed by Saint John Neumann, and then to Mount St. Mary's, Emmitsburg, where he graduated in 1859. He then went to Rome to study for the priesthood and was one of the twelve students of the newly founded North American College when it opened its doors on December 8, 1859. He was the first student to register in the college, and the first alumnus to become a bishop. He was ordained on September 19, 1863, by Cardinal Patrizi, the Vicar of Rome, and continued his studies until he obtained a doctorate in divinity in June 1864.

NEWARK

On his return to Newark in September 1864, Father Corrigan was assigned to teach dogma and scripture in the Seminary at Seton Hall, and began his meteoric rise to high office in the Church. In 1865 he was Vice President of Seton Hall and director of the Seminary. By June 1868 he was president of both Seton Hall College and Seminary, and in October 1868 was also Vicar General of Newark. He was administrator of Newark while Bishop Bayley was at the First Vatican Council (1869–1870), and again when Bayley left reluctantly for Baltimore in October 1872. In 1871 he was proposed for the vacant see of Cleveland. Made Bishop of Newark in February 1873, he was consecrated there on May 4th by Archbishop McCloskey in whose ecclesiastical province Newark belonged. The co-consecrators were Bishop Loughlin of Brooklyn and Bishop William McCloskey of Louisville, who had been rector (1859–1868) of the North American College in Rome.

The new bishop was the youngest in the country and soon showed himself to be one of the most active. The program he carried out in Newark was much the same as his program in New York later. His first task was a thorough visitation of every parish and mission, some of which had never been visited before. The pastors were notified in ample time of everything he intended to check, down to the last detail. His goal was to bring the diocesan organization and every parish into strict conformity with the laws of the Church and, where applicable, of the State. All the parishes were properly incorporated and all church property properly registered. Though the national depression of 1873 lasted in New Jersey until 1880, coinciding with his entire administration of Newark, he managed to make a substantial reduction in the debt, and, in a diocese of some 175,000 Catholics, opened sixty-nine new churches and missions, an increase of about a third. The Newark Synod of 1878, which dealt mainly with matters suggested by his visitations, urged pastors to put their solicitude for schools before all the other duties of their office. He was interested in higher education, too. He and his brothers saved Seton Hall from bankruptcy, and he encouraged the Jesuits to open St. Peter's College, Jersey City, in 1878. He retained the presidency of Seton Hall until 1876.

In spite of his evident competence in financial matters, Bishop Corrigan was far from being just a brick-and-mortar man. The regular clergy conferences and examinations became a reality. The correct and reverent celebration of the liturgy, the proper administration of the sacraments, and the fostering of the devotional life of the people were stressed and supervised. He demanded a high level of conduct from the clergy and religious. He himself gave an example of zeal not only by his methodical and unremitting toil but by his conduct of the visitations, at which he often heard confessions far into the night.

As early as 1876, the secular press was discussing the probability of a coadjutor of New York, and the Bishop of Newark was among those mentioned as likely candidates. Hence there was little surprise when it leaked out that his name was on the list sent to Rome in April 1880. He had qualms about accepting the offer if it came. According to Cardinal McCloskey, he tried to prevent it because he feared the responsibility, but was given to understand that if the appointment did come, he must accept. He was notified privately on September 28, 1880, and on October 1 his appointment as titular Archbishop of Petra and coadjutor Archbishop of New York with the right of succession was announced officially. Before leaving for New York, he began the process of dividing Newark by erecting the diocese of Trenton.

THE COADJUTOR OF NEW YORK

The new coadjutor Archbishop had many obvious qualifications for the major post he had attained so quickly. His outstanding characteristic was a deep and disciplined piety. He was intelligent, orderly, and a tireless worker. His grasp of detail came close to genius, and he had a remarkable ability to concentrate on the matter in hand. Though not the brightest student in his class, he was considered the one with the greatest over-all comprehension. A rapid reader with an exceptional memory, he was a lifelong student of the ecclesiastical sciences. For him, study was a duty, a delight, his favorite recreation, and an anodyne. He was fluent in Latin, Italian, and French and read Hebrew and Greek with ease. He was also interested in mathematics and astronomy. He was prompt in the dispatch of business, often answering letters immediately and in longhand. Simple in his tastes, austere in his habits, modest in bearing, and with excellent manners, he made a favorable impression on most of those who crossed his path. Cardinal McCloskey, who as a special mark of favor had given him Archbishop Hughes' pectoral cross, called him the humblest man he had ever met. Archbishop Bayley thought he had learning enough for five bishops and sanctity enough for ten. He was apparently unmoved by flattery and did not overvalue money.

These excellent qualities, which made him a model coadjutor, were not enough to steer him safely through the storms he encountered, and to a degree provoked, when he succeeded to New York. Nor were they the whole man. He had the limitations that went with his qualities and some that did not. Though he was always readily accessible to those who sought him out, his innate shyness and some quality in his enigmatic personality prevented him from putting ordinary people at their ease. It was a disadvantage that he had never spent an hour in parish life. He sometimes found this a problem in Newark and New York, in dealing with priests often much older than himself, who had spent their entire lives in parish work.

More important was his lack of interest in public affairs on the local, state and national level, and even in ecclesiastical affairs that were national or international in scope. He took part in them only when driven by a sense of duty and by a feeling they were unavoidable. Too often, they were to prove unavoidable in New York. If he had been left in Newark, he probably could have escaped almost all the controversies that marked his administration here. In dealing with matters that lay outside the field he had marked out as his own, he was unsure of himself and often showed a disconcerting lack of candor and consistency and a love of indirect methods that added greatly to his problems. These characteristics infuriated his opponents and bewildered his friends. His greatest handicap was that he was a poor judge of men and therefore maladroit in handling many of them. He was more at home with ideas and things.

Though Cardinal McCloskey welcomed his coadjutor warmly, he did not surrender control of the Archdiocese. He continued to make the big decisions almost to the end; when his health collapsed, big decisions were postponed. He governed through his vicars, with whom he associated Archbishop Corrigan, who fitted in gracefully and performed almost all the routine episcopal functions. He found time to acquire the exhaustive knowledge of the Archdiocese, its resources, needs, problems and prospects that became evident when he succeeded to New York. He was chiefly responsible for the New York Archdiocesan Synod of 1882, the Fourth Provincial Council of New York, 1883, and the introduction of the systematic triennial visitation of the parishes in 1883. The Synod reaffirmed, to the distress of some, the obligation of the clergy to wear the Roman collar, and Cardinal McCloskey dismissed all complaints by declaring that experience had shown quite clearly the value and necessity of that regulation. The Provincial Council of New York anticipated many of the decrees of the Third Plenary Council of Baltimore by which it was largely superseded.

Archbishop Corrigan's arrival in New York brought him onto a larger stage and involved him for the first time in church problems that were national in scope. His first two experiences of the kind, in both of which he represented the Cardinal, went very well. One was minor, the other major. The minor one was the threatened confiscation by the Italian Government of the North

American College in Rome. One of the consequences of the fall of Rome, September 20, 1870, was the theft of church property on a grand scale. In January 1884, the Italian Supreme Court upheld the right of the State to confiscate the property of Propaganda, including the money held in trust for the missions all over the world. Though the College building had been placed by the Holy See at the disposition of the United States bishops who maintained it and supported it, and though it was used exclusively by American students, it belonged technically to Propaganda and was included in the proposed confiscation.

The confiscation of the mission funds aroused great indignation throughout the Catholic world, and on March 2nd, 1884 a pastoral denouncing it was read in all the churches of New York. That evening, Archbishop Corrigan received a cable announcing the imminent seizure of the College. He arranged at once to have George Bliss, a prominent lawyer who was a convert to the Church, present a letter from the Cardinal to President Chester Arthur asking for his intervention. This was done by March 4. President Arthur discussed the matter with his cabinet and instructed the United States minister to Italy to intervene with the Italian government. Negotiations were underway by March 6th, and by March 28th they were finished and the College was saved. The whole affair was an example of how quickly things could be done when our government was smaller. That the Italian government was not entirely happy with its handling of the mission funds was shown when it made substantial but partial restitution in the Lateran Pacts of 1929.

Much more important was the work done in preparation for the Third Plenary Council of Baltimore and in the Council itself, which was a major event in the history of the Church in this country. By 1880 the Catholics in America were increasing at the rate of over 2,000,000 a decade, and even greater growth was easily foreseeable. Between the Civil War and 1880, their number had almost doubled and reached about 6,300,000. The growth was uneven, with the great urban dioceses increasing much more rapidly than the others.

It was not just a question of increasing numbers. There was a widespread feeling, shared by many who opposed the Baltimore Council, that a new chapter was opening for the Church. In fact, that chapter was to last until 1918, and the years 1880–1900 were to be marked by bitter controversies, several of which were carried on simultaneously and led by the same people. The reduction in anti-Catholic feeling and the growth in Catholic numbers and influence brought new opportunities and dangers, and led to a sharp division of opinion on how to meet both. The Catholics felt easier about quarreling among themselves and had some important things to quarrel about. The central problem, underlying all the others, was how to make the Church here conform to the still hostile society of which it was now an integral and permanent part without destroying or undermining its union with Rome and without altering or seeming to alter the faith. It was wider than the problem of Church and State to which Christ had supplied the answer: "Render therefore to Caesar . . ." etc. (Matthew 22:21).

The problem is perennial and confronts the Church in every time and place, with varying degrees of urgency and under such different guises that many make the mistake of thinking it is new. In America, near the end of the nineteenth century, it took the form of wondering how far and how fast to go with Americanization or assimilation, terms that meant different things to different people and left plenty of room for honest differences of opinion. The mission of the Church is to the world, which she cannot ignore, wishes to serve, and does not want to be alienated from. There is no theoretical solution that can be applied everywhere and no perfect solution anywhere. The more the Church is in the world, the more the world will be in the Church. The more closely the Church is identified with any particular historical or cultural era, the more surely it will be in conflict with its successor.

The Western and Midwestern bishops who wanted another Plenary Council found a receptive ear in Rome, which was distressed by the lack of unity and leadership in America and wanted to bring the American Church into closer conformity with the general discipline of the Universal Church. A Council was opposed by the major Eastern provinces such as Baltimore, Boston, New York, and Philadelphia, which suggested holding Provincial Councils first and working from the bottom up instead of from the top down. They felt the time was not ripe for binding decisions on several matters that were still developing. They feared that the Roman authorities, who had no personal knowledge of conditions here, would insist on imposing on America regulations drawn up for other countries in quite different circumstances and in times long past. Mindful of the Bedini affair and of the image of the Church here as a foreign body, they feared the appointment of an Italian apostolic delegate to preside over the Council, as it was clear to all that Cardinal McCloskey was too ill to do so.

In May 1883, all the archbishops except Alemany of San Francisco, who pleaded ill health and distance, were invited to Rome to discuss the agenda for the Council. Anyone who could not come was asked to send a bishop from his province. The meetings were scheduled for November and December. Archbishop Corrigan sailed for Rome on October 10th with Archbishops Gibbons of Baltimore, Feehan of Chicago, Ryan, Coadjutor of St. Louis who was soon to go to Philadelphia, and Seghers of Oregon City, among others. They had already met in Baltimore in September, had been in correspondence with one another and Rome for months, and continued their conferences en route, so they were amply prepared for their Roman stay. In all the formal sessions with the Roman experts, Archbishop Gibbons was the spokesman for the Americans, and Archbishop Corrigan, who was in his element, was active in the informal sessions. Both men made a very favorable impression in Rome.

One of the major topics for discussion was a problem that had been developing for years, and that James McMaster had been ventilating in *The Freeman's Journal* since 1870. It was how best to achieve a suitable measure of decentralization of authority that would give the lower clergy a voice in the administration of church affairs, including the selection of bishops, and security against arbitrary action by the bishops, while preserving to the latter ample power to fulfill their responsibilities. No one could forget the disorders that arose so quickly whenever the bishops were unable or unwilling to assert their authority. It was impossible to introduce the general law of the Church on parishes in the United States because conditions varied so widely, but it was also clear that in many American dioceses something more than the minimum legislation applicable to mission fields was feasible, necessary, and overdue.

Some of the Roman experts suggested the traditional European solution, the erection of Cathedral Chapters. The Chapters were groups of priests who lived with or near the bishop, sang the Divine Office in choir daily, advised the bishop on the spiritual and temporal affairs of the diocese, and had a voice in the selection of the bishop. Without exception, the Americans agreed such a solution was wholly impractical in this country.

Finally, in the face of Roman insistence that something be done for the lower clergy, a solution was found that had something for everyone. Instead of the Chapter, a new body called the Consultors was agreed to. These were priests, not less than two or more than six in number, depending on the size of the diocese, whom the bishop was obliged to consult with on a wide range of topics but whose consent was needed in very few. Six would be the normal number where the bishop had enough men to choose from. Three were to be selected by the bishop directly, and three from a list nominated by the diocesan clergy. In every diocese, ten percent of the parishes were to be irremovable rectorships, whose occupants together with the consultors were to nominate three candidates for a vacant see. The bishops of the province were also to nominate three candidates, and were free to accept or reject the candidates of the clergy. The consultors were an American idea that originated in the diocese of Mobile, Alabama, in 1829, and has now been incorporated into the general law of the Church for dioceses without Chapters.

When these and many other matters had been discussed, the Roman meetings ended in December 1883. It was announced that Archbishop Gibbons of Baltimore would be the apostolic delegate chosen to preside over the Council to be held in America in November 1884 after the United States presidential election was over. His predecessors in Baltimore, Francis P. Kenrick (1796–1863) and Martin J. Spalding (1810–1872) had presided respectively as apostolic delegate over the First (1852) and Second (1866) Plenary Councils of Baltimore. Moreover, in 1858, the Holy See, while refusing the petition that the Archbishop of Baltimore be made Primate of the United States, had granted him in perpetuity a "Prerogative of Place" that gave him precedence over all other American bishops who were not cardinals. Archbishop Gibbons was, then, the logical choice in the absence of Cardinal McCloskey, though some thought the coadjutor of New York could more suitably replace Cardinal McCloskey. They knew New York was then the largest and most important diocese in the country, with about four times as many Catholics as Baltimore, and judged wrongly that it should therefore take precedence.

The formal letter of convocation of the Council was issued on March 19th, 1884, and the opening was set for November 9th. In the intervening months, the committees of bishops and theologians assigned to prepare various items for discussion and to draft the proposed decrees were busy, and copies of the decisions reached in Rome were sent to all the bishops. The Mass at the official opening was sung by Archbishop Peter Kenrick of St. Louis, whose brother had been the apostolic delegate in 1852. The growth since 1866 was evident in the number of sees and bishops. Almost one-third of the sixty-four sees, including five of the twelve archdioceses, had been erected since 1866. Of the seventy-one bishops who attended, twenty-four were born in America. There were twenty from Ireland, eight Germans, six French, four Belgians, three Canadians, two Spaniards, and one each from Austria, Holland, Scotland, and Switzerland.

The Council laid down the rules by which the American Church would be administered until the Code of Canon Law took effect on Pentecost Sunday, 1918. Many of its regulations are still in effect, and its decrees were copied extensively in Australia, Quebec, and Scotland. It reaffirmed all preceding conciliar legislation that was not expressly revoked, accepted the decrees of Vatican I, and legislated on a wide range of topics, including faith, ecclesiastical persons, divine worship, the sacraments, clerical education, the education of Catholic youth, church property, ecclesiastical trials, Christian burial, and the care of immigrant and minority groups. It approved the foundation of a Catholic university and the preparation of the Baltimore Catechism. It established, too, the present list of Holydays of Obligation in this country. Almost a fourth of all the decrees dealt with education. The most famous and important of these reaffirmed emphatically the value of the parochial school and the Church's commitment to it. It ordered every pastor who could do so to provide one within two years. Failure to do so was to be grounds for removal. It accepted the agreement reached in Rome on the Consultors and irremovable rectors. It reaffirmed expressly the decree of the Provincial Council of Baltimore, 1849, that priests were to refrain from all political questions in the pulpit and in public life.

Archbishop Corrigan played an active role in the deliberations of the Council and in the solemn ceremonies. He sang the Mass on the closing day, preached at the Requiem Mass for the forty-seven bishops who had died since 1866, and was chairman of the committee that wrote the Pastoral issued by the Council. The other members were Bishop O'Farrell of Trenton, who was a former pastor of St. Peter's in Barclay Street, and Bishop Keane, then of Richmond.

The new era produced new leaders, and there were three especially with whom Archbishop Corrigan was to find himself in close contact, and often in conflict, during his entire administration. They were Archbishops James Gibbons of Baltimore, John Ireland of St. Paul, and John Keane of Dubuque. James Gibbons (1834–1921) was easily the outstanding Catholic in this country in the period between 1885 and 1921. He was born in Baltimore, educated there and in Ireland, ordained in 1861, and made the first Vicar Apostolic of North Carolina in March 1868. He became Bishop of Richmond in 1872 and coadjutor of Baltimore in May 1877. There he succeeded Archbishop Bayley in October 1877 and was made Cardinal in June 1886. He was essentially a centrist and did not enjoy controversy, but once engaged in it he was prepared to see it through. He rendered distinguished service to the Church by his skill in interpreting Rome to America and America to Rome, and by explaining so convincingly the essential harmony between Catholic principles and American political institutions. He played the key role in the establishment of the Catholic University of America, and in preventing the condemnation of the Knights of Labor which would have been taken as a repudiation by the Church of the Labor Movement in America. Though inferior to Archbishop Corrigan as a scholar and administrator, he was greatly superior to him as a judge of men and an interpreter of public opinion and the signs of the times. On most of the issues in which they were involved, he and Archbishop Corrigan were on opposite sides.

John Ireland (1838–1918) was born in Ireland, brought here as a child, educated in France, and ordained in 1861. He was a chaplain in the Civil War. He became Coadjutor of St. Paul (Minnesota) in 1875, Bishop of St. Paul in 1884, and Archbishop in 1888. A forceful, eloquent, and great-hearted man—one of the great builders among the pioneer bishops—he made a permanent mark on the church in Minnesota and the Dakotas. His interests were many and varied, and his impact was felt far outside the area of his jurisdiction. His naturally sanguine temperament and the astonishing progress he witnessed filled him with optimism about both the Church and America, to which he often gave enthusiastic, not to say extravagant expression. At the celebration of the centennial of the hierarchy in November 1889, he said: "The greatest epoch of human history, if we except that which witnessed the coming of God upon earth, is upon us, and of this epoch our wisdom and our energy will make the Church the supreme mistress." In 1893 at Cardinal Gibbons' episcopal silver jubilee, he said: "I preach the new, the most glorious crusade, Church and Age. Unite them in the name of humanity, in the name of God." More than once, in his desire to win his audience, he expressed himself so carelessly that he found himself in hot water with other groups, and spent much time explaining what he had said. His strong views on temperance and rapid Americanization rendered him suspect to the German Catholics. In a significant departure from the normal practice of the American Catholic clergy, he played an active role in party politics, in his case as a Republican, with consequences that were felt in New York. He, much more than Cardinal Gibbons (with whom he worked closely and who always helped to rescue him when he overshot his mark), was the real leader of the liberal camp in the Church in America, just as Archbishop Corrigan, whom he came to dislike intensely, was the reluctant leader of the conservative camp.

John J. Keane (1839–1918), also born in Ireland, was educated in Baltimore where he was ordained in 1866, and succeeded Bishop Gibbons in Richmond in 1878. He was appointed the first rector of the Catholic University of America in April 1887, and dismissed by the Pope in September 1896. Early the following year, he was called to Rome, made a titular archbishop, and a consultor of Propaganda. He remained there until his return as Archbishop of Dubuque, Iowa, in 1900. He resigned Dubuque in 1911. He was a warm-hearted, eloquent man of scholarly tastes who was wholly devoted to Archbishop Ireland and to the Catholic University. As he considered Archbishop Corrigan hostile to both, he in turn was consistently hostile to him. He fully shared Archbishop Ireland's patriotic fervor and optimistic estimate of the probable consequences of harmony between the Church and the Age.

ARCHBISHOP OF NEW YORK

The decrees of the Council were approved formally by Rome on September 10, 1885, and exactly a month later the Corrigan administration began in New York. Many watched closely to see what direction it would take. It soon became apparent that the new Archbishop relied especially on three strongly opinionated and strikingly dissimilar advisers. By the time this situation was changed by the death of two of these men, the main course of his administration had been set and a chain of events put in motion that was to burden him to the end of his life. It also became apparent as problems multiplied, that though he was essentially a loner he inspired an almost fiercely protective loyalty in those who worked most closely with him. The first in rank and influence among his close associates was Bishop Bernard McQuaid of Rochester, N.Y. The others were Monsignors Thomas Preston and Arthur Donnelly.

Bernard J. McQuaid (1824–1909) would have made his mark in any walk of life he chose to enter. His character was formed and tested by adversity. At a very early age, he had first-hand knowledge of deep personal sorrow, poverty, sickness and discrimination, all of which he took in stride without ever becoming embittered. He was born in New York City of immigrant parents; his mother died when he was three. When he was seven, the death of his father in an unsolved murder placed him in the Catholic Orphan Asylum, where he counted himself fortunate to come under the lasting influence of Mother Elizabeth Boyle. His health was so poor, he was not expected to live through his student years. As a boy and young man, for the asylum was his home until his ordination, he had on several occasions seen a mob gather to attack the Cathedral, which was across the street from the asylum. He was ordained at Fordham by Bishop Hughes on January 16, 1848.

For reasons of health, he was sent to the country. His first assignment was at Madison, N.J., where, after a short service, he became pastor. His parish contained all of three counties and parts of two others, so he became of necessity a roving missionary. An early sign of a lifelong enthusiasm was the school he opened in the church basement in Madison, and in which he himself taught for six months until he could find a teacher. It was the first parochial school in New Jersey. When Newark became a separate diocese, in July 1853, he was moved to St. Patrick's Cathedral there. In September 1854, Newark was swept by anti-Catholic riots organized by the Know Nothing Party and the Orangemen in which St. Mary's Church, the German parish, was wrecked. We may judge the temper of the times from the fact that the coroner's jury, which held an inquest on a young Irishman who died in the riot from bullet and knife wounds, brought in a verdict of death from cholera. Father McQuaid made strenuous efforts to protect his flock, but no one was punished and no compensation was ever paid. The episode made a lasting impression on him, though he was careful to draw the proper distinction between the rioters and the non-Catholic community as a whole. He was intimately involved in the two major achievements of Bishop Bayley's administration, the founding of Seton Hall College and Seminary in 1860 and, even more important, the founding of the Sisters of Charity of Convent Station in 1859. He became Vicar General of Newark in 1866 and the first Bishop of Rochester, N.Y., on March 3, 1868.

It was at Seton Hall that he became friendly with Father Corrigan, who had been one of his altar boys. He came to esteem him so highly that he suggested, urged, even demanded, and later, rightly or wrongly, took full credit for, his successive promotions to Seton Hall, Newark, and New York. For the whole of Michael Corrigan's adult life, Bernard McQuaid was his closest friend and advisor. He was also, for forty years, one of the outstanding members of the hierarchy, a man whose formidable personality and exceptional accomplishments were recognized by all. Once he took a stand, he stuck to it in spite of all opposition, and he rarely if ever changed his mind on people, principles, or practical matters. He never shrank from a fight. Like Archbishop Hughes, whom he resembled in many ways, he neither gave nor sought quarter. Predictably, these were the attitudes he urged on the Archbishop, to whom he sent such messages as "Be clear, strong and bold, and not afraid." He never forgot that he had been ordained for New York, and always took a keen interest in its affairs. He liked to recall that he had been baptized by Bishop Connolly, confirmed by Bishop Dubois, ordained by Archbishop Hughes, and consecrated by Archbishop McCloskey.

Thomas Preston (1824–1891) came from a very different background. He was born in Hartford, Conn., of English ancestry, and attended Washington (now Trinity) College there, where in 1843 he gave the valedictory in Greek. As a student at the General Theological Seminary in New York, he became so interested in the Oxford Movement that he was refused ordination to the ministry by the Episcopal Bishop of New York. Ordained an Episcopal priest in 1848 by another bishop, he served St. Luke's in New York City with Dr. John Murray Forbes with whom he was received into the Catholic Church by Father James R. Bayley in November 1849. They were ordained to the priesthood by Bishop McCloskey on November 16, 1850, at Fordham, and in 1851 after a short curacy at the Cathedral, Father Preston became pastor of St. Mary's, Yonkers. He was chancellor of the Archdiocese from 1853 to 1891 and Vicar General from 1873 to 1891. In 1861 he became pastor of St. Ann's on East 12th Street, founded in 1852 by Dr. Forbes, who returned to the Episcopal Church in 1859. During most of Father Preston's pastorate, St. Ann's was a blend of a fashionable residential area and a civic center. It contained Astor Place, where the first church stood, and Union Square. Both Cooper Union and the Academy of Music were within its boundaries. He was able to build a large new church, the present one, in 1870 and in the preceding year a parochial school. In May 1865 he held the first Forty Hours Devotion in New York.

For nearly forty years, he worked in close contact with three successive archbishops, each of whom found him a competent, reliable, industrious, and devoted collaborator. He had a high regard for Archbishop Corrigan, whom he described to Rome as the finest ecclesiastic he ever knew. He considered him the equal and in some respects the superior of both his immediate predecessors. Like the Archbishop, but for different reasons, he was less successful in personal relations than in administrative matters. In his case, this was due less to his exceptional austerity than to the inflexible rectitude and severity with which he applied the law to himself and all others. According to Father Richard Burtsell, a former assistant who was his severest critic, his strong point was the ability to decide. Though he was Archbishop Corrigan's candidate for New York in 1880, he had no desire for the episcopate and escaped it more than once. In 1886 he and Mother Veronica Starr, another convert, founded the Sisters of the Divine Compassion.

Arthur J. Donnelly (1820–1890) was born in County Kildare, Ireland, and brought here as a child of seven. He went to work at fourteen, spent several years working at Lord and Taylor's department store, ultimately went into business for himself, and prospered. Answering an appeal for vocations by Bishop Hughes, he entered the seminary at Fordham in 1846, stayed six years instead of the then-usual four, and was ordained on October 6, 1852. He was assigned almost immediately to establish Annunciation parish in Manhattanville, which he did so successfully that in 1855 he was assigned to Fordham with a double task—to be procurator of the seminary, and to establish a parish, under the title of Our Lady of Mercy, which was to use the seminary chapel as a base.

In 1857, Archbishop Hughes decided a new parish was needed on the west side between St. Columba (on West Twenty-fifth Street) and Holy Cross (on West Forty-second Street). He named Father Donnelly as pastor, assigned him the territory from Twenty-eighth to Thirty-eighth Streets, from Sixth Avenue to the Hudson, and selected St. Michael as the patron. There the young pastor found his final assignment. Though he started during the panic of 1857 and the parish, twice divided in his lifetime, was composed almost entirely of very poor people, he succeeded in building one of the largest parochial plants in New York. When the church was consecrated in 1886, after the debt was extinguished, it was pointed out that the pastor had raised and publicly accounted for the then immense sum of $1,400,000. His pride and joy was the school, which had 1,600 children by 1886. It was one of the largest parochial schools in New York, and for almost a century a great source of vocations. A notable event for both parish and school was the arrival from Ireland on September 8, 1874, of the Presentation Sisters, whose coming fulfilled Father Kohlmann's dream in 1814. In 1884 they opened St. Michael's Home, on Staten Island, to serve as a home for orphans from the parish and as a summer home to which the children of the parish were sent in relays.

Everyone knew how much the success of St. Michael's owed to the pastor. It was not just his conspicuous talent for administration. He was an austere, industrious, courageous and demanding man, whose zeal inspired all and communicated itself to many. His courage was shown during the Draft Riots when he dissuaded a mob, many of whom were his parishioners, from burning the local Presbyterian Church whose minister was said to be an abolitionist. His interests were not confined to St. Michael's. He was on the Archbishop's Council from 1870 to 1886 and a consultor from 1886 until his death. He became Vicar General in May 1887 and a domestic prelate in December 1888. He was a benefactor of John Gilmary Shea, the historian, and a close friend of Bishop McQuaid.

The first major achievement of the Corrigan administration was the Fifth Synod, in November 1886. Its purpose was to bring New York into strict conformity with the decrees of Baltimore III and to complete the organization of the archdiocesan offices. The Synod was the most important ever held in New York and was so complete and detailed that all the succeeding ones made very minor changes. Among its more important provisions were those dealing with the consultors, the permanent rectors, and the parochial schools. The first consultors were Monsignors Quinn and Preston, who were the

Vicars General, Monsignor Farley and Fathers Arthur Donnelly, James Dougherty, and Patrick McSweeney. All but the last two had belonged to Cardinal McCloskey's Council. Three were appointed directly by the Archbishop, and three nominated by the clergy who had submitted nine names. This gave the clergy, and (as his critics were quick to say) the Archbishop a wider choice.

The irremovable rectors prescribed by Baltimore III were chosen. By law they were to be ordained at least ten years, have passed an examination in theology, and given proof of competence to manage a parish. The Archbishop was to be the final judge of that competence. Actually, they could be removed, but only after a canonical trial and for a serious reason. The parishes to which they were appointed had to have a complete plant, including church, rectory, and school, and be financially sound. At first only ten parishes in Manhattan and three other parishes were designated as irremovable rectorships, though others were added fairly soon. The ten city parishes were those of Sts. Brigid, Gabriel, James, Joseph (Greenwich Village), Mary (Grand Street), Michael, Patrick (the old Cathedral), Peter, Teresa, and the Immaculate Conception. All but St. Michael's, then on 31st Street, and Immaculate Conception which was on 14th Street, were below 14th Street. The country parishes were St. Patrick's in Newburgh, St. Peter's in Poughkeepsie, and Immaculate Conception (St. Mary's) in Yonkers.

Every pastor who could do so was ordered to build a school within two years or submit his reasons for not doing so to the Archbishop, who was to be the judge of their validity. A School Board was established, and shortly afterwards a superintendent for the elementary schools. All teachers, both religious and lay, were to be examined for competence, and an attempt was made to standardize tests and texts. Other offices set up were those of the censor of books, the examiners of the clergy, the matrimonial tribunal, and the rural deans. The deans were to lighten the load of the visitations and bring the country parishes under closer supervision. All in all, about fifty posts were set up. Having greatly expanded the machinery of government, the Archbishop then had to use it well, and see that through it the law became the custom of the archdiocese. The decrees reflected his passion for order, precision, and regularity. The customary Pastoral at the close of the Synod made special mention of spiritualism, then enjoying a great vogue, as one of the rampant evils of the day.

THE McGLYNN CASE

On the eve of the Synod, Archbishop Corrigan became involved in the most famous controversy of his life. It was also the most protracted and bitter one, and one in which the clash of personalities obscured for many the principles involved. It became the most widely publicized dispute between a priest and his bishop in the history of this country to the present time, and its effects were felt for half a century or more. It was the case of Father Edward McGlynn. Though it began in the fall of 1886, the material for it had been accumulating for years.

The golden opinions Archbishop Corrigan won from his superiors and closest associates were not shared by all the clergy. An emphatic dissent was registered by a small group, mainly his contemporaries in Rome, who were the survivors of those who had opposed Archbishop McCloskey's appointment to New York. They were important for the effect they had on the Corrigan administration, to which they were opposed from the beginning to the end, and because they were the first spokesmen here for ideas that were to surface again and spread widely after Vatican Council II. Known as the "Accademia" and about half a dozen strong, they formed a close-knit body regarded by itself and others as an elite corps. They had their origin in an attempt to form an officially approved voluntary society for clerics interested in discussing theology.

In the beginning, they met at St. Joseph's in Greenwich Village, where they enjoyed the hospitality of Father Farrell. Many of the original members retired quickly, feeling the society was dominated by "a clique of Romans and abolitionists." Those who remained took themselves very seriously and always retained a high opinion of their own ability and importance. Several of them held Roman doctorates of which they were very conscious since non-medical doctorates of any kind were rare in this country. They were also conscious and proud that their views on a wide range of topics, both sacred and profane, differed greatly from those of most Catholics, and even in some instances from the formal teaching of the Church. In spite of their views, most of which they neither preached nor published, all of them persevered in the priesthood and most of them were in many ways successful pastors. None of them ever attained high rank.

In the religious field, they questioned the inspiration and inerrancy of scripture. They limited the former to "a slight extent" and to being the same kind as Dante's. They doubted papal infallibility until 1870, and therefore they doubted the Immaculate Conception because it was defined by the Pope without the formal consent of a General Council. They were highly critical of religious communities and especially of the vows that religious take, so they rejoiced in the misfortunes that overtook those communities in United Italy. They disliked the Latin liturgy, vestments, and the way in which the sacrament of Penance was administered. They favored general absolution without any obligation for individual confession, and thought it "absurd for a priest to be listening for five hours to the tomfooleries of servant girls." They thought nuns were incapable of educating girls who were to become wives and mothers. All but Father McGlynn doubted the value of celibacy, and he thought the Church should have forbidden whiskey instead of meat on Friday. They thought the Church needed the Holy See as a center for teaching faith and morals but not for discipline, and that a priest on his own personal responsibility could do as much good as he chose without the consent of the bishop, who could interfere only in the case of grave abuses.

Perhaps their most eccentric opinion was that "the most oppressive mystery of our faith is the promise of never-ending happiness. Eternity oppresses the mind accustomed to the variety found in time. We can hardly look forward to an eternal existence with pleasure. Annihilation seems almost desirable." They regarded most of the priests here as very poorly trained, and felt the only hope of the Church lay in the young clergy (by which they meant themselves) and in the converts. They thought "the Church must be ruled by converts, who alone comprehend the American character."

Their opinions in the secular sphere were, with the exception of their support of the Fenians, the dominant ones of the day. They were ardent supporters of the Union cause, and strongly approved of the entire Reconstruction program imposed on the Confederacy, for which they thought no punishment could be too severe. They were ardent abolitionists, too. By choosing to ignore the religious dimension of the question of the Temporal Power of the Holy See, they were free to join in the general satisfaction in non-Catholic circles at its fall and proclaim that it was the bane of the Church. They supported the Fenian Movement because it was a struggle for freedom, and it made no difference to them that it could not succeed. Hence, they disapproved of Archbishop McCloskey's warning against supporting it. They saw no inconsistency in supporting it themselves while maintaining that the Holy See, the Irish bishops, and the American bishops had no right to an opinion on it.

These ideas and many others were not due only to social and intellectual snobbery, the arrogance and intolerance of bright young reformers in a hurry, and a misunderstanding of the history and tradition of the Church, which are recurring phenomena. They were due mainly to an enthusiastic and indiscriminate admiration of all things American and to a serious misreading of the actual condition of religion in this country at that time. They were sure that "a free government produces automatic moral growth." They felt that "God had carved out this country on a gigantic scale to prepare for the gigantic moral growth of our people produced by our free government. It would be a great gain to have its energy and ability directed to the propagation of the truth. Our Catholic population needs to be taught the first page of the Patriots' Catechism." Their goal was to make America Catholic and they were sincerely convinced that could be done, but only if the Church became American first. That meant scrapping all Catholic traditions and customs that were unacceptable to American Protestants. The Church had only to divest herself of her European heritage (as if there were anything in the American religious and political heritage that did not come from Europe) and all would be well. The gaining of so great a prize justified great sacrifices, and anything that did not touch absolutely essential doctrine could be waived for a greater good.

Though Father Thomas Farrell (1823–1880) was not the actual founder, he was at least a prime mover in establishing the Accademia, but he did not lead it for very long. He was born in Ireland, ordained at Fordham in 1848, and was pastor of St. Joseph's from 1857 until his death. He was so keenly interested in the Civil War that he vowed to leave America if the South won. He was one of the first priests in New York to take up the cause of equality for the blacks, and in his will left $5,000 to found the first Catholic church here for them. He provided that if the church was not opened in three years, the money was to go to a Protestant orphan asylum for blacks. St. Benedict the Moor was opened in 1883 with Dr. Burtsell in charge. Father Farrell's views on the Temporal Power involved him in difficulties with Archbishop McCloskey who suspended him in 1871. He appealed to a special committee of six pastors who were unanimous in recommending his removal from St. Joseph's. The Archbishop relented, characteristically, and Father Farrell subsided. Ignoring St. Paul's teaching on the love of money (1 Timothy 6:10), he wanted on his tomb "Intelligence and knowledge overthrow all kinds of oppression: ignorance is the cause of all evil." He thought, too, that 12- to 16-year-old boys were too young to go to confession. Archbishop Corrigan described him as a "kind-hearted, amiable priest much beloved by his congregation notwithstanding his peculiar ideas in politics." Father Preston thought him "a man of little education and less wisdom." He had the distinction of being one of the three people known to have had a strong influence on Dr. McGlynn, who preached over him, praising "his hatred of tyranny, hypocrisy and sham." The other two were Henry Ward Beecher and Henry George.

The real leader of the Accademia was Father Richard L. Burtsell (1840–1912) who was born in New York City and belonged to one of the older and more prosperous Catholic families—a fact of which he was almost painfully aware. He was sent to Rome as a boy and spent nine years at "Propaganda" where he earned doctorates in philosophy and divinity and was ordained in August 1862. There he became a life-long disciple of Edward McGlynn. His first assignment in New York was as assistant to Father Preston at St. Ann's, where he remained until he founded Epiphany parish on East 22nd Street in January 1868. He was among the first of the few Americans who then took a special interest in Canon Law, and for many years was a skillful and successful counsellor of priests who were having legal problems with their bishops. Cold and reserved by nature and lacking magnetism, he had no taste or talent for popular oratory and definitely lacked the common touch. He was an industrious and competent man, a good administrator, and a notably loyal friend to the small group to whom he gave himself and for whom he provided a center. He came to be respected but was never liked by the general body of priests, who could not fail to notice his uniformly poor opinion of them.

He was also the very model of a brash young man. He said he could not take the Pope's opinions on theology seriously because Pius IX, unlike himself, had not had a thorough course in theology. It did not take him long to decide that the Archdiocese of New York was in bad shape and in the wrong hands. He felt that at fifty-five, the Archbishop was too old and too tired for his position. Taking advantage of his right as an alumnus of "Propaganda" to report on conditions in his area, he began to file reports to that effect in Rome. He and his friends were sure they knew the needs of the Church in New York much better than the Archbishop did because, they thought, "he had never mixed with the people." They seem to have known nothing of his years on the mission here and in Albany. They were insistent that the need for more churches be given top priority and were unimpressed when the Archbishop, who remembered when there was only one church in New York, reminded them that in proportion to its Catholic population it already had more churches than Paris. Actually, in his first five years he opened twenty parishes, but he could not locate them all in the city or concentrate all his resources on them. He in turn was unimpressed when told that Father Burtsell and his friends had a special mission "to alert him to the needs of his archdiocese."

Archbishop McCloskey's reaction to the Accademia was mild and firm and he dealt with them on an individual basis, rebuking them privately when he deemed it necessary, appreciating their good points, and giving them elbow room and plenty to do. His handling of Father Burtsell will do as an example. The latter was very anxious for a place of his own, and by 1866 had staked out territory near St. Stephen's as a suitable site. He was then in almost daily contact with Dr. McGlynn. He wrote for permission, only to receive a polite refusal. When he pressed for and even demanded an explanation, the Archbishop invited him to an interview on February 10, 1867, and explained the refusal. He expressed his regret that Burtsell had set himself up as the Inquisitor-General of the archdiocese, had written anonymously some severely critical newspaper articles on conditions here, and had leaked to the local press confidential information he had heard at private gatherings at which the Archbishop was present. He took this as proof of serious indiscretion. The young man's reaction was typical. He wrote: "I have learned this day to hold Archbishop McCloskey in contempt; he never suggested to me a spiritual motive for my future conduct." The matter rested there until December 3rd, when Father Burtsell returned, admitted his faults, apologized, and received permission to start the new parish. He did not challenge the Archbishop again.

The outstanding member of the Accademia was Father Edward McGlynn (1837–1900), born in New York of Irish parents. His father, a prosperous contractor, died early leaving his widow and eleven children quite secure financially. After preliminary studies in the public schools, he was sent to Rome, at age thirteen, by Archbishop Hughes. He lived at the "Propaganda" Seminary for nine years where he met most of the members of the Accademia, and a year at the North American College, where he first met Michael Corrigan. His health suffered at "Propaganda" as did that of many others. In December 1846, John Henry Newman, the future cardinal, who was living there described it as a most unhealthy place and said the young New Yorkers seemed to suffer most. Of eight students from New York in his time, only one or two survived. Edward was an outstanding student. He won the gold medal for excellence at the end of his course and was notably good in Latin and Italian. He was ordained in Rome on March 12, 1860.

On his return to New York City, Father McGlynn was assigned in significantly rapid succession to the parishes of St. Joseph, St. Brigid, and St. James, and in December 1861 became pastor of St. Ann's. A year later, partly because he was threatened by tuberculosis again, partly for what Hughes regarded as insubordination in going to Europe without permission, and partly to make way for Father Preston, he was removed from St. Ann's and assigned as chaplain to the Military Hospital in Central Park, where he remained until it closed at the end of the Civil War. At that time, Father Jeremiah Cummings, the founder of St. Stephen's parish, the senior Roman alumnus in New York and the first New Yorker to win a Roman degree, was dying and asked for him as his assistant and successor. He became pastor of St. Stephen's in January 1866, and was launched on his remarkable career.

Father McGlynn or "the Doctor," as he was called almost invariably, soon became one of the best-known men in the city. This was due less to his accomplishments at St. Stephen's, impressive as they were, than to his personality, the range of his interests, and the stand he took on a number of controversial issues. He was always ready to help any cause he thought would help the community, regardless of its sponsorship. In the parish, he completed the extension of the church to its present great size, opened a home for destitute children that ultimately had about 300 residents, organized a Sunday school that soon had some 1,600 students, paid great attention to the liturgy and music, and was deeply interested in the condition of the poor. In June 1881, in an innovation that did not survive the Synod of 1882, he introduced a low Mass at noon on Sundays. It was described by McMaster, who approved of it, as "the Mass of the Weak."

In spite of his excellent academic record, study was not his strongpoint. He was essentially an activist, a popular orator, a visionary, and even a crusader. His outstanding quality, which he possessed to a quite exceptional degree and which was the chief source of his influence, was the dangerous gift of great personal magnetism. Through it, he inspired in many of his followers a devotion that increased with his misfortunes. Like most popular orators, he needed an audience as much as it needed him, and was very sensitive to praise and blame. He gave an indication of that when he succeeded Dr. Cummings. On that occasion, his friends, who regarded his appointment as "triumph of progress over old-fogyism, of virtue over cunning," noted with regret that the Archbishop, when appointing him, at age 29, pastor of the largest congregation in the country (about 28,000), said no word of encouragement, thus showing himself to be, in their eyes, a man "with no feeling, no heart." He could have led the Accademia, but chose not to and was content to be its idol, accepting without protest the deference it paid him to the end of his life. Even when individual members disagreed with him, they could not bring themselves to admit it publicly, and they rarely admitted it privately.

The most conspicuous omission from his good works at St. Stephen's was a parochial school. This was due not to lack of need or means but to his lifelong opposition to Church-related schools. Repudiating all Catholic tradition, he maintained that the Church had no role in education outside religious instruction. The rest belonged to the State. He felt so strongly on the subject that he said that if he were ever ordered to build a school, he would ask the Pope to send him as a simple missionary to China or Japan or any other place "where he might still confine himself to doing the work of the Church and of charity without becoming the pedagogue." He made his views, which he never modified, clear in an interview in *The New York Sun* on April 30, 1870. In it, he advocated an amendment to the Federal Constitution that would forbid government on any level to help any church-related school or charitable institution in any way. He advocated, too, forbidding the appointment of chaplains of any kind to any public institution, and forbidding Bible reading, prayer, hymn singing, and worship of any kind in public schools. The interview raised the first of the many storms that were to be connected with his name. Father Preston called a meeting of the pastors in the city, in the absence of the Archbishop at the Vatican Council, and fifty-four signed a public protest against Dr. McGlynn's views. Only three refused to sign, all of whom belonged to the Accademia.

Dr. McGlynn's proposed amendment, which he linked with his concept of the total separation of Church and State, anticipated the amendment to be recommended to Congress (which rejected it) by President Grant in December 1875. Grant stressed that as the Republic began its second century it should reaffirm its commitment to popular education. He said that under our form of government it is of the greatest importance that "all should be possessed of education and intelligence enough to cast a vote with the right understanding of its meaning. A large association of ignorant men cannot for any considerable period oppose a successful resistance to tyranny and oppression from the educated few, but will inevitably sink into acquiescence to the will of intelligence whether directed by a demagogue or by priestcraft. Hence, the education of the masses became the first necessity for the preservation of our institutions." He wanted mandatory education for everyone through elementary school. He was willing to exempt church cemeteries and possible church buildings from taxation, but nothing else. His proposed amendment, introduced in Congress by James G. Blaine on December 14, 1875, was later to play an important role in New York State.

Archbishop McCloskey was surprised to discover in Rome in the early summer of 1870 that Propaganda was slow to accept criticism of Dr.

McGlynn, whose personality and academic brilliance had left a vivid memory there. The situation changed by 1874 when the first of what became a stream of complaints about him reached New York from Rome. In the beginning, they were about his liberal views in theology, and later mainly about his extravagant statements on the social problems. These complaints did not interfere with his being the spokesman for an American pilgrimage to Rome for the episcopal Golden Jubilee of Pius IX in 1877, or with his being featured frequently during the McCloskey administration on notable occasions as a prominent attendant to the Cardinal or as the speaker of the day.

Dr. McGlynn was one of the first priests in New York to see the size and importance of the rapidly developing social problems brought about by industrialization, and to warn against relying on charity alone to cure them. He saw that charity was not a substitute for justice, and that major structural changes were necessary. The great expansion of industry here after the Civil War brought an immense increase in the national wealth that blinded many to the suffering it imposed on the workers, who then had practically no legal defense against the rapacity of their employers and no social aid from the state. Here, as in Europe, they bore what Pope Leo XIII was to call in 1891 "a yoke little better than that of slavery itself." The failure of those who controlled the state to provide proper and timely solutions to ever-growing problems, or even to recognize that they were needed, led to widespread discontent. It opened the door, too, to false solutions. Three that were already in the field, Communism (condemned by Rome in 1846), Socialism, and Anarchism, received more attention than their importance here warranted. Their names were invoked freely and unfairly against many who advocated even the mildest alleviation of inequities that were obvious to all.

Dr. McGlynn found a new and absorbing interest when he espoused the cause of Irish nationalism and particularly the cause of Irish social and economic reform. Conditions in Ireland were even worse than usual in 1879. It was the worst year since the Great Famine. The substantial crop failure brought new attention to the wretched condition of most of the people and aggravated the chronic unrest, the extent of which can be judged from the passage of forty-two Coercion Acts between 1830 and 1870. It brought, too, a renewed demand for a thorough overhauling of the system of land tenure that was the root of the problem. Unlike their peers in England and America, the poor in Ireland suffered from too little industrialization rather than from too much. In 1880 the population was about 5,000,000, of whom nearly 4,000,000 were tenant farmers and agricultural laborers with their families. The farmers were chiefly tenants at will, who were denied leases longer than a year and were completely at the mercy of the landlords, many of whom were alien absentees. They were at least slightly better off than the agricultural laborers, who were, as Gladstone told Parliament in 1870, as badly off as they had been under the Penal Laws a century earlier. In 1868, Disraeli told Parliament one-fourth of the Irish people were paupers in a helpless condition. John Stuart Mill said that "almost alone among mankind the Irish cottier is in this condition that he can scarcely be better off or worse off by any act of his own."

In 1879 Michael Davitt founded the Irish Land League which had as its goal inducing or compelling the British Government to undo the confiscations of centuries by buying out the landlords and selling the land to the tenants. He agreed to work in harmony with Parnell, the leader of the Home Rule movement which was attempting to restore the old Irish Parliament and to undo substantially the Act of Union of 1800. It is noteworthy that although apparently the more radical of the two, Davitt's plan to transfer most of the land of Ireland from one set of owners to another by government action encountered less opposition than Parnell's. Home Rule was not achieved until 1922 and then only by violence and in truncated form, while Davitt's goal was achieved peacefully by 1903. In 1880 England was approaching the peak of her imperial power. Any weakening of the United Kingdom, the core of the Empire, was unthinkable to the majority of Englishmen. They held, too, with passionate intensity, the conviction that the Irish were unfit for self-government, an opinion shared very widely in America. It was a time when much attention was paid to the idea of Nordic, Anglo-Saxon, or Teutonic supremacy.

The distress in Ireland and the reform movements it fostered aroused much sympathetic interest among the Irish Catholics in the United States. In 1879 the bishops raised almost $5,000,000 for Irish Relief. In 1880 the American Land League was formed to help Davitt, and it soon supplied about ninety percent of the money for its Irish counterpart. Dr. McGlynn threw himself into the movement with his customary enthusiasm, and was much in demand as a speaker for both Home Rule and Land League meetings in all the large cities with substantial Irish populations. That same year brought two events that were to have a profound effect on him. The first, which turned out to be the most important event in his life after his ordination, was his sudden and total conversion to the economic doctrines of Henry George. The second was the appointment of Archbishop Corrigan as coadjutor of New York.

Henry George (1839–1897) was one of the many self-educated enthusiasts who, in various times and fields, have contributed so much to America. He was born in Philadelphia of Anglo-Scots background and had little formal schooling. He went to work at fourteen, sailed before the mast to Australia and India in 1855 for wages of six dollars per month, and in time became a journalist and economist. He read widely but unevenly. His name will always be associated with the theory of the Single Tax, which he did not invent but which he advocated so tirelessly that it became identified with him in the public mind. It is expounded in his book, *Progress and Poverty*, which was released to the general public in 1880, and was influenced by his experiences in Ireland as a correspondent for the New York *Irish World* for which he covered the events of 1879–1880. Briefly, his theory is that while private ownership of land is legitimate, profiting from that ownership is not. Thus, one may buy, sell, lease, inherit, or bequeath land, but one may not profit from it. The State is obliged to seize the entire profit by taxation. If it does, it will have so much money it can abolish all other taxes—hence the name Single Tax—and will have enough money for ordinary expenses and for a vastly expanded social program. Believers in the Single Tax were convinced their plan was applicable everywhere.

Only a handful of the advocates of land reform believed in the Single Tax. Davitt was perfectly willing to have the landlords compensated for their holdings and wanted many, many more, not fewer, people to own their own land. Even among the Single Taxers there was a division of opinion. Henry George and Dr. McGlynn differed on one essential point. The former did not deny the right to own land, but wanted to make such ownership unprofitable, while Dr. McGlynn wished to abolish all private ownership of land and refuse all compensation for it.

Progress and Poverty struck Dr. McGlynn with the force of a revelation from on high and made an indelible impression on him. His clerical friends, few of whom took it seriously, marvelled at his enthusiasm for it, though they should not have been surprised that a man who believed in 1860 that this country was ripe for conversion to Catholicism believed in 1880 that *Progress and Poverty* provided "the true, the only adequate prescription for the ills of modern civilization"—and that its concluding chapter "is more like the utterance of an inspired seer of Israel or of some ecstatic contemplating the great process of eternity than the utterance of a mere political economist." His admiration for Henry George's doctrines was strengthened, if possible, when he met their author for the first time in 1883. They formed a tempestuous but sincere friendship that survived all strains while both lived.

The likelihood of a conflict with the Roman authorities increased as Dr. McGlynn's involvement in the land problem deepened. The British Government, well aware of the danger presented by Home Rule and Land League movements, tried to avert it by invoking the aid of the Holy See against them. It kept Rome well informed of all excesses in word and deed connected with both movements and was helped in this by some highly placed English Catholics. Rome, unwilling to be used as a cat's paw by London, condemned such abuses as the "Plan of Campaign"—basically a rent-withholding scheme—in 1888, but it refrained very carefully from condemning the movements themselves. At the same time, it could not forget that England was then the most powerful country in the world and that her good will, or even her mitigated ill will, could be helpful to the Church in the vast areas of Africa, Asia, and the Pacific (then under British rule) that were opening up for missionary activity.

Not all the complaints came from England and Ireland. Several American bishops in whose dioceses Dr. McGlynn spoke at public meetings condemned and reported his increasingly extravagant statements. In September 1882, he electrified his audience by declaring that "a landlord is a thief." In that same month, Cardinal Simeoni, the Prefect of Propaganda, sent Cardinal McCloskey an order from the Pope to suspend Dr. McGlynn unless the Cardinal thought his attitude had improved. He thought it had improved and contented himself with a warning and with persuading Dr. McGlynn to promise to abstain "from all public gatherings of whatsoever kind in the future." Later, in February 1887, the Doctor said the promise was meant only for the Cardinal's lifetime and that he had promised to make no more Land League speeches, "not because I recognized the right of anyone to forbid me but because I knew too well the power of my ecclesiastical superiors to impair and almost destroy my usefulness in the ministry of Christ's Church to which I had consecrated my life." Whatever he meant at the time, he did not keep his promise, and in May 1883, after further complaints reached Rome, he was expressly forbidden to make any more political speeches. He was urged to go to Rome himself and discuss the situation with Propaganda, but declined, pleading that to do so would interfere with his efforts to reduce his parish debt. There matters rested until the death of the Cardinal.

The year 1886 was an unusually troubled one for New York and the whole country. The Labor Movement was struggling to get organized and was meeting widespread public resistance. The failure of a railroad strike led by the Knights of Labor and public dismay at the Haymarket riot in Chicago, in which a number of policemen were killed at an anarchist rally, increased the already widespread uneasiness. The Knights of Labor went from 100,000 members in 1885 to over 700,000 in the spring of 1886, but then declined rapidly. In New York City there was widespread unemployment and the public was angered by a long transit strike.

In these circumstances, the local election of 1886 aroused a special interest that was increased when it became known that Henry George intended to run for Mayor. He ran as the candidate of the United Labor Party, a new organization formed by the Socialists, the Central Labor Union, and some other reform groups. His candidacy was supported by a number of well-known people of widely different backgrounds, including Dr. McGlynn, Robert Ingersoll, the famous agnostic, and Samuel Gompers, who founded the American Federation of Labor in 1886. The Democratic and Republican candidates were respectively Abram Hewitt and Theodore Roosevelt. It was expected that, although Dr. McGlynn was a Republican, his endorsement would weigh heavily with the Irish Catholics who normally supported Tammany.

In September 1886, Dr. McGlynn had a national reputation and was at the height of his fame and influence. He was also an increasingly controversial figure about whom few who knew him professed to be neutral. Impatient with details, careless and often extravagant in speech, improvident in disbursing parochial and personal funds, a notably poor administrator, he was so habitually unpunctual he seldom ate with his assistants at St. Stephen's because they had to eat at fixed hours and he could not meet a schedule. He was described by his relatives as "the world's worst correspondent" because often he did not read his mail, much less answer it, and his executors were to find in his belongings trunkloads of unopened mail, some of it going back for many years.

A fluent extempore speaker, fully conscious of his great hold on the crowd, his quite exceptional magnetism, and of his fame, Dr. McGlynn was impressive in appearance and had a commanding presence. He was keenly interested in politics and in the social problems for which he regarded political action as the only cure, and was so confident of his own opinions he rarely asked and more rarely followed advice. Subject to generous enthusiasms and impulses, whose probable consequences were imperfectly thought out, and resentful of pressure or commands from superiors on any level, all of whom he tended to treat as his equals, he was—to many not under his spell— an angular, headstrong, disorganized, undisciplined, and exasperating man. To his disciples, who cheerfully ignored, denied, or forgave all faults and foibles, he was an inspired leader, a true Master in Israel, the Moses of the working man, and the authentic prophet of a new and better social order. All who knew him recognized his very special sense of mission which can fairly be called a messianic streak.

In all these points, both good and bad, he was the very opposite of Archbishop Corrigan and it would have been astonishing if they had not clashed. Three additional factors pushed them into conflict. One was the Doctor's strong dislike of the Archbishop, which was tinged with contempt and went back to their student days. Another was his defective sense of obedience in the Church. The third was his unshakeable conviction that, in the writings of Henry George he had found at last the long-sought panacea for the universal and immemorial scourge of involuntary poverty.

Dr. McGlynn's endorsement of Henry George and announced intention to campaign actively for him, beginning with a speech at a great meeting on October 1st, presented Archbishop Corrigan with a public challenge he could not ignore. Consequently, on September 29th he wrote to Dr. McGlynn, expressly forbidding him to attend the meeting or to take part in any other political meeting without the prior consent of Propaganda. Having explained to the Archbishop that he felt committed to the meeting but would take no further part in the campaign, the Doctor presented Henry George to a wildly enthusiastic crowd at Chickering Hall as "the most unselfish man of this country, formed by providence to preach the new gospel." He regarded the campaign as "the beginning of a pacific revolution which is destined to have upon the whole world a more beneficial effect than our first Revolution and the great Declaration which gave it its justification and battle cry." On the following day, he was suspended privately for two weeks. Archbishop Corrigan told him that "so flagrant an act of disobedience cannot be passed over" and reminded him that it had nothing to do with partisan politics but was "founded on the instructions of the Holy See and on the nature of episcopal authority on the one hand and sacerdotal obedience on the other."

Though the election of 1886 was the occasion for the confrontation between the Archbishop and Dr. McGlynn, it was surely not its cause, and soon turned out to be only one episode in a series of events that dragged on for years. Dr. McGlynn kept his word about making no more speeches in the campaign, though he did appear at some rallies, and on Election Day, November 2nd, toured the polling places with Henry George and Terence Powderly of the Knights of Labor. Hewitt won with about 92,000 votes while Henry George received about 68,000 and Roosevelt about 60,000. It was an unimpressive victory for the official Democratic candidate in an overwhelmingly Democratic city, and showed, all observers agreed, that Dr. McGlynn had influenced many Irish voters. He had done so in spite of an open letter from Monsignor Preston dated October 25th in which he stated that "the great majority of the Catholic clergy in this City are opposed to the candidacy of Mr. George. They think his principles unsound and unsafe and contrary to the teachings of the Church." He added: "His principles, logically carried out, would prove the ruin of the workingman he professes to befriend."

The real reason for the confrontation, as Archbishop Corrigan saw it, was the Doctor's teaching on private property in land, which he kept repeating with almost obsessive frequency. As a consequence of press interviews on that topic, his suspension was continued to December 31st and on December 4th, he was summoned to Rome by a cable to which he deferred an answer. On being pressed for one by the Archbishop, he replied on December 20th, refusing to go and offering three reasons: his poor health (a friendly doctor assured him a sea voyage might cause pneumonia), poverty, and the obligation to care for his recently deceased widowed sister's children. He added: "I have taught and I shall continue to teach in speeches and writings as long as I live that land is rightfully the property of the people in common, and that private ownership of land is against natural justice, no matter by what civil or ecclesiastical laws it may be sanctioned, and I would bring about instantly, if I could, such change of laws all the world over as would confiscate private property in land without one penny of compensation for the mis-called owners." The reasons given for not going to Rome were unconvincing, as was shown in March 1887 when he offered to go if all penalties were lifted and he was restored to St. Stephen's, and in June 1893, when he did go.

His persistent defiance of Archbishop Corrigan and the Roman authorities, and his repeated expression of his views on the ownership of land led to his removal from St. Stephen's on January 14th, 1887, and later, when he disobeyed a direct order from the Pope to appear in Rome within forty days of the receipt of the summons, to his excommunication, effective July 1st, 1887. The excommunication was based solely on his disobedience to the Pope and had nothing whatsoever to do with his views on private property in land, a fact that was consistently misrepresented by his followers for years. His removal from St. Stephen's revealed his basic problem, which underlay even the land question. It was, in his own words, his claim that he was entitled "to avow his political principles and to promote their adoption, a right that belongs to every American citizen, whatever his profession or his faith." In fact, it has never been true that "every American citizen" has that right. From the foundation of the Republic, special groups such as the armed forces and the judiciary have been barred from active participation in politics, and by now there are millions of government employees in the same situation. Moreover, Dr. McGlynn had been ordained for full-time service to the Church and had freely promised obedience to his superiors, to whom it belonged to say in what area that service was to be rendered.

Archbishop Corrigan was genuinely surprised by Dr. McGlynn's refusal to go to Rome, and by the intense excitement his removal from St. Stephen's caused there and in certain circles in New York and in other parts of the country. Himself, a most obedient man, he could not understand flagrant public disobedience to supreme authority. This was especially so when, as in the McGlynn case, the papal summons to Rome involved no adverse judgment on him or his doctrines. The Archbishop regarded the case as essentially a problem of ecclesiastical discipline which he had inherited from Cardinal McCloskey, who had failed to deal with it decisively when urged to do so by Rome. Since Rome, not New York, had begun the proceedings against Dr. McGlynn, Archbishop Corrigan regarded himself simply as Rome's agent and much time was spent in writing back and forth and waiting for further instructions. Probably that is why he made no personal effort to study Henry George's doctrines. Archbishop Walsh of Dublin, one of the few recognized experts on land tenure in Ireland, told Cardinal Manning that Archbishop Corrigan must have misunderstood Henry George's doctrine and could not have read his book.

Unfortunately for Archbishop Corrigan and his advisers, only a handful of those who took an active interest in the McGlynn case shared their view of it. At least one of Henry George's prophesies was fulfilled. In their one interview, on September 29th, 1886, he warned Archbishop Corrigan that if he touched Dr. McGlynn he would be portrayed as an enemy of the poor. Some adherents of each of the many good causes the Doctor had supported chose to view his censure as an attack on their cause. At a time when feelings ran very high about issues like the social problem and labor unions, Irish nationalism and land reform, the School Question here, the relations of Church and State, private property in land, and the place and image of Catholicism in America, few concerned themselves with the strictly legal aspects of the case. Archbishop Corrigan was inundated with abusive mail and was a target of the press for many years. Early in November 1888, a bullet was fired through his study window. He was, of course, not an enemy of the poor or of labor, whose very real grievances he had recognized in the Synodal Pastoral of 1886, which said: "True indeed in many painful instances, the rights of the toiler are trampled on and the fruits of his labor are snatched from his hand. True, this is done too frequently with the concurrence or at least the connivance of the law. This is an evil that needs redress, but such redress can never be brought about by denying a fundamental right or by perpetrating a radical wrong." He was sincerely convinced that the solution offered by Henry George and Dr. McGlynn was a false one. He knew, too, that rightly or wrongly it had no chance of being adopted here, so time spent advocating it was time wasted. It is improbable that if he had foreseen the storm he would have altered his course. He was not the man to shirk a disagreeable duty in the hope of avoiding adverse publicity.

If the Archbishop was surprised by Dr. McGlynn's reaction to the penalties, the Doctor was surprised by the penalties themselves, which he regarded as wholly unjust and motivated solely by malice. His reaction was that of a proud, sensitive, and very angry man, who struck out in all directions and this set the tone for his followers. He made no effort to calm the storm at St. Stephen's, which amounted to a substantial boycott of all services, and led to the withdrawal of Monsignor Donnelly, the temporary administrator, in ten days. He was replaced by Father Charles H. Colton (1848–1915), who had been an assistant there for ten years, was deservedly popular with the people, and who, while always friendly with the Doctor (who had helped him through the seminary), disagreed with his doctrine and conduct and was loyal to the Archbishop. He succeeded in restoring order and contentment in the parish.

On March 26th Dr. McGlynn and his friends founded the Anti-Poverty Society, which supplied him with a platform for years. He was the President, Henry George was the Vice President, and a number of socialists and radicals were the co-founders. It met in the Academy of Music on Sunday evening, and the program—usually presented to a crowded house—consisted of a collection, some hymns by members of St. Stephen's choir, and an address of two hours or more by the Doctor, who spoke without notes. Occasionally he carried the message to other cities—Boston, Buffalo, Chicago, Cincinnati, and even Rochester—with similar results. The most famous of all his speeches, "The Cross of a New Crusade," was given on March 29th, 1887, and repeated often in the next few years. On June 18th, a mammoth rally was held to demonstrate support for him and to protest or prevent the impending excommunication. A crowd estimated by some of the press at 75,000 and containing large numbers of women, then a rare thing, marched through St. Stephen's parish to Union Square. The highlight of the evening was a speech by Dr. McGlynn, who used for the first time a theme that was to be recurrent with him until December 1892. It was his denunciation of "the ecclesiastical machine" which had, he said, for "thousands of years" been "perpetrating blunders and mistakes, and committing crimes." Such a gathering for such a cause was an unmistakable sign of the enthusiasm the Doctor inspired in his followers. The extravagant remarks made by clever men who could and should have known better, and probably did know better, were another sign. The Doctor compared his own case to those of Galileo and Copernicus, and Henry George called him a new and greater Luther. A friendly Protestant minister called him "the first martyr to papal tyranny in America." Dr. Burtsell told Archbishop Williams of Boston that, "if Rome could stand not reinstating the Doctor, the Doctor could stand it too." Two other lectures that were well received were "The Pope in Politics" on January 3rd, 1888, a sharp attack on the Temporal Power, and "The Ecclesiastical Machine in American Politics" on January 22nd, 1888. Dr. McGlynn was less successful in his No Rent Campaign in New York City in June 1888.

The pressure in favor of Dr. McGlynn led to counter-pressure in favor of the Archbishop. On March 24th, 1887, in a gesture from Rome, he was made an Assistant at the Pontifical Throne and received, for the only time in his tenure of New York, the unanimous support of the hierarchy. All the bishops to whom Dr. McGlynn and his friends appealed, even Archbishop Ireland, gave the same advice: Go to Rome, go quickly, and go without trying to impose conditions on the Pope. Many of Dr. McGlynn's supporters were non-Catholics and some were anti-Catholic. Many non-Catholics supported the Archbishop. While many Catholics supported the Doctor, his followers were never even close to the majority and their number fell off sharply after the excommunication. The priests were more divided than the bishops, partly because so many of them knew Dr. McGlynn personally and admired some of his works. In April 1887, a declaration of support for Archbishop Corrigan was signed by fifty-five German priests. On May 14th, a similar declaration signed by 357 of 450 non-German priests was presented to him in a ceremony in the Cathedral. Some had signed under pressure, others refused because they felt Dr. McGlynn had been treated too harshly, others because they thought it unnecessary and undignified, and some because they disapproved of those in charge of it. Only two of New York's Romans signed. Naturally enough, the Archbishop was displeased with those whose refusal to sign expressed opposition to him, but it was tactless to indicate his intention not to promote any of them.

The McGlynn Case, in which it played a notable role, presented the press with a dilemma which it solved along easily predictable lines. After the excommunication but not until then, even in New York, the Catholic press supported the Archbishop solidly. Almost without exception, the secular and non-Catholic religious press disapproved strongly of Henry George's theories and of Dr. McGlynn's version of them. They applauded Archbishop Corrigan's condemnation of those theories and thought he had been very patient with Dr. McGlynn. At the same time, they could not help welcoming any sign of weakness and division in the Church. They were especially sympathetic to attacks on ecclesiastical authority and then, as now, any insubordinate, dissident, or fugitive cleric who was willing to attack it publicly was assured of at least one brief hour of fame. Dr. McGlynn's hour lasted much longer than most because he was already a celebrity when he started his attack and remained one when he stopped. Moreover, no one could deny that he was newsworthy since his flamboyant personality and extravagant speeches, effect on the crowd, and bitter personal attacks on the Pope and Archbishop Corrigan delighted the reporters, who gave him ample coverage in the news columns that in the minds of many readers outweighed disapproval on the editorial page.

After the excommunication, the McGlynn case was at a standstill for several years, and no one seemed to know how to end it. Archbishop Corrigan suggested a joint appeal to Rome in 1890 but nothing came of it. In the meantime, he was anxious to have Rome condemn Henry George's doctrines publicly, but was opposed successfully by Cardinal Gibbons, Archbishop Ireland, and many other bishops who told Rome that it would make them too important and that they were a passing fad. Rome straddled the issue in April 1889 by sending a private warning against the doctrines to the United States bishops. Other archbishops offered their good offices or were approached from time to time to effect a solution. Interest flared up occasionally and then died down but not out.

One flare-up came when Archbishop Corrigan disciplined Dr. Burtsell. At the beginning of the quarrel, the latter had given Dr. McGlynn three pieces of good advice privately. He urged him to avoid suspension since it would alienate many of his followers and weaken his effectiveness. He urged him to stay away from the great meeting on October 1st, 1886, giving Archbishop Corrigan's order as his reason, and to obey the papal summons to go to Rome. Having done that much, he became his lawyer and most active partisan and defended him from all critics to the end. Judging correctly that Dr. Burtsell— much more than Dr. McGlynn—was the center and chief fomenter of clerical opposition to his authority and policies, the Archbishop decided to remove him from the city. On December 6, 1889, Dr. Burtsell was transferred to St. Mary's, Rondout (Kingston). The transfer was immediately appealed to Rome which upheld Archbishop Corrigan in July. After a hard struggle with himself, Dr. Burtsell accepted the transfer reluctantly and arrived in Rondout in November 1890. Though he was too good a canonist not to know the Archbishop was entirely justified in moving him, for he, like Dr. McGlynn, was not an irremovable rector, he never forgave him for doing so, and for years carried out a series of appeals in Rome. He made an excellent record in Rondout, although for most of his time there he dreamt of and worked toward a triumphant return to Epiphany Parish, Manhattan.

Finally, a way was found to settle a conflict of which all concerned were weary. The Anti-Poverty Society was losing ground and in May 1891, in his famous encyclical on labor, *Rerum Novarum,* which Archbishop Corrigan welcomed warmly, Leo XIII had defended private property in land as "in perfect harmony with the law of nature," and had criticized as "obsolete" certain opinions that denied it. On October 12th, 1892, Archbishop Satolli arrived on a mission from Rome with authority also to settle the McGlynn case. His trip was managed by Archbishop Ireland with whom he spent much of his time, and through whose intervention Doctors McGlynn and Burtsell had an interview with the papal envoy in Washington on December 20th. They presented him with a very carefully worded statement—in Latin, Italian, and English—on Dr. McGlynn's views on private property in land, to which was added, on December 22nd, a statement of acceptance of the recent encyclical on labor. Archbishop Satolli in turn presented it to four professors at the Catholic University, who assured him that it contained nothing contrary to Catholic teaching. Accordingly, on December 23rd, he lifted the excommunication and restored Dr. McGlynn to good standing in the Church.

Dr. McGlynn and his friends had much reason to be grateful to Archbishop Satolli, and to regard his handling of the case as a sweeping vindication of their stand. The joy in their camp was only matched by astonishment and dismay in the other. No retraction was asked and no apology for the scandal given. No reference was made to the teaching and conduct of which the Holy See itself had complained for years, which had prompted all the steps Cardinal McCloskey and Archbishop Corrigan had taken against Dr. McGlynn in Rome's name, and which it was impossible to reconcile with the statement of December 20th. Rome was content with the Doctor's recognition of the papal authority he had been denouncing for years, with his promise to go to Rome, and with a very general apology for his attacks on the Pope "if" in fact such had been made. No reference of any kind was made to his attacks on Archbishop Corrigan. At huge victory rallies in Cooper Union on Christmas night and on January 8th, 1893, the Doctor stressed that no retraction had been made or asked for, and stated his determination to teach exactly as he had taught before. The only change in his speeches was an omission from that time on of all personal criticism of the Pope and Archbishop Corrigan, and all reference to "the ecclesiastical machine."

The end of the quarrel with Rome was not the end of Dr. McGlynn's quarrel with New York. Archbishop Ireland's hope that the restoration of Dr. McGlynn would break Archbishop Corrigan's "head and heart" was not fulfilled. Instead, he had welcomed the lifting of the excommunication, of which he learned from the press, but was surprised by the way it was handled. When he mentioned that to Archbishop Satolli, he was told in effect that, as the matter concerned the Holy See and Dr. McGlynn, it was none of his business. Under the circumstances, he decided to wait for an overture from Dr. McGlynn, who was living in Brooklyn where he was restricted by Bishop McDonnell, his former curate, to saying Mass privately for the first six months after his absolution. The Archbishop had to wait two years, during which the Doctor carried on his lectures and, in 1893, tried hard to be named the first United States Ambassador to Italy. On December 21st, 1894, they met for the first time since September 1886. The Doctor formally asked for an assignment specifically at St. Ann's, then vacant because of the untimely death of Monsignor Preston's successor. Archbishop Corrigan was determined not to give him a city parish, and especially St. Ann's. He offered St. Mary's in Newburgh, which was accepted, and set January 1st, 1895, as the date for his arrival there. The two met again on December 30th, 1894, at the consecration of St. Stephen's Church. Father Colton had fulfilled the Archbishop's hopes by building a large parochial school, extinguishing the long-standing debt, and uniting the factions of the parish. He was rewarded by being made Chancellor of New York in 1897, and Bishop of Buffalo from 1903 until his death in 1915.

The force of Dr. McGlynn's personality was felt to the end and even beyond it, though his activities were restricted by failing health. He received one of his greatest ovations at the funeral of Henry George, which was held in the Grand Central Palace on October 31st, 1897. He took as his text "There was a man sent from God whose name was Henry George," and said the Presidency of the United States was too small an office for so great a man. The end came on January 5th, 1900, after a long struggle with heart trouble and Bright's disease. Although for much of his time in Newburgh he was absent or ill, he had been invited by some responsible people to run for mayor, and the entire city turned out for his funeral. Many non-Catholic clergy attended and Dr. Burtsell preached. Immediately after the funeral, the body was brought back to St. Stephen's for a second Mass on the following day, at which Monsignor Mooney, a Vicar General, preached. There, nearly thirteen years to the day after his removal, about 40,000 people attended the wake and filled the church and the surrounding streets during the funeral. Archbishop Corrigan presided at both funerals. Dr. McGlynn was buried in Calvary Cemetery, and in 1918 a large bronze statue of him was erected in Woodlawn Cemetery. Memorial services were held for many years at both the grave and the statue.

In retrospect, it is clear that, as many saw at the time, mistakes were made by all parties directly concerned in the McGlynn case. Archbishop Corrigan made three mistakes, two major and one minor. Though his essential decisions—the suspension and the removal from St. Stephen's—were justified and even necessary, it was a mistake not to offer Dr. McGlynn a trial even though, strictly speaking, he was not entitled to one as he was not an irremovable rector. Offering a trial would have removed even the appearance of arbitrary or unjust condemnation. It would also have presented the Doctor with a difficult choice. To have refused a trial would have placed him in an awkward position. To have accepted and lost (and there was little hope of winning) would have sent the case to Rome, where it wound up ultimately. It is noteworthy that he never asked for a trial, in New York or in Rome, and was in fact determined not to have one, and successfully avoided one to the end. On April 8th, 1890, Dr. McGlynn reminded the Archbishop that he had never asked for a hearing in New York, that he never would, and that he repudiated any appeal anyone might have made in his name. No fully satisfactory explanation of his attitude has ever been documented. Probably it was a mixture of reluctance to be held accountable to anyone and a well-founded fear that, in the heat of the fight, other and more serious charges had been or would be made.

The Archbishop's second mistake was not to have made some provision for Dr. McGlynn upon removing him from St. Stephen's. When he first decided on the removal, the Archbishop had planned to send him to St. Joseph's, Middletown, as pastor. His sudden change of mind was an example of his lack of confidence in his own judgment. He should have given Dr. McGlynn a place, even if only as an administrator, pending a final decision from Rome. Failure to do so made many, and especially the priests, feel that he had been treated too harshly. If he had been offered a trial and given a place, much and probably most of the division and bitterness among the clergy which lasted for years would have been avoided. The third mistake was to make Monsignor Donnelly, an outspoken critic of the Doctor, administrator of St. Stephen's.

Rome blundered too. It was wrong to wait from October to July to take action, especially as the case had been building up, largely on Rome's initiative, for years. The Holy See was paralyzed by conflicting advice from this country and by the interdepartmental rivalry between the papal Secretariat of State (where Cardinal Rampolla was cultivated assiduously by Archbishop Ireland) and Propaganda, which normally had full charge of American clerical affairs. As the Secretary of Propaganda told the Archbishop on February 10, 1887, the Pope was acting with "meditated dilatoriness." Archbishop Satolli's faculties to absolve Dr. McGlynn came from Cardinal Rampolla, not from Cardinal Ledochowski, the Prefect of Propaganda.

The major mistake was made by Dr. McGlynn who must bear much the heaviest share of the blame for the whole affair. Had he gone to Rome in January 1887, as he did in June 1893, he and all concerned would have been spared much unnecessary suffering and things would have wound up much as they did in December 1894, without all the strife and bitterness of the intervening years.

As it was, he devoted much of his time and energy in those years to denouncing the Church he professed to serve, appealing consciously to every vulgar anti-Catholic prejudice, and doing his best to stir up dissension within and hostility without the fold. His attacks on the Pope were untrue, unworthy, and in marked contrast to his comments on the same subject after his trip to Rome in 1893. He had accused the Pope of being "senile" and "a poor old bag of bones, seventy-eight years old with one foot in the grave; poor absent-minded old man flattered by his worshippers with the notion that he is one of the greatest pontiffs that ever lived." After his 1893 trip, during which he was received in a private audience by the Pope, he returned full of praise for Leo XIII and Archbishop Satolli.

Equally untrue and unworthy were the charges that the "ecclesiastical machine" in New York was "a tail to the Tammany Hall Kite," and that the chief purpose of maintaining Catholic schools and charitable institutions was to provide a living for the religious who staffed them, who were, in his opinion, too incompetent to make a livelihood elsewhere. Characteristically, his impatience with those who believed charity was a substitute for justice led him into the opposite error that justice was a substitute for charity, and into a sharp attack on organized charity itself as well as those working in it. He stated his views with customary vigor in the *New York Tribune* of November 24th, 1886. He said: "You can go on forever with hospitals and orphan asylums and St. Vincent de Paul Societies, but with them you can't cure the problem. In a right state of society, there ought not to be any hospitals or asylums or charitable societies or else very few of them." His attitude gave justifiable offense to the staff, supporters, and beneficiaries of organized charities of every kind, and served to divert the attention of many from the soundness of his criticism of the existing social structure.

These, and things like his demand for full payment of his salary for the years in which he did not function as a priest, which was rejected by Archbishop Corrigan, are examples of the innate lack of a sense of proportion and of the failure to acquire adequate self-control that explains better than anything else the bitterness and frustration that marred his declining years. They prevented his undeniably great gifts from realizing their potential more fully, with proportionate satisfaction to him and profit to the Church and the community. He and his followers naturally put the blame on the envy, malice and blindness of lesser men. During his last visit from Dr. Burtsell, he complained that he was merely vegetating and asked for prayers, in which he had great trust. Apart from his conditional apology to the Pope in December 1893, there is no known instance of his having admitted a mistake. On February 3rd, 1890, when he thought he was dying, he said he had nothing to retract, and that all the steps taken against him were unjustified.

The McGlynn case was not the most important controversy in which Archbishop Corrigan was involved. While it lasted, he was carrying on simultaneously or successively several others that were in fact more important for the Church in America, though they had less direct effect in New York. Among them were those concerned with Secret Societies, the Knights of Labor, the Catholic University of America, the School Question, and the Apostolic Delegation.

THE SECRET SOCIETIES

The issue of Catholic membership in secret societies was first raised by Bishop Carroll in 1794 and continued to trouble the bishops until it was settled in 1895. There were many good reasons for the delay in coming to a decision. The Church's objection to secret, oath-bound societies was well founded and well known, and in the beginning its chief target here was the Freemasons. As the number of the secret societies increased, the application of the principle underlying the ban on Freemasonry became more difficult. Though many and possibly most of the new societies based their rules and rituals on the Masonic ones and were therefore suspect, they had in general very different purposes. Many of them were clearly fraternal and social in character, but others were so secret it was very difficult to obtain reliable information on exactly what they stood for, aimed at, and demanded of their members. It was not easy to know if their rituals were religious or not, if all members had to participate in them, and if so to what extent. The rituals and uniforms made a strong appeal when public life in America was wholly devoid of pageantry, and most Protestant Churches gloried in the plainest possible liturgies.

As the societies grew in number, the differences among many of them became more obvious and so did the difficulty of putting them all in one category. The Ku Klux Klan, for instance, was a sectional and political organization in which few Catholics were likely to be found. The Grand Army of the Republic (veterans of the Union Army) was national (except for the former Confederate States), and in 1880 its membership was twenty percent Catholic. The Ancient Order of Hibernians was Catholic and Irish, and had revised its constitutions in 1878 to eliminate all grounds for suspicion by the Church. In 1886 it had about 50,000 members in New York. The American Protective Association (A.P.A.) was a bitterly anti-Catholic society founded in Ohio in 1887. It revived all the old Nativist propaganda and was fueled by economic rivalry with second-generation immigrants. It had about one million members by 1896, but then declined rapidly. Among its announced goals was the exclusion from public office of Catholics and of non-Catholics with Catholic relatives.

It is significant that the growth in number and membership of the secret societies coincided with the growth of industry and urbanization. The figures on secret societies tell the story. In 1880 there were seventy-eight societies. They grew to 202 in 1890, and 338 by 1895. By 1900 there were 568 with a combined membership of about six million out of a total population of 75,000,000. Such growth in voluntary associations would be inexplicable if they did not meet some basic needs. Probably their chief attraction for the rank-and-file membership was that they were also mutual benefit societies. This was an important consideration when few other forms of insurance were available to most Americans. Active intervention by the government in this area lay almost half a century ahead.

Considering all the circumstances, the United States bishops were inclined to go very slowly in banning any secret societies other than the Masons. In this they reflected the attitude of Rome. In 1869, Pius IX had recommended tolerating any society that did not clearly have to be condemned. By the latter, he had in mind those that conspired against the Church and State. The Second Plenary Council of Baltimore (1866) had forbidden bishops to condemn any society by name without the prior consent of Rome. The Third Plenary Council of Baltimore had left the matter to a committee of all the archbishops with the proviso that if they were unanimous in a given case their decision would bind all the bishops. If they were not, the case would be referred to Rome. The bishops themselves were divided in this matter. Cardinal Gibbons and Archbishop Ireland were firmly opposed to any condemnation, as were their supporters. Archbishop Corrigan, supported by Archbishops Katzer of Milwaukee and Janssens of New Orleans, favored a stronger stand. Archbishop Corrigan was the moving spirit behind a report to Rome in 1894 that led to the condemnation of the Odd Fellows, the Sons of Temperance, and the Knights of Pythias. The Knights of Pythias had refused a request to explain their oath and ritual when they were asked to do so by some of the bishops who sought to avoid a confrontation. Even after the condemnation, there was trouble in getting the bishops to publish it. Archbishop Corrigan, along with Bishop McDonnell of Brooklyn and Bishop McQuaid of Rochester, did so at once. Finally it was agreed that enforcement would be left to the archbishops, and that they could permit passive membership in individual cases in order to prevent undue economic hardship.

The Knights Of Labor

The most famous case of a secret society the bishops had to deal with was that of the Knights of Labor, who were both a secret society and a labor union. Moreover, they were the first successful national union and a portent of things to come. Normally the Knights of Labor would not have presented a problem to the bishops because both the Second and Third Plenary Councils of Baltimore had exempted labor unions from the ban on secret societies. Special circumstances, however, made them a topic of major interest, not only to the Church but to powerful forces outside it that usually could not care less about what the Church approved or condemned.

Those forces represented the right and the left, both of which were anxious to use the Church for their own ends. On the right were the representatives of the ownership and management of industry and commerce. They were hostile to unions of any kind and on any level, and believed sincerely that glaring social and economic disparities were inevitable in this country and the necessary price to be paid for the growth of wealth and power in America. They were generally quite anti-Catholic but would have welcomed the Church's support in curbing the growth of unionism, which they regarded as a threat to their own interests.

On the left were assorted radicals, a small but increasingly vocal force who had representatives inside as well as outside the Knights of Labor. They would have welcomed a condemnation of the Knights by the Church because it would have confirmed or seemed to confirm their claim that the Church was by its very nature pro-Capital and anti-Labor. It would have helped their efforts to alienate the workers from the Church. The radicals were less interested in improving the actual conditions of workers than in using their justifiable and undeniable grievances as a lever with which to force substantial, if not revolutionary, changes in the entire social, economic, and political system. Like their opponents on the right, they were strongly anti-Catholic.

The most obvious thing about the Knights of Labor in 1886 was their sudden and phenomenal growth. They went from about 42,000 members in 1882 to about 71,000 in 1884 and about 700,000 in 1886. Some thought that 500,000 of these were Catholics. Their growth reflected, and to a degree caused, the social unrest characteristic of those years. It was also due in part to the hard times of 1883–1885. The thing that attracted special attention from the bishops was the condemnation of the Canadian branch of the Knights by Rome in August 1884. That came in response to an inquiry from Archbishop Taschereau of Quebec, who was soon to become the first Canadian Cardinal. The Roman decree said that, "after examining the principles, organization, and statutes of the Knights of Labor as they have been exposed, that society ought to be considered among those prohibited by the Holy See."

At first sight, it seemed reasonable to assume that the condemnation applied also to the United States, and among those who thought it did was Archbishop Corrigan. He was sure it was based on the nature and purpose of the society without regard to local circumstances. Others, including Cardinal Gibbons, hoped or thought not. Typically, Archbishop Corrigan thought chiefly of the legal aspects of the problem and of the principles involved, and the Cardinal of the actual circumstances and of the probable consequences of a condemnation in the United States.

The question of the Knights was one of the items of unfinished business left by the Third Plenary Council of Baltimore to the committee of all the archbishops. Since they were divided in their opinions and busy about many things, nothing was done for nearly two years. At the end of that time, the clamor for a definite decision one way or the other could no longer be resisted. Accordingly, at the meeting of the archbishops in Baltimore on October 28th, 1886, an attempt was made to reach a consensus on that subject among others.

Those who regarded the Knights with suspicion or reserve were not without serious grounds for their attitude. The organization was founded in Philadelphia in 1869 by Uriah S. Stephens, a Baptist in religion and a tailor by trade, who was also a Mason, an Odd Fellow, and a Knight of Pythias. The Knights of Labor grew very slowly, partly because of the great secrecy insisted upon and which they thought necessary for their protection from employers, and partly because of hostile public opinion. Their ritual and constitution were based very largely on the Masons and they were undoubtedly an oath-bound secret society.

In 1879 Uriah Stephens was replaced as Grand Master Workman by Terence V. Powderly (1849–1924) who was then still a Catholic and who remained in control of the Knights until 1893. He was anxious to avoid a clash with the Church, and through his influence the secret oath was replaced in September 1881 by a word of honor. The initiation rite was changed, and, as of January 1, 1882, the Knights of Labor surfaced, using that name publicly for the first time. Powderly had in mind a single organization that would include all types of workers except lawyers, bankers, professional gamblers, stock brokers, saloon keepers, and, prior to 1881, doctors. His plan was too inclusive, which explains why the Knights were supplanted by the American Federation of Labor, with its craft unions, and ultimately dissolved in 1917.

Among the factors the archbishops had to keep in mind when they met were the Masonic background and connections of the Knights, though that loomed larger in Rome and Quebec than in the United States. On April 20th, 1884, Leo XIII had issued the encyclical letter *Humanum Genus* in which he renewed and confirmed all preceding papal condemnation of Freemasonry. Of the eleven popes who reigned from the election of Clement XII in 1730 to the death of Leo XIII in 1903, seven—beginning with Clement XII in 1738—had condemned Freemasonry. The Church suffered much from the Masons in Europe and the entire Latin world.

The meeting on October 28, 1886 failed to reach the unanimity necessary to settle the case here instead of in Rome. All recognized the unfair burdens placed on labor and the way in which the scales were loaded in favor of capital. The question was: were the Knights of Labor a suitable instrument for redressing the balance? Archbishop Corrigan, who probably was influenced by their support of Henry George in the mayoralty campaign currently being waged in New York, thought the Knights "an unhealthy organization" but opposed condemnation until the situation developed further. The consensus was that whatever was objectionable in the Knights could be tolerated, and that the Church must face the underlying issue by recognizing the right and need of labor to organize.

When the vote was taken, nine of the twelve archbishops who voted in person or by proxy opposed condemnation. Archbishop Corrigan abstained and Archbishops Kenrick of St. Louis and Salpointe of Santa Fe voted to condemn. The matter was thus referred automatically to Rome, where the views of the bishops were presented by Cardinal Gibbons when he arrived there in February 1887 to receive his red hat. Archbishop Ireland and Bishop Keane were already in Rome working on the affairs of the Catholic University and had paved Gibbons' way.

His handling of the Knights of Labor's case in Rome was a major event in the life of Cardinal Gibbons, and many consider it his finest achievement. It was also a major event in the history of the American church and in the whole English-speaking world. In the report he handed to Cardinal Simeoni on February 20th, 1887, he pointed out that the Knights of Labor were no longer an oath-bound or secret society and were not hostile to Church or State. Hence, the organization did not merit the condemnation reserved for those who were. He showed his usual accurate judgment of the American scene by predicting that the Knights would not last as a major force, but that the problem they represented would. The emerging social problem was to become the dominant issue of the coming age, and both justice and charity required the Church to stand openly and firmly on the side of labor. Prudence did as well, for to condemn a movement in which so many of the Church's children were involved and in which they were so clearly right would be to risk alienating them from the Church as had already happened so widely in France. He cited the uproar over Dr. McGlynn as something caused mainly by the belief that he had been disciplined because he was a friend of labor. For these and other reasons, Gibbons thought, a condemnation would not be justified, necessary, or prudent and would actually be dangerous, ineffectual, and ruinous. He also pointed out that confessional unions were impossible in this country.

Cardinal Gibbons did not ask for formal approval of the Knights, which would have been difficult for Rome to grant and would surely have caused trouble elsewhere. He asked only that they not be condemned. His petition was granted because Rome judged his reasons to be sound and saw that he was supported not only by seventy of the seventy-five American bishops but also by Cardinal Manning of Westminster, England, who was already famous as an apostle of social reform. Accordingly, on August 16th, 1886 the Knights were given a conditional toleration that in effect left the matter in the hands of the American bishops. Although he did not mention it in Rome, Cardinal Gibbons could have cited, as an instance of the "heartless avarice" of capital which he criticized in his report, an episode he witnessed in Baltimore in February 1886. In that month, the workers on the local transit system struck against a seventeen-hour working day and he issued a public letter supporting the strikers. In April, they won a twelve-hour day. His intervention in Baltimore and for the Knights, while praised later, brought him some sharp criticism at the time from papers like *The New York Times* and *The Nation* (New York).

THE CATHOLIC UNIVERSITY OF AMERICA

It was easy enough for the Third Plenary Council of Baltimore to authorize the establishment of a national Catholic University, but not so easy to reach agreement on such basic points as its location, management, system of studies, and adequate financial support. These matters were left to a committee of which Archbishop Corrigan was a member. He was also a member of the committees that recommended the University to the Council and chose the first rector, Bishop Keane, and it was hoped that, because of his personal gifts and his position, he would take a sustained and active interest in the University itself. That hope was disappointed.

The first disagreement concerned the site. The launching of the University was made possible by a gift of $300,000 from Miss Mary G. Caldwell of New York who turned out to have definite views on several matters connected with it. Besides wanting Cardinal Gibbons to be chairman of the University Committee, she wanted the University itself to be an entirely new institution and to be located in Washington, D.C. When the Cardinal, who favored Philadelphia, polled the bishops, he found that, of the fifty-eight who answered, thirty-three favored Washington. Archbishop Corrigan thought it would be "a fatal site." Twenty bishops divided their votes among Baltimore, Chicago, New York, and Philadelphia, and the others gave no opinion but promised to accept the judgment of the Committee.

There were other disagreements. Archbishop Corrigan, who would have preferred Seton Hall or New York as a site, wanted to place the University in the hands of one religious order, the Jesuits, or to have it just as an examining body supervising and setting standards for all the existing Catholic colleges in the country. When these proposals were rejected and he saw it being influenced increasingly by Cardinal Gibbons, Archbishop Ireland, and Bishop Keane, he began to lose interest in it. His doubts were confirmed by Bishop McQuaid and Father Robert Fulton, the Jesuit provincial, to whom he turned for advice. McQuaid was strongly opposed to the University, which he thought unviable in the circumstances of the time. He disliked particularly the idea of having it in Washington, which he dismissed as a southern city with, presumably, no notable future. He foresaw correctly that the financial problems would become acute, and that ultimately the bishops would have to resort to an annual collection in the parishes, which he opposed strenuously. Father Fulton opposed the site chosen (it would compete with Georgetown), the management, and the proposed system of education.

Fortified by this advice, which he probably expected, Archbishop Corrigan began to disassociate himself from the University. His way of doing so showed his weaker side. Having signed with the other archbishops, the petition to the Holy See for the erection of the University, he then wrote confidentially to Cardinal Simeoni to warn him against it. It did not take the other bishops long to learn from Rome that there was opposition to the University "from an important source" and to guess who that source was. He resigned from the committee in November 1887 and returned a year later under heavy pressure, but he never regained his confidence in the project. He was less likely to do so after four of the University's professors provided the opinion needed to justify the restoration of Dr. McGlynn, and when he heard that in January 1893 Bishop Keane had given a banquet in honor of

Archbishop Satolli at which Dr. McGlynn was a prominently featured guest. He never shared Archbishop Ireland's view of the University as "the glory of the Catholic Church in America whose destinies were largely in its hands."

Archbishop Corrigan's attitude had important consequences for the University and himself. For the University, it meant the loss, at a critical hour, of financial support from the most prosperous archdiocese in the country, since Corrigan pleaded the prior claims of the Cathedral and the new seminary as an excuse for not allowing funds for the University to be collected. For himself, it meant that the exasperation of his colleagues on the committee overflowed into other important matters in which he had to work with them. More importantly, he had offended the Pope, who had taken a genuine personal interest in the University from which he hoped for great benefits for the American Church.

The University got off to a slow start. The formal opening, which coincided with the celebration of the centennial of the hierarchy, took place on November 13th, 1889, in the presence of President Benjamin Harrison. At that time, the Catholic University had ten professors and forty-one students. It started only as a graduate school, then a rare thing in this country, but in 1905 had to open an undergraduate department for financial reasons.

THE SCHOOL QUESTION

In July 1890, a sudden and wholly unexpected storm broke out over the proper Catholic attitude toward parochial and public schools, the role of the State in education, and kindred matters. The storm raged with great fury for three years during which it was watched with the closest attention, and stimulated, by the Catholic, non-Catholic, and anti-Catholic press. It was watched closely, too, in several European countries, notably France, Italy, and Germany, and with increasing bewilderment and alarm by the Vatican itself. It was started inadvertently by Archbishop Ireland when he addressed the annual convention of the National Education Association in St. Paul on the topic: "State Schools and Parish Schools." In his desire to achieve the first goal of an orator—to render the audience well disposed—he spoke first in most laudatory terms of the existing system, then of its defects, and then of what he thought it should be, and of how the Catholic schools fitted into the picture.

The reaction to the speech was swift and clear. The non-Catholics were pleased by his approval of compulsory education. They were glad to hear that no tax was more justifiable than the school tax and to hear the Public School hailed as the pride and glory of the country. They were especially pleased to hear: "The free school in America, withered be the hand raised in sign of its destruction." They were not pleased to be reminded of the injustice done to the Catholics by barring all aid to their schools and thus compelling them to bear the heavy burden of double taxation to support them. They were not pleased either by the Archbishop's solution to that problem: to have the State pay the Catholic schools for the secular education they imparted, as was done in several non-Catholic countries in Europe.

The Catholics were astonished by the lavish praise of the existing system and by the proposal to remove its basic defect—the barring of religious and moral instruction—by making it as Protestant as possible because that was the religion of the majority. Their uneasiness was increased when, in August 1891, two rural parishes in the Archdiocese of St. Paul—those at Faribault and Stillwater—rented their schools to the public authorities for a dollar a year. It seemed to many that such an arrangement was to become the norm, in spite of the Third Plenary Council of Baltimore's insistence on parochial schools.

Archbishop Ireland found himself in a painful dilemma, as well as in a sharp cross-fire. His speech, stripped of the rhetorical flourishes and extravagances, and read in the context of his other speeches was unexceptional, and could be explained and defended. The point was that it had to be explained to be defended. If he did too much of that, the Protestants would suspect that he was explaining it away and had not meant what he said at the convention, when in fact he did mean every word he said. If he did too little, he would be open to serious misunderstanding by the American Catholics and by the Holy See. He decided to stand by his speech and to carry the war against his Catholic critics to Rome. Consequently, he marshaled his supporters, both sides took their accustomed battle stations, and the fight was on. Once again, Cardinal Gibbons, Archbishop Ireland, and Bishop Keane led one group, and Archbishop Corrigan the other. The liberals were helped greatly by Monsignor Denis O'Connell, the rector of the North American College, who had the advantage of being in Rome and in close contact with many officials there. Archbishop Corrigan was backed once again by the Germans, led by Archbishop Katzer of Milwaukee, by the Jesuits in America and in Rome, and this time, as events would prove, by the great majority of the bishops.

The basic question—the relationship of the parochial and public schools, and the State's attitude toward the former—was and is a sensitive one. The opposition Archbishop Hughes had encountered was still there, even if usually couched in milder terms. It had flared up when President Grant proposed to bar all aid to religious schools, and the Republican Party Platform of 1876 endorsed that view. The Democrats, mindful of the Catholic vote, contented themselves with promising to maintain the Public School system and the separation of Church and State. The impetus given to the parochial schools by the Third Plenary Council of Baltimore was a further indication of Catholic dissatisfaction with the public schools and, as such, was offensive to the defenders of the public schools. Among the most strident of the latter was the American Protective Association, whose lecturers and literature for years had as part of their stock in trade sharp attacks on Catholic criticism of the public schools. They did so, not only because they believed what they said, but because they were seeking the support of the great multitudes outside their ranks who had similar views on that topic.

Apart entirely from the theoretical aspects of this problem and the principles involved, the Catholics had two compelling practical reasons for taking an active interest in the public schools: first, they were taxed to support them; second, and more important, the majority of the Catholic children were enrolled in them. Few believed that, even with ample State aid, the goal of every Catholic child in a Catholic school could be reached. In 1890, taking the country as a whole, fewer than a third of the Catholic children were in Catholic schools, and in New York it was only twenty-five percent.

In such circumstances, it was reasonable to investigate whether any compromise could be found that would permit reaching a larger number of Catholic children without imposing a crushing financial burden on their parents. That is what the Faribault Plan was about. It was in fact a copy of the Poughkeepsie Plan, so called because it started in St. Peter's Parish in Poughkeepsie, N.Y. There, from 1873 to 1898, in the successive pastorates of Fathers Patrick F. McSweeney (1839–1907) and James R. Nilan (1836–1902), both of whom were active members of the New York Accademia, the parochial school building was leased for a dollar a year to the public authorities. The municipality undertook to maintain the building, to hire and test the teachers, and to select the text books except in history, reading, and geography. Religious instruction was given after regular school hours, and all religious emblems were removed from the classrooms during school hours.

The Poughkeepsie Plan, which was approved by Cardinal McCloskey and Archbishop Corrigan, was terminated in 1898 by the public authorities on the ground that it was illegal. They objected also to the Sisters wearing a religious habit. The Plan had been copied on a small scale in fourteen dioceses scattered through the country. The main objection to it from the Catholic point of view was its uncertain duration. While an isolated instance here or there could be accepted by both sides and might last a relatively long time, the leases were always annual and could be terminated by either side. If the plan was adopted widely and was seen or thought to be substantially helpful to the Church, it would be sure to arouse the opposition of the anti-Catholics, and would be ended, as happened in Faribault in 1893.

The plan was not a long-term solution to a long-term problem, and it was not an acceptable substitute for the parochial school. It was the fear that it was intended to be such that roused most of the Catholic opposition to Archbishop Ireland's position. That opposition was in large part personal to him, for (as Cardinal Gibbons told Rome) the same ideas from anyone else would have aroused much less feeling. They would almost certainly have been expressed differently, and therefore they would have been interpreted differently by many who suspected unjustly that he was an enemy of the parochial school.

When Archbishop Ireland submitted his side of the controversy to Rome, he did not confine himself to the bare facts, which were not in dispute, but attempted to put the whole issue against the background of public opinion in the country as a whole. He said that any censure of him would be taken as censure of his Americanism and as proof that the Church was hopelessly out of harmony with American institutions. Going further, he added on March 23rd, 1892: "Unfortunately, now the question has been so ventilated, public opinion considers me as representative of the Church party in the United States in favor of the government, and consider my opponents as a foreign party to the United States and a great danger to the Republic. In case of an adverse decision, I have serious reason to be alarmed. We Catholics are only one in eight in the United States, without wealth and influence, and a much larger proportion of Catholics than this, both in point of wealth and influence, did not prevent the Kultur Kampf in Germany." This reference to Bismarck's war on the Church (1871–1890) was an attempt to frighten the Pope, who had spent much of the first twelve years of his pontificate attempting to end the quarrel he had inherited in Germany, and whose success in doing so on advantageous terms was rightly regarded as an outstanding and very difficult achievement.

Surprisingly, for he was usually moderate in speech, these extravagant statements were endorsed by Cardinal Gibbons. In urging the Pope to give Archbishop Ireland public proof of his confidence in him, he warned that the continued silence of the Holy See would be interpreted by the general public as a condemnation of the Archbishop's conduct and views, and if that happened: "I fear that the national sentiment would be excited and that measures obnoxious to Catholics would be proposed in school matters. There have been attempts in this direction: they have been checked for the present but it is important not to renew them in creating or maintaining prejudice against ourselves." Moreover, Cardinal Gibbons thought that, without exception, Archbishop Ireland's critics were prompted by low motives.

While the Roman authorities were, in their usual deliberate way, sifting and weighing the conflicting statements with which both sides inundated them, the battle was being fought in the American press—with pamphlets on the rights of the family, the Church, and the State, and with a number of planted storms and inspired leaks. Confidential documents to and from Rome appeared frequently in the press, sometimes in full and sometimes in garbled form or as slanted extracts. The *New York Herald* was the most frequent publisher of such material, much of which is thought to have come from Archbishop Ireland's German critics in St. Louis.

Archbishop Ireland went to Rome in January 1892 to press for a decision and was received warmly by the Pope, Cardinal Rampolla, and Cardinal

Ledochowski, the new Prefect of Propaganda. Sanguine as ever, he returned confident of a sweeping victory, but, on April 21st, 1892, Rome declared that, while the Faribault Plan could be tolerated, the Third Plenary Council of Baltimore's Decree on Parochial Schools stood unimpaired. This left matters much as they had been, so both sides argued over the precise meaning of "could be tolerated." This continued until Archbishop Satolli arrived in October 1892. On November 16th, 1892, he attended a meeting of all the archbishops in New York and presented them with a series of propositions on education to which he demanded their signatures. The propositions were much more favorable to Archbishop Ireland's views than the other archbishops were, so all except Archbishop Ireland refused to sign and appealed to Rome. In January 1893, the Pope ordered every bishop in the country to write directly to him giving his full opinion on the school question, and on May 31st he notified them that Archbishop Sattoli's propositions were not intended in any way to weaken the Third Plenary Council's Decree on the Parochial Schools. Seventy bishops voted against the Satolli propositions.

It is easy to sympathize with the Roman authorities and to admire the skill with which they steered their way to a sound solution of the school controversy and all the other controversies that developed in the United States. Not one of them had ever been here, few of them understood English, few had more than a casual acquaintance with most of the American prelates they dealt with, and all of them found this country's institutions quite different from any of which they had personal knowledge. They were well aware of and greatly pleased by the growth of the Church in America, and of the excellent work done by both contending factions and their leaders.

Two minor episodes in which Archbishop Corrigan was involved illustrate the problems of communication faced on both ends of the line from here to Rome. One concerned Propaganda, the other the Pope himself. In January 1892 Giovanni Cardinal Simeoni (1816–1892), who had been Prefect of Propaganda since 1878, died in Rome. He had met all the American archbishops several times, had influenced most of their appointments and had been in touch with some of them continuously for years. Through his work on the Third Plenary Council of Baltimore, he had acquired an excellent knowledge of conditions in America. He was succeeded by Miescyslaw Cardinal Ledochowski (1822–1902), a Polish aristocrat with a background of wide experience that did not include contact with the English-speaking world. After serving the Holy See in minor diplomatic posts in Latin America and Portugal, he became Nuncio to Belgium (1861–1866) and then (1866–1886) Archbishop of Gnesen and Posen in German Poland. He was imprisoned by Bismarck in 1874 for refusing to obey an order to have Polish children taught religion in German, which they did not understand. He was created a Cardinal to rescue him from Bismarck, and after his release from prison in 1876 was exiled to Rome. He resigned his diocese in 1886 to help with the reconciliation of Germany with the Holy See.

Cardinal Ledochowski became Prefect of Propaganda at the time Archbishop Ireland was in Rome pressing for a decision on the school question. To the new Prefect, this was only one of the problems he found crowding in on him from all sides. Moreover, while America was an important part of the area under his jurisdiction, it was only a part, and one of which he knew hardly any more than he knew about China or Equatorial Africa, which were also in his care. In December 1891, Cardinal Gibbons had sent the Holy See by mistake an inaccurate version of the meeting held the previous month by the archbishops in St. Louis, implying in it that all those present approved—or at least failed to disapprove—of Archbishop Ireland's stand on the school question. When this document appeared in the press, Archbishop Corrigan challenged it and invited many of those who had attended the meeting to join him in sending a correction to Rome. Out of regard for Cardinal Gibbons' feelings, several refused. Those who joined with Archbishop Corrigan were the archbishops of Chicago, Cincinnati, Milwaukee, New Orleans, Philadelphia, and Portland (Oregon). The new Prefect, however, chose to believe that they had been "beguiled" by Archbishop Corrigan, and that even if they (a majority of the American Archbishops) had not been "beguiled," he preferred the report as made by Cardinal Gibbons and Archbishop Ireland.

When Archbishop Corrigan learned that the Pope had been warned by Cardinal Gibbons and Archbishop Ireland that a rejection of Archbishop Ireland's position on the school question would expose the Church here to proximate danger of persecution, or at least a political attack on the parochial schools, he protested again. On April 25th, 1892, four days after the Roman decision on the Faribault Plan but before it was known here, the bishops of the New York Province sent a collective letter to the Pope. They implored him not to allow any decision that would endanger the parochial schools and not to let himself be influenced by talk of a threatened persecution, as such a danger was nonexistent.

The Pope replied on May 23rd, 1892, in a letter that was intended as a rebuke. In it he stated: "To confine ourselves however more closely to what was troubling your minds and moved you to write, we want to assure you that in this judgment no one suggested to us the suspicion that there was to be feared an impending dangerous persecution for Catholics if the action of the Archbishop of St. Paul, as regards the schools located in the town Faribault and Stillwater, was disproved by us. Since neither the said venerable brother nor anyone else made mention of this danger it is clear that a mendacious public rumor gave rise to the story that led you into that wholly inane and false notion." In spite of the papal letter, the New York bishops were correct, as was seen when the full text of Archbishop Ireland's Memorial of March 23rd, 1892 was published in the *New York Herald* on January 26th, 1893. The most probable explanation for the mixup is that because of the demands on his time and attention the Pope was given only a digest of most of the documents he was supposed to see. Archbishop Corrigan did not soothe any feelings in Rome by stating bluntly that the Pope was mistaken in his facts.

THE APOSTOLIC DELEGATION

The faulty communications with Rome that were so evident under Leo XIII, because there was so much business to transact, had been noted by both sides since the days of Bishop Carroll. As early as February 1808, before there was any expectation that he himself would ever come to America, Father Concanen had urged the Holy See to send a personal representative, preferably of low rank, to survey conditions here. As time passed, other solutions were advanced. Some favored a full-time Roman representative of high rank who could settle many of the canonical matters that dragged on for years in Rome. Others thought such a representative should be of low rank. Others thought there should be one only from time to time and for special reasons and occasions. Still others thought perhaps a full-time representative of the American bishops should be sent to Rome. The Roman authorities themselves continued to cherish the vain hope of full diplomatic relations with the United States which neither the Catholics nor the Protestants here wanted.

There were objections to each proposal. A permanent, high ranking representative might well be a continuous irritant to the non-Catholics and stimulate more anti-Catholic feeling, as Archbishop Bedini had when he visited. A temporary one of low rank might be ineffective because he would be outranked by every bishop. A temporary one of high rank, like Bishop Plessis of Quebec who came in 1820 to report on trusteeism in New York, or Archbishop Bedini in 1853 and Bishop Conroy of Ardagh in 1878, could not meet the needs caused by the ever-growing volume of business. An American representative in Rome might represent in fact only a faction among the bishops and might not be sufficiently objective in his description of conditions here. This objection applied equally to an American representative of the Holy See here. Under our system of government, full reciprocal diplomatic relations were undesirable though not actually impossible.

From the beginning of his pontificate in February 1878, Pope Leo XIII had in mind sending his own representative to the United States and was only waiting for a suitable occasion. When he was elected, he found the Holy See on bad terms with almost every government on the continent of Europe and lacking any official contacts with the English-speaking world. He wanted to change that. He was a diplomat by training and temperament and, like many others with the same gifts, he had high—some thought too high—expectations of what could be accomplished by diplomacy. He was not only a diplomat but an Italian diplomat, and not only an Italian diplomat but an Italian ecclesiastical diplomat. As such, he belonged to an ancient and valuable corps which has served, and continues to serve, the Church well, though some of its members are suspected of thinking that if a *Nuncio* had been sent to deal with Satan there would have been no occasion to send St. Michael the Archangel.

It was not only the underlying desire for diplomatic relations and the obvious need for more accurate information that prompted the Pope to act. It was also the steadily growing number of complaints from priests who had, or thought they had, legitimate grievances against their bishops. It was an undeniable hardship that many of them had to hire a lawyer in Rome, pay for the translation of documents, and often wait years for a decision. That most of those who appealed to Rome were justified in doing so is seen from the fact that, as Cardinal McCloskey told Archbishop Corrigan, ninety percent of the cases heard in Rome went against the bishops. That was due in some cases to the failure of the bishops to document their side of the case properly. The increase in litigation was due to the great growth of the Church here. When Archbishop Corrigan was born, there were sixteen dioceses in America, and when he died at sixty-two there were eighty-two. The delays were not all on this side of the water. In the first year of his administration of New York, Archbishop Corrigan sent Rome over twenty letters that were not answered. Some of the bishops had personal agents in Rome who tried to expedite matters for them. Archbishop Corrigan and Bishop McQuaid used Miss Ella B. Edes, a convert and a newspaper correspondent who lived in Rome for many years. Others used the rector of the North American College.

The suitable occasion for which the Pope was waiting came in 1889, when the centennial of the hierarchy and the formal opening of the Catholic University were celebrated. The Pope decided to test the water by sending a personal representative. The half-expected storm of protest did not occur. In October 1892, the same envoy returned as the papal representative to the forthcoming Columbian Exhibition in Chicago (to which he brought on loan the Vatican collection of maps and documents pertaining to Columbus) and his reception was all that could be desired. The Pope now felt the time was ripe. On January 16th, 1893, it was announced that Archbishop Satolli was to remain here as Apostolic Delegate. In making his move, the Pope was well aware that, almost without exception, the bishops, fearing another anti-Catholic storm and not being quite sure what his role here would be were opposed to a Delegate. The exception was Archbishop Ireland who knew who would be Delegate and hoped to influence him. Leo XIII felt it was a necessary step in the development of the American Church, and time has vindicated his judgment. The Third Plenary Council of Baltimore, the Catholic University, the decision on the Knights of Labor, and the Apostolic Delegation are the outstanding contributions of his pontificate to the Church in the United States. The only visible public reaction against the Delegation, the temporary surge in enrollment in the A.P.A. which peaked in 1896, was unimportant. The benefits were long range. It is safe to say that its very existence has prevented more litigation than the Delegation itself has settled.

In theory, the Apostolic Delegate, who was sent to the bishops and had no link whatever with the Government (as would a Nuncio), was supposed to be the Pope's personal representative and the official through whom most business with Rome would be channeled back and forth. He was not to supplant the bishops in the exercise of their authority and he was not supposed to be identified with any faction of the hierarchy. In fact, however, due to special circumstances and his own personality, this was not true of Archbishop Satolli. He arrived while the Church here was bitterly divided on several major issues, and he was identified from the beginning with Archbishop Ireland and his friends. His attitude on the school question was well known and widely resented. In April 1895 he shifted camps suddenly, with the result that henceforth he was distrusted by both. He was the object of unfriendly special attention from the press, both Catholic and non-Catholic. The situation at length reached the point where Archbishop Corrigan, who was thought to be his leading opponent, felt obliged, on August 15th, 1893 to disavow in Archbishop Satolli's presence, in St. Patrick's Cathedral, any opposition to the Delegate and to reaffirm his own loyalty to Rome.

An unexpected complication was provided by the Delegate's personal friendship with the Pope. Francesco Satolli (1839–1910) was born in the diocese of Perugia of which the future Leo XIII was bishop from 1846 to 1878. He was an excellent student and seminary professor and accompanied the new pope to Rome, where he taught philosophy and later became head of the papal diplomatic academy. His career was watched closely by the Pope, who personally selected him for the American mission. Some thought only an Italian Delegate would be acceptable to all the national groups in the Church here. Any disagreement with the Delegate was easily construed as opposition to his office and to the Pope himself, and reports to that effect soon flooded Rome. He had very great difficulty with the English language, and many marvelled at the assurance with which he spoke on complicated and controverted topics. He was made a cardinal in 1895 and remained here until October 1896. He had poor relations with Propaganda, which was not consulted about his appointment.

DEALING WITH THE IMMIGRANTS

One of Archbishop Corrigan's most useful gifts was his capacity to concentrate fully on the matter in hand. It enabled him to turn away, which he did eagerly, from the controversies that in his opinion absorbed too much of his time, and to make a truly notable record in his favorite field of work, that of a diocesan bishop.

The central fact with which he had to deal all during his administration was the rapid growth of the Catholic population, which practically doubled in sixteen-and-a-half years. It was simply the local manifestation of a national problem. From 1880 to about 1890 five million immigrants arrived in this country, and from 1890 to 1900 some four million more came. Between 1870 and 1880, there had been only about 2,800,000 immigrants, of whom a third were Catholic. But it was not just a matter of many more immigrants arriving; there was also a notable change in their places of origin. From 1783 to 1890 about eighty-five percent of all the immigrants came from Northern and Western Europe, but after that the balance shifted to Southern and Eastern Europe. From 1890 to 1900, the Italians were the largest group among the new arrivals. As usual, the Catholics were increasing more rapidly than the population as a whole. From 1870 to 1900 the number increased from about four and a half million to twelve million. Natural increase amounted for, in round numbers, four million, immigration for three million, and conversion for five hundred thousand.

While the new immigrants had some special problems, their basic ones were old ones with which the Church authorities here were all too familiar. The steady influx of such large numbers overtaxed the available facilities, resources, and personnel. The new arrivals, like the earlier ones, were unevenly distributed and usually desperately poor. In the beginning, they could do little to help themselves and to provide and staff the necessary churches, schools, and charitable institutions. Moreover, unlike those who came before them, very substantial numbers of them were unwilling to help. There was an acute shortage of priests and religious who could speak the necessary languages. The earlier arrivals who had established themselves or were striving to do so were not interested in carrying the entire burden, and in many cases were unable to do so.

In these circumstances, there was much opportunity for friction, and it is surprising that so little of it developed. Huddled under the broad umbrella of the Church, which was itself regarded with suspicion and hostility by the great majority of the population, were a dozen or more separate national groups. They differed from one another in language, political, and cultural background, educational and economic standing, and often very widely in their level of religious literacy and practice. It is understandable that some in each group tended to think they were inadequately appreciated by the others and especially by the majority group, which happened to be the Irish.

In the period between 1886 and 1892, when so many other controversies were going on, most of the friction was between the two major groups among the earlier immigrants, the Irish and the Germans, and actually between only some in each group. It did not involve New York directly, though it did involve Archbishop Corrigan. The Germans were convinced they were underrepresented in the hierarchy, which had a total of sixty-nine members in 1886. Of them, the Irish and Irish Americans had thirty-five members, the Germans fifteen, the French eleven, the English five, and the Dutch, Scots and Spanish one each. Father Peter Abbelen (1843–1917) of Milwaukee, a native of Germany, petitioned the Holy See in 1886 to insist on more national parishes and schools and on absolute equality between English-speaking and German-speaking parishes. He asked also that every diocese with many Germans have a German, or at least a German-speaking, vicar general. Except for the question of the vicar general, few took exception to his proposals. Few denied the need of more national parishes and the desirability of treating them like the others. If the Germans were entitled to a vicar general, however, all or many of the other groups would in time make the same claim. Some wondered if a largely German diocese with a German bishop would have to have an Irish vicar general.

A more serious problem was raised by Peter P. Cahensly (1838–1923), an apostolic layman who was a successful businessman and a member of the Prussian Landtag and the German Reichstag. For nearly fifty years, he gave much of his time and money to the St. Raphael Society for German Catholic immigrants, which he helped found in 1871 and which soon had branches wherever those immigrants went. In December 1890 its representatives in many countries met at Lucerne and adopted a series of resolutions that were presented to the Pope by Cahensly in April 1891 and which, to the genuine astonishment of their sponsors, caused an international storm. Most of the recommendations were reasonable and attainable, like the better supervision of immigrant ships. Others were desirable but in practice unattainable. The American bishops, hard pressed to supply even the minimum services in many areas, must have wondered, for instance, where the multilingual priests recommended for so many parishes would come from.

Like many reformers, the delegates to Lucerne overstated their case and on two particular points were vulnerable to criticism. One was a matter of fact, the other of policy. The first point was their claim that the Church here had lost ten million members by not taking proper care of the immigrants. Cahensly raised that figure to sixteen million. The second point was the proposal that the American bishops be selected on the basis of national origin, so that each immigrant group would be represented in the hierarchy in proportion to its share of the Catholic population.

The charge about "lost Catholics" could be rebutted easily. Cahensly's figure, for instance, far exceeded the total immigration in the period referred to. But the plan for the bishops is what caused the storm. It was seen as an obstacle to the naturalization of the Church in the United States, and as providing an opportunity for foreign governments to meddle in its internal affairs. This would have been harmful in itself and would have provided more ammunition for the A.P.A. and its allies.

The bishops were unanimously opposed to the Lucerne Memorial, but many of them regarded it as a very remote danger and felt sure it had no chance of acceptance in Rome. Archbishop Ireland and his friends, ever sensitive to the probable reactions of the non-Catholics, took it very seriously, overrated it greatly, and helped to organize a press campaign against it that made it seem that the Republic was in danger. Things reached the point where President Harrison himself told Cardinal Gibbons, on July 11, 1891, how closely he was following the issue in the press, how strongly he disapproved of the whole idea, and how pleased he was to hear the Church authorities both here and in Rome disapproved of it too. Cardinal Gibbons conveyed this information to the Holy See at once, with great pleasure. In their reply to the Lucerne Memorial, the bishops, while not denying substantial losses or claiming a perfect record, cited figures to show that great progress had been made in spite of all obstacles. Between 1842 and 1892, for instance, the number of bishops went from seventeen to eighty-eight, of priests from 582 to 9,000, of churches from 512 to 9,500. The Catholic school system had grown from one with thirty-one small schools to one with 303,000 students.

One reason why the controversy over immigration aroused so little feeling among New York Catholics, though the secular press gave it wide coverage, was that from the very beginning of its organized life in 1784 the Church here had been multinational. In 1885 it had, in round numbers, 60,000 Germans, 60,000 Bohemians, 50,000 Italians, 25,000 French, 20,000 Poles and smaller numbers of French-Canadians, Spaniards, Greeks, and Lithuanians, among others. Archbishop Corrigan had no trouble with the Germans. He shared their belief in the absolute necessity of the national parish and the parochial school. He did not believe in instant Americanization, and did not equate patriotism with the use of the English language.

Though he agreed fully with the bishops' opposition to the vulnerable points in the Lucerne Memorial and was, in fact, the author of the Latin version of their letter to the Pope repudiating them, he knew and esteemed Cahensly, whom he had welcomed to New York in 1883. Archbishop Corrigan had helped to found a local branch of the St. Raphael Society and the Leo House, its hostel for immigrants. Similar hostels were opened for the Poles, French, and Italians. He praised Cahensly's work and his motives in a speech on September 26th, 1892 to a convention in Newark of all the German-Catholic societies. It was the first public defense by a prominent non-German of the German side of the controversy, and he was very well received by them. He praised them for their loyalty to the Church, their support of the Catholic schools, and their patriotism. In referring to the last point, he observed that it was unnecessary to keep "trumpeting it in season and out of season." They reciprocated his friendship, and all during his administration gave him loyal and generous support in his undertakings and in his controversies here and in Rome.

For many reasons, the Archbishop's relations with the Germans could not be duplicated with the Italians. It was a misfortune for all concerned that the first great wave of Italian immigrants started when neither the Church here or in Italy, nor Italy herself (nor ourselves, for that matter), was able to give them more than a tithe of the help they needed. United Italy never became the paradise its creators envisaged and promised, and was never able to solve the economic and political problems that kept so many of her people in poverty and ignorance. At least she made no effort to prevent their departure.

Italian emigration to America got off to a slow start. The number of Italian natives in America had grown from 3,697 in 1850 to only 44,230 in 1880, an average annual gain of 1,350. By 1890 there were 182,580 and by 1900 there were 307,309 more. The last two figures, though showing a notable increase in a decade, were only a portent of what was to come. Between 1876 and 1930 over five million Italians came to this country. In 1881 they were only 2.3 percent of the total immigration for the year, but by 1901 they were 27.9 percent. About 80 percent of the total came from Sicily and Naples, the old Kingdom of the Two Sicilies.

A special feature of the Italian immigrants was the indifference or strong hostility shown by many of them to the Church. It could be explained and in measure condoned, but it could not be denied or ignored. It could not be removed without much effort and time, and was in fact a formidable obstacle for many years. From 1848 to 1929, the Church and State in Italy engaged in a bitter dispute over the apparently irreconcilable rights of the Italians to form a united national state, and of the Holy See to the political freedom necessary for the proper fulfillment of its mission. That conflict, which was settled by Pope Pius XI and Mussolini in 1929 by the Lateran Pacts, aggravated but did not cause the anti-clericalism that had been prominent in southern Italy for generations before it.

The Italians who came here had several handicaps that were, like their poverty and illiteracy, beyond their control. They were generally very poorly instructed in religion. Coming from a country where they were not expected to contribute to building churches, schools, and institutions, even the well disposed found it difficult to adjust to the Church's system here. Here too, for the first time, they encountered racial and religious prejudice. The literary and political circles here that had welcomed and even lionized those who came as political refugees after 1848 had no use for the ordinary laborers who came later. They felt they had nothing in common with the later arrivals and joined in the widespread contempt for just another horde of poor Catholics.

Moreover, many of the Catholics who were already here were not pleased with the Italians, whom they regarded as a burden instead of a reenforcement. Many of the Irish, Germans, and Poles, for instance, who had suffered so much for their religion, were disconcerted and even scandalized by the Italian attitude toward the Church. Archbishop Corrigan summarized the attitude and condition that distressed the non-Italian Catholics in a report to Rome in 1884, in which he said that of the fifty thousand Italians in this area not more than twelve hundred attended Mass even when it was easy to do so, and that ten of the twelve Italian priests working here were fugitives from justice in Italy. Considering the obstacles they faced, it is not surprising that so many immigrants retraced their steps at least for awhile, and that many left here for good. Between 1887 and 1890, ten percent returned to Italy, and from 1890 to 1900 thirty-four percent returned, and from 1911 to 1920 an astonishing eighty-two percent went back. Many did so to rejoin families they hoped to bring here eventually.

If the situation looked bleak, it was neither desperate nor hopeless, and it improved steadily in the Corrigan years. The Italians were like good but long-neglected soil which, when properly tended, yielded a rich harvest to the patient husbandman. They brought with them their inexhaustible vitality, their capacity for work, and their deep loyalty to family ties. Like those who went before and those who followed, they began on the bottom and worked their way up slowly to an important and respected place in the American community. The Archbishop turned to Italy for help and received it from, among others, three saints from Northern Italy, two of whom have already been canonized. The first was St. John Bosco (1815–1888), the founder of the Salesians, who was canonized in 1934. As early as 1883, Archbishop Corrigan tried to get him to come to New York, but he could not get away. He did the next best thing in sending his community. The second was the Venerable Giovanni B. Scalabrini (1839–1905), the founder of the Mission-aries of St. Charles, who are widely known as the Scalabrinis. He came him-self in 1900 on a visit and sent his community, which was founded to care for emigrants from Italy. He did the New York area another favor by urging Mother Frances Xavier Cabrini to come here.

Mother Cabrini (1850–1918) founded the Missionary Sisters of the Sacred Heart in 1880. She had intended to go to China, but Leo XIII told her to find her China in the West. Invited to New York by Archbishop Corrigan on the advice of Father Scalabrini, she arrived here on March 31, 1889. By April 21st, she had opened the orphan asylum on which her heart was set. At that time, she knew not a word of English. Since she arrived before the Archbishop expected her and insisted on opening an orphan asylum when he wanted a school, his sense of order was offended and there was a coolness between them at the start, but it soon passed. He became her loyal friend and helped her to open her first hospital, in September 1892. Tactfully, and with a fine sense of timing, she called it Columbus Hospital, knowing that all Italians here would use and help an institution named in his honor. She used the same name for all the other hospitals she founded in this country, although some here changed names—Columbus in New York is now Cabrini Medical Center. Before her death from malaria in Chicago, she had established sixty-seven schools and institutions here, in Central and South America, and in Europe, one for every year of her life. She was canonized on July 7th, 1946, and was both the first United States citizen and the first person who worked in this archdiocese to receive that honor. She is also the only canonized saint buried in New York. On September 8th, 1950 Pope Pius XII named her the patroness of all emigrants.

PARISHES AND SCHOOLS

The rapid and substantial increase in the Catholic population necessitated a corresponding increase in the number of parishes in order to keep the ratio of churches to people at the level at which Cardinal McCloskey left it. There was also a need for additional schools, and not only of more but of different charitable institutions and services to meet the changing requirements of the community. These developments depended in turn on the provision of more priests and religious, and on the amount of financial support the faithful could give. A steady, systematic, and simultaneous advance in all these areas was the major program of the Corrigan administration.

The parishes came first, for the people had to be able to attend Mass and receive the Sacraments. They had also to be formed into a community. The parish became for huge numbers the focal point of loyalty in religious and social matters. Neighborhoods meant more before the automobile, the movies, the radio, and television transformed the social habits and amusements of the people. The well-organized urban parish which strengthened the religious life of multitudes of immigrants, whether English-speaking or not, while guiding and assisting their assimilation of American ways, was a powerful force for good for both Church and State, and was a major achievement of the clergy of that day. The insistence on Sunday Mass and the regular reception of the sacraments, joined with the numerous devotions and societies, and, where possible, with the school, brought many to a level of practice that astonished the church leaders in many of the areas from which the immigrants came. Young people were prepared for confession four times a year and urged to receive Holy Communion monthly if they were old enough. Monthly Communion was stressed too by the Holy Name Society. The Archbishop was especially interested in the daily exposition of the Eucharist carried out by the Blessed Sacrament Fathers.

Profiting from his observations as coadjutor, Archbishop Corrigan had turned immediately to the problem of more parishes. In his first four years, he opened twenty-three and by 1902 had opened ninety-nine, plus about as many more chapels and stations (places, neither churches nor chapels, where Mass was said regularly). The population was unevenly distributed and so, therefore, were the new parishes. The counties now in the city limits got the lion's share. Manhattan, which went from 1,164,673 to 1,850,093 people between 1880 and 1900 got twenty-nine. The present Bronx, up in the same years from 51,980 to 200,507, got eighteen, in addition to its previous eight; Staten Island, up from 33, 991 to 67,021, added five to seven; Westchester, up from 131,348 to 184,257, added sixteen to its nineteen. On the other end, Putnam, which declined from 15,181 to 13,787 between 1880 and 1900 and continued to decline from 1870 to 1920, added one new parish.

It was not just an increase in numbers. Every effort was made to provide for the non-English speaking groups. By 1902, all of them had over fifty churches and chapels of their own and about fifty Italian-born priests. In addition, in many parishes in which an Italian-speaking priest could be found, they had the regular use of the basement church or chapel. Regional loyalties were so strong among them that sometimes a priest from the wrong province was hardly more acceptable to them than a non-Italian. The Poles had seven churches and eight priests. The Blessed Sacrament Fathers were working among the French Canadians and the Assumptionist Fathers among the Spanish.

Archbishop Corrigan was less successful with the schools, because of the lack of personnel and money. Still, he opened twenty-four schools and three academies in his first four years, and seventy-five schools by 1902. When he died, there were 55,000 children in the ordinary schools and 20,000 in the schools in charitable institutions. Catholic children in the public schools were not forgotten and a beginning had been made on Confraternity of Christian Doctrine classes.

THE CHARITIES

There was a notable expansion of charitable work. Though the Catholic Protectory, the New York Foundling Hospital, and the Orphan Asylum were watched with special care, and the last was moved to new quarters in Kingsbridge in the Bronx, the Archbishop had his eye on many other needs. He worked closely with the Protestant and Jewish charities and was well aware that their combined efforts could not meet the needs of the time. The changing social pattern is evidenced in the starting of five day nurseries. The Fresh Air Society was started in 1897 to send city children to the country for two weeks. Two maternity hospitals, two training schools for nurses, two tuberculosis hospitals, two convalescent homes, a residence for homeless women, separate immigrant bureaus to minister to the Irish, Italian, German, Austrian, Polish, and Lithuanian immigrants, schools for the blind and the deaf, the Guild of the Infant Savior to care for abandoned children, St. Benedict's Asylum for black children, expansion of the Catholic Home Bureau, which places school-age children in supervised private homes, two homes for working girls, two training schools for women, including the Grace Institute and the Apostolate of the Sea, indicate the range of needs to be met and the effort made to do so. From 1889 on, the St. Vincent de Paul Society had a full-time worker in the City Courts to help Catholic children.

Special mention must be made of the effort to deal with the growing number of cancer patients. The first cancer hospital in the United States, the present world famous Memorial-Sloan Kettering Hospital, opened in 1884 as the New York Cancer Hospital. It is probable that the growing incidence of cancer was caused at least in part by the elimination or alleviation of diseases that previously would have carried off early in life people who now lived long enough to develop cancer. The dread and horror inspired by the disease were felt especially by the poor. It was to help them that Mother Alphonsa Hawthorne Lathrop (1851–1926), the daughter of novelist Nathaniel Hawthorne and a convert to the Church in 1891, founded in 1900 a religious community, a branch of the Dominican Sisters, known as the Servants of

Relief for Incurable Cancer, which opened St. Rose's Home in Manhattan. In 1890, a group of Catholic widows founded the House of Calvary for the same purpose. Both these institutions are still flourishing, although the House of Calvary is now known as Calvary Hospital.

THE RELIGIOUS COMMUNITIES

Additional works of religion and charity were made possible by the increase in the number of religious communities and the expansion of those already here. Between 1886 and 1902, twenty-four new communities came to New York or were founded here. Eight were for men and sixteen for women. Four of these—the Salesian Fathers, the Scalabrini Fathers, the Society of the Catholic Apostolate known as Pallottines, and the Missionary Sisters of the Sacred Heart (Cabrini Sisters), worked exclusively among the Italians. The Benedictine Fathers (Collegeville, Minn.), who came in 1890 and left in 1976, never succeeded in founding a monastery here, and devoted themselves to parish work. One of the newcomers was a special protégé of Archbishop Corrigan. It was the Second Order of Dominicans, a cloistered order of nuns, and the first contemplative order to make a successful foundation in New York State. Archbishop Corrigan brought them from France to Newark in 1880, and in 1889 a subgroup from Newark founded Corpus Christi Monastery in Hunts Point, Bronx. They were brought here primarily to pray for the seminary and the priesthood in New York. By 1902 there were about seven hundred male religious, of whom about two hundred were priests, and about twenty-five hundred nuns working here.

Archbishop Corrigan seems never to have met or heard of the first New Yorker to enter a contemplative convent, though she was a contemporary of his and was also the first native-born American Catholic to be considered for canonization. The Venerable Adelaide of St. Teresa O'Sullivan (1817–1893) was born in St. Peter's Parish on October 8, 1817 and baptized by Father Malou. Her paternal grandfather was an Irish Catholic, from County Cork, who had been an officer in the British Army and came here after the Revolution. Her father, a lapsed Catholic, was the United States Consul to the Barbary States, where he met and married an English Protestant. Their six children were baptized Catholic. He died when Adelaide was seven. Though not encouraged by her family, she made her First Communion and was confirmed at thirteen. In 1835 her family moved to Washington, where she studied at the Visitation Convent, which she entered against her family's wishes in 1837.

In 1840, feeling a call to a stricter life, she left the Visitandine Nuns and at the suggestion of Father Varela, went to Havana, Cuba, where she entered the Discalced Carmelites. She had to flee Cuba because of the political situation and went to Guatemala, where she became Mistress of Novices in

1858 and Prioress in 1868. Driven from Guatemala by the anti-clericals in 1875, she returned briefly to Havana, and then went to Savannah, Georgia, in 1877. She arrived in Yonkers in 1879, hoping to establish a permanent monastery, but the necessary funds were unavailable. After a year, she abandoned the idea and accepted the hospitality of Sister Irene at the New York Foundling Hospital until she went to Spain, where the Bishop of Leon gave her a former Franciscan convent. She died there on April 15, 1893. After the diocesan inquiry into her possible beatification was finished, her cause was formally introduced in Rome in 1940.

THE LAY SOCIETIES

Indispensable as the religious communities were, they could never have carried on all their activities by themselves. Archbishop Corrigan counted on the active support of a growing number of involved lay people. Three societies were especially helpful in channeling the energies of the men. Many men belonged to all three, and these societies came to have members from almost every parish. These were the St. Vincent de Paul Society, the Holy Name Society, and the Knights of Columbus. The Archbishop knew the first of these societies from personal experience and leaned heavily on it. He was a regular attendant at the monthly meetings of the Superior Council, following their activities with the closest of interest. At his request, they added the regular visitation of the Tombs Prison to their other activities.

The Holy Name Society came to New York in 1867 when the Dominican Fathers founded the parish of St. Vincent Ferrer, but it was officially restricted to that parish for nearly twenty years because, in 1604, Pope Clement VIII had limited it to one branch in a city. Though the restriction was not enforced strictly, it tended to limit the growth of the Society. Nonetheless, by 1882, when the Archdiocesan Union was formed, there were fifteen branches. It was not until 1896 that Father Charles McKenna, O.P., a well-known preacher and missioner, supported in his petition by Archbishop Corrigan, succeeded in having Rome lift the limitation. By 1902 the Society had seventy branches and sixteen hundred active members in New York.

The Knights of Columbus was founded in New Haven in March 1882 as a fraternal and mutual benefit society for Catholic men. Its first branch outside New England was established in Brooklyn in September 1891, and a branch was established in New York in May 1895. The Knights were an effective force in defending Catholic interests in public life. Their work among the troops in the Spanish-American War was a foretaste of the work in World War I that brought them lasting fame.

The volunteer efforts of Catholic women, first mobilized here for the orphan asylum in 1817, were increasingly important as the number and variety of organized good works grew. The first Superintendent of Charities,

Father Thomas Kinkead who was appointed in 1898, tried hard to organize them for more effective service, and in March 1902 the Association of Catholic Charities was formed to prevent overlapping and duplication.

THE NEW SEMINARY

Fundamental to the success of Archbishop Corrigan's plans for New York was an increase in the number of priests. The number he found in 1885 had more than doubled by 1902, having risen from 383 to 820. The diocesan priests went from 264 to 574, and the religious order priests from 118 to 246. By 1902, the native American priests were being helped by recruits from Ireland, Germany, France, Poland, Belgium, Quebec, Italy, Austria, Hungary, Bohemia, and Syria. While these recruits were necessary and welcomed warmly, they represented a short-term solution. He knew he could not count indefinitely on replacements from the same sources. In the long run, he felt New York must supply most of its own needs, and with the increased population, the sound family life of so many of its members, and the help of the growing Catholic school system, he hoped that it would. His keen awareness of a long-term need and his confidence that that need could be met stimulated his interest in his greatest achievement and favorite project, the building of the new St. Joseph's Seminary at Dunwoodie, Yonkers.

Though there were compelling practical reasons for building a new seminary, Archbishop Corrigan would have wanted it anyway and had it in mind from the beginning of his administration. He modeled his administration as far as possible on the decrees of the Council of Trent (1545–1563) which had strongly favored a diocesan seminary. It had placed on a bishop a special responsibility for the proper maintenance of the Cathedral and the celebration of the liturgy, for the care and supervision of the seminary and for preaching. Archbishop Corrigan took all these responsibilities quite seriously.

Archbishop Hughes' hope that the seminary in Troy would be used and supported by all the bishops of the Province of New York had never been fulfilled. Brooklyn, Buffalo, and Newark had seminaries of their own. Boston took away most of the New England students when it opened its own seminary in 1884, and Rochester opened its own in 1891 after years of planning. Some bishops preferred to send some of their men to Montreal because they admired the Sulpicians who ran the seminary there, because the students could learn spoken French, and because it was cheaper. The New York priests complained that Troy was inconvenient for the annual clergy retreat, and all admitted that the chapel and library were inadequate. The building had been designed for other purposes and was damp, poorly heated, and poorly equipped, and many regarded it as unhealthy. The official history lists the names of fifty-nine students who died there in thirty-two years, and adds "and many others who are not recorded." Presumably most of them died of tuberculosis—not that the hazards to health were all in Troy. Father William J. Hussey, the first student ordained there (on December 17th, 1864), died in New York City on February 7th, 1865, of typhoid caught on a sick call. Still, Troy had rendered a great service. Nearly 750 of its students were ordained, and they were distributed among thirty-six dioceses and four religious communities. The Archdiocese of New York received 328, an average of about ten a year, which was not half enough to meet the needs.

The plan to build a new seminary was announced at the Synod of 1886 and was well received by all. Committees were appointed to find a suitable site and to plan the necessary fund-raising. The site selected was the Valentine property in Yonkers, which had been in the possession of that family since 1786. It was bought on March 6th, 1890, for $64,146.77. The land acquired, about fifty-four acres, was judged sufficient for all foreseeable needs. The cornerstone was laid on May 17th, 1891, Pentecost Sunday, by the Archbishop, who had invited the entire Catholic population, and the invitations were printed in ten languages. The railroads were unable to handle the crowd and service broke down, so that only about 80,000 people, half of those who started out, reached the site. The sermon was given by Archbishop Ryan. Fund-raising started in a serious way in June 1892. It was so successful that, in spite of the financial panic of 1893–1897, the construction of the seminary was not stopped even for a day. Beginning in January 1896, the Archbishop, Bishop Farley, and Monsignor Mooney, the Vicar General, divided the Manhattan parishes among them and appealed in each one for a generous response to an envelope collection. Estimates were that the seminary would cost a half million dollars but, as usual, costs rose and the final cost was about one million.

The building itself was planned on a large scale and nobly proportioned. It was built of stone found on the grounds, and everything in it was of the finest quality. As usual, no detail escaped the Archbishop. He paid special attention to the chapel and library which he made the heart of the structure. He accepted no gift, large or small, for the chapel, in which every item from the chapel building itself to the least part of its furnishings was his personal gift. He was even more interested in the faculty than in the building, and rejoiced that the Sulpician Fathers agreed to take charge, thus fulfilling the hopes of Archbishop Hughes. The Council of Trent had made formation and training, which included testing, the two-fold purpose of the seminary. The Archbishop's desire to equip the seminary as well as possible had a practical purpose. He wanted it to make up any deficiencies in the candidates that might be due to the variety of backgrounds from which they came. With ample equipment in the hands of a highly trained professional faculty, he felt he had done all he could do. The dedication of the completed building took place on August 12th, 1896 with a Pontifical Mass celebrated by Cardinal Satolli and the sermon preached by Bishop Farley. Archbishop Corrigan contented himself with blessing the chapel before the Mass and intoning the

Te Deum after it. Owing to the oppressive heat, the speeches were cut to five, including one in Latin by Cardinal Satolli. The seminary, which had room for 160 students, opened on September 21st, 1896 with ninety-eight, of whom eighty-four were for New York, and sixty-seven had come from the Troy seminary, which at its peak had 173 students.

THE CATHEDRAL

But the seminary at Dunwoodie and his other projects never distracted Archbishop Corrigan's attention from the Cathedral. The spires, which had been planned by Cardinal McCloskey and Monsignor Quinn, were started in the fall of 1885 and completed in three years at a cost of $200,000. Archbishop Corrigan began the systematic completion of the side chapels and furnished most of them. The chapel of St. John was his personal gift in memory of his four predecessors, all of whom bore that name. He installed the chimes in the spires and also the stations of the cross. His major addition was the Lady Chapel, finished under his successor, which was started in July 1901. It was a gift from the family of Eugene Kelly, the banker, who had married a niece of Archbishop Hughes. Renwick's original plan had included such a chapel, but it had been dropped for financial reasons. The present one was designed by Charles Matthews.

PUBLIC AFFAIRS

Archbishop Corrigan's own inclination, the ever-growing volume of diocesan business, and the ecclesiastical controversies in which he took part so reluctantly kept him from playing or attempting to play any notable role in public affairs, and from having any unnecessary contact with public officials on any level. Because he had a neatly compartmentalized mind, he was surprised to find that his ecclesiastical controversies sometimes affected public officials who seemed to him to have no connection, however remote, with them. He carefully avoided involvement in partisan politics on any level, and in local affairs contented himself with dealing with the various regulatory agencies.

He had more contact with the State authorities and, during much of his administration, the establishment of genuine freedom of worship for Catholics in charitable institutions run by the State or supported by it was a major problem. It was one in which Bishop McQuaid was the chief spokesman for the bishops. Though the Constitution of New York State declared that "the free exercise and enjoyment of religious profession and worship without discrimination or preference shall forever be allowed in this State to all mankind," it was often denied in practice. It was granted much more readily in some areas than in others, and attempts to have the legislature enforce it uniformly by appropriate laws met stubborn resistance. In June 1881, Governor Cornell vetoed "an Act to secure for the inmates of institutions for the care of the poor freedom of worship and to provide for the visitation of such institutions for that purpose." He did so on the ground that "such institutions must of necessity be managed with a view to economy and discipline, and that provision for religious worship must depend on circumstances peculiar to each case." What he really meant was that it must depend on the convenience of the management. After repeated efforts and in spite of steady opposition from such groups as the Evangelical Alliance and the League for the Protection of American Institutions which had great influence with the Republican Party, the Act was passed in April 1892.

An excellent example of what the Act was intended to prevent was supplied by the New York House of Refuge on Randall's Island, which was the first institution of its kind in this country. It was run on public funds by the Society for the Reformation of Juvenile Delinquents, which was founded in 1825. It claimed to be non-sectarian but was in fact strongly Protestant, though undenominational. It claimed to provide instruction in the basic principles of Christianity, barring only all forms of dogmatic or sacramental religion. It declined to admit that the Catholics had any valid complaint in being refused Mass and all the sacraments, and rejected John Gilmary Shea's statement of their irreducible claims. These were: (1) to be free from compulsory attendance at Protestant worship of any kind; (2) to be allowed an opportunity to go to confession in privacy before Mass; (3) to have a priest for the last sacraments. These modest demands were denounced quite sincerely by the management as an attempt to control the State and propagate the religion of the Vatican. An attempt to secure religious worship in the public insane asylum was denounced as "papal aggression." At the same time, the Catholic Protectory, which always had some Protestant children, was sending them to the nearest Protestant Church on Sunday and seeing that they had Protestant instruction.

The depth of the resentment caused by the controversies in which Archbishops Corrigan and Ireland led opposing factions was shown clearly in New York State in March 1894, in the dispute that erupted over what would normally have been a routine matter little noticed by the public and barely mentioned in the press. In January 1894 Bishop Francis McNeirny of Albany (1828–1894) died. He had been Chancellor of New York and secretary to Archbishops Hughes and McCloskey. He was the only Catholic among the nineteen Regents of the University of the State of New York, and it was generally agreed that his successor on the Board must be a Catholic. The bishops of New York suggested Bishop McQuaid whose lifelong interest in Catholic schools and active support of the Regents made him a suitable choice. All the Catholic schools in Rochester took the Regents Examinations even though for many years the Rochester City Public Schools did not.

Two other candidates entered the field. The first was Father Louis A. Lambert (1835–1910), a gifted, angular, and contentious man with a literary flair who was involved in litigation with Bishop McQuaid for years. His *Notes on Ingersoll* (1887) was a widely used rebuttal of rationalism. The other candidate was Father Sylvester Malone (1821–1899), who was for many years the best-known priest in Brooklyn. He was born in Ireland and was ordained at Fordham in August 1844 by Bishop Hughes. His first and only assignment was Sts. Peter and Paul, in the Williamsburg area of Brooklyn. During his time there, the parish was divided twenty-five times and he contracted cholera, ships fever, and smallpox in ministering to the sick. He was the only non-New Yorker in the Accademia and was a loyal and enthusiastic follower of Dr. McGlynn. The matter was settled by the active intervention of Archbishop Ireland, whose views carried great weight with the Republicans in the Legislature. Accordingly, they chose as the sole Catholic representative on the Board of Regents a priest, Father Malone, who was in open conflict with his own bishop, who had publicly described Archbishop Corrigan as a madman who could and would be removed, who wanted to abolish all Catholic schools, and who believed that "Henry George's theories of land tenure are destined to find complete acceptance among the intelligent people of this country." Their choice was recognized widely as a deliberate affront to the bishops of New York.

Much more important matters came before the legislature in the same year. The Constitutional Convention in August was confronted by conflicting claims. The Catholics pressed for a fair share of support for their schools from public funds. The anti-Catholics pressed for the elimination of all State aid to any kind of sectarian charity. A compromise was reached which left things as they were. State aid for children in charitable institutions was justified on the ground that the State, standing in place of the parents, was bound to respect their wishes for the religious education of their children. It was barred for children in ordinary schools on the ground that it would violate the separation of Church and State. The election was contested bitterly with the Democrats condemning the A.P.A. formally and emphatically, while the Republicans refused to do so, and in fact had almost a hundred of its members as delegates to their convention.

Early in October, the bishops of New York met and decided to take no public position on the election and to leave the people to use their own judgment and intelligence. They were astonished when, shortly after their meeting, Archbishop Ireland came to New York for several weeks and, ignoring Archbishop Corrigan, took an active part in the campaign as a spokesman for the Republican Party. The Republicans won and the so-called Blaine Amendment, prohibiting State aid for Catholic schools, became part of the State Constitution. This second intervention in New York affairs by the Archbishop of St. Paul was too much for Bishop McQuaid, and on November 25th, 1894 he delivered a carefully worded address from the pulpit of the Rochester Cathedral in which, citing chapter and verse, he rebuked Archbishop Ireland for his political activities, his discourtesy to the Archbishop of New York, and his unwarranted intrusion into New York's affairs. He welcomed the expected inquiries from Rome as a chance to elaborate his charges, and he successfully weathered the storm he had provoked.

The Federal Government played a much smaller role then than now, so Archbishop Corrigan had few direct contacts with it, and those he had were chiefly with the Armed Forces. He welcomed, in 1889, the appointment of Father Charles H. Parks of New York (1855–1907) as the first Catholic chaplain in the United States Navy. His chief business with the Army concerned the provision of a suitable Catholic chapel at the United States Military Academy (West Point). For many years, Catholics there were attended to by the pastor of Highland Falls. Mass was said on the military reservation in an old, one-story frame building that was used for many other purposes. It was inconveniently located, inadequate in size and equipment, and actually off bounds to the cadets, who needed special permission to attend Mass.

In August 1896, with the permission of the Archbishop, Father Cornelius G. O'Keefe (1853–1918), pastor of Highland Falls, applied for permission to build a permanent chapel on a convenient site. The offer included the transfer of full title of the chapel to the government, which would continue to own the site, and could move or destroy the chapel if expansion at West Point required it. All expenses were to be borne by the Church, and all the necessary funds were to be received before the work commenced. The design and the materials used were to harmonize with the rest of the buildings and were to be approved in advance by the Superintendent of the Academy. In return, the government was to guarantee to the Catholics the permanent and exclusive use of the chapel.

The Judge Advocate General of the Army found that no existing law allowed the government to give such a guarantee. He suggested instead a revocable license which in practice would not be revoked, and this was accepted by the Church. The revocable license was granted to the Archdiocese by the Secretary of War on March 3rd, 1897, and the matter appeared to be settled. Both the Army and Archbishop Corrigan had overlooked the A.P.A., which began a nationwide campaign against the chapel. The McKinley administration, which took office on March 4th, 1897, buckled under pressure, revoked the license, and threw the matter into the lap of Congress.

The critics of the proposed chapel ignored the fact that the government had already paid for the erection of a fine Protestant chapel which it maintained, and that it supplied the Protestant chaplain with a salary and a house. No one, Protestant or Catholic, had protested against that. The Catholics were to receive no money for the chapel, and the pastor of Highland Falls was not to be paid for his services. Moreover, Catholics were one-third of the total personnel at West Point, and Mass had been said there for many years.

Since West Point is a national institution and therefore concerns all the bishops of the country, Archbishop Corrigan felt justified in asking any bishop who could do so to lend a helping hand in presenting the case to Congress. On March 3rd, 1898, taking advantage of an unexpected visit from Archbishop Ireland, whose standing with the Republicans was well known, he sought Archbishop Ireland's intervention which was refused on the ground that it would only intensify the opposition of the A.P.A. The chapel was approved on April 8th, 1898, started a year later, and dedicated by Bishop Farley on June 10th, 1900. The storm died down as suddenly as it started and the issue, a classic example of old-fashioned anti-Catholic bigotry, was never revived.

As the nineteenth century came to a close, both England and the United States were engaged in aggressive wars against smaller and notably weaker powers that brought each of them valuable territorial gains and a storm of criticism outside their own and each other's boundaries. Both wars, the Boer War and Spanish-American, were fought for ostensibly high moral purposes and supported by domestic public opinion. Archbishop Corrigan took no public stand on the Spanish-American War and found himself in agreement with Cardinal Gibbons and Archbishop Ireland, both of whom opposed it. He congratulated the Cardinal on speaking out so strongly for peace. He was untouched by the hysteria that gripped so much of the country, largely through the influence of the Hearst papers.

Archbishop Keane, who was living in Rome and was well aware of the generally anti-American feeling the war inspired in Europe, defended the war in the name of "a higher law" by which humanity demanded that Spain relinquish her colonies. He thought the American cause represented "the interests of civilization." The easy victory over helpless Spain stimulated national pride and led to a strong resurgence of belief in America's Manifest Destiny. The prevailing mood was well expressed by Senator Albert Beveridge of Indiana when he told the Senate in January 1900 that God had chosen the American people "to lead in the regeneration of the world." His theme has been repeated in every generation in this century. Our territorial acquisitions at the turn of the century were seen by many as the visible fruits of divine favor.

AMERICANISM

Archbishop Corrigan's agreement with their views on the war against Spain did not prevent him from opposing Cardinal Gibbons and Archbishop Ireland in the last controversy of his administration, which concerned Americanism. The progress of the Church in America under a democratic republic attracted much attention in France, where the Catholics were bitterly divided on the question of their own republic. Most of them were royalists and were well aware of the anti-Catholic feeling and record of most republicans. The Pope had been attempting to persuade the Catholics to accept the republic and work within it for the defense of Catholic rights and values. Those who followed his advice often cited this country as an example of the harmony possible between the Church and a democratic republic and, to the intense indignation of their opponents, claimed that the American solution was not only acceptable but ideal and would work equally well in France. Archbishop Ireland's views were circulated widely, not only through his visits to France but through the tireless efforts of his admirers there. The controversy was waged briskly in the periodical press, and a substantial amount of literature on the subject was produced by both sides.

The controversy reached its peak with the translation into French of an abridged version of the biography of Paulist Father Isaac Hecker, who had died in 1888. The original edition, which no one attacked, appeared in 1891 in New York with the imprimatur of Archbishop Corrigan, who said Hecker's funeral Mass, and with a characteristically laudatory preface by Archbishop Ireland that portrayed Hecker as the model for the modern priest anxious to be in touch with his age, etc. The translation accentuated all this and gave some conservative French Catholics the chance they seized to attack the Americanists on doctrinal rather than on political grounds. All sides, each confident of victory, appealed to Rome, and all found some comfort in her answer.

The Papal letter *Testem Benevolentiae* was issued on January 22nd, 1899 and sent through Cardinal Gibbons to the American hierarchy. It distinguished carefully between the Americanism which referred to the general characteristics of American society and institutions, which was not under discussion, and certain doctrinal errors and tendencies against which Rome wished to warn the bishops. The basic principle of censurable Americanism was that the Church should modify her doctrines to suit modern civilization and to attract non-Catholics, passing over less attractive or important doctrines and adapting her teaching to popular theories and methods. Five points in particular were judged worthy of special mention: (1) the rejection of external spiritual direction as no longer necessary; (2) the extolling of natural over supernatural virtues; (3) the preference for active over passive virtues, a distinction the Pope rejected because there are in fact no passive virtues; (4) the rejection of religious vows as incompatible with Christian liberty; (5) the adoption of new methods in apologetics and in the appeal to non-Catholics. Though these errors were censured, the Pope did not say who held them, and he did not condemn the biography of Father Hecker.

The reaction to the papal letter was significant. The liberals, who tried hard to prevent it from being issued, insisted that it was unimportant and that no one in this country ever held such views. There were then fourteen archbishops. Three of them—Chicago, Dubuque, and Santa Fe—made no public comment of any kind. Four—Cincinnati, New Orleans, Philadelphia, and Portland—thanked the Pope for his letter but did not admit the existence of errors here. Five—Baltimore, Boston, St. Louis, St. Paul, and San Francisco—thanked him and denied the existence of the errors here. Two— Milwaukee and New York—thanked the Pope for checking the growth of the errors and thereby admitted their existence. No one defended any of the censured propositions. Some writers have referred to Americanism as a "Phantom Heresy" and suggested that it existed only in the minds of some ill-disposed and misinformed Frenchmen. That ignores the fact that the Pope issued his letter after much study and consultation, and that he sent it here instead of to France.

CHANGES IN THE CITY

While the Archdiocese was growing at a spectacular rate, the city itself was undergoing substantial and permanent changes. The population was changing in kind as well as in number. One of the major events of the time was the Jewish immigration, whose numbers increased from 60,000 in 1880 to 350,000 in 1897. Most of the Jewish newcomers came from Eastern Europe. This was the beginning of an influx that was to have an incalculable effect on every aspect of New York life. There was a remarkable growth in the size of the city, too. The first step had been taken in 1874 when the western part of the present Bronx County was taken from Westchester County and the city line reached Yonkers. When the eastern part of the Bronx was added in 1895, the city's original area had been tripled. The Bronx became a separate borough in 1898.

Serious attention was given to the city's perennial traffic problems, and two major innovations came at almost the same time. In 1900, work was started on the first subway, which had been under discussion since the successful opening of the world's first subway in London in 1863. The first one in America opened in Boston in 1897. From the beginning of the discussion, there were some who foretold disaster and were sure New Yorkers would never risk their lives on an underground train. The first automobile show in this country was held in Madison Square Garden in 1900. At that time, there were fewer than 14,000 cars in the entire country (up from 300 in 1895), and they were regarded as the playthings of the very idle rich and as a menace to the ordinary traveler. The speed limit for automobiles in the city was set at nine miles an hour in 1899, and in 1901 the City Fathers, ever alert to new sources of revenue, set a fee of one dollar for the annual license. In 1897 electric taxicabs made their appearance.

There were changes in the cultural area, too. The first college for women, Barnard, opened in 1889. Though the city had opened the first evening school in the United States in 1823 and the first evening high school in 1866, New York was the last major city in America to establish public high schools, which it did in 1897. In 1900, the entire city had about 500,000 pupils in the public elementary schools, but only 13,700 of them graduated that year. Some famous historical and cultural landmarks appeared. The Statue of Liberty, a steady attraction for tourists from the opening day, was dedicated in 1886. Carnegie Hall opened in 1891. A year later, in December 1892, the Episcopalians laid the cornerstone of their magnificent Cathedral of St. John the Divine. In 1896, Adolph Ochs bought the *New York Times,* which had a circulation of 9,000. It was to develop into the most important organ of militant secular humanism in this country. The Bronx Zoo opened in 1899. A sign of coming events was the introduction of the annual Columbus Day Parade in 1900.

Social conditions left much to be desired, and the housing situation was, as usual, very bad. In 1900, about seventy percent of the population of Manhattan (1,850,093) lived in tenements in which many paid exorbitant rents. Infant mortality was more than five times what it is today. Social legislation lagged. City workers had a ten-hour day. A law forbidding night work by women was passed in 1899, but it was declared unconstitutional by the New York Court of Appeals in 1909 on the ground that it deprived women unjustifiably of that liberty. There was great improvement in one area about which visitors had complained for almost a century after the street cleaning department was organized in 1895. It soon showed results, and every paved street in Manhattan was swept once daily, three-quarters of them were swept twice daily, and some in the heart of the commercial district five times daily. All this was done at a per capita cost of three cents weekly. The central shopping area of the city was still at 23rd Street, but the move to 34th Street had begun.

The most important and obvious of all the changes was the formation of Greater New York. This was due chiefly to Andrew H. Green (1820–1903) of Brooklyn who had been working for it since the Civil War. In May 1890 he persuaded the legislature to set up a committee, of which he became chairman, to consider the expedience of consolidating the municipalities within the present area of New York. His plan took effect on January 1st, 1898 after much opposition. Among the unrealized hopes and fears that were much discussed at the time were the domination of the State by the city, and its capture by the Republicans because of their influence in Brooklyn and Queens, a reduction of overlapping and duplication of government services with resultant economies, and a simultaneous reduction in taxes and rise in employment from which Queens and Staten Island would profit greatly. Some, dismissed as pessimists, thought that Greater New York was, and if not would soon become, entirely too big to be run competently.

New York became and remains the largest city in the country. In 1900 it had 3,437,202 people, and the population of Manhattan outnumbered all the other boroughs by a ratio of roughly nineteen to seventeen. Brooklyn, with 1,166,582, had almost two-thirds of the population of the four other boroughs. Only two counties outside the city, Westchester and Orange, had passed the 100,000 mark. Commuters were a permanent feature of life here. In 1898 there were, in round numbers, 100,000 from New Jersey, 100,000 from Brooklyn, and 118,000 from Westchester and Connecticut. The Catholic proportion in the larger city was smaller than in the old, in which they had a majority. Even then, invisible lines were recognized, for there were never more than two or three Catholics among the twenty-six members of the School Board, and it was noted that a Catholic had great difficulty in becoming the principal of a public school. The new city had over 2,000 farms that occupied almost a quarter of its area. Thirty-seven percent of the population was foreign born, and of these 25 percent were German and 22 percent Irish. There were 700,000 Jews, 145,000 Italians, and 60,000 Blacks. In that same year, 10,500,000 of the national population of 76,000,000 had been born in Europe, and 26,000,000 had been born of foreign or mixed parentage. Sixty percent of the total population lived on farms or in small towns. The first budget of the Greater New York amounted to $90,000,000. The city had a solid economic base that came to be taken for granted. In the decade from 1890 to 1900, the percentage of increase in gainfully employed persons over ten years of age was 24.7 percent in the whole country, 23 percent in New York State, and 117 percent in the city. That was the highest rate of growth it ever reached.

Archbishop Corrigan's capacity for work kept pace with the growth in the volume of archdiocesan business. He had the same number of people on his staff at the end as at the beginning. Every Friday morning, he met with the three Vicar Generals, each of whom was the pastor of a large parish. At regular and stated intervals, he received anyone who cared to come without an appointment. From his arrival in November 1880 until the appointment of his only auxiliary, Bishop Farley, in December 1895, he did practically all the confirming and performed almost all the ordinary episcopal functions. In that period, he confirmed about 194,000 people; later, his share varied from 6,000 to 9,000 yearly. He performed all the visitations in the city until 1895, and many after that. The pastor received a report in longhand shortly after each of them. The deans did the visitations in the country areas, but Archbishop Corrigan did the confirming until 1895, and some after it, so he visited every parish several times.

Though he was not a good speaker and said so, he preached in the Cathedral on the first Sunday of every month, and, of course, at all episcopal functions. He used to hope, quoting Bishop Lynch of Charleston, that "the purple will supply the deficit." It was noticed that, though he never used a manuscript when he preached, he always had one with him. In 1886 the Bahama Islands were placed in the care of the New York Archdiocese and every three years, with one exception, the Archbishop made a visitation there. Apart from those trips and long visits to Europe in 1890 and 1900, he rarely left New York except on Church business. His regular schedule alternated prayer, work, and study, and the only exercise he ever took was walking. He never kept a carriage. A pleasant break in his routine came with his Episcopal Silver Jubilee in 1898. On that occasion, the remaining debt on the seminary, $250,000, was cleared. Eloquent tributes were paid by, among others, two prominent Protestants—Elbridge Gerry (1837–1927), the outstanding spokesman for Protestant philanthrophy, and especially for the New York Society for the Prevention of Cruelty to Children, and Elihu Root (1845–1937) then Secretary of War and a future Secretary of State, Senator, and Nobel Peace Prize winner.

In spite of the limitations imposed by lack of personnel and money, the Corrigan administration made a commendable effort to keep pace with the growing needs of the Archdiocese. In April 1900, on the eve of his departure for Rome, the Archbishop issued a pastoral in which he summarized what had been done in the previous ten years. Every two weeks, from January 1st, 1890 to December 31st, 1899, a new church, chapel, school, convent, rectory, or some other charitable or religious institution had been opened. The total was over 250 buildings. One gets a glimpse of the devotional life of the people before the reforms of Pius X in the figures on the reception of Holy Communion. From February 1st, 1898 to January 31st, 1899, 2,231,947 people received Communion in the city's Catholic churches, 345,399 in the county churches, and 513,094 in the Catholic institutions. The following year brought an innovation that caused a stir, since there were still limitations on the hours at which Mass could be said. The Printers Mass, introduced to St. Andrew's Church in May 1901, was said at 2:30 A.M. every Sunday for the benefit of the printers who worked at night near City Hall. It was an instant success, soon copied in many other places. It took the Archbishop, prompted by Monsignor Luke J. Evers (1860–1924), the pastor, about four months to get permission and was apparently the first of its kind in the world. The attendance, which averaged about 1,400 a Sunday until the newspapers moved away from that area of the city, justified the innovation.

Like many others who had poor health early in life and learned to pace themselves, Archbishop Corrigan escaped serious illness until the end. In the spring of 1902, while visiting the Cathedral to inspect the progress made on the Lady Chapel, he suffered a very severe fall. Pneumonia set in but he seemed certain to recover, and had already received a cablegram from the Pope congratulating him on having done so, when his heart failed. He died swiftly and painlessly on the evening of May 5th, 1902 and was buried in the Cathedral. The immense crowds that turned out for the wake and funeral were an impressive rebuttal of the charge that he had alienated the ordinary people. Among those who visited the Archbishop's house to pay their respects before the body was moved to the Cathedral for the public wake was Bishop Potter of the Episcopal Diocese of New York. He described

Archbishop Corrigan as a dear friend and an underestimated man whom he had found brilliant and entertaining in private conversation. In the unavoidable absence of the Apostolic Delegate, Archbishop Martinelli, the funeral Mass was sung by Cardinal Gibbons. Archbishop Ryan preached. Archbishop Ireland was present, as were a number of non-Catholic clergymen. Bishop Farley was on a pilgrimage to Lourdes and was unable to be present. A wreath from President Theodore Roosevelt was placed near the coffin, and the simple Latin inscription on his tomb described the Archbishop as a "staunch defender of Christian Education."

The extensive press coverage of the funeral, with the customary résumés of his career, contained many references to his failure to receive the red hat. Very probably this was due to his feud with Archbishop Ireland, and the strong feeling it caused in both camps. Archbishop Ireland was openly anxious to be made a cardinal, partly because he saw in that a public vindication of his policies. At various times, he and his friends invoked the aid of Presidents Harrison, McKinley, Theodore Roosevelt, and Taft. They were active too for years in opposing the promotion of Archbishop Corrigan to the College of Cardinals since that would have been interpreted as a defeat for them. In such a situation, the Roman authorities promoted neither. They were well aware of the immense progress made in New York, then clearly the most important diocese in America, under Archbishop Corrigan. They knew too the achievements of Archbishop Ireland in a necessarily smaller sphere, of the valuable service he rendered in the settlement of Church-State relations in the former Spanish Colonies, and of his support of the papal program in France. To have chosen between two such candidates would have offended a powerful faction in America and would have been interpreted as overlooking great merit in the opposing camp. To choose both did not seem possible then when the number of cardinals was limited to seventy, and the American Church was not thought entitled to three of them. It was easier and less divisive to choose neither. There is no way of knowing how Archbishop Corrigan would have fared under Pius X or how Archbishop Ireland would have fared under Benedict XV. The latter Pontiff, the most loyal disciple of Cardinal Rampolla, knew and esteemed Archbishop Ireland. In 1892, when he was Cardinal Rampolla's secretary, he had written some anonymous articles defending Archbishop Ireland's stand on the School Controversy. They appeared in the OSSERVATORE ROMANO, the Holy See's semi-official newspaper. However, Benedict XV created no cardinals during World War I which the Archbishop did not survive.

CHAPTER 10

John Cardinal Farley

Even before the death of Archbishop Corrigan, the "Accademia" had been discussing his successor and had decided to propose the appointment of Bishop James E. Quigley of Buffalo (who became the Archbishop of Chicago in 1903). On the eve of the funeral, they added the name of Bishop John L. Spalding of Peoria to their very short list of suitable candidates. They were unanimously opposed to Bishop McDonnell of Brooklyn, who had been very close to the late Archbishop. In the discussion preceding the formal voting for the three names to be sent to Rome by the irremovable rectors and the Consultors, Dr. Richard L. Burtsell (whom Archbishop Corrigan had made an irremovable rector in 1898 and a Consultor, as Dean of Ulster and Sullivan Counties, in 1901) stressed that New York belonged to the whole country and should look for the best man in it. He tried to counter the strong feeling for "home rule" by saying that any candidate they picked, no matter whence he came, would be a product of New York.

In the voting on May 22nd, the electors rejected Dr. Burtsell's arguments and put Bishop John Farley in first place with nineteen out of twenty-two votes. Monsignor Joseph Mooney was second with sixteen votes, and Dr. Patrick McSweeny was third with twelve. Then, at the suggestion of Bishop Bernard McQuaid, who presided at the meeting, those nominations were made unanimous. Bishop Farley was also the first choice of the bishops of the New York Province and of the archbishops of the United States. By early August 1902, he had heard privately of his appointment, which was announced officially on September 25th. His was the first and last case in which the procedure laid down by the Third Plenary Council of Baltimore for filling vacant sees was applied to New York. Dr. Burtsell, who had voted to put Bishop Farley first on the list, worked hard in the intervening months for Dr. McSweeny. The latter discounted Monsignor Mooney as a candidate because he expected him to be made bishop of a new diocese very soon. In 1902, as in every vacancy of New York since 1864, there were strong rumors of the see's impending division.

All factions in the Archdiocese were pleased by the appointment of Archbishop Farley, though some were surprised that one so near his predecessor in age was chosen. He received the pallium on August 12th, 1903, from Archbishop Diomede Falconio. The long delay was caused by the slowdown in Rome as the long pontificate of Leo XIII inched to its close. The Pope died at ninety-three on July 20th, and then nothing could be done until the Conclave ended on August 4th. The clergy, to whom Bishop Farley was a well-known quantity, were especially pleased by Rome's choice for New York. He was less accessible than Archbishop Corrigan had been, was more inclined to stand on his dignity in dealing with them, and some thought him occasionally arbitrary and inconsiderate in making clerical assignments, but they felt generally that they understood and were understood by him better than had been the case with his predecessor. This was due to his personality, his training, and his long apprenticeship. No other occupant of the New York see has had as much time to study it at first-hand before taking possession of it.

John Murphy Farley (April 20, 1842–September 17, 1918) was born in Newtown Hamilton, County Armagh, Ireland, in the year in which John Hughes became the Bishop of New York. He was the fourth and youngest child of his parents, who kept a small store and farm. They died when he was very young, and the support of their children devolved on John's maternal uncle, Patrick Murphy, who had come to New York in 1830 and prospered in the furniture business. John attended the local schools and St. Macartan's College, Monaghan (the preparatory seminary for the diocese of Clogher), then followed his surviving brother and sister to New York and entered St. John's College, Fordham, as a junior. There he led his class so clearly that he won eight out of nine prizes, missing only the one for religion. After one year each at Fordham and the seminary in Troy, he was sent to Rome, where he was ordained on June 11th, 1870 by Cardinal Constantine Patrizi, the Vicar of Rome. He was there during the First Vatican Council and witnessed the definition of Papal Infallibility on July

20th, 1870. He left for New York on August 1st, thereby missing the fall of Rome on September 20th.

The turning point in Father Farley's life came in July 1872 when, after two years as an assistant in St. Peter's parish on Staten Island, he became secretary to Archbishop McCloskey, whom he had met during the Council. On assuming his new position, he changed the spelling of his name from Farrelly to Farley to match the prevailing pronunciation. Henceforth for forty-six years, including sixteen as archbishop, he was near or at the very center of the administration of the Church in New York. He climbed the ladder of preferment slowly but steadily, serving as secretary (1872–1884) and as both Vicar General and President of the School Board—succeeding Monsignor Thomas S. Preston (1891–1902). He was on Cardinal McCloskey's Council and was one of Archbishop Corrigan's Consultors (1886–1902). In 1884 he was made pastor of St. Gabriel's, East 37th Street, then a flourishing parish, with a large and mixed congregation (suppressed in 1939 to make way for the Queens Midtown Tunnel). There he acquired the wide pastoral experience circumstances had denied his predecessor, and deepened the sympathy for the poor that led later to his being called the "Cardinal of the Poor."

Appropriate honors came in due course. When he became a papal chamberlain in 1884, there were only about a dozen monsignors in the country, and three of them were in New York. He became a domestic prelate in 1892, and in 1895 successively a protonotary apostolic (the highest grade of prelate below the episcopate) and a bishop. He was the first auxiliary bishop, as distinguished from a coadjutor with right of succession, appointed to New York. He was consecrated titular bishop of Zeugma on December 21st, 1895, by Archbishop Corrigan who was assisted by Bishop Charles E. McDonnell of Brooklyn and Bishop Henry Gabriels of Ogdensburg. He was the administrator of the Archdiocese from May to September 1902.

Two-thirds of John Farley's priestly life were spent in close association with his two immediate predecessors, whose personalities and careers influenced him greatly. During four of his twelve years as secretary, they shared the same house. Both men, as he saw them, were men who sincerely shunned the limelight and disliked flattery and ostentation in any form, but who had very different public images. Cardinal McCloskey combined firmness, kindness, and prudence so skillfully that he lived at peace with everyone. Archbishop Corrigan's inability to do so and his consequent difficulties, even though due chiefly to the time in which his lot was cast, strengthened in his successor an already keen awareness of the advantages of doing so. Their heir admired both of them greatly but chose the Cardinal as his model.

The dominant traits of the new Archbishop, to which he was able to give free rein, were the love of peace and an almost excessive caution. When Archbishop Corrigan died, the controversies that had divided the Church in

America during almost all of his administration had ended, and acceptable solutions had been found for all of them. The Church in America entered a period of peace and steady growth that lasted until the end of Vatican Council II. Archbishop Farley profited greatly from the change. Spared the burden of controversy, he was able to give almost all his time to the affairs of New York. He was spared too the personal friction with some of the hierarchy that had been so prominent in the Corrigan years. He was, for instance, on very friendly terms with Cardinal Gibbons whom he had first come to know when serving as a notary at the Third Plenary Council of Baltimore and as secretary to the Council's Committee for the Catholic University of America. He sought and followed his advice when offered the mitre in 1895, and always acknowledged freely his preeminence in the Church in America.

There was peace on the local scene, too. Though he had never belonged or wished to belong to the Accademia, Archbishop Farley had maintained courteous and even friendly relations with its members as far as his position and their attitude allowed. He knew they tended to dismiss him as a "company man," as they did all who failed to agree perfectly with them, but he could afford to be magnanimous. He had supported Archbishop Corrigan loyally without concealing from him disagreement with some of his actions. He had disapproved of the failure to offer Dr. McGlynn a formal hearing, and of the Archbishop's attitude toward the Catholic University, of which he himself was always a champion. He had done his best to smooth relations with Archbishop Satolli. None of this had impaired his relations with the Archbishop. When he himself became Archbishop, he determined to pour oil on troubled waters and chose what was then a novel method in this country. It was to distribute papal honors on a wide scale to priests who were not in key positions and to include all factions. Early in his administration he announced eight promotions to the rank of monsignor, including Drs. Burtsell and McSweeny, his predecessor's most unsparing critics. This popular gesture helped to heal old wounds and to forestall criticism from those who so willingly accepted unexpected honors from his hands.

There was more to the new Archbishop than caution and the love of peace. Gracious in manner and dignified in bearing though small in stature, he was a pleasing speaker and had the gift of getting on with people of all types. He spoke Italian and French fluently and read Spanish. Though scholarship was not his field, he esteemed it in others. He was an enthusiastic traveler who prepared diligently for intensive sightseeing on each trip, and he knew the religious and cultural significance of each place he visited. He had a wide range of interests and a correspondingly wide range of contacts that included many non-Catholics. He was an able administrator, a hard worker, and a successful fund raiser. Above all, he was a man who enjoyed his position, accepted the responsibilities that went with it, and took an obviously genuine and deep interest in the problems and programs it entailed.

Since he knew the Archdiocese so well, no time had to be spent mastering the details before he could act. He knew New York was a well-organized, dynamic archdiocese. He knew too what needed to be done, what resources were available, and which collaborators he intended to use. He kept all Archbishop Corrigan's officials with whom he had worked for years, and he added three on whom he came to lean very heavily and who played prominent roles in New York for the rest of their lives. They were, in the order of seniority, Fathers Michael J. Lavelle, Patrick J. Hayes, and John J. Dunn. All three were native New Yorkers.

Michael J. Lavelle (1856–1939) was ordained at St. Joseph's Seminary in Troy on June 7, 1879, and assigned at once to the new Cathedral which had been dedicated on the preceding May 25th. There he spent his entire priestly life and was rector from May 1887 on. He was made a domestic prelate in 1904. For more than half a century, he was one of the most prominent priests in New York. He was much in demand as a speaker at both religious and civic affairs, was chairman of innumerable committees, and indefatigable in his attendance at functions of every kind. He was very popular with the clergy, who found him kind, approachable, and understanding, and always ready to fill in without notice if anything prevented the appearance of the scheduled speaker of the day. He was deeply devoted to Archbishop Corrigan, with whom he had worked closely and who had wished to make him a bishop. He was Vicar General from 1902 to 1918, succeeding the Archbishop in that office, and from 1934 to 1939. He founded the Lavelle School for the Blind and was active in the affairs of the Catholic Summer School at Plattsburg from 1892 until his death.

Patrick J. Hayes (1867–1938), the future Cardinal, was ordained in September 1892 at Troy. He became Bishop Farley's secretary in 1895 and Chancellor of New York when Father Colton became Bishop of Buffalo in 1903. He became a domestic prelate in 1907. He came to be so closely identified with Archbishop Farley that even seasoned observers wondered occasionally which of the two was really responsible for certain decisions.

John J. Dunn (1869–1933) was ordained at Troy in 1896, a member of the last class ordained there. He became the first full-time archdiocesan Director of the Society for the Propagation of the Faith in 1904, and was made Chancellor in 1914. He retained a lifelong interest in the missions. He was regarded as a vigorous, capable, shrewd, hard-headed man with sound practical judgment and a good head for business. He was made a papal chamberlain in 1912.

The program of the Farley administration was much the same as that of the previous administration because both faced the same conditions and problems. It coincided almost exactly with the largest wave of legal immigration in the history of the country. Since a very high percentage of the immigrants came through New York, the Archbishop had to give special attention to them and to the need for more churches and schools occasioned by the immigrants who remained in the city.

The years 1901–1910 brought 8,795,386 immigrants, the largest number ever to come in a single decade. The number passed the million mark for the first time in 1905, and 1907, the year in which immigration reached its peak, brought 1,285,349. Between 1911 and 1920, in spite of the interruption of World War I, 5,735,811 immigrants arrived, the second highest number for a single decade.

The Italians were the largest contingent among the new arrivals between 1901 and 1910, a total of 2,045,877 for that period, compared with the 705,408 who came between 1889 and 1900 (of whom 682,134 came through New York), and the 1,109,484 who came between 1911 and 1920. Nor were the Italians the only large contingent. The influx of Jews from Eastern Europe, chiefly from the Russian Empire, continued and increased. In New York City alone, their numbers increased from 350,000 in 1898 to 672,000 in 1905, and to 1,550,000 by 1912. In 1890 they represented 12 percent of the population and, in 1920, 29.2 percent.

That most of the immigrants were birds of passage as far as New York was concerned is clear from the figures on the actual growth of the city in those years. The population grew from 3,437,202 in 1900 to 4,766,883 in 1910 and 5,602,048 in 1920. In 1910 there were 1,900,000 foreign-born residents (of whom 422,000 could not speak English) and 1,800,000 children of foreign-born parents. There were also 91,000 Blacks and 6,100 Orientals. Though substantial in itself, the increment of 2,164,846 in the city's population between 1900 and 1920 was small in comparison with the number of immigrants during the same period. Moreover, much of the city's growth was due to natural increase and to the steady stream of newcomers from other parts of the country. In 1907 the birthrate was 34.5 per thousand, the highest ever recorded in the city.

Immigration

If the estimates for the Archdiocese itself are even approximately correct, its growth was not impressive and was certainly the smallest in percentage under any bishop to that time. It increased by only 20 percent or about 200,000. This was due in part to a changing pattern of growth in the city itself. Though few noticed it at the time, a significant and long-term change started in Manhattan, which had led all the other areas within the present city limits in growth since 1790. While Manhattan grew by 434,000 to 2,284,103 in 1920, it passed its peak in 1910 and began a decline that, with the single exception of a slight gain in the decade 1930–1940, has lasted to the present day. By 1913 the pattern of flight from Manhattan was firmly established.

The growth of the Bronx, where the population more than trebled between 1900 and 1920, going from 200,507 to 732,016, and on Staten Island, which went from 67,021 to 116,531, did not match the growth of Brooklyn, which went from 1,166,582 to 2,018,356, a gain of 851,774, and Queens which went from 152,999 to 469,042, a gain of 360,043. This was the first phase of a continuing development which was to bring the four counties of Long Island, now divided into the dioceses of Brooklyn (Kings and Queens) and Rockville Centre (Nassau and Suffolk), a notably higher Catholic population than the Archdiocese of New York. In the seven suburban or rural counties of the Archdiocese, there was no substantial growth except in Westchester, which went from 146,777 to 344,436. Putnam and Ulster counties declined between 1900 and 1920, and Rockland, Sullivan, Ulster, and Putnam declined from 1910 to 1920. In Dutchess and Orange the growth was only marginal.

The care of the Italians involved bringing more priests from Italy and persuading more of the religious orders to staff parishes for them. The great majority of Italian immigrants continued to come from southern Italy. From 1881 to 1910, about 75 percent of them were men who either were yet unmarried or who came without their families in the hope of earning enough money to send for them. Most of them (75 to 90 percent) were unskilled workers, many of whom were taken advantage of shamefully by employers who included some of their compatriots. In 1903 there were eighteen Italian parishes, six of which had schools. They were served by fifty-two priests, and claimed a membership of 133,000. By 1918 there were thirty-eight parishes (fifteen outside the city) and thirteen chapels, served by seventy-four diocesan priests and fifty-seven priests from religious orders. There were thought to be about 500,000 Italians in the Archdiocese, with a total of about 1,050,000 Italians in the area that included New York plus the dioceses of Brooklyn, Newark, and Trenton. About half the Italians in the country were in the Middle Atlantic States. Of the remainder, there were 15 percent in New England and about 15 percent in the North Central States.

The Liberal Catholics were not the only ones anxious to bring about the instant Americanization of the Italians. Several Protestant groups and especially the Presbyterians were active among them. They were convinced that both the country and the Italians would be better off if the latter were assimilated quickly and totally. They thought the best way to achieve that was "to Christianize" them by bringing them into the mainstream of American Protestantism. At the same time, and from the opposite side, the Socialists tried hard to make converts among them. The available figures indicate that only a fractional percentage of them were won by either group.

There were other ethnic groups that also needed help from the Church. By 1902 a dozen different nationalities had their own churches in the city. Between 1902 and 1918 inclusive, sixty-eight parishes and about thirty chapels were opened. Of the total, about one-third were for the Italians. Of the twenty-three parishes opened in Manhattan, sixteen (of which seven were Italian) were national, whereas from 1880 to 1902 eighteen out of thirty-eight were national. Of thirteen new parishes in the Bronx (none of which was opened after 1912), three were Italian. Of five on Staten Island, two were Italian. The rest were in the counties.

CATHOLIC EDUCATION

If Archbishop Farley had been able to choose just one field of action and to concentrate all his energies on it, he would surely have chosen education, which he supported on every level. In his first two years he opened twenty-six parochial schools and in the first five years, thirty-eight schools with 14,000 pupils. By 1918 he had opened fifty, and the enrollment had doubled. He welcomed the opening of New Rochelle College by the Ursulines in 1904, of Mount St. Vincent College by the Sisters of Charity in 1910, and of Manhattanville College by the Sacred Heart nuns in 1917. New Rochelle was the first Catholic college for women in New York. The first in the country was Notre Dame, Baltimore, which was chartered in 1896. He was pleased, too, when St. John's College became Fordham University in 1904.

He did not forget secondary education. Though the modern trend to high school education for all who qualify and to college education for millions of students (both young and old) had not started, the first fifth of this century saw a steady increase in the number of people able and willing to send their children on for post-elementary studies. There had always been a fair number, and their needs had been met by the private academies that replaced the Latin grammar schools of colonial days. In New York State there were nineteen academies in 1800, and by 1850 there were eighty-seven, with 49,328 pupils. These figures do not include the Catholic schools. The public high school met and stimulated a demand it did not create, and by its existence it accelerated the standardization of the existing academies that had been under way for some time.

In the beginning, the academies in New York State were incorporated individually by the Legislature, but in 1875 they were transferred to the jurisdiction of the Regents, who were authorized to charter and supervise them. At that time, there were wide variations in the program of studies, the length of the course, and other basic items. Gradually, standardization was imposed. A notable step was the introduction of the Regents Examination in 1878. Another, in 1895, was the recommendation, in fact the imposition, of a four-year course. Other regulations on the length of the school year, the equipment of the buildings, the qualifications of teachers, and on the number and content of the courses followed. The general high school as we know it took shape and seemed to have been there always. Other developments which had a marked effect on the private academies were the establishment of the Middle States Association, which admitted high schools in 1892, and the introduction of the College Entrance Examinations in 1901.

By 1902, the Archdiocese of New York was reasonably well equipped on the secondary school level. The number of private academies had risen from fewer than twenty in 1865 to more than forty in 1900. The number of pupils in 1902 is hard to determine because many of the girls academies had elementary departments and did not separate the two departments when reporting their enrollment, but by 1908 the high schools alone had 3,736 girls. There were more girls than boys in the system. In 1902 there were only 2,652 students in the three colleges for men and the six high schools for boys in the Archdiocese. In the same year, there were only 6,900 pupils in the public high schools in Manhattan, the Bronx, and Staten Island, and only 1,000 graduates from all the public high schools in the city. All the Catholic academies were run by religious communities and all of them had to charge tuition. All of them were able to adopt their course of study to meet new needs and standards, and all of them had as many pupils as they could accommodate. On the secondary level, the bulk of the work among the boys was done by the Jesuits and the De La Salle Brothers. Strangely enough, only one teaching order of men, the Marist Brothers, which opened St. Ann's Academy in 1892, came to New York between 1848 and 1903. The bulk of the work among the girls was done by the Sisters of Charity, which had ten academies. The Farley years brought re-enforcements on the secondary level from, among others, the Augustinian Fathers (1903), the Christian Brothers of Ireland (1906), the Holy Child Sisters (1904), the Religious of the Sacred Heart of Mary (1915), and the French Ursulines (1912).

The growth was in kind as well as in numbers. The Farley administration brought three special schools, each of which was a first in New York. One was the Cathedral Girls High School which opened on a very modest scale as a parochial high school in 1905. It did not charge tuition and, in its opening years, had to beg for pupils. The first parochial high school in New York was short-lived. It was St. Gabriel's, which was chartered in 1894, and had the full four years in 1898. When it opened it had a total of 1,485 pupils on both the elementary and academic levels. The rapid changes in the neighborhood led to the closing of the high school department in 1912. It charged tuition. The first central Catholic High School was opened at St. Peter's, Staten Island, in 1915. It was nominally a parochial high school but was intended from the very beginning to serve all the Catholics on Staten Island who could not afford the private high schools. The third special school was Regis High School for Boys which was opened by the Jesuits in 1914. It was and is the only strictly scholarship school maintained by the Church in New York and is tuition free. Its existence is due to the princely munificence of private benefactors.

CATHEDRAL COLLEGE

Archbishop Farley's major contribution to the Catholic school system in New York was the opening of the preparatory or minor seminary, Cathedral College, in September 1903. Although he is rightly considered the founder of the College, it is certain, as he himself made clear, that the plan and most of the preparatory work were due to Archbishop Corrigan, whose untimely death delayed the opening for a year. Clerical education was the dominant interest in Archbishop Corrigan's life because he saw how intimately it was linked with the shortage of priests that underlay so many of his other problems. He had turned his attention first to the new major seminary at Dunwoodie, which was incorporated on February 11, 1886, but all along he had both institutions in mind.

Planning Dunwoodie, a very much larger project, was easier in some ways than planning the College. For the former, once he had secured the Sulpician faculty, the chief task was raising the money and supervising the erection of the building. The Archbishop knew exactly what kind of a seminary he wanted, and if any problem arose he had only to consult the decrees of the Council of Trent and the subsequent decisions of the Roman Congregations. Things were different with Cathedral College. The Third Plenary Council of Baltimore had lengthened the major seminary course to six years, adding a year each of philosophy and theology to make them two-year and four-year courses respectively. It had also prescribed six years' study before entry to the major seminary but had not laid down a uniform standard. Trent had recommended a boarding minor seminary in which the students made all their preparatory studies from a very early age, but this plan had never been realized on a large scale beyond the confines of the Latin world.

There were practical objections to a boarding school, including the great expense entailed, but the Archbishop and his advisers rejected it on more serious grounds. They believed the complete separation at an early age from their families and all normal social ties, which is part of the Continental system, would deprive the students of training and experience necessary both for their own proper development and for their understanding of the people with whom they would have to deal later when they were priests. There was the added danger that they would lack a sense of responsibility and initiative; there was danger too that vocations nurtured in such a hot-house atmosphere would be unable to withstand the burdens of the active ministry in a largely non-Catholic society.

Finding a faculty and a site for the new school was easy. The Roman Catholic Orphan Asylum moved in 1902 to Kingsbridge in the Bronx, evacuating the block from Fiftieth to Fifty-first Street and from Madison to Fifth Avenue. The Archbishop bought the block front on Madison Avenue for $350,000, and the trustees of the Asylum donated the block-long building formerly occupied by the Boland Trade School. Father Patrick Hayes, who suggested the name Cathedral College, was appointed president. He was assisted by five diocesan priests and three laymen, and the College opened with fifty-five students. The faculty was always drawn from the diocesan priesthood, but frequently had help from religious order men and always included some laymen. Since Father Hayes continued to be Chancellor, and the building was large, the Chancery and a number of other diocesan offices shared it with the College. It was convenient to have the students so near the Cathedral, where they could be trained in the liturgy.

The curriculum was largely determined by the decrees of the Third Plenary Council of Baltimore. Religion was given the primary place followed closely by Latin and English. Each student had to acquire at least one foreign language and enough Greek to be able to read the New Testament. History (sacred and profane, with special attention to American history), mathematics and science came next. Finally, plain chant and bookkeeping were included, and the students were to be schooled carefully in etiquette and decorum. The schedule was exacting and was intended to be. The students were trained to meet the standards of both the ecclesiastical and the civil authorities, neither of which could be sacrificed for the other. There was a conscious attempt to meet the standard expressed by Pius XI in 1935: "The priest must be at least as well educated as the well-educated laity of his time and place." The student body grew quickly and the first alumni to reach the priesthood were ordained in 1913. Until very recent years, the College supplied the great majority of the diocesan priests for New York.

THE MAJOR SEMINARY

Archbishop Farley took almost as much interest in Dunwoodie as Archbishop Corrigan had done. He had shared in planning it from the very beginning, had worked hard to raise the necessary funds, and had been the active leader of the successful drive to liquidate the debt on the occasion of Archbishop Corrigan's Episcopal Silver Jubilee. Since the seminary was so new and so well equipped not much could be done to the building, but in 1907 a new wing accommodating fifty students was added. It had been planned by Archbishop Corrigan, who had been discussing it within an hour of his death. It was made necessary by a gratifying increase in the enrollment. The ninety-six students, with eighty-four for New York, of the opening day had grown by 1902 to 155, with 142 for New York. By September 1918 there were 267, with 237 for New York. Moreover, the clergy shared in the increasing life expectancy of the general public, which went from 50.23 in 1900 to 56.34 in 1920. This gave the Archbishop, who loved minor economies, a chance to abolish the custom of giving a new set of breviaries to each priest who reached the silver jubilee of his ordination. He said they were becoming too numerous. He also erected at the seminary an imposing statue of Christ the Light of the World as a personal tribute to his predecessor.

The changes in the seminary faculty were more important. From the beginning, the Sulpicians were short of men and had been unable to supply the full faculty. They had been helped by diocesan priests, including some of the Troy faculty, but the administration was entirely in their hands. There was an impression that the Archbishop was less enthusiastic about them than Archbishop Corrigan had been, and that a major reason for sending several young priests away for higher studies was his anticipation, if not his actual desire, that the Sulpicians would soon have to withdraw because of lack of numbers.

They were under heavy external and internal pressure at that time. They were a small community centered in France, with solid foundations in Canada and America. In France, the bitter dispute between the Church and the Third Republic which had been going on for years reached its climax between 1905 and 1908 and resulted in the breaking of diplomatic relations with the Holy See, the denunciation of the Concordat under which the Church received substantial financial support, the suppression of all religious orders engaged in teaching, and a wholesale confiscation of Church property which involved the seizure of the seminaries. The spirit in which these changes were brought about was well expressed by René Viviani, then Minister of Education, who told the Chamber of Deputies, on November 8, 1906: "Together and with a magnificent gesture, we have extinguished the lights in heaven, lights which none will ever be able to rekindle." Internally, the Sulpicians were threatened by the lack of vocations here and even with the breaking away of their North American provinces. This was due at least partly to the great and perhaps excessive caution they showed in giving some of their members permission to publish the results of their studies. That in turn was due to the danger presented by the Modernist Movement which flourished mainly in France and Italy, with small groups in England, Germany and America, in the latter years of Leo XIII, and the first years of Pius X.

Modernism, which affected the Protestants more than the Catholics, was an aspect of the then contemporary attempt to reconcile Christianity with the very latest developments in science, history, philosophy, and biblical criticism, with special emphasis on the last. The perennial difficulty of striking just the right balance led some Catholic scholars to concede too little and others to concede too much to the new learning. A distinguished French historian, Adrien Dansette, says of the latter group that "carried away by their anxiety to bring traditional and modern outlooks into harmony, or convinced of the superiority of the modern attitudes, [they] were inclined to abandon tradition without considering the risk that they might be sacrificing the fundamentals of Catholicism. A work of adaptation had been transformed into one of demolition."

The Modernists were not an organized group with a single center and a definite doctrine and program, and they were never numerous. They attracted mainly intellectuals and semi-intellectuals and had no contact with or influence among, and really no interest in, ordinary people. Most of the Catholic scholars were not Modernists and many of the Modernists were not scholars. They represented a spirit or temper of mind. The encyclical that

Above, Pope Pius VII, founder of the Diocese of New York, 1808; at *right*, Richard Luke Concanen, the first bishop, 1808-1810.

John Connolly, second bishop of New York,
1814-1825.

John Dubois, third bishop, 1826-1842.

5

John Hughes, coadjutor bishop of New York, 1838; fourth bishop of New York, 1842; first archbishop of New York, 1850-1864.

6

St. Patrick's Old Cathedral, Mott Street. An illustration from the *New York Mirror*, 1830.

7

John Cardinal McCloskey, coadjutor bishop of New York, 1844; bishop of Albany, N.Y., 1847; archbishop of New York, 1864-1885; created the first American cardinal, 1875. A painting by G. P. A. Healy.

8

Above, Sister Irene, S.C. *Below*, the New York Foundling Hospital which she established, 1869. *On opposite page, above,* Father John C. Drumgoole, founder of Mount Loretto Home for Children. *Below*, Father Edward McGlynn.

9

10

11

12

Michael Augustine Corrigan, bishop of Newark, N.J., 1873; coadjutor
bishop of New York, 1880; archbishop of New York, 1885-1902.

13

John Cardinal Farley, auxiliary bishop of New York, 1895; archbishop of New York, 1903-1918; created cardinal, 1911.

14

Patrick Cardinal Hayes, auxiliary bishop of New York, 1914; archbishop of New York, 1919-1938. He is shown here with Governor Alfred E. Smith.

15

In the picture *above*, Francis Spellman, then auxiliary bishop of Boston, is seen at the left in 1936 on a visit to Mount Vernon, Virginia. With him, from left to right, are Count Enrico Galeazzi, Monsignor Vagnozzi, a guide, the then Cardinal Pacelli, and Archbishop Cicognani. *Below*, as cardinal and archbishop of New York (1939-1967), Cardinal Spellman is seen with Archbishop Angelo Roncalli (Pope John XXIII, 1958-1963) at Istanbul, Turkey, in 1943.

16

17

Cardinal Spellman, with General Mark Clark and King George VI of
England at the war front in Italy, 1944.

condemned them was the first systematic statement of their teaching, and it is probable that not one of them accepted all the doctrines it condemned. Three things that most of them shared were a strong dislike of authority in the Church, an equally strong contempt for the intellectual capacity and attainments of the vast majority of their fellow Catholics, clerical or lay, and a high and unwavering regard for "the modern mind" which was normative for them. They were fond of dismissing Pius X as "the peasant Pope" or "the parish priest of the Vatican," and thought him incapable of understanding the complex religious issues on which they felt they had special insights.

It was improbable from the beginning that such views and attitudes would be tolerated for any length of time by the new Pope. The wholly unexpected election of Cardinal Sarto of Venice, which surprised him as much as everyone else, brought the Church one of the strongest and most capable rulers in its history. In his stormy and fruitful pontificate (1903–1914), Pius X, who was canonized in 1954, made more changes in the inner life and administration of the Church than any Pope since the Council of Trent (1545–1563). He gave the Roman Curia the greatest shakeup it has received since its main lines were drawn permanently by Sixtus V in 1588. The founding of the Biblical Institute, the beginning of the codification of Canon Law (a project completed after his death), the emphasis on proper catechetical instruction, and the reform of liturgical music through the revival of Gregorian Chant were major events. He is remembered especially for the decrees on Frequent Communion (1904) and early First Communion for children (1910).

In all his actions, Pius X was motivated by a deep pastoral concern for the ordinary people from whom he came and among whom he had spent his entire priestly life. Though he was born an Austrian subject, he had never been out of Italy, and he did not speak French. He knew little of diplomacy, which he neither ignored nor disdained, but put very definitely in second place. His pastoral approach explained his firm refusal to compromise with the avowed enemies of the Church in France and elsewhere, or to tolerate false teaching, especially in the seminaries. Faithful to the ancient Roman tradition, he gave doctrinal purity top priority. He was never deflected from his goal by criticism from circles inside or outside the Church that he felt would be in opposition anyway. When he died, *The Times* (London) described him as a man who knew how to exercise authority and to exact obedience. He knew how to be kind and patient but, when the time for action came, he knew how to be firm and thorough. This was shown in his handling of the Modernists.

They were more important because of the attention they received from the press—both Catholic and non-Catholic—than because of their doctrines, which were not really new. After all, they were neither the first nor the last to attack all or some of the basic doctrines of the Church, each of which has been denied by many since it was first taught. Even their then advanced views on Scripture were not original with them but were derived from the non-Catholic

Scripture scholars of the time. What was new and startling about them (for most of those concerned) was that such views were taught openly and with apparent impunity by priests in good standing. That was the main reason why they were so newsworthy.

Other reasons for the favorable publicity they received were their literary gifts and the ability to attract disciples shown by several of their members. Two who were outstanding will do as examples.

Alfred F. Loisy (1857–1940) was a distinguished French scholar who taught Hebrew and Scripture for many years at the *Institut Catholique* in Paris, from which he was dismissed in 1893. He was recommended to Archbishop Ireland in 1894 as "the outstanding scripture scholar in the Church." He was a polished and prolific writer and a tireless correspondent who kept in touch with a wide circle of admirers for whom he provided a center. Most of them remained loyal when several of his books were put on the Index in 1903. George Tyrrell (1861–1909) was born in Ireland and became a Catholic in England in 1879. A year later, he entered the English Province of the Jesuits where he became known as a facile and persuasive writer on religious topics. He was not really a scholar but he associated with and was esteemed by many who were, and he too had a wide circle of devoted followers.

Though the Modernist crisis was a major problem for the Church in those years, it would have passed New York by like a storm on another planet if, in January 1905, three members of the Dunwoodie faculty had not asked the Archbishop for permission to found a theological journal. It was to be called the *New York Review* and edited at Dunwoodie. They pointed out correctly that there was no scientific theological journal published in this country under Catholic auspices. The issues that were causing so much trouble in other countries were, or soon would be, felt here, and there was need of such a publication to deal with them. It was hoped that it would attract a readership large enough to make it self-supporting.

The Archbishop, putting his habitual caution aside for the first and last time, approved enthusiastically. He said he had long regretted the backwardness of Catholic writers here in matters of modern scientific interest and attributed it partly to excessive censorship. He was proud to have such a journal connected with Dunwoodie and warned that because of that connection it must be very good. He thought it was worth trying even if it failed. The Sulpician superiors, more keenly aware of the gathering theological storm in Europe, were less enthusiastic. Their chief concern was to insure that their Society had no responsibility for the new review. They wondered what the Archbishop's reaction would be if criticism became too loud and if a hint of disapproval came from Rome.

The Archbishop's support of the new project was due in part to his confidence in the exceptional men who were to be in charge of it. They were Fathers James F. Driscoll, Francis P. Duffy, and John F. Brady. James F.

Driscoll (1859–1922), the editor, studied in Montreal, Paris, and Rome before being ordained for his native diocese, Burlington, Vermont, in 1887. A year later, he joined the Sulpicians for whom he taught in Montreal, Dunwoodie, Washington, and Baltimore before returning to Dunwoodie as Rector in 1902. He was a devout, courteous, self-effacing man who was respected and liked by his students. He followed theological developments in Europe closely and was a personal friend of Loisy and Tyrrell. The latter, who dismissed American Catholic scholars as "crude" and lacking "culture and learning," thought him the best theological thinker in America at that time. Dr. Driscoll had close contact with a number of non-Catholic scholars in New York and lectured occasionally at Columbia and the Union Theological Seminary.

Francis P. Duffy (1871–1932), the associate editor, was born in Canada and educated on scholarship at St. Michael's College, Toronto. After his ordination in Troy in September 1896, he studied at the Catholic University in Washington before joining the staff at Dunwoodie. His early education was interrupted by poverty, and at thirteen he had to work for some time in a sawmill. He was an industrious, versatile, gregarious, and enthusiastic man with a strong character, a most winning personality, and the gift of leadership. Dr. Edward Dyer, S.S., the first Rector of Dunwoodie, described him as "one of the most efficient men" he had ever seen at work in a seminary—"near enough to the ideal professor and director to be it." He lacked the deep scholarship and solid foundation of Dr. Driscoll, but was a more successful teacher because he had the gift for inspiring and sustaining enthusiasm in his students. The influence his character and personality had on them foreshadowed his success later as chaplain to New York's 165th Regiment (the old 69th) in France in World War I, where he acquired a legendary fame. He received the Distinguished Service Cross and Medal, the Croix de Guerre, and the Legion of Honor. He died as pastor of Holy Cross Church on West Forty-second Street, and to date is the only Catholic priest whose statue has been erected on public property in the City of New York. His personal following was second only to that of Dr. McGlynn and, unlike the Doctor, he seemed to have had no enemies.

John F. Brady (1871–1940), the managing editor, was less conspicuous than his colleagues. He was born in New York City, graduated from Xavier College, and finished his medical studies before entering the seminary, where he was ordained in September 1898. After further studies in Washington, he was assigned to Dunwoodie where he served as vice-rector and a professor for many years. Though not a richly gifted man, he made his mark through his manifest strength of character, stability, and balanced judgment. He was an excellent example of the type the seminary hoped to produce, and from 1916 until his death was an outstandingly successful pastor at St. Francis de Sales, East Ninety-sixth Street. He had already founded the *Homiletic Monthly,* a trade journal for the parochial clergy, when the *New York Review* was started, and he was the only one of its editors with previous editorial experience.

The editors of the *New York Review* were understandably anxious to attract readers by publishing articles by or on famous authors and on the more important and controversial topics that were being discussed in theological circles in Europe. Unfortunately, most of the widely publicized authors and the topics they discussed were precisely the authors and topics being watched with increasing concern and suspicion by the Roman authorities. Not to have discussed them or published anything by them would have denied the latter part of the editors' claim to be publishing "A Journal of Ancient Faith and Modern Thought." To discuss and publish them, as their writings became ever more evidently incompatible with Catholic teaching, would have been to deny the first part.

Moreover, the financial support expected from a growing number of subscribers was not forthcoming. Taking those factors and the recent developments in Rome into account, it was decided to cease publication with the end of the third volume, in June 1908. The editors made it clear that the decision was theirs, that financial reasons were the chief ones, that the Roman authorities had not asked or ordered the closing, and that no one connected with it, and no article in it had been condemned by Rome. Looking back they could see that while the need was genuine, the project was sound, and the prospects seemed bright, their timing was bad.

While the *New York Review* was absorbing much of their attention, the editors were affected by important developments in Dunwoodie and Rome. In January 1906 the Sulpician Superior in America, Dr. Dyer, was distressed to receive a letter informing him that five out of the six Sulpicians at Dunwoodie were leaving the Society, and intended to accept Archbishop Farley's invitation to join the Archdiocese and continue teaching at Dunwoodie. They said that nothing would be changed in the existing order in the seminary, and that they were leaving then because it was the least inconvenient time for all concerned to make a change that was bound to come eventually. They added that they wished to avoid introducing a third element of division among the clergy which would come if there were three groups of alumni, the Trojans, the old Dunwoodians, and the new.

The Sulpicians could hardly help regarding this move as "a very grievous and unmerited wrong" and an unfriendly act, especially as it came so near the impending disaster in France, but they admitted the Archbishop did not regard it as such. He said he could not make the Dunwoodie Sulpicians remain in the Society; that, if they were to leave Dunwoodie, neither he nor the Sulpicians could replace them at once; that the seminary could not be run with so many vacancies on the faculty, and that closing it was unthinkable. He would have welcomed having the Sulpicians retain charge of the spiritual direction and the discipline of the house on a permanent basis. They preferred to sever all links, and Dunwoodie passed to and has remained under the direct control of the Archbishop.

The news from Rome was more momentous and made a deeper impact. The long-expected reaction to the Modernists came at last and was all the more severe for having been delayed so long. On July 4, 1907, the Holy Office issued the Decree *Lamentabili* in which sixty-five erroneous teachings of the Modernists were set forth and condemned. On September 8th, this was followed by the Encyclical *Pascendi,* a lengthy analysis of Modernism itself accompanied by precise instructions on eliminating it and all who favored it from the seminarians and theological faculties. It also tightened the censorship. It was a highly technical document that required a careful and expert interpretation which it failed to receive in many quarters. It was greeted by a storm of protest in the non-Catholic press. The Pope had discounted this in advance. Some, but by no means all, of its targets were innocent or less guilty than they seemed. Loisy and Tyrrell were excommunicated by name for attacking it and both of them died outside the Church. It says much for the personal appeal of the former that the allegiance of some of his Catholic friends survived his open admission that for many years before he was unmasked the only article of the Creed he accepted was "he suffered under Pontius Pilate." During all that time, he said Mass daily and was meticulous in performing his duties as chaplain to a Catholic school. The condemnation of Modernism was effective and it disappeared until the aftermath of Vatican II. Tyrrell appealed, in an angry letter, to Cardinal Mercier of Belgium "to let the light of a new day strike into [the Church's] darkest corners, and the fresh wind of heaven blow through its mouldy cloisters."

The new papal regulations for the seminaries, which included a tightening of the discipline, suggested a change in the rectorship, and in September 1909 Dr. Driscoll, who was not a disciplinarian, retired. He died as pastor of St. Gabriel's, New Rochelle. He was succeeded as rector by Father John P. Chidwick (1863–1935), who was ordained at Troy in December 1887 and served as an assistant at St. Stephen's (1887–1895) during the trying years after Dr. McGlynn's removal. He became a United States Naval Chaplain and was the only chaplain on the *Maine* when she sank on February 15, 1898 in Havana Harbor. He was not a scholar and made no claim to be one. The testimony of those who knew him as a naval chaplain, as a seminary rector, and as pastor of St. Agnes (East Forty-third Street), where he died, was that he was a man of radiant integrity who was very definitely a leader. In the Navy, he got along equally well with officers and men, an unusual thing, and in Dunwoodie he did the same with the faculty and students. He was not popular at Dunwoodie in the beginning because he was sent there to tighten up and the students regretted Dr. Driscoll's departure, but he came to be deeply respected. No other rector made so lasting and favorable an impression on the students of his time.

Though Archbishop Farley was disappointed by the failure of the *New York Review,* he did not lose interest in promoting scholarship. He welcomed and helped the editors of *The Catholic Encyclopedia,* the first of its kind in

English, and a major achievement at the time. It was published in New York between 1907 and 1914. The chief editors were Charles G. Herbermann (1840–1916), Condé B. Pallen (1858–1929), and Father John J. Wynne, S.J. (1859–1948). Father Wynne, a prodigious worker, was chiefly responsible for the founding of *America,* the Jesuit weekly magazine (1909–), the expansion of *The Messenger of the Sacred Heart* and the Apostleship of Prayer, the canonization of the Jesuit Martyrs of North America, and the development of their shrine at Auriesville, N.Y. The Archbishop would have welcomed the establishment of a Catholic daily paper in New York. He recognized the value and the limitations of a weekly like *The Catholic News* (1886–1981) which was founded by the Ridder family.

THREE MAJOR CELEBRATIONS

Archbishop Farley showed an unexpected flair for organizing big celebrations and had three in four years. They marked the centennial of the see, the consecration of the Cathedral, and his own elevation to the Sacred College of Cardinals. The Centennial came first. Although the actual anniversary fell on April 8th, 1808, the celebration filled the week of April 26th to May 2nd in which each day had at least one special function. Every effort was made to include as many participants as possible and to see that no group, however small and inconspicuous, was overlooked. The pioneers were not overlooked either. Their heirs were reminded of what they had suffered and were urged to "remember the early days and keep the early years in mind." In a sermon at the Cathedral, Monsignor Lavelle recalled the "No Irish need apply" signs which, as he said, really meant "No Catholic need apply." On Sunday, April 26th, a special Mass of Thanksgiving was offered in every parish and institution in the Archdiocese.

The main event of the week was the Solemn Pontifical Mass at the Cathedral, which was attended by about half the American hierarchy. The celebrant was Michael Cardinal Logue, Archbishop of Armagh and Primate of All Ireland, the successor of St. Patrick. The preacher was James Cardinal Gibbons who spoke not only as the Dean of the Hierarchy but as the successor of John Carroll, the first bishop of this part of the world. Archbishop Farley read messages of congratulation from the Pope and from President Theodore Roosevelt, made all the usual acknowledgements, and had a special word of gratitude for the cordial messages of good will from the leaders of the other religious groups in the city and for the generally fair, sympathetic, and extensive coverage given to the celebrations by the secular press. In the evening, the Apostolic Delegate presided at Solemn Vespers and Archbishop John Glennon of St. Louis, the rising orator among the bishops, preached. Both at the Mass and at Vespers the Cathedral was packed and the surrounding streets were filled by a friendly and enthusiastic crowd.

Cardinal Gibbons' sermon was, as the occasion demanded, a review of the history of the Church in New York. He paid a just tribute to the successive occupants of the see, to the clergy and religious who worked under them, and especially to the laity who cooperated so wholeheartedly with them. He stressed the difference between this country and Europe. Here, everything was supported by the people, with rare assistance from the rich and powerful. The work accomplished by the Church in New York was due chiefly to the immigrants of the preceding century. They, whom he described as a "heterogeneous and unorganized mass of Christian worshippers," would have disintegrated under adverse circumstances if they had not been "marshalled and coordinated, nourished and sustained, by the zeal and piety of a devoted and enlightened clergy."

Speaking to an audience which included Archbishops Ireland and Keane and Monsignors Burtsell and McSweeny, he described Archbishop Corrigan as "a man of many-sided attainments: so learned in speculative theology yet so practical; so courtly yet so humble; so gentle yet so strong. He was a man of most methodical habits, never wasting a minute, and was eminently conspicuous for administrative ability. In all questions affecting canon law and church history as well as the venerable traditions and usages of the Apostolic See, he was an authority and a living encyclopedia among his colleagues."

The celebrations ended with a parade on Sunday, May 2nd, in which over 40,000 men marched. They represented every area, and every male organization in the Archdiocese. The parade itself took over three-and-a-half hours to pass the reviewing stand at the Cathedral. The press commented favorably on the perfect order and great good humor of the marchers and the spectators.

The press gave wide coverage to the statistics that showed the growth of the Church here in a century. In the Archdiocese itself, there were about 1,200,000 Catholics. The imperfect figures at our disposal suggest that some 515,000 of them were born here. In very round numbers the foreign born included 300,000 Italians, 140,000 Irish, 40,000 Germans, 25,000 French, 20,000 Spanish speaking, 18,000 Bohemians, and 9,500 Poles. There were also contingents of Austrians, Belgians, Canadians, Croatians, Hungarians, Lebanese, Lithuanians, Ruthenians, Slovaks and Syrians, and there were about 5,000 converts yearly. Monsignor Lavelle said that there were seventeen languages spoken in the Archdiocese. The *New York Times* estimated that the Catholics made up about a third of the total population of the city. The Archdiocese had 317 churches, of which 179 were in the country, and 186 chapels. There were 65,152 children in the parochial schools, of whom only 6,004 were outside the city. There were 894 priests, of whom 596 were diocesan and 298 religious order men. (Statistics on Sisters are not available.) The figures for the original limits of the diocese of New York were even more impressive. The one church, three priests, one school, and 15,000 people had grown mightily. There were now eight dioceses, with 1,546 churches, 2,710 priests, 583 parochial schools with 251,383 pupils, and about 3,162,309 people.

Though the centennial celebrations were a great success and were long remembered, they left no permanent memorial. When a group of priests mentioned that to the Archbishop, he, practical as ever, was ready with a solution. He suggested that the debt on the Cathedral be extinguished so that it could be consecrated. His suggestion was so well received that in two years the entire amount, some $850,000, was raised and the debt paid. When we recall the value of money then—a recent study puts the 1977 dollar at fourteen cents in relation to the 1897 dollar—and that the money was raised without a special drive and without diverting funds from other works, it can be seen how remarkable an achievement that was. The celebration focused on a single event, the Consecration itself, which took place on October 5, 1910. This time the Archbishop himself was the celebrant, and the long, complicated but splendid ceremony was carried out to the last detail. After it, Cardinal Gibbons sang a Pontifical Mass and Archbishop Glennon preached in the presence of most of the hierarchy. The ceremony was enhanced by the presence of Cardinal Logue and Vincenzo Cardinal Vannutelli. The latter was returning from Montreal, where he was Papal Legate to the Eucharistic Congress of 1910.

The consecration of the Cathedral was intensely gratifying to Archbishop Farley for personal as well as official reasons. In his early years as secretary, he had seen the walls rise and the structure roofed. He had accompanied Archbishop McCloskey on his trips to Europe to supervise the making of the furnishings, and he had been master of ceremonies on the great day of the dedication. He had watched with the deepest interest Archbishop Corrigan's methodical completion of the interior, and he himself had the satisfaction of completing one project Archbishop Corrigan had started and another he had planned. These were the construction of the Lady Chapel, in which the first Mass was said on Christmas 1906, and the installation of electric light in 1904. Few who visit the chapel would suspect it took five years to build because the work was done so carefully and involved excavating the space occupied by the very extensive underground sacristies. The installation of electric light had been under discussion for years and had baffled the experts, who finally came up with a plan they thought gave the maximum security against fire. The consecration seemed to be the crown of all the work the Archbishop had witnessed and shared.

The third great celebration marked the Archbishop's elevation to the Sacred College, which was received with extraordinary enthusiasm here. On October 30, 1911, it was announced officially that Pope Pius X had included three American citizens among the nineteen new Cardinals who were to be created in the consistory of November 30th. They were Archbishop Farley, Archbishop William H. O'Connell of Boston (1859–1944), and Archbishop

Diomede Falconio, O.F.M. (1842–1917), who was the Apostolic Delegate here from 1902–1911. Archbishop Falconio was born and educated in Italy, where he joined the Franciscans, but was ordained in Buffalo, N.Y., in 1861 and was engaged in teaching, parish, and mission work for twenty years before returning to Italy. He had a better personal knowledge of this country when he arrived as Delegate than any occupant of his office up to the present time. Archbishop O'Connell enjoyed the special favor of the Pope and the Secretary of State, Rafael Cardinal Merry del Val. It was announced that instead of receiving the red biretta here, as had been done by Cardinals McCloskey, Gibbons, and Satolli, the new cardinals were summoned to Rome for all the ceremonies involved in their elevation. Another feature of the Conclave that was very unusual at the time was that only six of the eighteen names published were Italian. The nineteenth name, which was not published until 1914, was that of the Patriarch of Lisbon who had been exiled by the Portuguese anti-clericals.

Although by present-day standards Cardinal Farley made a very leisurely trip to and from Rome, he did not consider it such. Mindful of his student days and his trips with Cardinal McCloskey, he was glad to be able to reach Rome in only nine days. Taking Cardinal Falconio with him, he sailed for Cherbourg on a German liner on November 14th. The Germans flew the papal flag in honor of the Cardinals. It was a minor courtesy that would then have been unthinkable on an English, French, or Italian liner, a point underscored by the attention it received from the Pope in the Consistory of November 29th and from the press.

In his speech to the Private Consistory on November 27th, the Pope spoke of the suffering of the Church in Italy and Portugal, which he attributed largely to the Freemasons. He said they had engineered the fall of the Portuguese Monarchy (1910) to pave the way for an all-out attack on the Church. He spoke too of the persecution in France. In his speech on November 29th he spoke of the demonstrations of good will in New York and Boston which, he noted, were not confined to the Catholics, and referred to America as "that hospitable land which receives all the peoples of the world and with well-ordered liberty provides for the universal well-being." Cardinal Farley received the same titular church, Santa Maria Sopra Minerva, as Cardinal McCloskey. When he took formal possession of it, he recalled having been present when Cardinal McCloskey did the same in 1875. At the formal audience granted to Cardinal Farley and his party, the address of homage was read by Monsignor Burtsell.

The Cardinal's arrival in New York, after a twelve day trip from Naples, was hailed by huge crowds. His ship, which was greeted by all the ships in the harbor, docked at Hoboken, N.J. He went to the Battery at the tip of Manhattan, and thence in an open carriage, up Broadway and Fifth Avenue to the Cathedral for the solemn liturgical welcome. It was estimated that 500,000 people watched the procession and that hundreds of buildings and offices, possibly taking a leaf from the German steamship, flew the papal flag. The Cathedral itself, illuminated at night for a week with 50,000 bulbs covering the whole outline of the building, drew large crowds. In his reply to the speeches of welcome, the Cardinal stated that most of the progress of the Church in New York since 1815 was due to the sacrifices made by the poor.

A unique event in the series of festivities that marked the Cardinal's return was the dinner given in his honor by a group of distinguished non-Catholics. It was a tribute to his personal talent for getting on with people of different backgrounds and beliefs, and to the enhanced position of the Church in New York. It was held at the Waldorf on January 12, 1912. The dinner was arranged by a group of seventy-five, who had approached him before he left for Rome. Each member was allowed to bring one guest—a non-Catholic— and a small group of Catholics was invited to accompany the Cardinal. The guests represented the leadership of the business, professional, academic, and political life of the city. Mr. Oscar Straus, a former Ambassador to Turkey, spoke for the Jewish community.

The speakers included Governor John A. Dix of New York and Mayor William J. Gaynor. The Governor, speaking with the euphoria excusable on such occasions, spoke of the years since 1842 as "the grandest in the history of the world," in which "the almost incredible advances in material and scientific affairs were surpassed by the extraordinary developments in the social and moral orders." He took as one of several auguries of future blessings the improved condition of Ireland, which was "soon to receive full justice from the ancient enemy, now enlightened under the leadership of that great man of Celtic blood, the Welshman Lloyd George, assisted by a man who carries in his veins the best blood of New York, Winston Churchill." He had spoken earlier in the week of "assisting at the burial of the blue-beard of bigotry in our country." The Mayor, himself an ex-religious and a lapsed Catholic who died an Episcopalian, said, reflecting on its purpose and guest list, that it was the most extraordinary dinner ever held in New York.

President William Howard Taft sent a letter regretting his inability to attend, and praising the non-denominational character of the dinner as "an indication of the great progress which has taken place in the direction of mutual tolerance and of brotherhood among those who support and maintain different religious faiths and organizations." He added that, "in its sturdy opposition to anarchistic doctrines and its powerful support of law and order and constitutional authority, all non-Catholics may properly express a high appreciation of the good influence of the Catholic Church in our Community."

POLITICAL REFORM

In the political field, the second half of the Farley administration saw a number of reforms on the national and local levels. The Cardinal himself was so anxious to avoid involvement in politics that he never voted, but that did not mean lack of interest in what was going on. On the Federal level, there were important changes. The vanity and ambition of Theodore Roosevelt split the Republican Party in 1912 and practically handed the presidential election to the Democrats. Their candidate, Woodrow Wilson (1856– 1924), then Governor of New Jersey, won a sweeping victory in the Electoral College, but had only a plurality of the popular vote. He interpreted his victory as a mandate to promote a series of reforms that would curb the excessive influence of big business, finance, and commerce. The substantial Democratic majorities in Congress supported him and in a few years had passed the Federal Reserve Act and the Clayton Anti-Trust Act, had cut the Tariff, and had established the Federal Trade Commission. The Federal Constitution, untouched since 1869, was amended four times in six years. Two of the new amendments had passed Congress under President Taft. In 1913, the XVI Amendment, which had been proposed in 1909, was ratified. It legalized the Federal Income Tax. A proposal to limit the tax to four percent was rejected as unnecessary. The XVII Amendment, providing for the direct election of United States Senators, proposed in 1912, also took effect in 1913. The XVIII Amendment, establishing National Prohibition, was proposed in December 1917 and ratified in January 1919. The XIX Amendment, providing for woman suffrage, was ratified, after a long discussion, in August 1919.

THE CHARITIES ROW

The friendly relations with the community at large that were shown and strengthened by the Catholic celebrations were strained by the one big controversy that arose during the Farley administration. It concerned the proper relationship between the Catholic and other private charitable institutions and the city. It reflected sharply divergent views of the role of the government (local and state, for no one then dreamed of a federal role in such matters) in the relief of the poor and dealt with very sensitive issues like the proper care of orphans and abandoned children. The issues were exploited by contending political factions, provided abundant material for a sensation hungry press and for a number of bigots, and lasted several years, arousing strong feeling in every camp.

The first phase was simple enough. In 1910, the City Comptroller, William Prendergast, permitted the Bureau of Municipal Research to examine the financial records of all the private institutions in the city. The Archbishop thought the ultimate purpose of the investigation was to attack the charitable institutions. He countered by having an outside firm of auditors examine the accounts of every Catholic institution that received public funds in the years 1906 to 1909. The problem was settled in October 1912 by a compromise arranged by a group of representatives of the institutions and a group of businessmen and lawyers who proposed proper rules of procedure. A uniform system of bookkeeping suggested by the auditors who had made the survey covering 1906 to 1909 was imposed on all Catholic institutions by the Archdiocese. Until 1912, the Sisters and Brothers had received no salaries as individuals serving the institutions but were content with their keep. Henceforth, to avoid all possible misunderstanding, they agreed to accept a salary. The difference between what they were paid and what they were worth was to be considered a "donated service."

The basic problem the Cardinal faced in dealing with the many-sided problem of the charities was administrative rather than financial. They had grown in number and variety to the point where the existing supervisory machinery was clearly inadequate. There was need not only of better supervision but of coordination, direction, and planned expansion. All agreed there was overlapping and duplication in some areas, and therefore some inefficiency and waste, and that this was due only in part to the language problem. There were fields in which the Church was not represented and areas of the Archdiocese that were covered inadequately. Gradually, a consensus was formed among those in charge that what was needed was a central office with a trained staff and a central fund from which new as well as old needs could be met. These needs were easier to see than to meet, and in fact the problem was not solved until the next administration. It could not have been solved then without the experience gained by trial and error in the Farley administration, out of which came a development that was to have far-reaching consequences for the Church in New York and in the entire country.

By 1912, the Archdiocese had 122 institutions serving the sick, the aged, the handicapped, dependent children, homeless adults, and other dependents. They were supervised by priests, brothers, and nineteen communities of sisters. Their position in relation to the city varied widely. Some Catholic hospitals, eleven in all, received partial public support which covered about a quarter of their expenses. Others, eight in all, were supported entirely by their own efforts and by private charity. Some institutions, such as convalescent homes, homes for the aged, houses for immigrants, the Blind Asylum, and four settlement houses, received no public funds. Others, twenty in all, received grants for the subsistence, and in some cases for the education, of their residents. Three were homes for deaf mutes, two were reformatories for women, one a home for friendless women, and fourteen were child-caring houses.

The child-caring homes, to which children were assigned by the city courts, were paid $2.50 weekly for the maintenance of each child plus seven cents daily for each child's education and an additional seven cents if vocational training were given. In 1911, these homes received a total of $2,061,451.96 from public funds and spent $2,682,133.62. By 1908, the Catholic institutions were spending about one million dollars from private sources which, given the declining value of money, compares favorably with the present state of affairs.

Each of the Catholic institutions or charitable organizations had a loyal corps of volunteers. Some of these groups were very large, others very small. The most effective were the Society of St. Vincent de Paul, which from 1900 to 1910 was easily the most important factor in the development of organized Catholic charity in New York, the Catholic Protective Association, and the Ladies of Charity, which had been founded as the Association of Charities in 1902 but affiliated with the world-wide Ladies of Charity (centered in Paris) in 1912. The Ladies of Charity were active in a number of good works, about twenty-four in all, which were loosely federated. The Catholic Home Bureau, which placed dependent Catholic children in private homes, was the beginning in this country of the systematic placing of Catholic children.

To unify and coordinate these groups without injuring local initiative and the sense of personal involvement essential to the continuance of many of them would be difficult, but it was necessary to try. Monsignor Denis J. McMahon (1855-1915), the pastor of Epiphany parish and the supervisor of Catholic Charities for years, said that besides running his parish he had to attend over twenty-five meetings a month and carry on a voluminous but inadequate correspondence without proper secretarial help.

The Cardinal decided to try. On October 12, 1912, he held a meeting at the Astor House of representatives of societies claiming a total of more than 100,000 members. There and at a later meeting, he outlined and developed his plan. All existing organizations and charitable activities were to be kept intact but were to join an organization called the United Catholic Works. In April 1913, a bazaar and exhibition were held and an attempt was made to raise $100,000 with which to start additional day nurseries and clubs for young people. It was hoped to raise that sum yearly from 100,000 people. The drive was unsuccessful and brought in only $70,000. The plan had to be revised and the attitude of many Catholics changed before a second and successful attempt could be made.

In dealing with the Society of St. Vincent de Paul, of which he was spiritual director for many years, and in all other works of charity, the Cardinal, like Archbishop Corrigan, leaned heavily on Thomas M. Mulry (1855-1916), who was the most representative Catholic layman of his time in New York. He was an able, vigorous, and industrious man of sound practical judgment and wide vision. He was also a deeply devout, charitable, and self-effacing man who sought none of the distinctions that came his way and used them only to promote the numerous good works he found time to help. He was educated in the parochial schools, the LaSalle Academy on Second Street, and at Cooper Union. He then joined his father's successful contracting business and later became President of the Emigrant Industrial Savings Bank.

Mulry joined the Society of St. Vincent de Paul at seventeen and was an active member until his death. He was a lifelong advocate of close cooperation among all charitable groups, Catholic and non-Catholic alike, and was the first Catholic member of the Charity Organization Society (C.O.S.) founded in 1882 to bring such cooperation about. The C.O.S. helped to coordinate the activities of 138 charitable groups, including the city Department of Public Charities and Correction. He was on the New York State Board of Charities (1907–1916), was president of the National Conference of Charities and Correction, and, in 1909, was one of the committee of three appointed by President Theodore Roosevelt to organize the first White House Conference on Children. Cardinal Gibbons thought him one of the leading Catholics in America; Cardinal Farley thought him the leading Vincentian; and Archbishop Hayes described him in 1919 as the "one who had done more in the interest of Christian charity than any other American layman in his generation." His own happy family life—he was one of fourteen children and had thirteen of his own—deepened his constant interest in any and all aspects of child welfare, and he was a tower of strength to many child-caring institutions. Though Mulry was outstanding, he was not alone. Among the prominent men who often appeared as the Catholic spokesman on public occasions were John D. Crimmins (1841–1917), a successful contractor who was a consistently generous benefactor of the Cathedral, Corpus Christi Monastery, and several charities; Morgan J. O'Brien (1852–1937), a Judge of the Appellate Division; and James A. O'Gorman (1860–1943), a Judge of the Supreme Court, who became the first member of the Archdiocese elected to the United States Senate (1912–1918).

The pressure needed to convince many Catholics that a reorganization of their charities was overdue came unexpectedly from outside their ranks. It was a by-product of a local political storm, without some understanding of which the charities row is incomprehensible. From 1910 to 1918 the city lived through one of its spasmodic attempts at reform, and two successive one-term mayors, both long since forgotten, dominated the political scene. As usual, there was much to reform and the reformers were not agreed on their goals, their priorities, or the proper division of the spoils of victory.

In 1909 the Democratic leaders, well aware of the growing public impatience with their performance, astounded their followers and stole the thunder of their opponents by nominating William J. Gaynor (1849–1913) for mayor. He was a capable and abrasive man with a notably sharp tongue who had a reputation for great severity as a Supreme Court Judge and was regarded as an incorruptible political independent. The Fusion candidate, Otto T. Barnard, was a respectable man who lacked popular appeal. The race was made the most exciting since 1886 by the intervention of William Randolph Hearst (1863–1951), the famous newspaper publisher, who supported Gaynor in the beginning and then ran himself as an independent. He was an intelligent, forceful, and ambitious man who was a notoriously unreliable ally. He was also a master of invective and a top-flight journalist. The rank-and-file Democrats were not sure what kind of a Democrat Gaynor was, and the Fusionists bitterly resented his accepting the Democratic nomination. Still, their candidate was lackluster and a substantial number in all camps mistrusted Hearst. The campaign was enlivened by the latter's unsparing attacks on Gaynor who paid him back by dismissing him as "a rich young man with the face of a sheep and the eyes of a pig." On election day Gaynor got 43 percent of the vote, Barnard 30 percent and Hearst 27 percent. Gaynor was the only Democrat elected to a major post. The Democrats lost every seat on the Board of Estimate and the five Borough Presidents' posts. It meant a divided and largely paralyzed administration for the next four years.

The Democrats refused to renominate Gaynor in 1913 and chose instead Judge Edward McCall. The Mayor, who by then had succeeded in alienating every kind of organized political support, decided to run as an independent. He had been shot in the throat and wounded badly in August 1910 by a demented former employee of the city, and he had not recovered fully. Hearst, who had kept up his campaign against Gaynor, resented the charge that his action had something to do with the attempted assassination and maintained the bullet had affected Gaynor's mind, not his throat, and had had no effect whatever on the Mayor's "evil temper and lying tongue." The Fusion forces rallied behind John Purroy Mitchel, the President of the Board of Aldermen. His position was strengthened greatly by the Mayor's sudden death on September 12, 1913, and he won by the largest majority since the formation of Greater New York. He carried all five boroughs. It was a bright beginning to an unsuccessful administration.

John Purroy Mitchel (1879–1918) was born in Fordham (Bronx, N.Y.) of mixed Irish and Spanish background. His relatives on both sides were civil servants. He was educated at Fordham and Columbia and showed an interest in politics soon after finishing law school. He was an intelligent, energetic, ambitious, and notably personable man who was the youngest mayor in the history of the city, the 1913 model of the man in the grey flannel suit. Like many with similar gifts, he attracted very loyal support and was inclined to interpret all criticism as opposition. He failed to estimate correctly the magnitude, durability, and complexity of the problems he hoped to solve, and the strength of the opposition he was sure to encounter. His basic mistake was to believe that the city could be run wholly or chiefly on business lines.

In 1914 there were reasons for wishing the city could be run just that way. New York was in bad shape. The new administration found it deeply in debt and was shocked at having to pay six percent for an emergency loan from reluctant bankers. Unemployment was high and the city tried to help by establishing a temporary work program for 5,000 people in which men were paid fifty cents a day and women sixty. The public schools took 20 percent of the budget and critics pointed out that from 1903 to 1914 the school population had increased by 40 percent and costs by 60 percent. Many felt that the public school system was too independent of the mayor and the city administration and there were complaints about the Police Department.

In these circumstances, it is understandable that efficiency and economy became the watchwords of the day and that one of the first places in which they were put into practice was the Department of Public Charities. The new commissioner, John A. Kingsbury, a former general secretary of the Association for Improving the Condition of the Poor, believed sincerely that the most effective form of charity was private charity and that public assistance should be kept to the absolute minimum. His views were shared by many, including some social workers, some big contributors to charity like the Russell Sage Foundation, and above all, the Mayor, who appointed him precisely because he believed a man with such views would practice economy in that Department. A friendly critic says that the Mayor was more interested in running the charities efficiently than generously and the schools cheaply rather than well. On such matters there were, of course, many other opinions. The Catholics, having more poor and much less money, thought public assistance should be increased. Another group was not opposed to public assistance to private charities but was opposed to giving it to Church-related institutions. Others disliked giving it to Catholic institutions. Some yearned for a government monopoly which they themselves would administer and others wished to substitute philanthropy for religion.

Kingsbury (who remained Commissioner throughout the Mitchel administration) appointed an Advisory Committee which conducted an investigation of all the child-caring institutions in the city. Its report, published November 1914, approved of only twelve of the thirty-eight examined. Of the twenty-six disapproved, twelve were Catholic and fourteen Protestant. No Jewish institution was disapproved. Disapproval meant simply that the institutions in question did not meet the standards laid down by the Committee, not by the law. In most cases it was conditional and would be altered if suggested changes were made. Since each of the disapproved institutions had already been approved by the State Board of Charities, the stage was set for a conflict between the city and the State Board. In May 1915, Mitchel asked Governor Charles S. Whitman to investigate the State Board, which was accused of "laxity in the performance of its duty" and of "inspecting private institutions with both eyes closed." The Governor responded by appointing Charles A. Strong to do so.

The Strong Commission regarded its mission as two-fold: (1) to find a simplified system of control of the charitable institutions in the State; and (2) to determine the quality of the inspections made by the State Board of Charities. It held hearings from January 23rd to April 24th, 1916, in which the Kingsbury Commission had a chance to justify its charges against the State Board by proving that conditions in the private institutions were substandard. The hearings turned out to be sensational and received extensive coverage in the press, which was as usual more interested in what was charged than in what was proved. Every evening, Strong himself held a press conference in which the more serious charges were repeated and corrections and refutations were rarely mentioned.. Things were not helped by an anonymous pamphlet, collecting all the more striking headlines and critical editorials from the leading papers all through the State, which was distributed very widely. It turned out to be the work of Edward A. Moree, the Secretary of the State Charities Aid Association. It admitted that some of the charges were inaccurate and unjust.

While the Kingsbury and Strong Commissions were doing their work, important changes took place in the administration of the Archdiocese. The Cardinal's first auxiliary bishop, Thomas F. Cusack (1862–1918), had been appointed in March 1904. Though he was popular with the clergy, who admired his exceptionally strong character, his appointment was a surprise as he had never held any administrative position. He was the first Superior of the New York Apostolate (1897–1967), a band of diocesan priests who specialized in parish missions. By 1914 the Cardinal felt the need of additional help. His choice fell on Monsignor Patrick J. Hayes, who was appointed auxiliary bishop in July 1914, and was replaced as Chancellor by Monsignor John J. Dunn. In July 1915 Bishop Cusack was transferred to Albany. The Cardinal's health was then failing visibly, and, while he was kept informed of everything, the conduct of affairs passed increasingly into the hands of Bishop Hayes and Monsignor Dunn. This was true especially of the charities affair.

The Cardinal and his advisers were firmly convinced that the Strong Commission was conceived and organized to discredit private charitable institutions, especially Catholic ones, and that it was intended to pave the way for a public monopoly of charitable work that would exclude all private and religious groups. Bishop Hayes believed the essential point in the whole affair was the quarrel between the State and the city Boards of Charities, and that those engaged in it had no concern for the rights and reputations of other interested parties. He, more than Monsignor Dunn, who was more visible in it, was the guiding spirit behind the Catholic response to the Strong Commission. He freely admitted the right and duty of the public authorities to investigate the institutions and said the Church would welcome constructive criticism. He felt that much of the criticism it was receiving at that time was unfair and inaccurate. He did not claim that everything was perfect in each institution. He knew too that, while the Catholic institutions bore the brunt of the attack, they were not the only ones under fire. Bishop Burgess of the Episcopal Diocese of Long Island was sharply critical of the attacks on institutions in his care and said the false press reports were doing irreparable harm.

The Catholics' response to Strong's manipulation of the press and to the Moree pamphlet included the circulation of a series of pamphlets written in defense of the institutions, by Father William B. Farrell (1867–1930), a Brooklyn priest who had been interested in organized charity for many years. Despairing of obtaining a fair hearing from much of the press, the New York Chancery office gave out over 700,000 copies at the church doors all through the Archdiocese. Monsignor Dunn said they were issued in reply to "a malicious and scurrilous" attack on the Catholic institutions.

The Mayor took a very different view. He was convinced that the essential point in the dispute was an attempt by a small group of Catholics—among whom he was careful not to name the Cardinal or Bishop Hayes—to control or widely influence the city authorities. His emotional and ringing declaration that this would not be allowed while he was mayor, and that the city in turn would not try to influence Church affairs, brought favorable comments from some elements of the community. He came to believe, with Kingsbury, that Father Farrell did not write the pamphlets published over his name, and, in searching for proof of that, invoked a relatively new weapon—wiretapping. After their telephones had been tapped by the Police Department, he had Monsignor Dunn, Father Farrell, and several others indicted for perjury, criminal libel, and conspiracy to obstruct justice. They countered by complaining of illegal wiretapping and Kingsbury and his deputy were indicted for it. In September 1916, Judge Samuel Greenbaum dismissed all the charges brought by Mitchel as unfounded and stated that Kingsbury and his deputy were responsible for the circulation of the Moree pamphlet which contained untruthful attacks on the Catholic institutions. In another court, the wiretapping charges were dismissed because, though they were factual, there was no proof the offense had been committed with "bad faith or evil intent."

The Charities controversy died down after the Strong Commission filed a report in October 1916, endorsing the methods of the Kingsbury Commission which, it said, was trying to establish suitable standards for institutions aided by the city. It then went out of business. It had both long-term and short-term consequences. Among the former were the establishment of the Catholic Charities organization in New York that is the chief legacy of the Hayes administration, the establishment in Albany of an office maintained by all the bishops of the State to watch over Catholic interests in the Legislature, and the opening in 1916 of the Fordham School of Social Service. The short-term consequences included the black eye suffered by private religious charitable institutions, which, though painful at the time, was soon forgotten, and the Commissions' major role in ending the political career of Mayor Mitchel.

Looking back on the whole controversy on March 30, 1918 (a year-and-a-half after it had subsided), one of those most closely involved in it stressed a practical point that was generally overlooked in the excitement of the time, though it explained why conditions in some institutions were substandard. Robert H. Hebbard was the Secretary of the New York State Board of Charities during the controversy and had held that position for sixteen years.

Previously he had been New York City Commissioner of Charities for four years. He was one of those indicted with Monsignor Dunn. He spoke at the unfurling of a service flag at the Mission of the Immaculate Virgin on Lafayette Street, an institution that had been accused of allowing the children to eat from the same plates as pigs. He praised the Mission highly, spoke of the excellent annual reports it received all during his years of service, and commented that those responsible for the campaign of calumny against it allowed $2.50 weekly for the support of a child and demanded in return services that twice that amount could not provide. On the same occasion Bird S. Coler, the new Commissioner of Charities, promised to be fair and cooperative in dealing with the private institutions.

When Mitchel ran for reelection in 1917, he was better known than any of his rivals and was supported by almost the entire press, except for the Hearst papers, which then had the largest circulation. He had a few handicaps too. He had alienated the Catholics and had failed to solve any of the important problems he had inherited, his one lasting legacy being the zoning ordinance that took effect in 1916. He was blamed unfairly for the inflation that sent the cost of food up by 47 percent between 1913 and 1917. The election brought the first primaries ever held in New York. Mitchel won the Republican primary, only to have his victory overturned by the courts because of fraud, and his rival, William M. Bennett, was declared the winner. It was a bad start for a reformer. The Democrats nominated John F. Hylan (1868–1936), a non-political Supreme Court judge from Brooklyn and an ex-Republican who had no enemies. Mitchel ran as an Independent.

In spite of an endorsement by Theodore Roosevelt, who described him as "the man who now in New York stands foremost as an embodiment of true Americanism," and a campaign that stressed the patriotic theme (he claimed he was running against "Hearst, Hylan and the Hohenzollerns" to help President Wilson win the war), Mitchel was swamped by Hylan, who carried the five boroughs with a margin of at least two to one. Observers noted that Hylan's campaign cost $122,000, and Mitchel's over $1,000,000. While seeking a role after leaving office, he tried for a commission in the Air Force and on July 6, 1918, while practicing a solo flight without wearing a seat belt, fell out of his plane. He was buried from the Cathedral, to which the funeral procession marched from City Hall. It was probably the first in the city to be accompanied by an airplane dropping flowers.

SOCIAL REFORM

Social legislation, which got off to a slow start in both New York State and City, made genuine progress in the Farley years. The first Factory Act regulating the labor of women (1881) had required the owners to supply seats. In 1886 the ten-hour day for female factory workers aged twenty-one or over was introduced, and all minors under eighteen and women under twenty-one were forbidden to work more than sixty hours a week except to make necessary repairs. No child under thirteen could work in a factory at all, but this did not apply, except in the cities, to a plant employing fewer than five people. In 1903 children under sixteen were limited to nine hours a day. It was generally accepted that these laws were loosely enforced and that factory inspections were very lax. Conditions were worst in the garment industry, the city's largest, which was notorious for its sweatshops. In 1900, the International Ladies Garment Workers Union (I.L.G.W.U.) had been founded but was very weak. The police and the courts, reflecting public opinion in general, were usually hostile to strikers.

As is often the case, it took a spectacular disaster to focus public attention on the problem and to create a climate of opinion in which government officials were forced or induced or permitted to pass and enforce remedial legislation. In this instance, it was the Triangle Fire on March 25, 1911, which has often been described. The Triangle Shirtwaist Co., a well-known sweatshop, occupied the three top stories in a ten-story building near Washington Square. It had six hundred employees, mostly Jewish and Italian women and girls between thirteen and twenty-three. They had to pay for the needles they used, rent their chairs and lockers, and were fined for any damage, however slight, to the material they worked on. Just at closing time on the day of the disaster, a fire of unexplained origin broke out and in ten minutes had destroyed the premises. There was no sprinkler system, the Fire Department ladders reached only to the sixth floor and its hoses to the seventh. Many of the victims jumped in flames from the building. The death toll reached 141, of whom 125 were young girls.

Public opinion was deeply moved, both by the fire and the revelation of bad working conditions. A Legislative Commission, of which the chairman and vice-chairman were Robert F. Wagner and Alfred E. Smith, two rising young politicians, began an investigation that led later to wholesale changes in the factory code. In the meantime, in 1912, the work week for factory women was reduced to fifty-four hours, and in 1913 they were forbidden factory work from 10:00 P.M. to 6:00 A.M. One of the most surprising aspects of the whole affair was that the Triangle Company's owners, who were tried for manslaughter, were acquitted in a jury trial.

The reform movement was not restricted to politics and the labor movement. Increased attention was being given to the young people who were not problem children and to the public health. The Boy Scouts were established here in 1910 and the Girl Scouts in 1918. A great impetus was given to the camping movement. In 1907 the St. Vincent de Paul Society, which had started work on behalf of juvenile prisoners in 1904, developed the Catholic Probation League from a Boys Club. This led later to the Catholic Youth Organization (C.Y.O.). The water supply was chlorinated in 1910, and the pasteurization of milk began in 1912.

Another reform which was to spread far beyond anything foreseen in 1915 was the anti-discrimination movement. It started modestly. For a long time, there had been widespread and often open discrimination against Catholics applying for teaching positions in the public schools. This was especially true outside the city. The Knights of Columbus took the matter up in 1915, and in 1918 the New York State Legislature passed a bill forbidding discrimination in public employment by reason of race, creed, or color. It was a step forward on a long road. A more surprising and less important one was the brief appearance of the first Catholic Governor since Thomas Dongan. This was Martin H. Glynn of Albany (1871–1924), who became Lieutenant Governor on January 1, 1913 and in the following October succeeded Governor Sulzer when the latter was impeached. Glynn was defeated in November 1914. His chief claim to fame is having supplied the slogan "he kept us out of war" that played an important role in Wilson's narrow margin of victory in the presidential election of 1916. In 1910, in a still more surprising development, the second (and to date, the last) Catholic to become Chief Justice of the Supreme Court of the United States had been appointed. He was Edward Douglas White (1845–1921) of Louisiana, a former United States Senator and a Confederate veteran who had gone to war at the age of fifteen. He was appointed to the Court in 1894.

Another and less desirable development in 1915 was the revival of the Ku Klux Klan. Though it copied all the externals and the name of the Klan, it was really a revival of Nativism. The bitterly anti-Catholic spirit it represented was expressed in *The Menace,* a periodical that was circulated extensively. The Catholics responded by a huge rally in Madison Square Garden, on August 20th, 1916, at which Cardinal O'Connell, speaking in the presence of Cardinals Gibbons and Farley, spoke strongly on the full religious liberty due to Catholics under the Constitution and urged them to demand it.

THE MISSIONS

One of Cardinal Farley's major interests was the Society for the Propagation of the Faith (S.P.F.), from which his predecessors had received substantial and timely help which he was anxious to repay. Although the situation of the Church in this country was quite uneven and there were many dioceses which would welcome help from the Society for years to come, there was a growing feeling that at least some of the larger dioceses could do more for themselves and for other American dioceses as well as for the needs of the Universal Church. If they could and did, it would be welcomed warmly by Rome. In 1903 the national office of the S.P.F moved to New York from Baltimore, and in 1904 a separate archdiocesan office was founded, with Father Dunn in charge. A marked improvement became evident very soon. New York had given about $3,800 in 1903, but by 1908 it gave $70,000 and by 1918 about a quarter million. In October 1905, the Catholic Church Extension Society was founded in Chicago under the patronage of the entire hierarchy to help the home missions, especially the rural areas.

There were some who doubted that young Americans had the spirit and the stamina needed for survival in the foreign missions. Among those who were sure they had were Fathers James A. Walsh (1867–1936) of Boston and Thomas F. Price (1860–1919) of Raleigh who founded the Catholic Foreign Mission Society of America (Maryknoll) in 1911 and located its headquarters in New York. They were helped from the beginning by Mary J. Rogers (1882–1955) of Boston, the foundress of the Maryknoll Sisters of St. Dominic, who were organized in 1912 and erected canonically in 1920.

One of Maryknoll's first recruits was Francis X. Ford (1892–1952), a native of Brooklyn and a graduate of New York's Cathedral College, who entered in 1912. He was one of the small band of Maryknollers sent to China, their first mission field, in 1918. He became a bishop in June 1935, and died in Canton at the hands of the Chinese Communists.

These developments coincided with Rome's decision, announced in 1908, to remove the entire English-speaking world, except Australasia, from the jurisdiction of Propaganda, on the ground that it was no longer a genuine mission area. Another fruitful development was the conversion to the Church of the Fathers and Sisters of the Atonement on October 30th, 1909. They had been founded in 1898 in Graymoor, N.Y., by, respectively, Paul Wattson (1863–1940) and Lurana White (1870–1935). Each group was allowed to enter as a body and preserve its own organization and identity. They had started out as Anglican Franciscans and through the intervention of Archbishop Falconio were allowed to form independent branches of the Franciscan family. Their conversion was a unique episode in the history of the Church in America. In 1908 they started the Chair of Unity Octave to work for the reunion of all Christians, which has since spread all over the world and plays an important role in the Ecumenical Movement.

In his concern for the missions at home and abroad and for relations with non-Catholics, the Cardinal did not forget the neediest portion of his own flock. In 1912 he brought the Holy Ghost Fathers to St. Mark's, Manhattan, where, aided by the Blessed Sacrament Sisters who came in the same year, they expanded the Black apostolate. They are still working fruitfully in it.

Popular Devotions

The devotional needs of the people were not neglected and were met in additional ways. On December 31st, 1903, the Nocturnal Adoration Society held its first meeting at St. Jean Baptiste Church under the auspices of the Blessed Sacrament Fathers. On October 20th, 1906, the first noonday devotions ever given in this country were started at St. Peter's, Barclay

Street. In December 1904 the Monthly Day of Recollection for the clergy was inaugurated, and on January 16th, 1906, the Priests Choir was organized to help the revival of plain chant ordered by the Pope in November 1903. The Lenten Pastoral of 1904 urged abstinence from all hard liquor in memory of the Sacred Thirst of Our Lord.

The chief change was made by the new decrees on the reception of Holy Communion, which were enforced energetically all through the Archdiocese. The cult of the Eucharist was strengthened by bringing in the Reparatrice Nuns from Italy in 1910 and the Sacramentine Nuns from France in 1911. Closed Retreats for Laymen were started at Fordham on July 9th, 1909, and moved to Mt. Manresa, Staten Island, in July 1911. They were due chiefly to the labors of Father Terence Shealy, S.J., who was aided substantially from the beginning by the Knights of Columbus. Closed Retreats for women were already available at, among other places, the Cenacle Convent opened by Archbishop Corrigan. The contemplative life was strengthened by the coming of the Poor Clares in 1915. Unknown to all but a handful of obscure people, Father Solanus Casey (1870–1957), a priest whose intellectual gifts were so limited that he was never allowed to preach or hear confessions, was serving as porter in various Capuchin houses in New York from 1904 to 1924. The process of his beatification was opened in Detroit in 1976.

Changes In The City

While all these events were taking place, the city continued to develop and more of its most famous landmarks appeared. As usual, the traffic problems received special attention. On October 27th, 1904, a red-letter day in the city's history, the long-awaited subway system opened. It ran from City Hall to Grand Central Station, over to Times Square, and up to West 145th Street, and soon proved to be indispensable. In 1908 the subway system was extended to Brooklyn, and the first Hudson Tube providing rail service under the Hudson River to New Jersey was opened. The City Fathers, ever anxious to make it easier to get out of the city as well as into it, opened both the Queensboro and Manhattan Bridges in 1909. The increased use of the automobile was noted too. The first year in which there were more cars than horses in New York was 1917, with about 115,000 cars to 109,000 horses. New York's position as the financial and business center of the country was strengthened in 1915 when the transcontinental telephone service was introduced. The first example of New York's most distinctive architectural style, the skyscraper, was the Flatiron Building, which opened in 1912. The New York Public Library at 42nd Street and Fifth Avenue, which took nine years to build, opened on May 23rd, 1911, and took rank at once as one of the finest buildings of its kind in the world. Transit, business, and local government profited when three monumental structures opened in 1913.

They were the new Grand Central Terminal, the Woolworth Building, and the Municipal Building. Pennsylvania Station, which was replaced in 1968 by the latest Madison Square Garden, was opened in 1910.

WORLD WAR I

Undoubtedly the most important event in the public life of the country during the Farley administration was America's entry into World War I. The outbreak of war in Europe in August 1914 took the general public there and here by surprise, though there had been a series of crises since 1905. It was the first general war in Europe since the fall of Napoleon and it involved all the Great Powers because of the system of military alliances established to preserve the balance of power. Italy, an ally of Germany and Austria in 1914, remained neutral until May 1915 when it switched sides and joined England, France, and Russia.

Not everyone was surprised by the war. The Holy See, under both Leo XIII and St. Pius X, had been warning of its coming for years. It hastened the death of Pope Pius, whose successor, Benedict XV (1914–1927), was elected on September 3rd, the morning of the first day of the Battle of the Marne, the first great battle of the war. He was a highly trained diplomat who was able to steer the Church through the storm successfully. Cardinal Farley was in Switzerland when the war broke out, so he had no trouble reaching Rome on time for the Conclave at which he was the only American present.

One reason for the general surprise here was the strength of the Peace Movement. Both in 1899 and 1909 the Hague Conferences on Peace, called by Nicholas II of Russia, had encouraged the belief that war could be curtailed, if not eliminated, and the Peace Palace, erected at the Hague in 1913 to house the Court of International Arbitration (and paid for largely by Andrew Carnegie of New York), was a symbol of the widespread belief in the cause. Many who considered themselves more sophisticated than their neighbors believed war was outmoded. In the beginning, the war was regarded here as an aberration and as an event of major importance that was too remote from our vital interests to make it likely that we should or would enter it. President Wilson proclaimed a policy of strict neutrality, and few students of the period doubt that the prevailing popular opinion then was strongly in favor of non-intervention. This was true, clearly, until well after the election of 1916.

It is probable that America would have entered the war no matter who won the election of 1916, because very powerful forces at home and abroad were pushing or pulling in that direction, but it would have done so in a different way if the Republicans had won. Their candidate, Charles Evans Hughes (1862–1948), a former governor of New York and a future United States Secretary of State and Chief Justice, was not the stuff of which prophets are made, but Woodrow Wilson surely was. Wilson was the first of the secularized evangelists of this century who, having come to power in important countries, turned the world upside down. He presented the war to the American people as a crusade to "make the world safe for democracy," to "protect the rights of small nations," "to preserve the sanctity of treaties," and—and this was probably the most popular theme—as "the war to end war." He evoked an astonishing response. Criticism and opposition were muted, and there was a greater display of solidarity and national unity here than ever before or since.

It is impossible now to recapture adequately the mood of the time and the enthusiasm with which people of all backgrounds threw themselves into the common effort. The former pacifists matched or outdid in fervor those who had been preaching preparedness, with an eye to intervention, since August 1914. The enthusiasm for American intervention was even greater abroad in countries that had borne the brunt of the war from the beginning and were in imminent danger of collapse and defeat. They saw salvation coming from the West and were moved appropriately. One example will do. The Abbé Louis Duchesne (1843–1922), the outstanding ecclesiastical historian in his time and a man known not only for immense erudition but for his sceptical mind and ironic wit, wrote to Archbishop Ireland that "through President Wilson, the world has heard the voice of a people that was truly the voice of God."

The Catholics joined enthusiastically in the war effort in which they were welcomed warmly in many but not all areas, and the bishops placed all the resources of the Church at the disposal of the Government. There were two fields of action that called for prompt attention and in both of them New York took the lead. The first was to supply a sufficient number of chaplains for the Armed Forces, which went from a few hundred thousand to almost five million in about eighteen months. In April 1917, there were only sixteen priests in the regular Army and nine in the National Guard, or twenty-five for about 300,000 troups. By November 1918, there were 1,023 priests in all branches of the Service, and 500 more had already been cleared for duty as of January 1st, 1919. To handle this immense expansion, the Holy See created the Military Diocese on November 24th, 1917, and made Bishop Hayes the Chaplain Bishop. He understood that, if he wanted other dioceses with fewer priests to supply a fair quota of chaplains, New York must set an example. It did so handsomely, for while its quota was forty-nine, it had eighty-seven in service when the war ended. The expenses of the new diocese were met largely by the Knights of Columbus.

The Knights were indispensable in meeting the second need, which was to provide proper recreational facilities of every kind for the military personnel here and abroad. It was agreed that the Knights would be the agent in this work of the National Catholic War Council (N.C.W.C.), which was established by the hierarchy to coordinate Catholic efforts to help the war. They worked in the same field as the Salvation Army. From the very start, the Knights held firmly to two rules they were often urged to bend or break, rules that were summed up in their slogan: "Everybody Welcome, Everything Free." Cardinal Farley wanted their drive in New York run under the auspices of the N.C.W.C. It was the first Catholic drive here that was professionally organized and run, and that had adequate publicity. Each parish had a quota and a corps of well-supervised volunteers. The goal was $2,500,000 and there was general rejoicing when the total raised exceeded $5,000,000. Of that amount $3,250,000 was placed at the disposal of the Knights and the rest went to the N.C.W.C. The Knights had drives all over the country, but not at the same time in order not to interfere with others like the Liberty Loan, War Bond, and Savings Bond drives. They raised nationally about $14,000,000, of which about $5,000,000 came from New York State.

In May 1917, Cardinal Farley underwent serious surgery and withdrew very largely from the public view. His last public function was the formal blessing of Gate of Heaven Cemetery on July 14th, 1918. On the weekend before his death, prayers and messages of sympathy came from a number of Protestant and Jewish congregations. He died of pneumonia on September 17th, 1918, and was buried in the Cathedral. The Mass was sung by Archbishop John Bonzano, the Apostolic Delegate, and the eulogy was given by Bishop Thomas Hickey of Rochester. For the third and last time, Cardinal Gibbons was the ranking prelate at the funeral of an Archbishop of New York.

CHAPTER 11

Patrick Cardinal Hayes

On July 25, 1916, Pope Benedict XV changed the procedure for recommending candidates for the episcopate in this country that had been established by the Third Plenary Council of Baltimore. He did so mainly because it was too slow, as experience had shown. He substituted a system whereby every two years the bishops of each province meet and draw up a list of candidates which they forward to Rome. Provision was made for ascertaining the opinion of the Consultors of a vacant diocese, but opinions were to be obtained from them singly, in writing, and in the strictest confidence. The new plan took effect at the beginning of Lent in 1917 and so was in effect when New York fell vacant in September 1918. In its first application in New York, it was slower than the old plan, a fact attributed to the pressure of business in Rome in the aftermath of World War I (which was not officially over) and to the personal attention the Pope himself wished to give so important an appointment.

As usual, the long vacancy, during which Monsignor Joseph F. Mooney was Administrator, gave ample time for many rumors, including one that Cardinal O'Connell would come from Boston. The prevailing opinion, however, was that a local candidate would be chosen, and on February 16, 1919 the press printed a dispatch from Rome announcing that Bishop Patrick

215

J. Hayes, the only obvious local candidate, had been appointed to New York. The official documents were delayed so long in transit that he obtained permission to proceed without them and was installed on March 19th, the feast of St. Joseph. He received the pallium from Archbishop Bonzano on May 8th.

The new Archbishop was well received. He was the first occupant of the see whose entire life was spent in New York. His years at Cathedral College had given him a greater personal knowledge of the young priests and of many of the seminarians than any of his predecessors or successors had had a chance to acquire. His service as Chancellor had brought him in contact with most of the other priests. As secretary to Bishop Farley, whom he accompanied to confirmations and visitations, and as his successor in that work, he had visited almost every parish and institution in the Archdiocese. His active association with all those engaged in Catholic charitable work of any kind and with all the Catholic fund-raising activities during the war had brought him into personal touch with many of the laity.

His position as Cardinal Farley's other self, which he played down as much as possible, was recognized by the public authorities and the leaders of other groups in the city as well as in Catholic circles, and he could fairly claim to be acquainted with every section of the Catholic community and with many outside it. While all acknowledged his acceptability to the priests and the people, his knowledge of New York, and his personal qualities, many thought his promotion was due chiefly to his successful handling of the charities controversy and his performance as Chaplain Bishop. Another reason, to which the Apostolic Delegate alluded in his sermon at the installation, was Cardinal Farley's earnest wish that it be so.

Patrick Joseph Hayes (November 20, 1867–September 4, 1938) was born on City Hall Place on the lower East Side of Manhattan and was baptized the following day in St. Andrew's Church. Both his parents were born in Ireland. His father, a longshoreman and an active member of the Society of St. Vincent de Paul, called his first child Patrick in protest against the anti-Irish feeling of the time. His mother died when he was four and he was brought up by a maternal aunt and her husband who lived nearby and had no children of their own. They kept a small grocery store in which as a boy and a student he helped after school and in vacation time. Patrick, whose father remarried, had a full brother and a half sister with whom he was always on friendly terms.

After a brief interval in a public school, Patrick was transferred to the parochial school of Transfiguration parish. When he had finished there, his guardians decided that as he had shown a genuine aptitude for study they would send him to La Salle Academy on Second St. and to Manhattan College, both of which were and are conducted by the Brothers of the Christian Schools. Their decision represented a substantial sacrifice for people of their means, but it was made willingly and accepted gratefully. His years with the Brothers brought him a solid grounding in the traditional classical education of the day and won them his lifelong devotion. Among his friends and contemporaries in the very small student body at Manhattan were Austin Dowling (1868–1930), the future Archbishop of St. Paul, George Mundelein (1870–1939), the first Cardinal Archbishop of Chicago, and Joseph P. Donahue (1870–1959), a future auxiliary bishop and vicar general of New York under Cardinal Spellman.

At Manhattan, as elsewhere, Patrick was a diligent and conscientious rather than a brilliant student. He was not distracted by athletic or social interests and graduated with prizes in philosophy and the classics. He entered the seminary at Troy in September 1888 and near the end of his course was chosen for higher studies at the Catholic University in Washington. He was ordained ahead of his class, on September 8, 1892, by Archbishop Corrigan and was a student in Washington when Dr. Edward McGlynn was absolved by Archbishop Satolli. When he returned to New York in 1894, he was sent as an assistant to Monsignor Farley at St. Gabriel's. It was considered a good assignment in itself and turned out to be a very good one for him. When, a year after his arrival, his pastor became a bishop and needed a secretary, he chose his junior assistant. That was the beginning of an association that grew closer while both of them lived and brought the younger man to the very edge of the archiepiscopal throne.

His secretarial duties left ample time for the parochial work for which St. Gabriel's offered so many opportunities and which he found congenial. His experience there, where he saw the poor at very close range, strengthened the convictions and deepened the impressions about the poor, and the central role that relieving them must play in the life of the Church, that he had acquired very early in life. It deepened too, as he saw its members at work, the respect for the Society of St. Vincent de Paul that his father and uncle had instilled in him.

Father Hayes' active participation in parochial work was interrupted in September 1902 when he accompanied Archbishop Farley to the Archbishops' House. There his double role as Chancellor and President of Cathedral College gave him plenty to do. His duties were changed but hardly lightened when he became a bishop. When Cardinal Farley asked for a second auxiliary, he asked for something that was then very rare. Both he and the new bishop attributed the granting of his petition largely to the active intervention of Cardinal Gibbons who helped to push the nomination through the prescribed channels. The new auxiliary and titular bishop of Tagaste was consecrated by Cardinal Farley on October 28, 1914. The co-consecrators were Bishop Thomas F. Cusack and Bishop Henry Gabriels of Ogdensburg. The latter had been rector of the seminary in Troy, 1871–1892. In July 1915, Bishop Hayes ended twenty-one years in the Farley household by replacing Bishop Cusack as pastor of St. Stephen's. He was the third and last of Dr. McGlynn's immediate successors who was or became a bishop.

At St. Stephen's, he had of necessity less direct contact with the poor than he had at St. Gabriel's, but he had wider and stronger contacts with those who were helping them. He was there during much of the time in which he was involved in the Charities Row, and during the whole of his tenure there he was the archdiocesan spiritual director of the Society of St. Vincent de Paul. His days were full, for most episcopal functions fell to him and he was increasingly active as a stand-in for the Cardinal in other things as well. Thus it was with a certain reluctance that he accepted two additional assignments, both caused by the World War, which took him away from his ordinary duties for the first and last time, and obliged him to play an active role in the national affairs of the Church. The first was the office of Chaplain Bishop and the second was membership on the executive committee of the National Catholic War Council. Both assignments were due to the importance of the Archdiocese of New York and to the recognition here and in Rome of his position in it.

THE CHAPLAIN BISHOP

When the Military Diocese was erected in November 1917, its first bishop found a great deal of work that needed to be done quickly and he had no precedents here to guide him. He had to survey the existing situation, estimate foreseeable needs, get in touch with the bishops and religious superiors who could supply priests, provide and maintain suitable places for religious worship and activities, and establish communications with each chaplain. He had also to establish a center from which instructions could be sent and in which the necessary records and reports could be kept, and to keep in close touch with the higher officials of the Armed Forces whose cooperation was needed for the successful completion of his mission. He received excellent cooperation on every level, inside and outside the Armed Forces, and was indebted especially to the Knights of Columbus and the Chaplains Aid Society. The latter was founded in New York in 1917 and soon had chapters all through the country.

The jurisdiction of the Chaplain Bishop included the Armed Forces of the United States at home and abroad and their civilian assistants who lived at military or naval installations. It was estimated that he had about one million people in his charge. Before April 1917, the quota for Catholic chaplains in the Army was 24 percent of the Chaplain Corps but it was raised to 37.8 percent during the war. Both figures were far above the Catholic percentage of the general population and reflected the percentage of Catholics in military service. After the war, the quota was lowered to 25 percent. It was never more than 25 percent in the Navy.

His first step was to divide the diocese into five vicariates and to appoint a vicar general for each. The names of the vicariates suggest the immensity of the areas covered. They were the Atlantic Seaboard (New York), the Great Lakes (Chicago), the Pacific (San Francisco), the Gulf (New Orleans), and the Overseas (Paris) Vicariates. The last, which was closed in 1919, covered all of Western Europe and the Mediterranean. The next step was to establish a chancery, which was located in New York, and to appoint an Executive Secretary who would live in Washington and maintain daily contact with the Armed Forces. The last step was to visit as many as possible of the military and naval posts in America. Though his plan to visit the troops in France was announced in May 1918, Bishop Hayes never went to the Overseas Vicariate, partly because of the illness and death of Cardinal Farley, whose dependence on him at that time was total.

When hostilities ceased, the Catholic Chaplain Corps shrank as rapidly as it had expanded, but never went back to its pre-war numbers. By 1924 it had only ninety-six members on active service. Since he himself had had no previous contact with the Armed Forces and knew nothing of the problems of chaplains, Bishop Hayes had to rely in the beginning on the advice of those who had the necessary contacts and knowledge. He found one chaplain so useful that he came to regard him as indispensable, made him Vicar General and Chancellor, and after March 1919 left him in full control while both of them lived. This was Father George J. Waring (1872–1943), who was born in England, educated in New York and Washington, ordained from Dunwoodie for Dubuque, Iowa, in 1903, and served as a chaplain in the Regular Army (1905–1920). He became a prelate in 1919, and in June 1923 pastor of St. Ann's (Monsignor Preston's parish), where he established the headquarters of the Military Diocese and remained until his death. He was a capable and aggressive man whose exceptional personality was long remembered, not always favorably, by those who worked most closely with him.

THE NATIONAL CATHOLIC WAR COUNCIL

Very shortly after America entered the war, it became obvious that some kind of national organization was needed to coordinate the war-related efforts of all the Catholic societies, which numbered about 15,000. In August 1917, at the suggestion of Father John Burke, C.S.P., who was the editor of *The Catholic World* and the founder of the Chaplains Aid Society, representatives of sixty-eight dioceses and twenty-seven national organizations met at the University in Washington and formed the National Catholic War Council (N.C.W.C.). Its success indicated the need and the possibilities of an organization including every diocese and recognized by the hierarchy as the official Catholic agent in matters of common concern.

The Archbishops of the country had been meeting annually since 1890, but it was felt they were too numerous and too busy to supervise the

N.C.W.C. effectively, and that its importance and urgency required special handling. Consequently, at the suggestion of Cardinal Gibbons and Archbishop Glennon, it was decided to enlarge the N.C.W.C., make it the official spokesman for the hierarchy, and put it under the control of an administrative board of four bishops who would function under the archbishops. The four selected were Bishops Peter J. Muldoon of Rockford, Ill., William T. Russell of Charleston, S.C., Joseph Schrembs of Toledo, Oh., and Patrick J. Hayes. They accepted the assignment and by January 16, 1918, the new and enlarged N.C.W.C. was in operation. It worked closely with the Knights of Columbus Committee on War Activities and the committees that had been formed by its predecessor.

The manifest utility of coordinating Catholic efforts on a national basis led to the suggestion that the wartime organization be continued, and this was agreed to by the Holy See and the hierarchy. Part of the new plan was an annual meeting of all the bishops, and this was inaugurated on September 24, 1919. On that occasion, ninety-two of the ninety-eight heads of dioceses in the country met in Washington and voted to establish the National Catholic Welfare Council. Since "Council" could be misunderstood both here and in Rome, "Conference" was substituted for it at the suggestion of Archbishop Hayes. Cardinal Gibbons regarded the establishment of a permanent N.C.W.C. as the most important development in the organization of the Church here since the Third Plenary Council of Baltimore. It has no coercive power and its chief function is to coordinate and unify all Catholic activities on a national scale. In the beginning it set up departments to deal with Education, the Press, Social Action, Legal Affairs, and Lay Organizations. It is now known as the United States Catholic Conference (U.S.C.C.).

In addition to performing its tasks successfully and paving the way for the present U.S.C.C., the enlarged N.C.W.C. issued, on February 12, 1919, a statement called *Social Reconstruction, a General Review of the Problems and Survey of Remedies.* It contained a program of action to meet the widely expressed demand for extensive post-war social changes involving capital and labor. It called for minimum wage legislation, public housing, progressive taxes on incomes and inheritance, control of monopolies, the spread of cooperatives, labor participation in management, and other reforms, most of which have since been adopted. At the time, it was considered very advanced in its thinking and gave great offense to many. It was chiefly the work of Father John A. Ryan (1869–1945) of the Catholic University, who was then and until his death the most widely known Catholic spokesman for social reform. The Executive Committee accepted his plan wholeheartedly and made it its own.

ARCHBISHOP OF NEW YORK

Bishop Hayes' appointment as Archbishop of New York gave him a welcome chance to withdraw from the Administrative Board of N.C.W.C., for which he was no longer eligible, and to devote himself entirely to his new assignment. His reluctance to assume responsibilities outside the Archdiocese was not due solely to his well-founded belief that he had an important and urgent task in New York. It was due partly to his awareness of his own limitations, and to an understandable desire to avoid unnecessary involvement in areas in which he was unsure of himself and had no special interest and competence. He had all and more of Cardinal Farley's caution and Archbishop Corrigan's lack of interest in matters that lay outside the immediate concerns of a diocesan bishop. He was in fact a man of narrow range who had one major, overriding and almost exclusive interest, Catholic Charities, to which he was drawn by a strong natural attraction, by experience, by his recognition of its great and growing importance, and above all by a deep religious conviction that after divine worship, the preaching of the Gospel, and the proper administration of the sacraments, it was the primary work of the Church.

Though he was less gifted than any of the preceding Archbishops, he had strengths of his own. In his chosen field, in which he felt entirely at ease, he moved with a sureness of touch, a clear view of his goals, a grasp of principles, an eye for detail, a talent for organization, and an unwearied interest that made him a resounding success. He wanted the Catholic Charities to be as good as possible for the sake of the people they exist to serve, for the spiritual welfare and good name of the Church, for the benefit of the community at large, and to provide a model for the Church in other parts of this country. He achieved all those goals.

He succeeded partly because of his personal qualities which made it possible for him to enlist the necessary cooperation of others. People on every level responded warmly to his notably uncomplicated personality. He was slightly under middle height, had prematurely white hair, was dignified in bearing and had a very gracious and benign manner. Until his health failed, he was readily accessible. Those who tried to draw him into water he sensed was beyond his depth often found him preoccupied and unresponsive. He impressed them as a man whose energies and resources were taxed to the limit by his existing commitments. He needed and received in abundant measure the assurance, often couched in very flattering terms, that all was well with him and his administration. His great personal popularity and his own temperament made him very sensitive to criticism or opposition within the fold, and on that account unlikely to forget it.

Catholic Charities was not the only field in which the Archbishop shone. He was superb in the celebration of the liturgy. The effortless ease, correctness, relish, dignity, and reverence with which he moved through the complicated and majestic pontifical ceremonies of the pre-Vatican II Tridentine Rite made a lasting impression on all who watched him in action. He embodied for them the traditional concept of the great high priest. He was helped in that by his pleasing and well modulated voice and his evident piety.

Like his three immediate predecessors, Archbishop Hayes had an excellent knowledge of the Archdiocese when he took office. He found it well organized and in generally good condition. Since he was not an innovator outside the field of charity, his policy was to preserve the *status quo* and, in order that he might be free to devote himself to his favorite work, to leave routine matters in the hands of trusted subordinates with whom he had worked for years. In the whole course of his administration, only one or two people whom he had not known really well before his appointment became close to him.

He contented himself with what would later be regarded as a skeletal staff, and was sparing in the distribution of honors. He had only one auxiliary bishop and one vicar general at a time, and for ten years one man held both positions. His first auxiliary was Monsignor John J. Dunn, who was consecrated on October 28, 1921 and became Vicar General when Monsigor Joseph Mooney died on May 13, 1923. He in turn was succeeded as Chancellor in October 1921 by Monsignor Joseph P. Dineen (1883–1923) whose untimely death on May 11, 1923, removed a major irritant to the clergy. Ordained from Dunwoodie in 1908, Monsignor Dineen became secretary to Bishop Hayes in 1915 and soon became as useful to him in archdiocesan affairs as Father Waring was in the Military Diocese, with similar results. He was regarded as able, industrious, overbearing, officious, and abrasive. His successor, Monsignor Thomas G. Carroll (1885–1934), a former secretary of Cardinal Farley, was immensely popular with the clergy who regarded him as a much valued link between them and the Archbishop.

CATHOLIC CHARITIES

From the very first days of his administration, Archbishop Hayes made it clear that the reorganization of the Catholic Charities was to be his Number One project. In June 1919 he spelled out his plans (to which he had referred in his speech at the reception of the pallium) to the priests attending the annual clergy retreats at Dunwoodie. The first thing to do was to collect all the facts, which had never been done adequately. He announced his intention to have a survey made by experts who would examine the field thoroughly and give him a clear, accurate, and detailed account of the existing situation with all its strengths and weaknesses. In planning the survey, he turned for help to friends he had made while serving on the N.C.W.C. and to Father William J. Kerby (1870–1936), a classmate during his student days in Washington who headed the Sociology Department at the Catholic University from its inception in 1897 until his death. They supplied the plan and suggested the top personnel, and the Archbishop provided the necessary funds from the purse the clergy gave him when he received the pallium. It was the first gift he received on his appointment and he wanted it to go to charity. The survey was directed by Dr. John H. Lapp of the N.C.W.C., who had experience in that field, and by two young priests of the Archdiocese, Fathers Keegan and McEntegart, who had studied under Father Kerby and, at his suggestion, at the New York School of Social Work at Columbia University, the first full-time professional school for social workers in this country.

Robert F. Keegan (1888–1947) graduated from Cathedral College, where he was allowed to skip a year, in 1911, and was ordained on September 18, 1915, by Bishop Hayes, who had been following his career since they first met at the College. He returned from Washington in 1916 with high praise from Father Kerby, and lived at St. Stephen's rectory while continuing his studies. In June 1919 he was named Secretary for Charities, a new post, and in August was made Executive Director of the survey. Under different titles, he was the dominant figure in the day-to-day operations of Catholic Charities until his death. Though the Archbishop kept ultimate control and took a deep interest in it until the end, there was no doubt who his right-hand man in that work was. The Executive Director was an exceptionally able administrator, a hard-driving and imperious man who knew exactly what he wanted to accomplish. He soon acquired a national reputation as an effective and even formidable representative of Catholic Charities, the work to which he gave his undivided attention, and was regarded as the most gifted man in the Hayes administration.

Bryan J. McEntegart (1893–1968) graduated from Manhattan College in 1913, was ordained on September 8, 1917 by Cardinal Farley, and was appointed to the committee making the survey in the summer of 1919. He headed the division of Child Care until 1941 and then went on to be, in succession, national secretary of the Catholic Near East Welfare Association, Bishop of Ogdensburg, Rector of the Catholic University of America, and finally Archbishop-Bishop of Brooklyn, a post from which he retired shortly before his death. It is worth noting that, when they were placed in charge of a major work which was intended to be of national significance, Father Keegan was ordained not quite four years and Father McEntegart not quite two.

The survey was intended to make a thorough study of the social, recreational, institutional, and preventive work being carried on by the Archdiocese of New York and to outline a program for constructive work in the future. In the beginning, many of the institutions were wary of it because of their vivid memories of the Kingsbury Commission, and the Archbishop had trouble convincing them it was a survey, not an investigation. He told them he wanted to find out from them not only what they were doing but what they wanted to do, and how much help they needed. He said he did not want to eliminate any existing charity but to give them all more to do and more to do it with. He told them too that whatever they told him would be held in the strictest confidence.

The actual survey was made by a team of forty-two salaried professionals, aided by a number of priests, many of whom were relieved of parish duties for its duration, and a large number of lay volunteers. They used questionnaires and personal visits, divided the work topically into hospitals, child care, health, delinquency, recreation, and county activities, and were careful to consult the local public officials as well as the private agencies. They examined 175 works of charity in 297 parishes. In February 1920, they submitted a composite report about two thousand pages long, a summary suitable for release to the general public and the press, and a separate report on each of the following—twenty-six hospitals, three dispensaries, four sisterhoods devoted to nursing the sick poor in their own homes, twenty institutions (with thirty-two branches) caring for dependent, defective, delinquent, and neglected children, twenty-four day nurseries, three institutions for delinquent girls, five homes for the aged, the Catholic Protective Society, the Society of St. Vincent de Paul, ninety-three agencies doing benevolent but unpublicized work, and twenty-nine ladies auxiliaries.

The conclusions and recommendations of the survey confirmed and underscored what the Archbishop had known since the early days of the Mitchel investigation. The Catholic Charities lacked a single unified plan and a central office that would supply guidance and coordination. They lacked, too, sufficient funds for necessary improvement and expansion. There was duplication and overlapping, with a consequent waste of personnel and resources. An example of the lack of coordination was that four Catholic agencies that placed children in foster homes did so without any consultation among themselves.

Though the main thrust of the reports was not new, there were some surprises among the details they supplied. The Society of St. Vincent de Paul, still the chief agency for Catholic charitable work and relief, was established in only 117 of the 301 parishes. The amount of money that Catholics gave annually for charity was much greater than anyone had believed. It was estimated at $4,424,207. The agencies helped by the State and City received an additional $2,622,245. The financial statistics were especially surprising to the anti-Catholics who had been claiming for years that the Catholic institutions were supported mainly if not entirely by public funds, and that this was due to an unholy alliance between the Church and Tammany Hall.

Even before the survey was finished, the Archbishop, who had been following it very closely, moved ahead with his plan to reorganize the Charities. He was determined to bring them under unified control, to make all the recommended changes, and to raise the necessary funds. The last required obtaining the active cooperation of the laity on a scale previously unknown in New York, but he was confident that it could be done. In his mind these reforms, while indispensable, were not the whole story. He viewed the Charities as the work of the entire Catholic community, and he wanted to involve as many as possible of its members in the common effort. That participation, and whatever sacrifice of time and money it required, would benefit the donors as well as the recipients. He felt also that a disproportionate share of the burden had been carried for too long a time by the religious communities. He counted on the survey, and especially the summary, which was to be widely publicized and was awaited with friendly interest by social workers in many parts of the country, to give him a solid platform from which to appeal to the people and to carry out ideas he had been turning over in his mind for years.

In January 1920 he presented his plan to the Federated Catholic Societies, to which Cardinal Farley had appealed unsuccessfully, and on March 12th to a special meeting of the priests. He told both groups that the existing charitable institutions and work were to be coordinated, standardized, and extended. In the interest of efficiency and in recognition of his own accountability to the public to which he was appealing, they were also to be centralized. The field of charity was to be divided into six areas: Relief, Children, Health, Protective Care, Social Action, and General Administration. He intended to establish on a permanent basis the Archbishop's Committee of the Laity, which he hoped would ultimately reach a membership of 20,000. Their task would be to make personal contact with 100,000 other Catholics and enlist their support for the Catholic Charities of the Archdiocese of New York, which was incorporated legally on June 12, 1920. They would have their chance to do so in the week of April 18–24, in an archdiocesan drive that was to be planned and supervised by professionals.

The Archbishop's methodical and painstaking preparation for his big venture was richly rewarded. The summary of the survey, which was released in March, achieved the intended effect. The drive, which was run by the people who ran the Knights of Columbus drive in March 1918, was surprisingly successful. It used the parish as the unit and each parish had a clerical and a lay director. The national parishes were not overlooked and active lay committees were formed among the Albanians, Belgians, Bohemians, French, Greeks, Hungarians, Italians, Lithuanians, Maronites, Poles, Ruthenians, Slovaks, Spanish, and Syrians. The lists that were drawn up served many parishes as the beginning of a parish census. Monsignor Dunn was chairman of the Enrollment Committee, a post he retained until his death. On April 11, 1920—Easter Sunday—the Archbishop devoted his pastoral letter to the drive, inaugurating a custom that lasted during his administration.

The response of both workers and donors exceeded all expectations. By the end of the first week, 125 parishes had raised $503,274. In two weeks, 16,668 volunteers visited 233,000 prospective donors and brought in $917,219.84. The workers compared favorably in number with the 37,000 who helped the Knights of Columbus drive because the latter group had the advantage of the unprecedented solidarity the wartime emergency produced. The initial goal had been $500,000 for each of three years, but the response was so great and the recognition of a long-term need so widespread that the drive became a permanent feature of New York Catholic life, and people came to forget what an innovation it was. While he never discouraged large gifts, the Archbishop did not stress them and was pleased by the great number of small ones.

Though the funds raised by the charity drive were important, they were never the chief consideration in the Archbishop's mind. He had very definite ideas about the role his new organization was to fill. It was to be a scientific, central clearing house that would supplement, not supplant, the existing fund-raising activities. Its chief contribution was to be service, not the direct relief for which the Society of St. Vincent de Paul was to be the official Archdiocesan agency. He never thought the maximum conceivable Catholic effort could meet the existing needs and he was anxious to work closely with the other private agencies. In this, he followed in the footsteps of his two immediate predecessors and especially of Archbishop Corrigan. In 1916 Cardinal Farley, when making his fortieth and last appearance at the annual Christmas Party at the Foundling Asylum, had made an earnest plea for cooperation in charitable work by all religious groups.

Archbishop Hayes welcomed too the still modest role of the public authorities in charitable and welfare work and was pleased to see it expand. The work required and stimulated the growth of a relatively new group of technicians, the professionally trained social workers, who were needed in both the private and public sectors. He was well aware that, as Pope Pius XI would soon be saying, "piety does not permit us to dispense with technique," and that the Church must always be "healthily modern." He was anxious that the Catholic social workers, religious or lay, be at least as well trained as the others, and for that he relied especially on the Fordham School of Social Service with whose founding he had much to do. It is the second oldest Catholic school of its kind in the country, having been preceded by two years by the one at Loyola University in Chicago. In addition to being well trained, the Catholic social workers were to have the most up-to-date equipment and methods at their disposal. Examples of his interest in that area are the opening of a venereal disease clinic in one of the Good Shepherd Homes in 1920 and of a psychiatric clinic in St. Vincent's Hospital in 1922.

Highly as he valued good organization, competent administration, careful planning, professional training, adequate financing, and an awareness both of contemporary needs and of sound developments in the treatment of the myriad social evils of the day, there was one thing the Archbishop valued even more highly, and that was the religious dimension of genuine charity which to him was the heart of the matter. While he wanted Catholic social workers to be well-trained professionals, he wanted the non-religious social workers, whose numbers he foresaw would increase, to recognize and respect the importance of religion in the lives of great numbers of those with whom they had to deal. He feared, as he said in his eulogy of Thomas Mulry, the growing trend to the secularization of charity and philanthropy and that the whole matter of relief might become "a state or city function without any higher ideal than an economic or social one." One sign of the stress he placed on the link between religion and social work was his approbation of the Parish Visitors of Mary Immaculate, a community devoted to social work, which was founded in New York City on August 15, 1920, by Mother M. Teresa Tallon. It was the first religious community founded in the Archdiocese during his administration and followed by a month the arrival of the Discalced Carmelite Nuns from Baltimore on June 15, 1920.

While Archbishop Hayes was engrossed in planning, starting and consolidating the major work of his life, the national and international political scene, from which he held aloof entirely, was changing rapidly and unexpectedly with consequences for the Church and the country that were felt with special force in the first half of his administration. Whatever view one took of them, the war and the peace were of paramount importance.

THE REACTION AGAINST THE WAR AND THE PEACE

Almost everyone recognized, as the speakers at his installation stressed, that the World War had closed a long chapter in the history of the Western world, and that the new one then opening offered not only great opportunities but many uncertainties and dangers. The triumph of democracy and nationalism, the fall of the German, Austrian, Russian, and Turkish Empires, the establishment of the League of Nations and the universal weariness of militarism and war seemed to many to offer the prospect of an age in which at last the lion would lie down with the lamb. With more justification than many who have had the same idea before and since, people felt they were living at an immensely important turning point in human affairs. The Allied military victory had already been won and only a few perceptive people in Europe saw that it was not permanent. No one seemed to have foreseen how America's decisive intervention—her first major role as a Great Power—would turn out. Few thought the Communist regime established in Russia in November 1917 could last.

The change in public opinion in America surfaced in November 1918 when, just before the Armistice of November 11th, the Republicans carried both houses of Congress, an event seen by many as a rejection of President Wilson and his policies. The enthusiasm, hysteria, and national unity evoked by the war could not be sustained when the fighting stopped. The growing desire to liquidate the war as quickly as possible became irresistible when the peace treaties revealed the gap between what the electorate here had been promised and what had actually been achieved. This was all the truer because during the war the press here had glossed over the difference between the Allied war aims and our own. The reaction against the war would result in a revival of Nativism that was to affect Catholic interests here for the next decade. The enthusiasm with which Catholics were welcomed into the collective war effort waned. In some areas, the Catholics felt like the "temporary gentlemen" who filled the gap in the British Army officer corps until the war ended, and they reverted suddenly to their previous inferior status.

When Woodrow Wilson, who chose to ignore the danger signals flashing so clearly here and in Europe, sailed for France on December 4, 1918, he was confident he would bring back a settlement based on the Fourteen Points he had proclaimed on January 8, 1918. He was counting on public opinion in the allied countries to overcome the reluctance of their leaders to accept his plans for the peace. No other person in the history of Europe has received the spontaneous, heartfelt, and almost universal acclaim with which he was received when he landed. He was hailed, Herbert Hoover tells us, as the Second Messiah and was considered by millions in the Allied countries and even by many in the conquered ones as the First Citizen of the World. Within a year, the high drama of the Paris Peace Conference, his conflict with the United States Senate, and his physical collapse had been played, and in an astonishing reversal of fortune he had been repudiated at home and abroad and was a broken and discredited man. America, hailed so recently as the Savior of the World, was being denounced by millions as Uncle Shylock.

The story has often been told of how President Wilson and the Allied leaders compromised when the basic incompatibility of their goals could no longer be concealed and decisions could no longer be postponed. They agreed in effect that the Wilsonian principles were to be applied only where they would weaken the defeated Central Powers (Germany, Austria and Turkey) and Russia, but not where they would weaken England and France. The Allies accepted the League of Nations, which they did not take very seriously, in order to get America to accept the Treaty of Versailles, which ended the war with Germany largely on their terms. Wilson accepted the Treaty in order to get them to accept the League, on which he pinned all his hopes for the elimination of war and of the balance of power policy with its necessarily interlocking military alliances. He saw the defects of the Treaty but was convinced that, once passions died down, the defects would be corrected by the League. He insisted on linking the League and the Treaty so closely that to reject one was to reject the other.

The Treaty was signed in Paris on June 28, 1919, and on July 10th was sent to the Senate which rejected it on November 19th after a long and acrimonious debate. The main obstacle to ratification was Article X of the Covenant of the League, which bound each member to respect and preserve the territorial integrity and political independence of each of the others. This required automatic American involvement in every boundary dispute in which force was used. The Senate, unwilling to reject the Treaty outright, attempted to attach reservations with which it would have been ratified. The President, who was through with compromise, insisted that it be taken or left just as it was. This gave the Senate no choice but to reject it, and each side blamed the other. Meanwhile, the President, having decided to take his case to the people, suffered a massive stroke on September 25th in Pueblo, Colorado. He was taken back, his doctor said, "to the restful atmosphere of the White House," and for the remainder of his term was incapable of conducting public business, an important fact that was largely concealed from the public by a sympathetic press.

The Allied leaders, Lloyd George of England, Clemenceau of France, and Orlando of Italy, were not without understandable reasons for their attitude. Their countries had fought longer and harder than America had, and had suffered incomparably greater losses of life and property. France with a population of about 40,000,000 lost 1,363,000 men and 73.3 percent of all its mobilized troops were killed, wounded, captured, or missing. The corresponding figures for America with a population of about 105,000,000 were 126,000 fatalities and eight percent casualties. The European Allies were determined to obtain and did obtain substantial practical advantages, on which they had agreed in 1915, from the victory America made possible later. They were, too, the prisoners of their own propaganda. They had made promises to their own electorates that were incompatible with the lip service they had paid the Fourteen Points while American aid was indispensable. England and France especially had raised the anti-German feeling of their people to fever pitch (Lloyd George had won the election of 1918 with a promise to "Hang the Kaiser") and they were expected to deliver the goods. Moreover, they were certain they understood Europe's problems much better than Wilson did and they did not think he had the right to dictate the peace.

Closer acquaintance had not improved their opinion of their great benefactor who was now dismissed by Lloyd George, himself a notorious cynic and double-dealing schemer, as "the most extraordinary compound I have ever encountered of the noble visionary, the implacable and unscrupulous partisan, the exalted idealist, and the man of rather petty personal rancors." Clemenceau, a bitter anti-Christian who was, if possible, a greater cynic than Lloyd George, derided Wilson by saying: "The good Lord had only Ten Commandments, who is this American Schoolmaster with Fourteen?" He was one of those who did not believe in the permanence of the victory of 1918, and in September 1919 told Herbert Hoover there would be another war in Europe in twenty years and that Hoover would be needed there again to administer relief.

Many of Wilson's domestic critics admired his objectives but were sincerely convinced they could not be achieved. Some others, partly because of his compromises, doubted his sincerity. Success would require the simultaneous cooperation of a number of sovereign states, many of which had conflicting interests and ambitions and some of which had strongly held hereditary antipathies to their neighbors. The Peace had been written against the interests of the Germans, on whom it had been imposed, and of the

Russians, who had been ignored. Many doubted that arrangements opposed by the two most numerous peoples in Europe could last very long.

The American Catholics were generally less disillusioned by the outcome of the war than other Americans because they had expected less from it. Though they had supported it loyally and even enthusiastically, they had never really regarded it as a crusade. They had not taken England and the Third French Republic (not to mention Tsarist Russia) seriously as the defenders of Christian civilization. They were not hostile to Austria-Hungary and they, and especially the Germans among them, rejected because they knew it to be false, the grotesquely distorted view of German culture and morality spread by wartime propaganda. They were mindful of the immense prestige Imperial Germany enjoyed in American academic and business circles from 1870 to 1914 and remembered, as a sign of that, the fulsome tributes the American press and public leaders had paid the German Emperor—suddenly transformed by propaganda into the Beast of Berlin—in 1913 when he celebrated his silver jubilee, the theme of which was twenty-five years of peace.

The Irish-Americans noted that the principle of self-determination, used to justify the breakup of Austria-Hungary and the restoration of Poland and the Baltic Republics, did not apply to Ireland. There, from 1919 to 1921 the British were attempting to suppress forcibly the demand for self-government that culminated in the partition of Ireland (a major cause of the present situation in Ulster) in 1920 and the erection of the Irish Free State in 1922. The Italian-Americans, less active politically than the Irish and the Germans, resented what they considered to be the inadequate recognition of Italy's territorial claims at the Peace Conference, which they blamed on Wilson.

The attitude of all the major allied leaders to the Church was another reason why ordinary Catholics expected less from them than other Americans did. As usual, each of the opposing camps sought to use the Holy See for its own purposes, but the new Pope refused to be drawn into their schemes. From the very day of his election, Benedict XV worked for peace. He maintained strict impartiality, did everything possible to help the victims of the war, especially prisoners, deportees, and refugees, without distinction of person, nationality, or religion, and made repeated appeals for the cessation or limiting of hostilities. He condemned the atrocities on both sides, the bombing of open cities as well as the German treatment of Belgium. When he judged the time was ripe, he issued on August 1, 1917, his Peace Note, with specific proposals for a negotiated peace. Some of his proposals were later in Wilson's Fourteen Points. A negotiated peace at that time would probably, as things turned out, have averted the Bolshevist Revolution in Russia and Hitler's rise to power. Both sides rejected the papal plan, partly because it was a papal plan and partly because each was confident of military victory.

His attitude toward the war brought Benedict XV the proverbial reward of the peacemaker in this life. He was denounced by many in each camp, including many Catholics. Each side accused him of being the paid agent or unwitting dupe of the other. In the Secret Treaties of 1915 which brought Italy into the war, he was expressly barred from the Peace Conference lest he bring up the Roman Question. Meanwhile, his help was sought for the afflicted in every area, as, for example, by the American Jewish Committee of New York which asked him in December 1915 to help the Jews in Poland. In 1916 he began, through Cardinal Gibbons, the custom of appealing to the Catholic school children of America to help their peers in wartorn lands. He distributed his meager resources so freely that the Holy See had to borrow the money for his funeral and the Conclave that elected his successor. His generosity and impartiality were not entirely unappreciated, however, and shortly before his death the first of the very few monuments to him was erected at Constantinople by popular subscription. In a most exceptional gesture of good will, the ceremony was attended by the Turkish Crown Prince and a number of other high-ranking Moslems as well as by the Orthodox Patriarch of Constantinople.

It would be wrong to suppose that the American reaction against the war was caused solely by dissatisfaction with the peace. The war affected the United States more than any event since the Civil War and imposed heavy social and financial burdens. The national talent for organization was shown in the speed and efficiency with which an immense army was raised, equipped, and shipped to Europe, but that could not be done easily or cheaply. The first American troops reached France in June 1917 but they were only a token force. They were, however, the harbingers of unlimited supplies of men and material and of final triumph if the Allies held out. By July 1918, one million and by November two million Americans had landed. Four million men, ten percent of whom came from New York, were drafted. At the same time, the national debt was rising from about one billion dollars in 1916 to $25,234,496,274 in August 1919, and the interest then was higher than the debt had been in 1916. Inflation was rampant, and by 1920 the 1914 dollar was valued at forty-five cents. That may explain why 1918 brought the Foundling Asylum its first deficit.

These things help to explain why Warren G. Harding swept the presidential election of 1920 with his pledge of a return to "normalcy" and a slogan like "Let's be done with wiggle and wobble." That goal was unattainable. The prolongation of the war had brought about a fundamental shift in the balance of power that was concealed from many by the temporary weakness of Germany and Russia and the consequent illusion of great strength in England and France. England had ceased to be the Number One power and America was unwilling to assume that role, so a period of uncertainty and drift followed. America, which had entered the war as a debtor, emerged as a creditor, and New York City became the financial center of the world.

DISTINGUISHED VISITORS

One pleasant by-product of the war was the arrival of distinguished visitors who came to express their countries' gratitude for America's aid. Among them were three authentic heroes whose reputations remain untarnished by subsequent revelations, who were received with extraordinary enthusiasm wherever they went, and who were of special interest to the Catholics. They were Albert I (1875–1934), King of the Belgians, Desiré Cardinal Mercier (1851–1926), Primate of Belgium, and Ferdinand Foch (1851–1921), Marshal of France, who was Supreme Commander of the Allied Armies in 1918.

The King, the first reigning European monarch to visit America, had been here as a young man before his accession and had been a house guest of Archbishop Ireland in St. Paul. His character and his courageous attitude toward the German invaders made him seem to his contemporaries the personification of chivalry. The Marshal, whose career had been impeded for years by his refusal to soft pedal his Catholicism and to sever relations with his Jesuit brother, received the greatest ovation given here to any Frenchman since Lafayette's triumphal tour in 1824.

The Cardinal's reception was more surprising. The warrior king and the successful soldier are enduring types, but Cardinal Mercier's position was different. Though he had received worldwide acclaim for the moral leadership he gave the people in occupied Belgium, no one could have complained if his popularity had not cut across all lines in America as did those of the King and the Marshal, but in fact it did. He arrived on time to review the great victory parade in which General Pershing led the First Division of the American Expeditionary Force up Fifth Avenue on September 10, 1919. The whole city turned out to welcome them home from France, and a highlight of the day was the moment when the General dismounted at the Cathedral to pay his respects to Cardinal Mercier.

After a brief visit to Baltimore to call on Cardinal Gibbons, and a stop in Washington, the Cardinal returned to New York to preside at the first anniversary Mass for Cardinal Farley and to receive the honors the city had in store for him. They were the Freedom of the City, a special Medal of Honor, and a civic banquet at the Waldorf. He was the first and last priest or prelate to receive any of the three. The banquet was attended by a notably distinguished group drawn from almost every sector of New York life. Archbishop Hayes showed his devotion to the routine duties of his office and his lack of interest in public affairs by missing it because he had a date for confirmation in the country that he was unwilling to reschedule.

The official honors heaped on Cardinal Mercier were matched by the unofficial ones, and there, too, he set a record. The non-Catholic academic world, with which relatively few New York Catholics had any contact, was notably cordial and generous, partly to express its disapproval of the wanton destruction by the German Army of Louvain University, in which the

Cardinal had taught for years. In a single week, he received honorary degrees from Harvard, Yale, and Princeton. In a single morning at Hartford, he received degrees from Yale, Wesleyan University, and Trinity College. Harvard held a special convocation—the fourth in its history—in his honor, and thus ranked him with Washington, Marshall Joffre, and King Albert. The University of the State of New York did the same, and ranked him with Elihu Root, Jules Jusserand (the French Ambassador to the United States during the war), and Thomas Edison. He was hailed at Princeton as "a majestic figure in the world of heroism, a brilliant figure in the world of ideas," and at Columbia as "the spiritual hero of the greatest of Wars."

Other groups joined in what seemed to be a universal chorus as the Cardinal went from one unique event to another. A dinner billed as "An Interracial Tribute" was sponsored by representatives of thirty-three different races or nations, presided over by Charles Evans Hughes and held at the Plaza Hotel. The non-Catholic clergy, acting through their Clergy Club, gave a lunch at the Commodore Hotel which was presided over by Bishop William T. Manning of the Episcopal Diocese of New York and attended by about 350 ministers, rabbis, and Orthodox priests. The Cardinal was accompanied by the Archbishop and a handful of priests. Nothing could have exceeded the courtesy and warmth of the audience, which the Cardinal reciprocated when, on the eve of his departure from the country, he placed a wreath on the tomb of Bishop Potter in the Cathedral of St. John the Divine.

Although America rejected world leadership, the Treaty of Versailles, and the League of Nations, and renounced for a time its desire to impose its standards on the rest of the world, it did not lose interest in helping the victims of the war, a work in which it made a golden and unequalled record. Between 1914 and 1923, about six billion dollars in food and supplies went to Europe. The American Relief Administration, established by Congress early in 1919 and directed by Herbert Hoover, sent about four million metric tons of food to twenty-one countries, including Soviet Russia. In the beginning, the defeated powers were barred from this assistance, but their condition became so desperate they had to be included. The Anglo-French food blockade of Germany was continued until March 1919 against the wishes of America. Hoover denounced it as "a crime against statesmanship and against civilization as a whole." The American government welcomed the help of all the private agencies that had been so active during the war, including the Red Cross, the Y.M.C.A., the Salvation Army, the Joint Jewish Distribution Committee, the Knights of Columbus and others, many of which kept up their good work after government aid ended.

THE CARDINALATE

The Catholic share in America's wonderful response to the cries for help from Europe (including Russia) and the Middle East had much to do with the timing of Archbishop Hayes' elevation to the Sacred College of Cardinals, though it was morally certain it would come eventually. On March 6, 1924, it was announced in Rome that the Archbishops of New York and Chicago would be elevated in the Consistory of March 24th. That raised American representation to four, as Archbishop Dennis J. Dougherty of Philadelphia (1865–1951) had received the Red Hat on March 17, 1921, a week before the death of Cardinal Gibbons.

The appointments were well received and were reported widely and extensively. The press stressed that both prelates were natives of New York and had graduated from Manhattan College. Archbishop George W. Mundelein, the first German-American to receive the Hat, was born in the oldest German parish in New York, St. Nicholas on Second Street, and was ordained for Brooklyn, where he was auxiliary bishop when promoted to Chicago in 1915. The Roman papers made much of his being the first Cardinal who lived west of the Alleghenies and referred to him as "the Cardinal of the West."

The sudden and rapid departure of the Cardinals-elect (who sailed on March 8th) prevented any organized farewell, but every detail of their voyage—from their rough crossing to France through their return seven weeks later—was given extensive coverage. They reached Rome on March 17th and were caught up at once in the usual round of ceremonies. America's interest in the Consistory of 1924 was heightened by the American flavor Pius XI gave it. No other country was represented in it and, to give it special prominence, it was held in St. Peter's (which was filled for the occasion) instead of in the Vatican. After the customary tributes to the personal merits of the heroes of the day and the importance of their sees, the Pope paid a special tribute to the filial piety and fraternal charity that had won the American Catholics primacy in charity in the Universal Church. He said that, finding it impossible to express adequately in words what he felt about the calamities of recent years and the no less historic, even epic, charity that had relieved them, he determined to express his feelings by an act that would be visible and clear to all, "especially to the great and noble people and country which gained so laudable a primacy in such a glorious undertaking." He added that "if the act is extraordinary, the moment which inspired it is also extraordinary and unexampled."

Cardinal Hayes, who was assigned the Church of Santa Maria in Via, sent his Easter pastoral on charity from Rome on March 25th, and was back in New York on April 28th. His welcome equalled Cardinal Farley's. A huge and friendly crowd watched his motorcade pass up Broadway, with a detour through City Hall Place, to the solemn reception in the Cathedral. He was grateful for all the signs of affection and goodwill and for the congratulatory messages that came pouring in. One that pleased him especially was from the Grand Street Boys Association—a group four thousand strong, drawn from past and present residents of the Lower East Side who had made good—who hailed him proudly as one of their own. Henceforth, he was known widely as the Cardinal of Charity.

DOMESTIC REFORM

The movement for domestic reform was aided rather than hurt by the war, as was seen in the adoption of the Prohibition and Woman Suffrage Amendments. They, and the crusading aspect of the war, illustrate the facet of the national character Pope Pius XII had in mind when he referred to the Americans as a people "by nature inclined to grandiose undertakings and to liberality." In a little over three years they attempted to eliminate by force and legislation the great and ancient evils of war, alcoholism, and corruption in politics.

In the public mind, both amendments came to be associated with the war, but they had been in the making for a long time. Prohibition stemmed from the Temperance Movement that started in the 1840s and was given a powerful boost by the Woman's Christian Temperance movement, which was organized in 1874, and the Anti-Saloon League, organized in 1893. Though the movement's fortunes waxed and waned and waxed again in different areas, it had achieved total or partial success in twenty-six states (thirteen of which were bone dry) by 1917. The wartime atmosphere gave it the needed push, and the Prohibition Amendment was ratified by forty-six states. Ratification was aided by the claim that it would help win the war, and by the refusal of the liquor industry to set its house in order.

The Catholic reaction to Prohibition was mixed, but most Catholics opposed it. Their attitude was well expressed by Archbishop Glennon, who said the Church would rather take the man from the drink than the drink from the man. Cardinal Gibbons described himself as a temperate man rather than a man of temperance. No one could deny the immense amount of suffering and evil caused by the abuse of alcohol, but the Catholics had never regarded that abuse with the peculiar horror it inspired in many Evangelical Protestants. They were aware of the large vein of fanaticism in many supporters of Prohibition and that many of them were strongly anti-Catholic. They were not convinced it could or should be made to work, and they regarded it as a questionable means to an undesirable and probably unattainable end. In a number of places it was hard to get altar wine and in 1926 the government issued a special form requiring priests to apply for a permit for it.

There was less agreement among Catholics on Woman Suffrage. One of the arguments advanced in its favor was that "women are people," which few cared or dared to deny. Another was that women would not tolerate corruption in politics and would put an end to it when they began to play an active role in public life. Cardinal Gibbons, expressing the mind of many and perhaps most Catholics, opposed it fearing it would weaken family life, but when it passed he urged the women to regard it as a duty as well as a right and to use it wisely. Some thought it would do nothing more useful than double the electorate and thereby further entrench the local political machines. Some were repelled by the fanaticism of some of its supporters, and by such antics as chaining themselves to public buildings or pouring acid into mail boxes to show that they were responsible citizens.

Like most of their fellow citizens, the Catholics were less interested in the League of Nations than in domestic matters like Prohibition and Woman Suffrage. They went along with the prevailing opinion, and America's participation in the League never became an issue with which they were strongly identified. Cardinal Gibbons, reflecting the papal desire to see some machinery established that might diminish or eliminate the danger of war, was in favor of it, but in this rare instance his attention seemed to focus on what should be rather than on what almost certainly would be true in a political matter.

The Cardinal did not go as far as Father John A. Ryan—a man described by a sympathetic biographer as being "remarkably ignorant of foreign affairs"—who was the spokesman for the Catholics, usually in academic circles, who supported the League. Father Ryan could find no flaw in the project. He scoffed at all critics of the League, and was sure that the people will "henceforth be the makers of national policies and interpreters of national interests and they will conceive national interests in terms of popular welfare, not in terms of national power, conquest and economic gain for a few special groups. In other words, national interests will henceforth be interpreted as bound up with peace and international justice." Those who considered this view to be hopelessly unrealistic came to be regarded as people who hoped the League would not succeed.

Just as the war ended a chapter in American history, the death of Cardinal Gibbons, on March 24, 1921, ended an era for the Church in this country. He had become the last survivor of Vatican I and the Third Plenary Council of Baltimore. He celebrated his episcopal golden jubilee in February 1919—belatedly because of the war and the influenza epidemic—and it had a strong international as well as national flavor. The Pope sent a special personal envoy and there were representatives or greetings from the Irish, English, Belgian, French, and Canadian hierarchies. The French and even the Italian governments sent greetings, as did a host of non-Catholic leaders in this country. He had survived all his companions in arms in the great controversies of his episcopate and felt especially the death on September 25, 1918, of Archbishop Ireland whose funeral he was unable to attend and whose promotion to the Sacred College he had never ceased working and hoping for.

Since 1884, James Cardinal Gibbons had been in fact and since 1886 in title the outstanding representative of the Church in America. In those years the Catholic population had grown from about 7,000,000 in 1884 to

17,886,000 in 1920. The number of dioceses had grown from sixty-four to ninety-eight, the number of priests from about 7,000 to 21,643. In 1920 the 6,551 parochial schools had 1,771,418 pupils and 1,552 high schools had 130,000. The Cardinal himself had come to be regarded almost as a national institution. He departed amid a chorus of praise from all quarters—the *New York Times* called him "one of the wisest men in the world"—and there has been no successor to his role as the freely accepted and internationally recognized spokesman and representative of the Church in America. His successor as dean of the hierarchy was Cardinal O'Connell of Boston, a very able man who chose to restrict his interests and activities mainly to New England. Neither he nor any of the other archbishops, least of all Archbishop Hayes, attempted to play a national role.

A Changing City

The city took its new status in stride as something altogether fitting and predictable. The new era got off to a bad start when the great influenza epidemic of September to November 1918 struck. The worst disaster of its kind since the Black Death ravaged Europe in 1347, it was felt all over the world. On a global basis it took some 21,000,000 lives (the war took 8,543,515) and is thought to have affected about half the total population. In this country it killed about 550,000, of whom some 20,000 were in New York State. The city toll was 12,562, of whom over eight hundred died in one day. Though the number of deaths was the highest ever recorded here, the percentage was lower than that of some of the cholera epidemics.

While the wealth and population of the city continued to grow, there were significant changes in population patterns. In 1920 the total population was 5,602,048, including 2,290,000 foreign-born. By 1940 the total had risen to 7,454,995, but 1,328,398 of the additional 1,852,947 had come between 1920 and 1930, and only 524,549 in the 1930–1940 period. On a national basis, the percentage of foreign-born had remained stable for forty years: 86 percent in 1880, 86.4 percent in 1900, and 86.8 percent in 1920.

The change in the rate of growth locally was only part of the story. The other part was the sharply altered distribution of the people. Manhattan with 2,284,103 was still the leading borough in 1920 though it was followed closely by Brooklyn which had 2,018,356. By 1930 Manhattan had lost 417,000 and was 693,089 below Brooklyn, which had gained 542,045, and reached 2,560,401. By 1940 Manhattan had risen from 1,867,312 to 1,889,924, but Brooklyn had reached 2,698,285. In the same years, 1920 to 1940, Queens went from 469,042 to 1,297,634, a gain of 828,592; the Bronx from 732,016 to 1,394,711, a gain of 662,695; and Staten Island from 116,531 to 174,441, a gain of 57,910. In the same period, the population of New York State went from 10,385,227 to 13,479,142.

The shifting of the population had a marked effect on the Archdiocese. Its three urban counties (Manhattan, the Bronx, and Staten Island) had only 326,426 of the 1,852,947 the city gained in 1920–1940, and of course they were not all Catholics. The seven suburban or rural counties gained only 324,332 in those years, and 246,841 of them were in Westchester. This shifting pattern explains why the Hayes administration saw a sharp drop in the Catholic population. The estimated Catholic population fell from 1,250,000 to 1,000,000. In those years, Nassau County went from 126,120 to 404,888 and Suffolk County from 110,246 to 195,540. New Jersey gained almost a million, going from 3,155,900 to 4,148,562. From 1920 to 1930 New Jersey gained 28.1 percent while New York State gained only 21.2 percent. The composition of the population was changing too. The Jews continued to grow in number though their percentage of the national population did not change appreciably. It was 3.27 percent in 1917 and 3.53 percent in 1927. In New York, things were different. The Jewish population went from about 350,000 in 1897 to 1,765,000 in 1927 and 2,035,000 in 1937, when there were about 4,770,647 in the entire country. In 1890 they were 12 percent of the population of Greater New York, but by 1920 the percentage was 29.2. Their distribution also changed. From 1910 to 1930 their numbers in Manhattan sank by a third, and from 1927 to 1937 from 465,000 to 351,037. In the Bronx, the number rose by 421.5 percent between 1910 and 1930 and from 420,000 to 592,185 from 1927 to 1937. In the same years (1927–1937), they went from 797,000 to 974,765 in Brooklyn and from 75,800 in Queens to 107,855. Their gains in Richmond County were small, from 7,200 to 9,158.

By 1930 there were over 500,000 foreign-born Italians and about 600,000 Italian-Americans born in the United States in Greater New York. They were about a fourth of all the Italians in America. Other groups, among whom the Russians, Poles, and Germans were mainly Jewish, were listed as 950,000 Russians, 460,000 Poles, 600,000 Germans, and 535,000 Irish. The number of Blacks was also increasing: from about 150,000 in 1920 to 327,700 in the city, from a total of 413,000 in the State. In 1930 Manhattan counted 224,670 Blacks and the Bronx 12,930.

A great era ended when Congress, urged on by the Nativists and the labor unions, passed the Immigration Act of 1924 which set drastic limits to immigration from Europe. It established quotas which were altered from time to time and abolished in 1968. In the 1920–1930 period, 2,477,853 of the 4,107,209 immigrants were from Europe and 1,516,716 from Canada, Mexico, and the rest of Latin America. From 1930 to 1940 only 348,289 of 528,431 immigrants came from Europe.

The decline in the Catholic population did not eliminate the need of new parishes. Provision had to be made for the growing areas, and in this matter as in many others Archbishop Hayes followed the programs established by his predecessors. In the first half of his administration, he opened sixty parishes and in the second, five. They included twenty-three in the Bronx, sixteen in Westchester, fifteen in Staten Island, seven in Manhattan, two in Dutchess, one each in Rockland and Ulster. There were no new parishes in Orange, Putnam, or Sullivan counties. Sixteen of the new parishes were Italian.

EDUCATION

While the Charities remained the Cardinal's major interest, the Hayes administration saw real progress on the educational front. Many of the new parishes opened schools. By 1938, the Archdiocese had 218 of them with 90,787 pupils, of whom 18,414 were in the counties. The growth on the high school level was less marked, though by 1938 the sixteen schools for boys had 5,491 students and the forty-four for girls had 4,838. In all this development the Archdiocese itself played a minor role. It was responsible, through the influence of Monsignor Lavelle, for the new building erected in 1925 for the Cathedral Girls High School, which was the only archdiocesan high school and the first monument to Archbishop Hughes. A boys' department, taught by the Christian Brothers, was in a separate building. It offered a two-year course until the class of 1929; in 1941 it was merged with Cardinal Hayes High School. All other new schools were built by the parishes or the religious communities.

The period between the two World Wars—the long armistice, as some called it—saw a very substantial growth in education on the public high school level both in New York City and in the entire country. During the same years, the number of Catholic high schools in the country increased by about a third to 2,105 and almost trebled their enrollment, which reached 311,000. In the city, the number of public high schools had grown from twenty-one in 1920, with an average daily attendance of 68,000, to fifty-one by 1940 with an average daily attendance of 253,348. The figures on high school graduates are significant, too. In 1900 the number in the entire country was only 94,883, but by 1920 it was 311,266, and by 1940 1,221,475. In each period, substantially more girls than boys graduated and America was the only country in the world in which that was true. The figures are even more striking when given in percentages. The percentage of eligible children enrolled in the public high schools in 1870 was 1.2 and it had grown only to 3.3 by 1900. By 1920 it was 10.2 and by 1940 it was 26. In 1920 New York State had only 729 public high schools, with 77,799 boys and 88,789 girls enrolled. The 645 private schools had 8,500 boys and 9,489 girls.

Things were different at the college level where the men retained their lead in numbers, though the percentage of women increased steadily. In 1870 only 9,371 students in the entire country graduated from college, and only 1,780 of them were women. By 1900 the respective figures were 25,324 and 8,104; by 1920, they were 48,633 and 16,642; and by 1940 the figures were

186,500 and 76,954. In New York State in 1918, there were only thirty-five colleges and universities. The fifteen for men only had 7,682 students, the nine for women only had 4,822, and the eleven mixed schools had 9,656 men and 6,212 women. By 1938 the Catholic colleges in the Archdiocese had 1,500 men and 1,745 women, and Fordham University (which accepted both) had 7,500 students.

One development in the educational world that gave the Archbishop much pleasure concerned the De La Salle Brothers. When they were founded in 1680, their primary purpose was "the gratuitous instruction of the poor through the medium of the vernacular." There were then other groups that attended to the needs of those going on for higher studies, for which Latin was then indispensable. Neither of those two requirements, free schools and a ban on Latin, could be met in this country because of the needs of the Church, and as early as 1854 the Brothers, who came here in 1848, received permission to give up both. So marked a departure from the original purpose of the Institute was bound to arouse opposition in areas that did not have to face the problems the Brothers faced in America, and in 1894 the General Chapter ordered that Latin be phased out of the curriculum as quickly as possible. This decision was upheld by the Holy See in December 1899, because it felt unable to interfere with an attempt by a religious community to adhere strictly to its original rule.

The elimination of Latin was opposed strongly by the American archbishops and the American Brothers, but their repeated appeals had no effect. Their worst fears were realized as the enrollment in the Brothers' schools plummeted. In 1904 Manhattan College had only forty-seven students in the Arts course, their second secondary schools were hard hit, and vocations to the priesthood from the Brothers' schools fell off sharply. Finally, in April 1923, Pope Pius XI repealed the ban. The exemplary obedience and patience of the Brothers here was then rewarded by a great flowering of their schools.

In his attitude toward the Seminary, which he left unvisited for years and in which, with one minor exception, he took no visible interest, Cardinal Hayes stands alone among the Archbishops of New York. The exception was a villa, opened in Suffern in July 1923, in which the third-year and fourth-year theologians spent most of the summer. It was inadequately housed and equipped, relatively expensive, unpopular with the faculty and many students, and was closed quietly after a few summers. Apart from that, the Cardinal's chief concerns were that the students abstain from smoking and that the Seminary be run as cheaply as possible.

Various explanations of his attitude, apart from his absorption in the Charities, were advanced from time to time by a puzzled clergy. Some thought it was due to his having concluded, in the light of his vivid and apparently happy memories of his own student days at Troy, that by comparison Dunwoodie was run on too lavish a scale. Others recalled that in

1906 the Dunwoodie Sulpicians had referred to the tension between some of the Troy alumni and the Dunwoodians, which was based on the former's view that the latter were favored unduly by Archbishops Corrigan and Farley. Others thought he was convinced the faculty had opposed his appointment to New York. Though all these explanations were true, a more basic one was that he never outgrew the extreme frugality of his early years. He lived very simply, saw no reason why those under him should not do the same, and was sure that even in its most spartan days Dunwoodie was better equipped and run than Troy had ever been.

What is certain is that within a few weeks of his appointment he sent a new procurator with instructions to cut expenses to the bone. No one who lived there at any time between 1919 and 1940 could forget the single-minded devotion, the enthusiasm, and the ability with which that mandate was carried out, or the mingled astonishment, indignation, and amusement with which his victims beheld the growing virtuosity which the all-powerful procurator displayed as he brought the art of stretching a dollar to ever greater heights.

How firmly the Cardinal's attitude was fixed may be seen from the fact that Dunwoodie was the only archdiocesan major seminary in the United States to which Cardinal Pacelli was not invited when he paid his historic visit to this country in November 1936. The omission was all the more obvious because he was driven past it on his way from lunch with President Roosevelt at Hyde Park to a private reception at the Joseph P. Kennedy home in Bronxville. The austerity and strict discipline of the seminary did not discourage vocations, and the enrollment, which passed three hundred in 1931, was never as high. The students ordained during the Hayes administration numbered 656, a record unequalled there before or since in the same number of years. Moreover, judged by post Vatican II standards, they had an astonishingly high level of perseverance in the active priestly ministry.

Apart entirely from local affairs, the Hayes administration witnessed some major developments that helped to clarify and safeguard the constitutional and legal rights of Catholic and other private schools and of the parents who choose to use them. On the national scene, the Nebraska and Oregon cases were outstanding. Both were occasioned by the revival of Nativism that was stimulated so greatly by the popular revulsion against World War I.

In 1923 the Nebraska Legislature enacted a law, which was upheld by Nebraska's highest Court, that forbade any school, public or private, to teach a foreign language to a child below the eighth grade. A teacher in a Lutheran parochial school who claimed that the law was an unjustifiable interference with his constitutional rights appealed to the United States Supreme Court which decided unanimously in his favor and nullified the law.

The Oregon School Case was even more important. The Scottish Rite Free Masons of the Southern jurisdiction adopted a resolution in May 1920 calling for the free and compulsory education of all children in the public primary schools. In November 1922 this proposal won in a referendum in Oregon and was to become law on September 1, 1926. It was supported vigorously by the Free Masons and the Ku Klux Klan and opposed not only by the Catholics, who were obviously its chief target, but by other religious groups and by all other owners of private schools. The Catholics were fortunate that the bill was so inclusive that many who might not otherwise have sided with them had no choice but to do so in self-defense. The Sisters of the Holy Names of Jesus and Mary, a Canadian community that had gone to Oregon in 1859 and had many schools there, appealed to the United States Supreme Court which, on June 1, 1925, handed down a landmark decision in their favor.

In its decision, which was unanimous and was based on the Fourteenth Amendment, not the First, the Court stated that: "The fundamental theory of liberty upon which all governments in this Union repose excludes any general power of the State to standardize its children by forcing them to accept instruction from public teachers only. The child is not the mere creature of the state; those who nurture him and direct his destiny have the right, coupled with the high duty, to recognize and prepare him for additional obligations." This statement was quoted with approval by Pope Pius XI in his encyclical on Education *Divini Illius Magistri* of December 31, 1929, and contrasted with the attitude of the growing number of countries imposing a state monopoly of education.

Had these decisions gone the other way, what was done in Nebraska and Oregon would surely have been copied in some other States and, even where it was not copied, the private schools on all levels would have existed solely at the pleasure of the local authorities. In the intervening years, some members of the Supreme Court may have regretted those decisions, but the Court itself has never retreated from them and seems unlikely to do so now.

There were developments on the State level too. In 1936 the age at which children could quit school legally was raised to sixteen in New York. At the time, that was generally regarded as a step forward, although it has since come to be questioned by many. Two other changes were more controversial and led to years of bitter litigation in New York and other states. They were the Released Time Program and state-supplied busing for parochial school pupils. The idea of releasing public school children from class to allow them to attend religious instruction in church institutions originated in Protestant circles, and the program began in New York City in 1906 in a Lutheran parish. The first legal test came in 1925 when a program in Mount Vernon, New York, was declared illegal because the forms used to apply for membership in the program were printed by the school, and this was judged to be a wrong use of public property. Exception was taken, too, to regular absence from class as a violation of the compulsory attendance law. Two years later, in a White Plains case where forms were not supplied by the school, the New York State Court of Appeals upheld the Released Time

Program and at the same time took a less restrictive view of the compulsory attendance law.

The Busing Bill aroused more interest among the general public. In 1935 the New York State Legislature passed a bill, sponsored by the Knights of Columbus, that gave parochial school pupils the same busing service provided for the public school children. This was particularly useful in rural areas. It was vetoed by Governor Herbert H. Lehman on the ground that it was "a departure from public policy." He signed it when it was repassed in 1936. It was rejected on constitutional grounds by the Court of Appeals in 1938, but in 1939 an amended law was upheld. The Busing Bill revealed, even more than the Released Time Program, the strength of the anti-Catholic feeling that was sure to surface whenever aid of any kind was given to the children in Catholic schools. No one denied that the Catholic parents paid their share of the taxes that supported the school-bus programs, but it was claimed that the sacred principle of the separation of Church and State required that their children be denied the use of the program.

In spite of the 1918 act against discrimination, some continued to question the right of Catholics to teach in the public schools, and a particularly flagrant instance of that occurred in October 1929 in Harriman, New York. A qualified Catholic teacher, Miss Anna Mulholland, applied for a position in the public school and was rejected on the stated ground that she was a Catholic. The pastor of Harriman, Father Patrick F. MacAran (1859–1930), aided by the Knights of Columbus, filed a complaint with the State educational authorities and won in April 1930. The offending principal was removed and, in March 1932, Governor Franklin D. Roosevelt signed a bill forbidding inquiry concerning the religious affiliation of candidates for employment in the public schools.

Public Affairs

Like Archbishop Corrigan, Cardinal Hayes intervened in public affairs reluctantly and only when he felt an inescapable obligation to do so. One such occasion arose when Congress passed the Child Labor Amendment in 1924. It was opposed by all the bishops of New York State on the twofold ground that it was so loosely worded it gave the Federal Government excessive control of everyone under eighteen years of age, and that it was unnecessary as child labor was already being eliminated rapidly. The available figures sustained the bishops' stand. Taking the country as a whole, the gainful employment of boys from ten to fifteen years of age dropped from 26.1 percent in 1900 to 6.4 percent in 1930, and of girls from 10.2 percent to 2.9 percent. The figures for New York State and City were even lower. In the city, the employment of boys dropped from 16.7 percent to 2.1 percent, and of girls from 12.6 percent to 1.4 percent. The Amendment was not ratified by the requisite number of States.

A second occasion was presented by the spread of the campaign for artificial contraception. In 1930 the Lambeth Conference, a worldwide gathering of the bishops of the Anglican Communion, had sanctioned the use of artificial contraception by married couples. This was rightly hailed as a notable breakthrough by the advocates of birth control, and was one of the reasons why Pope Pius XI issued his Encyclical on Marriage, *Casti Connubii,* on December 31, 1930. In it, he expressly condemned the use of artificial contraceptives of any kind and under any circumstances and repeated and confirmed the traditional Catholic teaching on marriage.

On December 2, 1935, a mass meeting was held at Carnegie Hall under the auspices of the American Birth Control League and on December 8th the Cardinal, who rarely preached in the Cathedral, did so, referring to the meeting and voicing what he called "a measured, deliberate, and emphatic condemnation of the effrontery of those who at this meeting advocated birth control for families on relief." His targets, whom he described as "Prophets of Decadence," hit back, and a lively controversy followed. An earlier effort to have the police enforce the laws against contraceptives caused a momentary stir and brought him much criticism from people who chose to ignore the fact that the laws were there and had been passed long ago when the Catholics had very little influence on the Legislature.

Not all of Archbishop Hayes' difficulties came from outside the fold. Early in his administration, he was involved quite innocently in a minor controversy that amused some of his closest advisers, who knew how cautious he was. It is worth mentioning only for the light it throws on some sectors of public opinion here at that time. On November 3, 1920, a Mass was sung at the Cathedral for Terence MacSwiney, the recently deceased Lord Mayor of Cork, whose death after a prolonged hunger strike had focused international attention on the deplorable situation in Ireland. It was one of a series of Masses being held in the major cities of the English-speaking and Catholic worlds. Wishing to give the occasion added solemnity and to show his own sympathies, Archbishop Hayes decided to preside himself, have Monsignor Dunn, the Chancellor, offer the Mass, and Monsignor Mooney, the Vicar General, preach.

All went well until the congregation was leaving. Some of them noticed that the Union Club, then on the northeast corner of Fifth Avenue and Fifty-First Street, was flying a Union Jack (apparently without any intention or awareness of being provocative). They noticed too that the street was being repaired and that the workmen had left a supply of paving blocks nearby. Temptation was too strong for some, and in a few minutes the club's windows were smashed.

The press, here and elsewhere, played the episode up and some reacted as if the city were facing a renewal of the Draft Riots. The Archbishop was surprised to receive a letter from a group of well-known Catholics, spiritual heirs of Archbishop Hughes's "timid souls," deploring the attack on the club, which no one defended, and by implication rebuking him for having allowed and attended the Mass that provided the occasion for it. He replied in a firm and temperate letter defending his conduct and rebuking them for bad manners in sending a letter to him to the press before he received it. There were unverified rumors at the time that they wanted him to give the Cathedral a less controversial, by which they meant a less common, name than Patrick.

Years later, in 1927, in another episode related to Ireland, but this time in an attack from a sensational non-Catholic paper in London, the *Sunday Express,* the Archbishop, by then a Cardinal, was accused of having condoned publicly the murder of Kevin O'Higgins, a prominent member of the Irish Government, on the stated ground that the victim was "an English hireling." He sued for libel and won an unconditional apology and his legal expenses.

THE REVIVAL OF THE KU KLUX KLAN

The revived Nativist Movement did not confine its attention to immigration and education, and for several years it was an important political force. That was unavoidable because of its great and rapid (though uneven) growth, the skilled leadership that guided and exploited it, and the fact that its rise coincided with the first serious discussion by a major political party of the selection of a Catholic candidate for the presidency of the United States. Since its most conspicuous manifestation was the Ku Klux Klan, many made the mistake of thinking the Klan caused Nativism, but of course it was the other way round. The Klan articulated the deep feelings of millions of Americans and provided them with an instrument with which to compel an attentive hearing from some political leaders on every level of government; but when it faded away and Nativism subsided, the feelings to which both appealed remained and are still strong.

The growth of the Klan was impressive by any standard. Starting on a small scale in Georgia, and remaining a local movement for several years, it spread rapidly after 1920. By 1925, when the national population was estimated at about 115,000,000—of whom some 18,000,000 were Catholics, 4,000,000 were Jews, and 11,000,000 were Blacks—it had about 5,000,000 adult white male members. The Klan was bipartisan and was as strong in the solidly Republican Middle West as it was in the solidly Democratic South. Its slogan—"Native White Protestant Supremacy"— really meant Northern European White Supremacy. It disliked Latins and Slavs. It disliked Jews too, but they were not as old or as numerous an enemy as the Catholics. Still, a Klan paper denounced Alfred E. Smith as the candidate of "Jew York." Its militant Protestantism led to militant anti-Catholicism, which it expressed in the "No Popery" literature that flooded the country during the 1920s. Though the Klan had little support in the major cities, it was not limited to the rural areas. It was strong in the small and medium sized towns and in the suburbs of several metropolitan centers. The urban population had passed the half-way mark in 1920 when it constituted 51.4 percent of the national total as opposed to 40 percent in 1900.

The Klan was never as strong in New York State as it was in California and had no chance in New York City, but it was active in such suburban New York areas as Rockland, Nassau, and Suffolk Counties, and in New Jersey. Its chief interest for most New Yorkers was that the presidential candidate it fought so bitterly and successfully was the Governor of New York and the most prominent lay member of the Archdiocese.

Alfred Emanuel (Al) Smith (December 30, 1873–October 4, 1944), a typical example of the American success story, was born on the lower East Side of Manhattan. His parents, both of whom were born in New York, were very poor; his father was a truckman who worked along the docks. Al's formal education ended when he left St. James parochial school at thirteen. He then went to work as a newsboy and in the Fulton Fish Market—which he used to claim as his alma mater—to help support his recently widowed mother and his sister. He started his political career in 1895 serving jury notices and rose steadily through the ranks. He served in the State Legislature, of which he was the Speaker in 1913, in the city government (as sheriff of New York County in 1915 and as President of the Board of Aldermen in 1917), reaching the State Capital as Governor in 1918. He was the first Catholic elected to that office.

Al Smith was an excellent and very popular governor. He was regarded as an able administrator, a good organizer, and a fiscal conservative who promoted sound social legislation and reform. He was defeated in 1920 but reelected in 1922. Viewed from outside his own state as a candidate for the national presidency, he was vulnerable to criticism from several quarters. He was a product of the New York City Democratic political machine, a fact for which (like Harry Truman in a similar case) he felt no need to apologize, though New York Democrats who aspire to higher office have usually found it expedient to disavow it. He was an open and consistent opponent of Prohibition, the dominant fanaticism of the day, which he regarded as unwise and unworkable. He was largely unknown to the country at large and had not made a point of acquiring and expressing views on most of the current national issues. His most obvious handicap was that he was a devout Catholic who never thought of soft-pedaling the role the Church played in his life.

His first appearance on the national stage in a major role was at the Democratic Convention of 1924, which was held in New York City from June 24th to July 9th. It was the first national convention held in the city by either party since 1868 and the last until 1976. Though not the most important, it was the longest and the most disorderly on record. It was also the most expensive up to that date and one of the best remembered. Unlike the Chicago Convention of 1968, in which the disorders took place outside the Convention itself, in 1924 the raucous and even riotous demonstrations took place within the hall.

Though sixty names were placed in nomination, the Convention was divided from the beginning between two factions of almost equal strength. Since the rules of that time required the successful candidate to win two-thirds of the votes, each faction could block the other. The first test of strength came after the preliminary formalities which included an invocation by Cardinal Hayes, who was introduced as "Cardinal Farley." The Republican Convention had ignored the Klan, but the Democrats were unable to do so and were confronted with two conflicting resolutions. One was to condemn it and the other was to give it mild approval. The Convention chose the latter by a vote of 546.15 to 542.85.

The triumph of the Klan brought the religious issue to the fore, but it was not the only major issue. The failure of Prohibition had not yet been seen or accepted by many who had so recently favored its adoption, and those who were for it were bound to be anti-Smith. To be anti-Smith was to be for McAdoo, his chief rival. William G. McAdoo (1863–1941), a son-in-law of Woodrow Wilson and a former United States Secretary of the Treasury, was a former southerner who had moved through New York and Washington to California, where he had a solid political base. He was the avowed candidate of the Klan and the Prohibitionists. There were sectional differences, too. Smith never had more than one vote from the entire South or more than twenty from west of the Mississippi. There was strong anti-New York sentiment to which McAdoo, who had lived in the city from 1892 to 1913 and made a fortune as promoter of the Hudson Tubes, appealed. He described it as "the imperial city—reactionary, sinister, unscrupulous, mercenary, and sordid, devoid of conscience, rooted in corruption, directed by greed, and dominated by selfishness."

The religious issue was not as simple as it seemed. While all the anti-Catholics were anti-Smith, not all the Catholics were pro-Smith, which surprised some of his enemies. Few Catholics could have agreed that there should never be a Catholic President, but many felt that having one was not a matter of great urgency and, like those Archbishop Hughes criticized for excessive meekness, were willing to postpone it to a quieter day. Some did not wish Smith to be the first one chosen for that honor. Some opposed him because of his attitude toward Prohibition. Among them was Thomas J. Walsh (1859–1933), a United States Senator from Montana, who was Permanent Chairman of the Convention. He was a much respected man of national stature who had helped draft the Prohibition and Woman Suffrage Amendments, and was one of those chiefly responsible for the exposure of the Teapot Dome Scandals of the Harding era. Some Catholics opposed Smith on strictly political grounds. Among them was James D. Phelan (1861–1930), a former United States Senator from California, who nominated McAdoo at the Convention. He was a munificent patron of Catholic charities and schools, to which he later bequeathed additional millions. Just as it was considered prudent to have McAdoo nominated by a Catholic, it was considered prudent to have Smith nominated by a Protestant with impeccable Establishment credentials. The one chosen for that task was Franklin D. Roosevelt, who hailed him as "The Happy Warrior," a title that stuck.

As the length, cost, and bitterness of the Convention increased, many Democratic leaders began to fear an irreparable split in the party and begged both Smith and McAdoo to withdraw in favor of a candidate acceptable to both. They agreed reluctantly, and on the 103rd ballot the exhausted delegates nominated John W. Davis of West Virginia and New York, a wealthy corporation lawyer, with Charles W. Bryan of Nebraska, a brother of William Jennings Bryan, as his running-mate. The wounds inflicted during the Convention could not be healed by November and the Democratic ticket suffered a crushing defeat. The election returns gave the professionals in both parties food for thought. Coolidge, though victorious, got fewer electoral and popular votes than Harding. He had hardly bothered to campaign, and "Keep Cool with Coolidge" was his chief slogan. Davis, though he added Kentucky to the eleven southern and border states won by Cox in 1920, received almost a million fewer votes. A third party, Robert M. LaFollette's Progressives, carried only his native Wisconsin, but received almost five million votes.

The Democratic Convention of 1924 had great educational value and brought about permanent changes in America's political campaigns. It was the first convention broadcast from coast to coast. Millions of Americans sat glued to their radios listening to the seemingly interminable roll calls and to the descriptions of the proceedings, which Arthur Krock of *The New York Times* called "the snarling, cursing, tedious, tenuous, suicidal, homicidal roughhouse in New York." The Catholics in New York, long insulated by their numbers and position from what Catholics outside the other great urban centers had to put up with, were astonished by much of what they heard. Not since the pre-Civil War days had such bitter anti-Catholic sentiments been expressed so openly here. On the other hand, many delegates from the West, the Middle West, and the South had their worst opinions of New York City confirmed, and left convinced it was the Babylon, if not the Sodom and Gomorrah, of the Western Hemisphere.

Al Smith's drive for the presidency was like a two-act play in which the interest aroused in the first act survived a very long intermission. To the distress of many Catholics, it kept the Catholic issue alive politically for several years. When the second act opened with the Convention of 1928, his position in his party had improved considerably and on the surface the country seemed much calmer. He had been reelected governor in 1924, in spite of the Coolidge sweep, and again in 1926 and was the first New York governor since DeWitt Clinton to serve four terms. The Klan had declined very rapidly and many of its former supporters seemed ashamed of its excesses. There was no danger of a third party movement like LaFollette's, and the Democratic leaders, determined to prevent another fiasco like the previous Convention, had laid their plans carefully. Accordingly, the Convention, which was held in Houston, Texas, in June was limited to three days. Smith, who did not attend, was nominated again by Franklin D. Roosevelt and won on the first ballot.

Those who hoped the religious issue would go away if they ignored it were disappointed but should not have been surprised. It was important to millions of Americans whose deepest prejudices had been excited deliberately for several years, and it cut across all social barriers. Smith hoped it had been defused by an exchange of letters for which the *Atlantic Monthly* provided a forum in April and May of 1927. The first was from Charles C. Marshall, a distinguished Episcopalian lawyer, who stated in courteous and temperate terms the difficulties seen by many Protestants in the traditional Catholic teaching on the relations of Church and State. Smith's reply, which was drafted with the help of Father Francis P. Duffy, restated that teaching as it was understood by most American Catholics, and showed the basic harmony between Catholic teaching and American political principles and institutions. Prior to its release, his reply was submitted to Cardinal Hayes who pronounced it "good Catholicism and good Americanism." Events were soon to show that discussions on that level were wholly irrelevant to millions of voters.

The bitter anti-Catholic campaign for which the election of 1928 is best remembered must be seen in perspective. The Republicans began with many advantages and were clearly in the lead from the start. They were still the majority party and had won twelve of the sixteen presidential elections since 1860. Only two Democrats, Cleveland and Wilson, had been elected in that time and each of them had won both of his terms with a minority of the votes cast. The country was prosperous and at peace. The Prohibitionists, who were still very strong and commanded a major bloc in Congress (including many so-called "drinking Drys"), were largely in the Republican camp that year. They were grateful for Hoover's oft-quoted description of Prohibition as "a great social and economic experiment, noble in motive and far-reaching in its purpose."

The Republicans had a strong candidate in Herbert Hoover (1874–1964) who was an example of a version of the American success story that differed greatly from Smith's. Born in rural Iowa, the son of a blacksmith and orphaned early in life, he had worked his way through Stanford University where he earned a degree in mining engineering. He practiced his profession so successfully that he acquired a substantial fortune. Unlike Smith, who had never been outside this country, he had lived in China, the Malay States, Australia, and Europe. He had acquired great fame as Director of American Relief in Europe, and knew many world leaders. He had been a successful

Secretary of Commerce in the Harding and Coolidge administrations and had a deservedly high reputation for intelligence, integrity, and administrative ability. He was not anti-Catholic and had received warm personal thanks from Benedict XV for his work in Europe. He had opposed the adoption of Prohibition but felt that it must be given a fair trial and enforced as long as it was the law of the land. Like Smith, he had been nominated on the first ballot.

If the Republican leaders had been too highminded to use the religious issue, and they surely were not, it would still have been important and it was used widely by the Democrats too. The party leaders and the Convention had accepted Smith, but they were unable to deliver their troops to the polls and the Democrats soon broke ranks. Within a week of the Convention, over ten million pieces of anti-Catholic literature had been distributed, and that flood continued until after the election. The Klan paper, *The Fellowship Forum,* had an immense increase in circulation and it was not hard to guess where the money came from. Mrs. Mabel Walker Willebrandt, an Assistant United States Attorney General, devoted herself to rousing the various Protestant Ministers Associations. Many of them, scenting an unholy alliance between Romanism and Rum, threw themselves eagerly into the fray.

The Evangelical press had a field day too. Many Baptist, Methodist, and Lutheran papers were openly hostile to Smith because of his religion, but the Episcopalians were generally more moderate. A Methodist paper said correctly that he had a constitutional right to run for president even though he was a Catholic, and his opponents had the same right to oppose him on the same ground and intended to do so. A Baptist paper in Arkansas posed the question, "Is the Catholic Church a Christian Church?" and answered, "No, it is a brutal, hell-born power and its priests are money-grubbing scoundrels."

All the old anti-Catholic canards—from the Inquisition and Foxe's *Book of Martyrs* (1563) down through *Maria Monk*—were revived. Since the campaign was better organized and financed than earlier ones, the worst excesses of the Know Nothing propaganda were surpassed, though this time there was no violence. There was something on every level and for every taste and nothing seemed too extravagant or absurd to be said or believed. The bogus "Knights of Columbus oath" which included such purple passages as, "I will spare neither sex, age nor condition and I swear that I will hang, waste, boil, flay, strangle and burn alive those infamous heretics"—warned Protestants of their impending doom, as did the charge that guns were being stored in Catholic churches to await the time set for the great massacre. It was alleged, too, that a million dollars had been taken from the funds raised by the Knights of Columbus fund drive in 1917 and sent directly to the Pope.

There were a few new items too, of which three examples will suffice. On November 12, 1927, the Holland Tunnel, which connects New York City with Jersey City, was opened in the presence of the governors of both states. After Smith's nomination, thousands of pictures of him at the tunnel's New York entrance were distributed in Georgia with a notation that it was designed to go through to the Vatican when Smith entered the White House. A community of Sisters bought a large house on the Jersey shore and it was widely publicized as the new papal summer residence. Two ancient decorative cannon in front of Georgetown University were described to the Senate by Senator Heflin of Alabama as having been placed there in preparation for a papal order to bombard the Capitol. The attitude that underlay all these charges, whether old or new, was well expressed by the Methodist Bishop of Buffalo, who was also the head of the Anti-Saloon League in New York State, when he said, "No Governor can kiss the papal ring and get within gunshot of the White House."

The ordinary Catholic reaction to all this was a mixture of incredulity, bewilderment, and anger, with an underlying regret that so many ordinary decent people could be so ignorant of the Church and her teaching. They recognized the sincerity of most of the anti-Catholics and their leaders and saw, too, how they were being manipulated for political ends by people who knew exactly what they were doing.

The excitement engendered by the campaign was reflected in the sharp rise in the number of votes cast, which went from about 29,000,000 in 1924 to about 36,500,000 in 1928. Hoover carried forty states, with 83.6 percent of the electoral vote, but his 21,391,381 votes were a smaller percentage of the popular vote than Harding's. Though it broke for the first time since Reconstruction, Smith salvaged about half the Solid South, in which he carried Alabama, Arkansas, Georgia, Louisiana, Mississippi and South Carolina. His other two states were Massachusetts and Rhode Island, which, except for 1912, had been Republican since the Civil War. The loss of New York was a hard blow, even though the vote—2,193,344 to 2,089,863—was close, and Hoover got only a plurality as the fringe parties garnered 122,409. Smith carried the five counties in New York City but only four—Albany, Rensselaer, Clinton, and Franklin—of the remaining fifty-seven. His vote in the city was due in part to his great popularity in the Jewish community, from which he drew some of his closest friends and admirers and which knew that many of his enemies were their enemies, too. He carried the twelve largest cities in the country—a portent missed by many—and got 6,000,000 more votes than any preceding Democratic candidate. His 15,006,443 votes, 40.8 percent of the total, far exceeded the country's Catholic and Jewish vote, which did not all go to him, so it is clear that millions of Protestants voted for him.

It is impossible to determine precisely the degree to which the religious issue influenced the election and therefore there will be different opinions, but it seems clear that the issue aroused more feeling than any other, that it was decisive in certain areas and important in others, and that it worked both ways. If it cost Smith half the South and probably New York, it brought him Massachusetts and Rhode Island, the two most Catholic states in the Union. Hoover, the first Quaker to seek or reach the White House, was unfairly attacked on the ground that no Quaker could fulfill the President's obligations as Commander-in-Chief. For a substantial but indeterminate number, the religious issue conflicted with their dislike of Prohibition, which Smith denounced during the campaign. Perhaps H. L. Mencken put it best when he said: "Those who fear the Pope outnumber those who are tired of the Anti-Saloon League."

THE DEPRESSION OF 1929

Within a year, the Great Depression, which began on Wall Street on October 29, 1929, and was the worst in the history of the country, gave Smith, the Catholics, and the Democratic Party reason to congratulate themselves on his defeat. Though unperceived by most of the experts, it was already in the works when Hoover took office on March 4th. Had it occurred in a Smith administration, nothing could have prevented it from being blamed on his being a Catholic and a Democrat with consequences that would be felt even today. Millions of his contemporaries would have believed—and succeeding generations would have been taught by the experts—that, if a man of Hoover's gifts and experiences had been in office, the situation would have been saved. As it was, the Depression and its child, the New Deal, made such sweeping and permanent social, economic, and political changes that they may fairly be said to have affected the country more than any event since the adoption of the Federal Constitution. Two of their early and obvious political effects were: (1) that the Democrats became the majority party and, except for two short intervals, have controlled Congress since January 1931; and (2) that, to the relief of millions of Catholics and non-Catholics, the religious issue was put aside for a generation or more.

One reason for the great impact of the Depression was that it was so unexpected. After recovering from the depression or recession of 1921–1922, the country had entered a period of uninterrupted prosperity and growth. Taxes and the public debt were reduced regularly. Every available index showed a steady and substantial rise in the standard of living, and many had come to believe that the situation was to be permanent. Even Hoover, a matter-of-fact and cautious man with no trace of demagoguery, felt able to promise in his acceptance speech that poverty would vanish from the land.

The most obvious social effect of the Depression was the widespread unemployment, which put an almost unbearable burden on the private charitable organizations and on the very limited public funds then given for relief. There had been progress in social legislation in New York since 1920 but nothing like what was needed to meet the Depression. As always, public opinion lagged behind events. Small indications of a changing attitude were the change in title of the New York City Department of Charity to the Department of Welfare in 1920, and of the State Superintendent of the Poor to the State Commissioner of Welfare in 1929. More substantial steps were the passages of a Workmen's Compensation Act in 1928 (an earlier attempt was declared unconstitutional in 1911), the codification and expansion in 1929 of all the State's welfare legislation, which made it the most liberal in the country, and the passage of the Old Age Pension Act in 1929. In 1931, New York became the first State to help the local government units meet their welfare needs by giving them grants of money and in 1933 the first to have a minimum wage.

Like all the other private agencies, Catholic Charities was hard hit by the Depression because there were fewer contributors to meet more requests for help. The small contributors the Cardinal valued fell off sharply in 1930, and many of them needed help. By 1933 he had to make a permanent change in his fund-raising procedure and he formed a Special Gifts Committee which was headed by Al Smith. It solicited gifts from large donors, private or corporate. Aid came, too, from some of the foundations that used Catholic Charities as a dispensing agent. The Cardinal put all their contributions in a separate account so that all concerned might see that every dollar went for relief and not for religious purposes. The first Federal Emergency Relief came in 1931, but under it public funds could not be given to unemployed persons who were not in institutions. In April 1932, over 800,000 people in the city were being aided by public or private charity.

As the election of 1932 approached, the Republicans found themselves in an unenviable position. They had claimed credit for the prosperity of former years and could not avoid blame for the Depression. Moreover, it was clear that Hoover, whom they had to renominate, lacked the capacity for leadership and the manipulative skills our political system requires of a president in times of crisis. Those qualities were conspicuous in his Democratic opponent, Franklin D. Roosevelt (1882–1945), Al Smith's chosen successor as Governor of New York. The Democrats swept the country but Hoover, who carried only six states, all in New England and the Middle Atlantic, got more popular votes than Smith got in 1928. The religious issue had no place in the campaign and the South returned gladly to its Democratic allegiance.

The advent of the New Deal, with its program of "Relief, Recovery and Reform" brought a flood of social legislation and put the Federal Government squarely in the center of the picture in that area. A Federal Relief Program was started in 1933. At first, welfare recipients were given relief orders for food instead of cash, but this was soon changed and expanded to include rent, clothing, fuel, and medical care. Though the figures vary, it was estimated that in March 1933, there were 14,762,000 people, a third of the entire working force, unemployed. Things were worse than those figures indicated because, while the employed workers declined by a third between 1926 and 1933, the total payroll declined by 56 percent. In 1934 there were about 1,000,000 persons on relief in New York City. In that year, the city adopted a

2 percent sales tax to help meet the cost of unemployment relief which was then costing $19,000,000 a month. It also began to receive huge Federal grants under the new Relief and Recovery Program.

Three major developments in 1935 that lay outside the field of relief were the Wagner Act, which protected labor's right to organize; the Social Security Act; and the opening of the first public housing project in the country—a federally funded project built in New York by the City Housing Authority. At that time, about 2,000,000 New Yorkers were living in substandard housing. In 1938 the Federal Minimum Wage Act, which set a forty-hour week at forty cents an hour, was introduced. Cardinal Hayes, whose active interest in politics was limited to voting in all presidential elections and some others, approved wholeheartedly of all the social reforms of the New Deal. He thought the need was urgent and obvious and that the government's functions and responsibilities could not be limited to protecting life and property.

One of the most popular reforms of the New Deal was the repeal of the XVIII Amendment, which took effect on December 5, 1933. Prohibition, though noble in motive, was a spectacular failure that left deep and lasting scars on the country. It almost destroyed the Temperance Movement, which has never regained its former strength. It made drinking popular with young people and encouraged in them and their elders a disrespect for law that became very fashionable and spread far beyond the field of liquor. It greatly weakened the moral authority of the Evangelical Protestants who had put such effort into it and thus it hastened the dechristianization of the country. It placed immense sums in the hands of organized crime, which operates in the United States today on a scale unknown in any other part of the civilized world and has acquired influence on every level and in every branch of government that renders it substantially immune to prosecution.

The New Deal opened many doors that had hitherto been closed to Catholics and Jews, who formed a major part of the coalition Roosevelt had put together. One instance among many affecting Catholics was the appointment of Catholics to the Federal Cabinet, to which only six had been appointed between 1789 and 1932. Roosevelt appointed three and a fourth, Senator Thomas Walsh of Montana, had died before his nomination as Attorney General could be confirmed by the Senate. The three were James A. Farley (1888–1976), the first from New York, as Postmaster General; Frank C. Walker (1888–1959), also from New York, as Postmaster General; and Frank Murphy (1890–1949) of Michigan, as Attorney General. Perhaps less important but more surprising was the appointment of a Catholic (and even an Irish Catholic) as Ambassador to the Court of St. James, in the person of Joseph P. Kennedy (1888–1969) of Boston.

Another sign of the changed political and social climate was the President's appearance at the National Conference of Catholic Charities, to which he spoke on October 4, 1933. He had shown a friendly interest earlier when, on April 9, 1932, he and Al Smith spoke at the lunch that launched the annual Charity Drive. The Conference was held in New York, at the Waldorf, at the Cardinal's invitation, and at his suggestion it celebrated the centennial of the founding of the St. Vincent de Paul Society, which he said had "quietly and unobtrusively been the bulwark of Catholic Charities in the United States not only in the field of relief but also in cooperation with other welfare organizations." The National Conference had been founded in 1911 largely at the instance of Thomas Mulry, to whom the Cardinal paid another warm tribute.

The 1933 Conference, which was attended by Catholic leaders from all over the country and by representatives of many of the major non-Catholic workers in the same field, was made the occasion of a national tribute to the leadership the Cardinal had supplied and to his substantial achievements in New York. A number of those present remembered the Mitchell investigation and were able to measure the progress that had been made and the changed attitude of the press and much of the public. It was also the occasion for an appeal by the recently arrived Apostolic Delegate, Archbishop Amleto G. Cicognani (1888–1973), for support of the Legion of Decency, a national organization established in Chicago and then moved to New York in 1936, which for a number of years gave effective moral guidance on motion pictures. In 1965 it became the National Catholic Office for Motion Pictures. The Cardinal was grateful to the President for attending the Conference and was pleased that Mrs. Eleanor Roosevelt accompanied him. As things turned out, it was one of her very rare appearances at a Catholic gathering.

CHANGES IN THE CHARITIES

The growth of the Catholic Charities was steady but not spectacular. By 1938 it included 214 agencies. As the government's role increased, it began to assume responsibility for some areas such as the probation system in the Court of General Sessions, which the city took over in 1926, and parole work, which became a State function in 1930. But as some doors closed others opened, and every effort was made to recognize and meet long-term needs and to avoid concentrating too much of Catholic Charities' limited personnel and resources on any one of them. Among the developments in the Hayes administration that merit special mention are the Catholic Youth Organization, an umbrella agency for all non-academic youth activities, which was founded in 1936; the opening in 1934, on a very small scale, of St. Clare's Hospital on West 51st Street, which was to become the second largest hospital in the Archdiocese; the building of the Frances Schervier Home and Hospital in Riverdale in 1932; and the founding on September 15, 1929, by Mother Angeline Teresa, of the Carmelite Sisters for the Aged and Infirm.

Improvements in medicine and a rising standard of living led to a notable increase in the life span, which rose from 50.93 in 1900 and 54.1 in 1920 to 59.12 in 1930 and 68 in 1940. A serious problem was presented to the Archdiocese by the growing number of people whose slightly higher economic status barred them from the care the Little Sisters of the Poor were bound by their rule to restrict to the destitute elderly poor. These others needed care their families could not, and in some cases would not, supply. Moreover they would have overtaxed the facilities of the Little Sisters and diverted them from the special apostolate they carry out so well. The situation was complicated by the growing number and percentages of married women working outside the home. The War had given that movement a great impetus. By 1920 there were 1,920,281 married women (23 percent) among all the gainfully employed women fifteen years of age or older. By 1940 their numbers had soared to 5,040,000 or 36.4 percent of all working women. This was an irreversible trend.

The Cardinal's solution to what he saw as a long-term problem was the founding of a new community that would devote itself entirely to meeting that need. The Carmelite Sisters, whom he helped, opened their first foundation, St. Patrick's Home, at Van Cortlandt Park, in 1931. They have gone from strength to strength and spread thoughout the English-speaking world. In the same year, the Cardinal, rejecting the advice of some of his closest advisers, who told him that because of the Depression money was unavailable, approved a drive for $1,000,000 to help the Franciscan Sisters of the Poor move from their dilapidated quarters on Fifth Street to Riverdale. Once again his judgment in his own field was vindicated by events.

CATHOLIC ACTION AND THE MISSIONS

The Hayes administration coincided mainly with the pontificate of Pius XI (1922–1939), which was pre-eminently the pontificate of Catholic action and the missions. The Pope, a learned, courageous, and masterful man and an exceptionally vigorous leader, was summed up well by the motto "Intrepid Faith" assigned to him by the pseudo-Malachian prophecies. Mindful of the dictum often quoted by St. Pius X that all that was needed for evil to triumph was that the good do nothing, he wanted to mobilize the spiritual resources of the ordinary Catholics, to make them aware of their responsibilities to the Church and the community, and to induce them to play an active role in the defense and spread of Christian values. He felt that the circumstances of his time made it both easier and more urgent to put that ancient idea into practice.

There were already many active lay organizations in New York but some very helpful new ones were established. The Catholic Lawyers Guild was founded in 1927, and the Catholic Evidence Guild in 1928. In the beginning, the Evidence Guild was restricted to the radio and to talking to private groups, but street preaching was allowed from 1936 on. The Legion of Mary was started in New York in 1935 by Father Anthony Rothlauf of St. Anthony of Padua in the Bronx. Three other organizations addressed themselves in quite different ways to the racial and social problems that were then becoming more acute. The one with the most difficult task was the Catholic Interracial Council, founded on Pentecost Sunday, 1934, and the first group of its kind in the country. Its guiding spirit was Father John LaFarge, S.J. (1880–1963), who used as its nucleus the Catholic Laymen's Union, a Black professional and businessmen's group he had founded in 1927. The Association of Catholic Trade Unionists was founded in 1937. Its task was to train workers to help themselves and it did so by sponsoring labor schools and lectures. It was a response to the papal appeal to properly informed and motivated laymen to identify and treat the causes of the social unrest of the day rather than content themselves with relieving the misery that flowed from it. The laymen who founded A.C.T.U. owed much to the inspriation and guidance provided by Father John P. Monaghan (1890–1961). He combined a firm grasp of the papal teaching, a deep love of justice, and the capacity to inspire lasting enthusiasm for a good cause. His influence on a substantial percentage of the younger priests who had been his students at Cathedral College brought the A.C.T.U. much needed support. The A.C.T.U. was preceded by a year by the Xavier Labor School, which owes so much to Father Philip A. Carey, S.J.

The third movement, The Catholic Worker, was co-founded by Dorothy Day (1897–1980) and Peter Maurin (1877–1949) in May 1933, and was followed in 1934 by the opening of St. Joseph's House of Hospitality, the first of a number of such establishments in the major cities. The movement made no attempt to modify the existing social structure, though it stressed the principles on which it believed major changes should be made. Its appeal for farming communes fell largely on deaf ears. Its chief work has been and is to care for the urban poor who for various reasons, good and bad, are beyond the reach of organized charity or welfare. Not content with being good to them, it goes an extra mile by identifying with them and sharing their way of life.

There was a marked growth of missionary activity under Pius XI, who attached great importance to it. Following resolutely the path marked out so clearly by Benedict XV, he promoted the growth of a native clergy in every mission field, not only as something good in itself but as a safeguard against the day when European political control would end. One area that opened up for the first time in centuries was the Near East. The fall of the Turkish Empire lifted a heavy yoke from the Christian Arabs, who came under the protection of England and France. To help them recover from generations of oppression, the Pope turned to America for aid and in 1926 he established the Catholic Near East Welfare Association. It absorbed all the existing Catholic organizations interested in that area and became the chief support of the Sacred Congregation for the Oriental Church, the agency the Holy See uses in dealing with Russia, the Balkans, the Near and the Middle East. Its headquarters were located in New York and in 1931 the Cardinal became its president.

There were other developments in the Archdiocese, too. The Catholic Medical Mission Board, which sends medical supplies all through the mission fields, was founded in 1928 by Father Edward Gareché, S.J. (1876–1960), who also founded, in 1935, the Daughters of Mary Health of the Sick. The Bahama Islands, now the diocese of Nassau, were detached from New York on March 21, 1929, and made a separate jurisdiction as the Prefecture Apostolic of the Bahamas. In 1891 they had been entrusted by Archbishop Corrigan to the Benedictines of Collegeville, Minnesota, who still staff them. New York's annual contributions to the Propagation of the Faith continued to grow—from $261,380.78 in 1919 to $509,404.86 in 1938. Contributions peaked at $656,134.42 in 1929, sank to $356,181.26 in 1934, then rebounded, though in cheaper dollars. One of the first economic reforms of the New Deal had been the devaluation of the dollar by forty percent, a measure that brought Roosevelt much less criticism from the general public than Hoover received for cutting the size, not the value, of paper money in July 1929.

THE UNIVERSAL CHURCH

If it was a time of growth for the Church in many areas, it was also a time of bloody persecution in Russia, Mexico, Spain, and Germany, and of renewed tension with Italy following the settlement of the Roman Question in February 1929. It would never have occurred to Cardinal Hayes to organize a public protest against such things, as Cardinal Farley did in 1907 against the persecution in France. He took so little part in public affairs at home that it would have been quite out of character for him to do otherwise in international affairs, religious or secular, even when they were followed with passionate intensity in opinion-making circles in New York.

He made no comment on Roosevelt's recognition of Soviet Russia in November 1933, or on the President's refusal, in the same year (on the stated ground that he could never interfere in the internal affairs of a friendly country), to ask the Mexican Government to moderate its persecution of the Church. The Mexican persecution, Marxist in origin, was the longest (1917–1940) and the most severe in the history of Latin America, and it left deep wounds on the Church and Mexican society. Pius XI, comparing it to the worst persecution under the Roman Empire, condemned the conspiracy of silence in the world press that covered it up. Much was made at the time of Russia's willingness to allow one American priest to function in Moscow under the protection of the French Embassy and of a solemn assurance, which the President accepted at face value, that Russia would never engage in subversion or espionage here. Many expected great economic benefits to flow from the opening of the Russian market to American businessmen.

Though all the persecutions were real and of major concern to the Church, the center of interest was Europe where they were regarded by most non-Catholics as aspects of the three-sided struggle for political control of Europe (and, therefore, at that time of much of the world) that was to lead to World War II. The liberal democracies, led by France and England, had lost ground since 1919 and were on the defensive. They were under pressure from Communism on one side and Fascism in its different forms on the other. By the early 1930s, Stalin, Mussolini, and Hitler seemed firmly entrenched. Each of the three camps was basically incompatible with the other two.

The Pope, judging all three by the same norms, found them defective in differing degrees, and passed judgment on them in a series of encyclicals. In May 1931, in *Quadragesimo Anno,* he found much to criticize in the social conditions in the Liberal camp. The following month, in *Non Abbiamo Bisogno,* he condemned Italian Fascism. In March 1937, in *Mit Brennender Sorge* and *Divini Redemptoris,* he condemned, respectively, National Socialism in Germany and Communism everywhere. In 1932 and 1933 he also condemned the persecutions in Mexico and Spain. He singled out for special condemnation in the totalitarian powers the renewal of the pagan worship of the State which was used to justify their worst excesses. One reason for the canonization of St. Thomas More in May 1935 was that, not since his execution by Henry VIII in 1535, had the rights of conscience been invaded as ruthlessly as they were then being attacked by the totalitarian powers.

ROUTINE ADMINISTRATION

In the improbable event that Cardinal Hayes considered any significant alteration in the course on which he had embarked so deliberately in March 1919, two considerations would have deterred him. The first was the growing pressure on the Catholic Charities as they expanded to meet the demands caused by the Depression. They absorbed all his resources and caused him to postpone any development in other areas that was not truly unavoidable. The second was his failing health. In June 1932 he attended the International Eucharistic Congress held in Dublin to commemorate the fifteen-hundredth anniversary of St. Patrick's arrival in Ireland. During the Congress, at which he was a guest in the American Legation, he suffered a massive heart attack from which he made only a partial recovery. Henceforth, his activities were restricted and routine affairs fell increasingly into the hands of his closest associates, who tried to protect him and to lighten his burden.

When Bishop Dunn died on August 31, 1933, he was succeeded as Vicar General by Monsignor Lavelle and as auxiliary bishop by Monsignor

Stephen J. Donahue (1893–1982), who was ordained on May 25, 1918 in Rome. Bishop Donahue was the Cardinal's secretary from 1919 to 1932, and had known him since beginning his studies at Cathedral College in 1906. The new auxiliary bishop was consecrated on May 1, 1934, and took over at once most of the episcopal functions. Monsignor Thomas Carroll, the Chancellor of the Archdiocese, died in September 1934 and was succeeded by Father J. Francis A. McIntyre (1886–1979), the Vice-Chancellor, who had been ordained on May 31, 1921. After two years at St. Gabriel's, he joined the Cardinal's household and soon became indispensable to him. In view of the Cardinal's health and Monsignor Lavelle's great age, the new Chancellor was soon recognized as the man to see and the one through whom all matters, great and small, outside the Charities, reached the Cardinal.

The inner circle had a number of lay members in whom the Cardinal inspired a deep affection and loyalty and who gave him generous and competent assistance to the end. Several besides Al Smith deserve special mention. George J. Gillespie (1870–1953), his lawyer, joined the Society of St. Vincent de Paul in 1891 and was an active member until his death. He succeeded Thomas Mulry as its national president, 1916–1952. He served also on the New York State Board of Charities and, in 1944, as president of the National Conference of Catholic Charities. George MacDonald (1869–1961), a successful businessman, gave the Cardinal companionship as well as financial assistance. Victor J. Dowling (1866–1934), a judge of the Appellate Division for years, was active in many good works. John S. Burke (1889–1962), longtime head of B. Altman and Co., was a pillar of Catholic Charities. Alfred J. Talley (1872–1952), a judge of the Court of General Sessions, was president of the Catholic Club several times, was active in the Marquette League for Indian Missions, and was the spokesman for the laity at the archdiocesan reception for Cardinal Pacelli. Prominent among the rising younger men was John A. Coleman (1901–1977), a stockbroker, who was vice chairman of the Special Gifts Committee of Catholic Charities from its formation in 1931 to 1944, and then chairman until his death. There was hardly a charity or good work in the Archdiocese that did not benefit in some way from his assistance.

Routine affairs, especially after 1929, meant mainly the existing parishes. The pattern of parish life was firmly established but there were always variations. There were also changes in the devotional life of the people. The last Mass on Sunday moved to one o'clock in many parishes. High Masses became less frequent and vespers practically disappeared. Two devotions from France became very popular. One, to St. Thérèse of Lisieux or the Little Flower, swept the Catholic world after her canonization in 1925. The other, the Miraculous Medal novena, became the leading Marian devotion here. At Holy Cross parish, West 42nd Street where it was introduced in 1934, it was attended by thousands each week.

The Cardinal respected local autonomy and initiative and left the pastors relatively free in the management of the temporalities. He maintained a strict standard of clerical discipline even in minor affairs. Curates who wanted to keep a car had to have personal permission from him to do so, and it was not given automatically. In the beginning, pastors were appointed at an earlier age than was possible when the opening of new parishes practically stopped. Cardinal Farley's policy of appointing them to the country for their first pastorate was kept as a guide, not a rule. Priests from other dioceses and members of religious communities found it very difficult to be accepted as priests of the Archdiocese.

While the pastors welcomed the autonomy, some of them found it a burden because it meant they were left not only to themselves but on their own. They and all managers of good works outside the Charities were on notice that, barring truly extraordinary circumstances, they could expect no financial assistance from headquarters. One example of the way that policy worked was the Harlem Apostolate. By 1925, the church of St. Benedict the Moor, which had moved from Greenwich Village to West 53rd Street in 1898, was no longer in the center of Black New York, which had moved to Harlem. The 1920s brought a sharp increase in the Black population of the City. In Harlem itself 118,792 whites left and 87,417 Blacks arrived. The Cardinal moved Monsignor Thomas M. O'Keefe (1863–1933) from St. Benedict's to St. Charles Borromeo's on West 141st Street in 1925, and encouraged him to raise funds from other parishes if he could, but gave him no direct help. He did not notice that the grinding poverty in which the work had to be carried on made progress almost impossible. When Monsignor O'Keefe (who spent forty-six years working among the Blacks) died, he was replaced by Father William R. McCann (1893–1949), who began an aggressive campaign for converts that was successful for a time. However, in 1940 there were only about 7,000 Black Catholics in Manhattan. The Blacks were not the only newcomers to Harlem. The Hispanics were beginning to arrive in large numbers, and in 1926 the Milagrosa Church at 114th Street was opened by the Spanish Vincentians to supplement the work being done at Our Lady of Guadaloupe (1902) and Our Lady of Esperanza (1912).

Another example, which had lasting consequences for a much larger number of people, was the case of radio station WLWL. In the early 1920s, before the commercial potentialities of radio had been widely grasped, it was relatively easy for religious and educational groups to obtain a license to operate a broadcasting station. The Paulist Fathers did so in January 1925; on September 25th the Cardinal opened their first program on the air. As the work developed, it became increasingly expensive and too heavy a burden for the Paulists to carry alone. They appealed to the Cardinal only to be told that "it would not be within the scope of diocesan policy" to make the station a diocesan obligation. They had no choice but to sell it to commercial interests, which they did on April 6, 1937. It was an irreversible setback one could not imagine Cardinal Spellman permitting.

No one, and least of all the Cardinal, supposed his refusal to help the Paulists would drive Catholic preachers off the air, and of course it did not. Several of them achieved national reputations on it. The National Council of Catholic Men began sponsoring The Catholic Hour in 1930, a Sunday afternoon program that brought a number of speakers to the attention of millions, and it was not the only available forum. Three preachers who had very large followings in New York and elsewhere differed notably in background, technique, message, and durability. Father James M. Gillis, C.S.P. (1876–1957) was the editor of the *Catholic World* (1922–1948) and a speaker on The Catholic Hour (1930–1941). He was an austere, scholarly man, an able controversialist, an eloquent speaker and a fine columnist, with a good bit of John the Baptist in his make-up. Fulton J. Sheen (1895–1979), a priest of the diocese of Peoria, began to teach at the Catholic University in 1926 and soon attracted attention as a public speaker. He became, and remained until his death, the outstanding preacher in the history of the Church in America. His fine and well-trained mind, his thorough professionalism as a speaker, his gift for popularization, and his personality kept him at the top for more than half a century on the platform, the radio, television, and in the pulpit.

Father Charles E. Coughlin (1891–1979) of Detroit started on the radio in 1926 and soon attracted a following that grew into millions when the Depression came. He became a controversial figure, partly because of the vehemence with which he stated his case, long before his involvement in politics in 1936 gravely impaired his influence and usefulness. His main topic was the social problem and his great merit was that during the Depression he made millions of people, who would normally have been beyond the range of the Church's voice, aware that it had a solution for that problem. Neither friend nor foe could deny that he had a great following and that it included millions of non-Catholics.

The only exception to the Cardinal's policy of rigid economy outside the Charities was the Cathedral, and it was more apparent than real, for he used funds left for that purpose. The extensive improvements which he had in mind as early as 1922 included a marble floor for the entire building, a new baptistry, the installation of the choir stalls and screen, the two new organs, and the enlarged choir loft and new pews. All but the main organ, which was dedicated in February 1930, were ready for the golden jubilee of the dedication, which was not celebrated.

MORE CITY LANDMARKS

New York City continued a great building program in spite of, and in some cases because of, the Depression. The Port of New York Authority was established in 1921. Transportation was given top priority, as usual. The

Eighth Avenue Subway opened in 1932, and the Sixth Avenue Subway was started in 1936. The Goethals, Outerbridge, and Bayonne Bridges linking Staten Island and New Jersey were opened between 1928 and 1931. The Triborough Bridge was finished in 1936. The Empire State Building, Rockefeller Center, and the George Washington Bridge opened in the same year, 1931, which also brought the first city-owned airport, Floyd Bennett Field.

DEATH OF CARDINAL HAYES

The careful husbanding of his strength enabled the Cardinal to fulfill most of his major engagements and even, in June 1935, to act as Papal Legate to the National Eucharistic Congress in Cleveland. His inability at the last moment to perform the annual ordinations on June 11, 1938, the first he ever missed, was an ominous sign, but he rallied and on June 19th attended a belated ceremony commemorating the fiftieth anniversary of the death of Father John Drumgoole, whom he had known. It was his last public appearance. He died suddenly in his sleep on September 4, 1938, while resting at St. Joseph's Camp in Monticello, New York. He had been ill so long that many were surprised to find he was only seventy. Even some of his close friends were surprised by the outpouring of affection and veneration his death evoked in multitudes on every level who had seen him only from a distance but who obviously felt a genuine sense of personal loss. The general feeling was expressed in *The New York Times* editorial tribute. It said: "The sincerest tribute that can be paid to any man is to be mourned by the poor. Cardinal Hayes will be so mourned. He had them always in his heart. He rose from among them and went back among them again and again, ever on errands of mercy and charity."

The funeral Mass was sung by George Cardinal Mundelein and the sermon was given by Archbishop Joseph F. Rummel of New Orleans who filled in for Archbishop John J. Mitty of San Francisco. All three were close friends of the Cardinal and the latter two were former New York pastors who became bishops in his time. The interment took place in the Cathedral.

CHAPTER 12

Francis Cardinal Spellman

The vacancy created by the death of Cardinal Hayes was the first one in New York that coincided even partly with a vacancy in the Holy See. That coincidence, an apparently trivial one, had momentous consequences because the change in popes led to the most important appointment to New York since that of John Hughes in August 1837. That appointment was due chiefly to the new Archbishop's Roman contacts and experience and they in turn greatly influenced his administration of New York. Pope Pius XI died on February 10, 1939. Indomitable to the end, he had begged his doctors to prolong his life for a single day so that on February 11th, the tenth anniversary of the Lateran Pacts, he could deliver to the Italian Hierarchy, which had been summoned to Rome for its first general assembly to hear it, another denunciation of Fascism and all its works. He had been in failing health for several months, which explained the delay in filling New York, but it is believed that his choice had fallen on the Archbishop of Cincinnati, John T. McNicholas, O.P. (1872–1950), who had been a pastor in New York from 1913 to 1917, and was chairman of the administrative board of the N.C.W.C. for years.

Though the death of Pius XI was greeted with undisguised satisfaction in the Nazi, Fascist, and Communist camps and by some important sectors in the liberal West, it was generally recognized that a very strong leader had departed, and he was given a genuinely, if somewhat grudgingly, respectful farewell salute outside Catholic ranks. The Church mourned a great Pope. Because of the ominous situation in Europe, the Conclave was watched by the non-Catholics and anti-Catholics with greater interest than they had shown in generations. Each camp hoped for a pope it could influence even if it could not bend him to its will. Europe was still the center of the world and, as the composition of the Sacred College of Cardinals showed, it was also the center of the Church. Of its sixty-four members, fifty-seven, including thirty-five Italians, were from Europe, four were from North America, two were from South America and one was from Syria. Another reason for the interest was the increased prestige the vigorous leadership of the late Pope had won for the Holy See.

The press was full of speculation, with each camp tending to see what it wanted to see. The best known of all the candidates was Eugenio Cardinal Pacelli (1876–1958), who had been Secretary of State from 1930 to 1939. He was clearly the favorite of Pius XI, who had done everything in his power to call attention to his merits. He had sent him as Legate to France twice, to Argentina and to Hungary, and had sanctioned his visit to America. He had also made him Archpriest of St. Peter's Basilica and the Camerlengo of the Holy Roman Church (the official charged with preparing the Conclave when the Pope died). Normally, as some well-informed observers were quick to point out, these quite exceptional signs of favor would not have helped and there would have been a swing of the pendulum away from the policies and collaborators of a notably active Pope, as had happened after Pius IX, Leo XIII, and Pius X. Moreover, there is a long-standing tradition, to which very few exceptions have been made, of not electing a Secretary of State. But the times were not normal. The Cardinals knew World War II was already in the works, that it would break out on September first, and that it would be started by Hitler. They knew, too, that of all their number Cardinal Pacelli was the one best equipped to deal with Germany. He had been Nuncio there (1917–1929), and, ever since Hitler's rise to power in January 1933, he had been intimately involved on a day-to-day basis with the problems and tribulations of the Church in Germany. In the eyes of many, his fitness was underscored by the violent campaign against him in the Nazi and Fascist press. Wishing to offer him the greatest insult in their power, the Nazis said he was a Jew. Pius XI, whom he was accused, absurdly, of dominating, was let off with being only half Jewish.

Accordingly, the Conclave of 1939 was one of the shortest on record. It opened later than usual because Pius XI, responding to the vehement protests of William Cardinal O'Connell, who had missed the Conclaves of 1914 and 1922, had extended the period allowed before the opening so that the American Cardinals could arrive on time. It began on the evening of March first, shortly after the arrival of Cardinal O'Connell and the two South

Americans, and on the following day, on the third ballot, elected Cardinal Pacelli. He chose the name Pius XII as a sign of continuity of policy. Washington's pleasure at the outcome was shown by the presence at the coronation, for the first time, of a Special Representative of the United States, a role filled by Ambassador Joseph P. Kennedy who was sent from London for the occasion. When all the formalities connected with the coronation were over, the Pope turned his attention to the unfinished business that had accumulated, and on April 24th it was announced officially that Bishop Spellman, the auxiliary of Boston, had been made Archbishop of New York. He had known since March 2nd that it was probable and since April 12th that it was certain.

Francis Joseph Spellman (May 4, 1889–December 2, 1967) was born in Whitman, Massachusetts, in the Archdiocese of Boston. Both his parents were born in America, but all his grandparents were born in Ireland. He was the oldest of five children and had two brothers, both of whom became doctors. His father kept a grocery store in which the boys helped after school. There was no parochial school in Whitman so Frank, as he was always known by his family and friends, went to the public schools.

After graduating from high school, he came to New York, to Fordham College. There, in a student body of 105 which received the undivided attention of a faculty consisting of ten Jesuits, no pupil could get lost in the crowd and each received individual attention. The outlander from New England soon made his mark. He was an average but well-rounded student who took part in a number of extracurricular activities, such as debating, dramatics, journalism, and sports. He showed an exceptional memory, especially for people, a very strong competitive spirit, and great self-assurance. Near the end of his senior year, he realized he had a vocation to the priesthood and that year, in a competition open to the entire student body, he won the gold medal for religion.

Since his parents, who received the news of his vocation with joy, were able and willing to finance his studies, it was decided after consultation with the local clergy that he should go to the North American College in Rome. This was approved by Cardinal O'Connell and in September 1911 he set forth on his great adventure. The College is really a hostel rather than a school. From its opening in December 1859 to the fall of 1933, when its students were switched to the Gregorian University, the Americans attended the courses at the "Propaganda" University.

The faculty at Propaganda was drawn mainly from the diocesan clergy and was predominantly Italian. Membership in it was regarded as an honor and often as a stepping-stone. Many of its members rose to very high office in the Roman Curia and were able to help the careers of former pupils who had won their approbation and interest. This was well known to the students and those among them who were ambitious for high rank set their sights accordingly. Not all succeeded, but among those who did Francis Spellman was outstanding in his generation—and even among all the American priests who have ever studied in Rome. He formed lasting friendships with, among others, Domenico Tardini, a future Cardinal Secretary of State, and Francesco Borgongini-Duca, a future Cardinal in Curia. The latter played an indispensable role in fostering his career.

Even by the standard of the American seminaries of 1911, life in Rome was rugged. The College building was small, poorly equipped and maintained, and overcrowded. The food was a continual source of complaint and became even worse when Italy entered the War in May 1915 and major shortages developed. There were compensations. Hardships endured in common forged strong friendships. The Americans were drawn from all over the country, and their peers at Propaganda came from a large part of the world. Rome, with its unrivaled and inexhaustible treasures and its incessant activity as the center of the Catholic world, made a lasting impression on all but the most insensitive and obtuse.

There were weightier problems that varied from student to student. The young man from Whitman had two: the disfavor of his superiors in the College and serious illness. Both the Rector and the Vice Rector thought him too forward and even aggressive and felt he must be put and kept in his place as they saw it. He, for his part, saw no reason why, once he had accepted a call to the priesthood, he should not wish to be successful in its internal and external forums, or why he should not wish to meet and cultivate important people. He knew his superiors had not reached their positions in the College entirely without effort on their part.

The illness was more important. For almost six months in 1914 he was in hospitals in Milan and Rome with what was variously described as "a weakness in the lungs," pneumonia or pleurisy. No one used the dread word "tuberculosis." He was always very grateful for the care he received from the doctors and the nursing sisters. He was less grateful for a visit from the Rector suggesting that he return to Boston where, the Rector was sure, the Cardinal would ordain him ahead of time if necessary so that he could say Mass a few times before he died. He recovered and was ordained on May 14, 1916 by Archbishop Giuseppe Ceppetelli, the Latin Patriarch of Constantinople and assistant Vicar of Rome. He said his first Mass at the tomb of St. Peter. His first Mass in America was said in the Lady Chapel of the Cathedral in New York and the first Mass in Whitman on July 23rd.

If in the summer of 1916 there were any prophets among the priests of Boston, they were either asleep at their posts or absorbed in what they mistook for more important matters, for Father Spellman's return went unnoticed by all but a handful of relatives and friends. After a brief chaplaincy in a Home for Aged Women, he became the second assistant at All Saints, Roxbury, a thriving parish with a number of active societies. In February 1918 he applied for a naval chaplaincy and was rejected as "temperamentally unfit" by a non-Catholic chaplain who resented his attitude. In August he was accepted as an Army chaplain, but at the last moment Cardinal O'Connell withdrew his permission and assigned him to *The Pilot,* the archdiocesan paper, with residence at the Cathedral. In his time there, he met and became very friendly with another young special worker, Father Richard J. Cushing (1895–1970), whose career was to be linked closely with his own. His task, which he performed for several years, was to visit a different parish each Sunday, speak at every Mass, and drum up subscriptions. In May 1922 he was assigned to a minor desk in the Boston Chancery, and later was demoted, in the common estimation, to the post of archdiocesan archivist. It was evident that he had incurred the displeasure of the Cardinal.

In all this there was no injustice. Father Spellman never claimed, and, as Cardinal Spellman, would never have allowed a subordinate of his to claim, that the authorities were obliged to tailor the post to the man. He was too clearheaded not to see that the Cardinal was entirely within his rights in acting as he did. He himself was too mature and resilient for self-pity or sulking, too sensible to give his critics ammunition by neglecting humdrum work, too many-sided in his interests and too energetic to be bored or idle. He accepted each assignment dutifully, did his best, kept his thoughts to himself, and awaited events. He acquired an extensive knowledge of the Boston clergy, of whom he had known only a few, because he never attended the schools in which most of them were trained, and of the Archdiocese. The Job's Comforters among his friends thought he had been buried with the archives in the basement of the Boston Chancery. Others, who knew him better, were not so sure.

The lean years stretched beyond the scriptural seven and had reached nine before rescue came in an unexpected way but not really from an unexpected source. In 1925 Father Spellman received permission to join an official Boston pilgrimage to Rome for the Holy Year. The group was surprised to be greeted on arrival by Monsignor Borgongini-Duca, now one of the two Under Secretaries in the Vatican Secretariat of State, and even more surprised to hear he had really come to greet his old friend and pupil, Father Spellman. A few days later, Pius XI spoke at length to an audience consisting solely of American pilgrims. When he had finished, he suddenly asked a young priest, a total stranger to him, to translate his speech into English. The translator did so well that the Pope, who understood but did not speak English, was impressed and asked about him. He was told he was Father Spellman of Boston.

The chance encounter with the Pope made the next step easier. In 1920 Benedict XV had asked the Knights of Columbus for help in providing playgrounds in Rome and they had responded generously. The work was one of the many things supervised by Monsignor Borgongini-Duca and, as it expanded, he felt the need of help. He had in mind a young American priest who would work closely with him, understand the Knights of Columbus, and be quite acceptable to them. He would be attached to the Secretariat of State and to the Knights. It seemed a suitable opening for Father Spellman. The plan was submitted to the Pope who, recalling the episode of the translation of his speech, approved. Cardinal Gasparri, the Secretary of State, was instructed to write to Cardinal O'Connell in the Pope's name, outlining the project in Rome and asking that Father Spellman be released from his duties in Boston and sent to Rome for at least a year. Refusal was impossible and so on November 1, 1925 he left for Rome to resume his astonishing career there.

His duties, which he performed faithfully, were not taxing and he had plenty of time to study at close range the personnel and policies of the Secretariat of State, in which he was the first American to serve. He had other contacts. As his position in the Vatican was consolidated, he met almost every American bishop who visited Rome and a growing number of other important English-speaking people, Catholic and non-Catholic, all of whom found him helpful, tireless, and tactful. Through Cardinal Bonzano, a former Apostolic Delegate in Washington, he met Mr. and Mrs. Nicholas F. Brady of New York, a devout and childless couple of immense wealth whose lives were dedicated to good works. They spent part of each year in Rome and he became their unofficial chaplain. At their home, he met many of the most important people in ecclesiastical Rome and in the diplomatic world. An even more important contact, the most important in his life, came through Monsignor Giuseppe Pizzardo, the other Under Secretary of State, who invited him, in September 1929, to accompany him on a short holiday in Germany. They were guests of Monsignor Pizzardo's close friend, Archbishop Pacelli, in the Nunciature in Berlin. Monsignor Spellman, who had received the purple in October 1928, was convinced that their host would be the next Secretary of State and the next Pope. When, in December 1929, the Nuncio relinquished his post and returned from Berlin as Cardinal-elect, he was met by only three people—his brother, Monsignor Pizzardo, and Monsignor Spellman.

Monsignor Spellman's normal duties did not bring him to the attention of the general public, but three special assignments did. Two of them were due to Cardinal Pacelli with whom he was in close touch and with whom he was so friendly that they spent their vacations together. All three brought him to the favorable attention of Pius XI. February 11, 1931 marked the formal opening of the Vatican Radio Station, which was built under the personal supervision of Guglielmo Marconi. At the conclusion of the Pope's highly polished Latin speech, which was carried almost universally, it was repeated in all the modern languages. The English translation and broadcast were both made by Monsignor Spellman, who was heard all over this country.

A more difficult task came in June 1931. When the Encyclical Letter *Non Abbiamo Bisogno* (June 29, 1931) was being prepared, the Holy See realized that the Italian Government could and probably would suppress it in Italy outside the confines of the Vatican. To forestall that, it was decided to publish it outside Italy and with no prior public notice. The text, which Pius XI wrote in longhand, was printed with special secrecy in the Vatican and, on June 29th, the official date of publication, Monsignor Spellman received it from the Pope himself. He also received from the same source most precise instructions for his journey to France. He was to travel as a Vatican courier bringing confidential documents to the Nuncio in Paris and to return with documents from him, which he did. His real mission was the publication of the encyclical. The various international press agencies had been alerted to expect big news and were delighted with the form it took. The encyclical was actually published on July 4th and it received worldwide coverage. The effect was all the Pope had hoped for. The coverage in America was notably extensive and Monsignor Spellman got ample attention as well.

The third task was the easiest. It was to accompany Cardinal Lauri to the Eucharistic Congress in Dublin in 1932, as a member of his official party. The Cardinal, the second papal Legate to visit Ireland since 1148, which was before the first Norman invasion, wanted him as his interpreter and personally asked the Pope to assign him to that role. (The first Legate was Vincenzo Cardinal Vannutelli who consecrated the Cathedral of Armagh in 1904). The Congress was a huge success and brought an ingathering of pilgrims of Irish extraction from all over the world. The Legate and Monsignor Tardini were used to splendid ceremonies and official functions. What impressed them most was the enthusiastic and reverent participation of great masses of ordinary people. In his report to the Pope, the Legate said: "I had prepared myself to witness something extraordinary, but I am obliged to say in all truth that what has occurred is beyond anything I could have conceived as possible."

AUXILIARY BISHOP OF BOSTON

By the summer of 1932, the small but growing band of Spellman watchers was waiting impatiently to hear he had been made a bishop. They were sure he would be, but they wondered when and where. No one in his position could escape the rumor-mongers who were busy with his name and who were not always wrong. He himself knew the authorities had considered him for the post of Bishop of Portland, Maine, and of Manchester, New Hampshire. In May, Bishop John B. Peterson, the auxiliary of Boston, was promoted to Manchester and many wondered who would succeed him. It was thought unlikely that Cardinal O'Connell would ask for Monsignor Spellman or that a man of his rank would be given an auxiliary he did not want. The unexpected happened, and on July 25th Monsignor Spellman was told by Cardinal Pacelli that the Pope himself had selected him for Boston.

Apart from having him consecrated by the Pope, then a rare event, nothing was left undone to give him a good send-off and to show the esteem in which he was held in the highest quarters in Rome. He was consecrated titular bishop of Sila on September 8, 1932 by Cardinal Pacelli. The co-consecrators were Monsignor Borgongini-Duca, then a titular Archbishop and Nuncio to Italy, and Monsignor Pizzardo, also a titular Archbishop and still Undersecretary of State. The bishop-elect wore as a gift, the vestments worn by Cardinal Pacelli when he was consecrated by Benedict XV on May 13, 1917, the day of the first apparition at Fatima. By special favor, the ceremony, the first ever held in St. Peter's for an American, was performed at the altar of the Chair. After it, Bishop Spellman was received by the Pope, who recommended that he take *Sequere Deum* (Follow God) as his episcopal motto. Later, he sent him a valuable ring and cross. There was time for a round of farewell visits in Rome and a short holiday with Cardinal Pacelli before leaving on September 25th to face an anticipated storm in Boston.

William Cardinal O'Connell gave his new auxiliary a frigid reception, partly because he resented having had no voice in selecting him and partly because of a temperamental incompatibility with him. They were the two most remarkable men the Church in New England has produced and no diocese in the world was big enough to hold them both comfortably. Though there were striking differences, they had more in common than either of them admitted or, perhaps, saw. Both were able, ambitious, and hardworking men who were quite willing to accept great responsibilities and to use the authority that went with them. Both had a natural aptitude for administrative work and public affairs. Both had a strong affinity for successful people in many walks of life. Both came to expect and to accept as a simple recognition of fact the lavish praise given to their personal qualities and their achievements. Both were wholly dedicated to the service of the Church, to which each in his time and place made an outstanding contribution. The Cardinal was the Moses of the Catholics in New England, whom he led across the tracks. Like his greater namesake, Daniel O'Connell, he could say justly that by the end of his life his people's position was so much better than it had been when his work began that they, forgetting the past, could not appreciate the extent of the change or the effort required to bring it about.

There was so great a similarity in the careers of both men that, making due allowance for minor differences, the second seemed almost a carbon copy of the first. The Cardinal had studied at the North American College, fallen seriously ill with chest trouble, been ordained early and sent home because of his health. After ten years as a curate in Boston, he had been recalled to Rome as Rector of the College. His career owed much to the interest taken in it by a former professor at "Propaganda" who, having risen to high rank in the Curia, remained his friend and became his patron. In his case it was Cardinal Satolli. The younger man was objective enough to acknowledge that his patron, to whom he was always devoted, was deficient in the knowledge, patience, sound judgment, and tact needed for success as Apostolic Delegate in

America and that, in his major differences with Archbishop Corrigan, the latter was right.

As Rector, Monsignor O'Connell had cultivated a number of important friends, clerical and lay, Catholic and non-Catholic, in Rome. He had attracted the friendly notice of two popes, Leo XIII who made him a bishop and St. Pius X who personally selected him for Boston. He had carried out a diplomatic mission for the Holy See as Special Envoy to Japan. Finally, his appointment as coadjutor of Boston had been a bitter disappointment to Archbishop John J. Williams who had done all in his power to prevent it.

Though Bishop Spellman's position was difficult, it was never intended that it be made impossible and in fact it was far from that. His relations with the Cardinal remained distant but were always correct. Both of them had too strong a sense of duty and propriety to let them be less than that. Both knew that the bishop could have left Boston on promotion if he wanted to. After six months' residence in the seminary, he was given a medium rank parish, Sacred Heart in Newton Center. He had much to do there and on the confirmation circuit, but always had time to pursue his own interests. It was generally assumed that he would succeed the Cardinal and he was treated accordingly by the clergy and the community at large. There were other rising stars in Boston at the time and their paths crossed frequently. In the early days of the New Deal, Joseph P. Kennedy was beginning the career in politics and high finance that was to make his family the richest and most prominent Catholic family in the history of the country. James Roosevelt was thought to be planning a political career in Massachusetts. It was through both of them that Bishop Spellman was called to President Franklin Roosevelt's attention and then met him.

The outstanding event in Bishop Spellman's time as auxiliary in Boston was Cardinal Pacelli's visit to America (October 8–November 7, 1936), which aroused much interest. Part of the interest was due to the visit's exceptional character. Cardinal Pacelli was the first Secretary of State to leave Italy since Cardinal Consalvi attended the Congress of Vienna in 1815, and all his other trips had been clearly official and to great Catholic gatherings. The fact that he came to the United States because he had a chance to come and because he was anxious to see this country, seemed to many to be too simple and too obvious to be the real reason, so various other explanations of his journey were advanced. Since he came in a presidential election year, some thought he came, possibly at the President's request, to silence Father Coughlin whose vigorous denunciations of Roosevelt's policies were a prominent feature of the campaign. Others thought he came to invoke American aid for the Church in Mexico or Russia, and still others that he wanted to establish diplomatic relations with the United States. The American bishops were just as puzzled as the general public.

The visit was planned first as a private visit to Mrs. Brady's home on Long Island, with some moderate sightseeing, but, even before it was announced on September 30th, Bishop Spellman doubted that that would be possible. The reaction to the announcement showed it would not. Invitations poured in from all parts of the country from important people who could not be ignored. It was clear that the Cardinal would need a guide who knew him and the country well, had appropriate rank and the proper contacts, could make the hard decisions needed to choose among conflicting claims, and could allot the available time without overtaxing him. Only one person met those requirements, and Bishop Spellman soon found himself in complete charge.

The proposed quiet visit became a very active one, of which the statistics give an inadequate idea. After a short rest on Long Island it opened, tactfully, in New York where on October 11th the Cardinal presided at the Pontifical Mass to mark the anniversary of the consecration of the Cathedral. Then, after visits to Boston, Newton Center, and Whitman, came a strenuous whirlwind tour of the entire country that would have been impossible without the airplane, which he was the first of his rank to use in America. He visited twelve of the sixteen archbishops in their sees, met seventy-nine bishops with them, saw most of the important Catholic institutions, and found time for civic and scenic points of interest like Mount Vernon, the Grand Canyon, and San Francisco's Golden Gate. He himself was astonished at how much he saw and did in the time at his disposal.

As the visit proceeded, attention turned from speculation about its purpose to the visitor himself. He was, as the German Emperor had said in 1917, "a man of aristocratic, likeable, and distinguished appearance, with great intelligence and impeccable manners, the perfect model of a high prelate of the Catholic Church." He was also eloquent. In Washington, he impressed the National Press Club with a carefully prepared speech in perfect but heavily accented English, given from memory, without the use of notes. Unlike Archbishop Bedini, he was received everywhere with friendly interest and great courtesy, which he reciprocated.

All during the Cardinal's tour, the presidential election campaign was being fought vigorously, with mounting intensity as election day approached. It ended on November 3rd with Roosevelt's greatest electoral triumph. He carried forty-six states, losing only Maine and Vermont, and won 98.59 percent of the Electoral College and 60.8 percent of the popular vote. He had been notified of the Cardinal's visit before it was announced, had welcomed it, and had expressed a desire to meet him. Both sides saw that a meeting had to await the end of the campaign, so it was set for November 5th. On that day, the Cardinal, accompanied by a small party that included Bishop Spellman, Bishop Stephen J. Donahue, and the Joseph P. Kennedys, went to Hyde Park for lunch and the President and the Cardinal had a long private conversation.

From the point of view of the press, the visit with the President was the highlight of the tour. The reporters would expect any visiting Cardinal to call on the American bishops and to see some Catholic institutions, but a private lunch with the President of the United States was another matter. The significance of the Hyde Park visit was well understood in Rome, which knew that in no other major country in the world would such a meeting have been possible. The success of the entire American visit was deeply gratifying to the Pope and Cardinal Pacelli. They gave most of the credit to Bishop Spellman, who accompanied the latter every inch of the way. It confirmed their confidence in him and widened his contacts with the other bishops here.

Archbishop Of New York

When Bishop Spellman accepted the appointment to New York, he knew the Pope wanted him to accept and that, if he refused, he was certain to be the next Cardinal Archbishop of Boston. He knew, too, that in some important ways his position in New York would from the beginning be different from that of any of his predecessors. He was already more firmly established in the inner councils of the Holy See than any of them ever had a chance to be, and he had closer contacts with the White House than any of them had ever wanted. His standing in Rome and Washington was not enhanced appreciably by his becoming Archbishop of New York, and with one important exception it did not broaden the scope of his activities. The purely archdiocesan work he did in New York would have been much the same if he had succeeded to Boston.

The appointment of an outsider as archbishop disappointed many New York priests, but it should not have surprised any of them who had paid attention to the administrative policies of Pius XI. He had appointed thirteen Archbishops in this country and only one of them, Floersh of Louisville, had been ordained for the Archdiocese he headed. In his case it had been unavoidable because he had already been Bishop of Louisville for years when it became an Archdiocese. There was a feeling in some quarters that New York was ripe for a change and even a shake-up, because each successor of Bishop Dubois in turn had been a member of his immediate predecessor's official family and had been legally or presumptively his heir apparent. Handing on the succession had become a tradition here. Pius XI and Pius XII had the same plan for New York but different candidates.

Another tradition was for the clergy to give an outsider a cool reception. Bishops Dubois and Hughes got one and Monsignor Lavelle thought that Archbishop Corrigan owed some of his difficulties to being considered a foreigner from Newark. That tradition still held in 1939. Archbishop Spellman was received by the clergy as a body with reserve. Very few of them knew him personally and some of those who did, chiefly schoolmates from Fordham and Rome, were not friendly with him.

The longest vacancy in New York since the one following the death of Bishop Connolly ended on May 22, 1939, when the Archbishop-elect arrived, presented his credentials to Bishop Donahue, who had been the Administrator since September 7th, and took the oath of office. On the following day, he was installed formally by the Apostolic Delegate, Archbishop Cigognani, in a long and splendid ceremony in which a large and representative delegation from Boston occupied a prominent place. He did not receive the pallium, which was delayed by the war in Europe, until March 12, 1940. Cardinal O'Connell, with whom his relations improved greatly when they no longer lived in the same diocese and there was no chance of his succeeding to Boston, had agreed to confer it but fell ill. Cardinal Dougherty of Philadelphia took his place.

The new administration, which turned out to be the longest and most active in the history of New York, began quietly. All incumbent officials were confirmed in their posts and no new programs were announced. The policy Archbishop Corrigan (who was not the first to use it) recommended to new pastors—always speak well of your predecessor and make no unnecessary changes for several months—was followed, and in the meantime the actual conditions and needs of the Archdiocese were studied carefully.

While the Archbishop was surveying his new field of labor, his immediate entourage and the clergy in general were watching him closely and their first reactions were mixed. He had the advantage, which he did not always appreciate, of being underestimated by many at first sight. He was short and stocky, unimpressive in appearance and bearing, offhand in manner, a poor speaker and a worse singer, and he tended to become impatient during long ceremonies. Only a very superficial observer could miss his intense awareness of his own authority and his determination that it be recognized and accepted by his subordinates on every level. He could be, as a number of them learned, very demanding and even inconsiderate of them as he often was of himself. At the same time, few could miss his sense of duty, his capacity for work, his grasp of affairs, his willingness to settle things promptly, his quite exceptional confidence in his own judgment and in his ability to handle any problem that arose, and the range of his interests. For the first time, New York had an Archbishop who was not only able and willing, but determined to play a leading role in ecclesiastical matters on a national and international level and in public life. He was already immersed in them when he arrived here as a mature man with a wide experience of men and affairs.

Though the initial reserve of the clergy proved to be lasting, it was not based on ill will, for they admired his programs and achievements, and it did not prevent their giving him full cooperation. They realized that the incessant activity required by his contacts and commitments inside and outside New York made it literally impossible for him to become friendly with more than a tiny fraction of the local clergy, even if he had had a strong desire to do so. He tried hard to know at least who they were and where they were stationed, and was satisfied with that relationship. As his administration developed, he distributed papal honors among them on an unheard-of scale, but he never tried, and presumably never wanted, to put them at their ease in his presence.

His aloofness did not indicate lack of interest in their welfare. He was the first Archbishop of New York to make proper, systematic, and often quite generous provision for sick priests. Though he was well aware of how subjective that determination can be, he wanted to be sure that no one found himself in a position in which he was genuinely unhappy, and that no one had reason to feel he had been passed over for promotion without just cause. Priests who had personal problems, culpable or inculpable, that came to his attention found him firm in discipline but also understanding, practical, anxious to be fair, and willing, when the case suggested it, to go far beyond the call of duty to be helpful. He was willing to correct a mistake when he recognized it, even though that might be done very indirectly.

Three months after his arrival, the Archbishop had decided on a plan of action and was able to tell the clergy what his first steps would be. Essentially his plan was to give all the other activities of the Archdiocese the close supervision Cardinal Hayes had given the Catholic Charities, which were to be kept up and expanded but were no longer to be the sole major interest. Such supervision would require coordination and centralization and was prompted by a desire to make the best possible use of the limited resources at his disposal by insisting on a united effort.

He began with the financial problem, on which so much else depended, and especially with the debt. He came with what New Yorkers think of as a typical New Englander's dislike of debt, though it mellowed as things improved. He was distressed to find that a single bank held $28 million in mortgages on church property and thought it was doing him a favor by charging only six percent interest. He was able to borrow $10 million at 2.5% in New York, and millions more in Boston, so that a substantial saving in interest was achieved very quickly.

Though the Archbishop was anxious that the debt be liquidated, or at least reduced, as soon as possible, he knew that that could not be done easily—or at all—in some parishes because the Depression was still on. The New Deal had lowered but not eliminated unemployment which in 1939 was still more than nine million in a population of about 131 million. The problem was not solved until the government was able to invoke the time-honored expedients of rearmament and war. The failure to solve unemployment was not due to lack of effort or money. The public debt had doubled in six years, going from $19.5 billion to about $40.5 billion. Per capita it had gone from $156.12 to $308.29. In 1939 Federal expenses were $9,268,338,030 (two-thirds the current budget of New York City) and some pessimists feared the government had embarked on a program of deficit spending that would last indefinitely. The formula "tax and tax, and spend and spend and elect and elect" was effective at the polls.

The debt was only one aspect of the archdiocesan financial problem.

Others were the control of building, insurance, real estate, purchasing, and in-house financing. These required permanent supervisory or advisory personnel and the Chancery staff was expanded to include the Building Commission (1939), the Archdiocesan Service Corporation for insurance (1939), The Institutional Commodity Services, a central purchasing agency (1941), and the Archdiocesan Reciprocal Loan Fund (1943). The insurance office found, as expected, that some parishes and institutions had too much, others too little, and a few no insurance. Most of it was fire insurance. The plan now was to see that every parish and institution conformed strictly to the legal requirements, and carried such coverage as liability and workmen's compensation. Other things were added later. The central purchasing agency made substantial economies possible and obtained supplies, especially during the war, that individual purchasers could not have obtained. The Loan Fund was especially helpful in the beginning to parishes that could not meet the requirements laid down by the banks for obtaining a low interest rate. These agencies, all of which had long been in existence in other dioceses, were a curtailment of the pastors' autonomy but they also ended their isolation and they were welcomed by most as the lifting of a heavy burden.

There were other innovations which pleased the clergy. Henceforth, anyone assigned to found a parish would be given the site debt-free and a sum of money sufficient to launch it without a crippling debt. Any good work to which the Archdiocese gave formal approval would be subsidized to the extent necessary to enable it to fulfill its purpose adequately. The Archbishop himself would back it and, as his commitments increased, he became of necessity a tireless fund raiser. A useful rule, to which suitable exceptions were made and which did not bind the Archbishop, was that a pastor must have half the money on hand before any building program would be approved.

The new regime gave early indications of its interest in areas outside the Charities such as the Cathedral, the seminaries, high school education, the hospitals, and new parishes. Two different anonymous donors had offered to replace the main altar of the Cathedral and the altar in the Lady Chapel. Both gifts had been declined by Cardinal Hayes and strongly opposed by Monsignor Lavelle for sentimental reasons. Hearing soon after the latter's death that both offers still stood, the Archbishop accepted them and in April and May 1942 had the pleasure of consecrating the present altars. In the same year, beautiful new windows were installed in the clerestory and the apse. The old main altar was given to the Fordham University Chapel in memory of Cardinal McCloskey.

The Seminary received a new procurator and began a program of methodical modernization and expansion that took years to complete. It was necessary to relocate Cathedral College, which found its position on Madison Avenue near the Cathedral ever less suitable because of the traffic. It was also necessary to make a start on meeting the insistent demand for

Catholic high school education for boys. At first, the Archbishop hoped to do the two at once by merging the preparatory department of Cathedral College with the new Cardinal Hayes High School and putting the College department in a separate wing of the new building; but later he announced that both institutions were needed and separate plants would be provided for each.

The new Cardinal Hayes High School, which opened at its present site on the Grand Concourse in the Bronx in September 1941, was the first school in the New York Archdiocese, apart from the seminaries, to be run by the diocesan clergy. They were assisted by Marist, Xaverian, and Irish Christian Brothers. The administrative staff and a large part of the Cathedral College faculty provided the nucleus of the Hayes faculty. They were replaced at the College, which opened in its new building on 87th Street and West End Avenue in September 1942. A former private school was donated by the McCadden-McQuirk Foundation and renovated so thoroughly that the College found itself housed adequately for the first time. There and at Dunwoodie, the Archbishop earned the title of the Second Founder.

The first in a long line of additions to the Catholic hospital system was the Spellman wing at St. Vincent's, Manhattan, which was begun in September 1941. Less could be done about new parishes, partly because of the restrictions on new building that were imposed by the war, and in his first eight years the Archbishop opened only three. St. Gabriel's, Riverdale (1939), replaced Cardinal Farley's parish when it closed. Our Lady of Victory, near Wall Street (1944), was a shrine church with a large daytime congregation and a handful of residents. St. Helena's in Parkchester, the Bronx (1940), was the first of its kind in New York. It was one in which thousands of people had moved almost simultaneously into new buildings erected on hitherto vacant land, and needed a huge and complete plant at once. There was no time for the pay-as-you-go and build-as-you-grow policy that was followed in most parishes. Parkchester itself was built by the Metropolitan Life Insurance Company on the extensive grounds vacated by the Catholic Protectory. A notable feature of all the new buildings was the fine quality of the material and, as far as it was available, of the workmanship that went into them. The architectural level was also high. The Archbishop was prepared to pay for the best and expected to get what he paid for.

PUBLIC AFFAIRS AND WORLD WAR II

While these new policies and programs were being initiated, the Archbishop kept in close touch with the official and public reactions to the growing threat of war and of American involvement in it. His attitude to them was affected by his relations with President Roosevelt. Like many normally hard-headed men in other walks of life, the Archbishop felt the force of charm and flattery laid on by a master hand. They met on several occasions before the Archbishop came to New York. On February 17, 1937, after an overnight visit to the White House, he said Mass there. The purpose of that visit was to help James Roosevelt prepare a radio speech urging Massachusetts to ratify the Child Labor Amendment, which Cardinal O'Connell opposed.

The President, who had already described him as "my favorite Bishop," was the first person outside the Spellman family informed of the appointment of the new Archbishop of New York. He returned the compliment gracefully with a handwritten letter thanking him for the message, for which he said he had been hoping and praying, and inviting him to use Hyde Park as a base when fulfilling his episcopal engagements in Dutchess County. The unexpected death of Cardinal Mundelein, October 2, 1939, of which the President himself notified the Archbishop by telephone, brought them closer. The death of the Cardinal, an ardent New Dealer from the beginning and the President's closest friend in the hierarchy, left a void the Archbishop of New York filled. Henceforth he was the bishop closest to the Pope and to the President, and was often the intermediary between the two.

The first order of business was the question of an American representative at the Vatican. The President had been thinking of it on and off for years and the outbreak of the war in Europe made it seem urgent to him. His visit from Cardinal Pacelli helped too. He turned with relief from the economic problems that baffled and bored him to the field of diplomacy in which he felt he had a very special competence. He foresaw and desired American entry into the war and wished to establish contact with all the anti-Hitler forces, among which he gave the Church an important place. The Vatican had never denied its desire for relations with Washington and, as it foresaw disaster in Europe, was even more anxious than usual for direct contact with the strongest non-European power.

The problem was to find a way to establish relations without causing too strong a political reaction in the United States. The President was equal to the task. On December 24, 1939 he wrote to the Pope announcing his intention to send a personal representative to the Vatican who could help coordinate plans for peace and the relief of suffering after the war. Similar letters were sent to the Protestant and Jewish leaders here. It was noted that Myron C. Taylor, the President's special representative, was not an ambassador, that no embassy was being established, that his mission was temporary, for the duration of the war, and that, as Italy was still neutral, he would spend most of his time in his villa in Florence. These explanations diminished but could not eliminate all the irritation the Taylor Mission caused, and it remained a source of grievance for years.

The ordinary Catholics were puzzled by the whole affair and many of them wondered just how the special representative would spend his time. Others wondered what it would mean for the Church. An example of that was the President's intervention in the selection of Cardinal Mundelein's successor.

He was anxious that his great admirer, Bishop Sheil of Chicago, be given the appointment and felt ill used when his candidate was passed over, though that happened not because he was his candidate, but because the Pope thought Archbishop Samuel Stritch of Milwaukee was better suited to that major post.

A much more important matter that concerned the President and in which the Archbishop could help him was the Catholic attitude toward the political situation in Europe. Roosevelt was well aware that public opinion in the United States was strongly opposed to American participation in the general European war that seemed ever more probable as Hitler's plans unfolded. The memory of World War I was vivid to millions who recalled the false promises and disappointed hopes connected with it. The strength of that opposition was reflected in the Neutrality Acts of 1935, 1936, and 1937, all of which were passed by overwhelmingly Democratic Congresses. They attempted to close all the loopholes their sponsors thought had led to our entry into the war in 1917. They forbade, among other things, the shipment of arms abroad, the granting of loans or credits of any kind to belligerents, and travel in war zones by American citizens. The public attitude was not changed by Hitler's seizure of Czechoslovakia in March 1939 or even by his pact with Stalin in August 1939, though the former showed there was no discernible limit to his territorial ambitions and the latter sealed the fate of Poland and made a general war inevitable.

The outbreak of war in Europe was preceded by intense diplomatic efforts to avert it. On August 24th, in a radio appeal for peace, Pius XII issued a prophetic warning to the German government that "Nothing is lost by peace. Everything can be lost through war." But the long-laid plans for war were already in motion and hostilities began on September 1st. They were to take 22,060,000 lives among all the armed forces. The civilian total will never be known. They led immediately to the proclamation of American neutrality and the declaration of a limited national emergency, followed by the amendment of the Neutrality Acts on November 4, 1939 to permit the sale of arms and war supplies. It was the first step toward American involvement in the war. Others followed very quickly. The fall of France, which followed Hitler's spectacular victories in Scandinavia and the Low Countries, made a deep impression here and the ignominious performance of the French was all the more startling because the American public had been assured by the experts that the French Army was invincible.

Congress reacted by appropriating a billion dollars for defense and by reviving the draft, for one year, in September 1940. The United States Army, which had been reduced to 150,000, was increased by November 1940 by 921,722 draftees. By December 1941 a total of 17,388,000 had been registered. In August 1941 Congress passed (with a majority of one vote in the House) a bill extending the draft to eighteen months. After Pearl Harbor, it was extended to six months after the cessation of hostilities. By the end of the war, 10,110,104 men had been drafted and another five million had been called up as reservists or had enlisted.

In the meantime, a vigorous propaganda war was being fought all over the country. In many ways, it was a rerun of World War I. Only a handful of insignificant people supported Germany and no one suggested that we help her. Hitler had outraged or offended and clearly menaced, not only the Jews, who were his most conspicuous victims, but the Protestants, the Catholics, the Liberals, the Socialists, the Communists, the Trade Unions, the International Bankers, the Free Masons, and every other group he could not hope to dominate. The question was how much America could or should do to help his enemies. Not all here who opposed him wanted war. Many thought it possible to sympathize with his victims, to admire the resistance offered by the British, then led by Churchill, and even to assist them, without thinking it necessary or desirable to enter the war. Others thought our entry was unavoidable and still others that it was also desirable.

The political situation here in 1940 had many similarities to the situation in 1916. Once again, there was a national election the incumbent President had to win before he was free to move decisively to war. Once again, because of the strength of the anti-war feeling, the campaign was run on a peace platform and the rearmament program was described as strictly defensive. Once again, the public, faced with a real emergency, was urged to follow the old adage about not swapping horses while crossing a stream. The Wilsonian campaign slogan, "He kept us out of war," was matched and surpassed by Roosevelt's famous promise delivered in Boston shortly before the election: "Fathers and Mothers of America, I tell you again and again and again your sons are not going to fight in foreign wars." Roosevelt won handily, by a much larger margin than Wilson, and was helped by an unconvincing and inexperienced opponent.

In general, the Catholics shared the prevailing opposition to intervention except in what seemed to many to be the improbable event of an attack on this country. The dominant attitude among them was expressed by two representative voices in New York. Father James Gillis, in his widely syndicated column, his lectures, and his radio talks was one. The other was Patrick F. Scanlan (1894–   ), the editor of The Brooklyn Tablet, a diocesan paper with a national circulation, who was supported by his bishop. They sympathized with the America First Movement which had been started to oppose intervention. They stressed the disillusionment that had followed the last war and feared a repetition of it on a larger scale if we entered the current war. They were not impressed by the sympathy shown the German Catholics by people who had ignored, condoned, or even approved the contemporary persecutions of the Church in Russia, Mexico, and Spain. Hitler's was the first persecution of the Catholics that was generally condemned by the non-Catholic American press, and even his elaborately staged "immorality trials" of monks and nuns fell flat and were recognized as fraudulent. That reaction was very different from "the conspiracy of silence" about the situation in Mexico that Pope Pius XI deplored more than once.

Another reason for the general Catholic lack of enthusiasm for intervention was the significant change made in some segments of public opinion and in government circles by Hitler's attack on Russia on June 22, 1941. Undoubtedly it was an immense advantage to the West, but it brought with it the problem of how best to use it without compromising fatally the moral principles for which the war was allegedly being fought. In September 1939, those principles seemed very clear. The two great totalitarian powers, each led by a monster, had combined to destroy Poland, to upset the balance of power and to pose a grave threat to the rest of the world. Each was perceived as a mortal enemy of all the values professed by the Christian West, and it was impossible to maintain the pretense that Fascism and National Socialism, both of which came into existence as antidotes to Communism, were genuinely Conservative or right wing movements.

The Nazi-Soviet Pact had disillusioned many, but by no means all, of the American liberals who for years had accepted the Communist line about life in the Workers' Paradise and whose credulity had survived such widely publicized events as the mass starvation of the Russian peasants and the Moscow Trials of 1934–1938. Stalin's crimes were on a larger scale than Hitler's, were as well known, and had been going on for a longer period, but they never evoked the same emotional response in this country that Hitler's did. That was due to a combination of factors including, among others, an understandably greater interest in Western than in Eastern Europe, an awareness that Fascism, especially in its German form, was a greater immediate menace to the West, the failure of many and the refusal of some to understand and accept the reality of the Communist menace, and the intellectual and emotional inability of many to cope with more than one enemy at a time. The ease with which American liberals combined denunciation of Hitler with praise of Stalin was due in part to the capacity for selective indignation that is their hallmark and outstanding characteristic.

The liberals were not the only ones who shifted their position after June 22, 1941. The Communists, who had been strongly against intervention until Stalin was attacked, instantly discovered great merit in it and used all their influence to promote it. Suddenly there was a stream of propaganda fed from liberal and Communist sources, downgrading Stalin's crimes and attempting to sell a largely skeptical public an improved image of the Soviet system and even of Stalin himself. These things were observed with distress by many Catholics who remembered the recent (March 19, 1937) warning of Pius XI that Communism is intrinsically evil and cooperation with it in any way is to be avoided. Their uneasiness was not allayed by the assurance given by Archbishop McNicholas, as spokesman for the hierarchy, that in helping Stalin we were not really helping Communism but were helping the Russian people defend themselves against unprovoked aggression.

Though he shared the general reactions to the results of World War I, Archbishop Spellman did not share the uneasiness in Catholic circles as America's entry into World War II approached. He regarded war as inevitable and thought it necessary in defense of liberty. It was just a question of how and when it could come. He was sure things would go better the second time around because the country was in better hands. His reading of the situation was still influenced by his relations with Roosevelt by whom he continued to be deeply impressed, and whom he judged able and willing to avoid past mistakes and to achieve the high goals he set before the people.

He thought, too, with millions of others, that the President was the only available candidate capable of handling the crisis. He did not believe Roosevelt was using the war crisis as an excuse to prolong his tenure in the White House or that he wished to prolong his tenure in order to get us into war. Hence he welcomed the rearmament program and the third term though he could give no public sign of approval of the latter. What he could do publicly, he did. In September 1940, speaking to the American Legion Convention in Boston, he made an appeal for preparedness that was regarded as a strong endorsement of Roosevelt's policies. To show where his sympathies lay he had special and separate Masses in the Cathedral for the suffering people in France, Poland, and England in the spring of 1941. They were attended by the ambassadors of those countries.

An important part of mobilizing the people for war in a democratic society is a statement of war aims that they can support and that appeal to their idealistic side. This was especially important in 1940–1941, because Americans still felt safe within their own boundaries and were largely self-sufficient economically. They had seen that Hitler, like Napoleon, was unable to cross the English Channel. In this task, Roosevelt's personality and oratorical gifts helped him greatly. On January 6, 1941 he proclaimed the Four Freedoms—of speech, of worship, from want, and from fear—which were to exist everywhere, and on August 14, 1941 the Atlantic Charter was proclaimed by Roosevelt and Churchill. It forbade territorial aggrandizement and territorial changes that did not accord with the freely expressed wishes of the inhabitants. It proclaimed the right of all peoples to choose the form of government under which they lived, promised to restore freedom to all the conquered nations, and urged all nations, for realistic as well as spiritual reasons, to abandon the use of force.

Like Wilson's Fourteen Points, these goals were hard to quarrel with, global in scope, and pointed to a new political order different from anything known in the history of mankind. Between the two declarations came the Lend Lease Act of March 1941 which gave the President a free hand in sending supplies of every kind to any nation whose defense he judged vital to our security. This was advanced with a straight face as a peace measure. America was to be "the Arsenal of Democracy" and Churchill was saying, "Give us the tools and we'll finish the job."

Though Pearl Harbor, which did not surprise Roosevelt and his closest advisers, was an initial disaster, it did the President the immense political favor of enabling him to lead a united country to war. Domestic dissension took second place to the war effort for the duration of hostilities, though the contending factions did not change their minds. It was recognized that the struggle would be longer, harder, and more expensive than the last one, but few doubted our capacity and will to win. Apart from the internment of all the Japanese-American citizens, a truly extraordinary measure that could be justified only in a grave national emergency, and which went unchallenged by all but a few, there was relatively little hysteria. No one matched Theodore Roosevelt's statement in 1915 that a "mother who is unwilling to raise her son to be a soldier is unfit for citizenship," or revived the claim that Christ had been crucified by German mercenaries in the Roman Army. There was no ban on German and Austrian music, nor were all non-diplomatic aliens moved out of Washington, D.C., as they had been in May 1918. The crusading spirit was weaker than in 1917 but it was strong enough for the government's purposes, and it was sustained by an incessant and all pervasive propaganda aimed at convincing millions that this time victory would surely bring us to the Promised Land.

Even before Pearl Harbor, the mobilization of such large numbers of men led to the revival of the voluntary supportive activities that had been so promiment in the previous war. This time things were done in advance. The government imposed a larger measure of coordination by forming the United Service Organization (U.S.O.) and in April 1941 the bishops established the National Catholic Community Service (N.C.C.S.) as an umbrella agency for all Catholic efforts. The Knights of Columbus submerged their efforts in those of the N.C.C.S., which continued their policy of "everyone welcome and everything free," and again provided much-appreciated help for the chaplains. The Chaplains Aid Society expanded its efforts and this time the government provided the chapels. The Knights were active, too, in the War Bond Drives and in the Blood Bank. In New York City, the Archbishop opened the Cathedral Canteen in August 1941. In its first three years, it served over 630,000 members of the armed forces. It continued until the U.S.O. was deactivated in 1947 and it was reopened for the Korean War. A substantial majority of those who used it were non-Catholics.

The Military Vicar

Archbishop Spellman could not have foreseen the lasting change the war would make in his own life. It opened a new, long and very important chapter, making him easily the best known member of the American Hierarchy. It brought him a global recognition through its effect on the office of Military Vicar of the Armed Forces (Chaplain Bishop) in which he had succeeded

Cardinal Hayes on December 8, 1939. Some thought had been given to moving the entire operation of the Military Vicariate to Washington but the Holy See decided to leave it in New York for the time being, and years later, on September 8, 1957, decreed that henceforth the Archbishop of New York is always to be the Military Vicar.

Archbishop Spellman's first step as Military Vicar was to prepare for the anticipated expansion. Monsignor Waring was replaced on December 9th by Father John F. O'Hara, C.S.C. (1888–1960), then president of Notre Dame University, who was made a bishop at once. As the work increased he was joined, on January 2, 1943, by Father William T. McCarty, C.SS.R. (1889–1972), who was also made a bishop at once. Henceforth, the Military Ordinariate (the Military Diocese) was never without at least two auxiliary bishops. In December 1939 the Army and Navy had fifty-three chaplains, five of whom were from New York. The Air Force Chaplain Corps was not established until 1949. By December 7, 1941 (Pearl Harbor) there were five hundred chaplains on active duty and by the end of the war 3,270 (of whom 150 were from the Archdiocese of New York) had served or were serving. They were helped wherever that was appropriate by about two thousand civilian priests.

The chaplains, like the military personnel, came from every area of the country, and every diocese and religious community was represented in their ranks. New York was able to supply the largest contingent because of a temporary surplus of vocations. Cardinal Hayes was the only Bishop or Archbishop of New York who felt even for a day that he had too many priests. He did so because in the last few years of his life, when expansion seemed impossible, he ordained more priests than he felt he could use effectively. Archbishop Spellman found a reservoir of young priests on which he could draw for chaplains for the armed forces and for teachers in the new high school.

Since the Military Ordinariate, which became one of the great enthusiasms and most successful efforts of his life, had about four times as many priests as the Archdiocese of New York and more than twice as many Catholics, and, since it soon reached every continent, it was impossible for the Vicar, who had many other responsibilities, to give it the personal attention he felt it deserved. He determined to make up for that by visiting as many bases and meeting as many chaplains and military personnel as possible in the time at his disposal. In August 1942, he visited Alaska and the Southwest and met three hundred chaplains as he visited ninety-two posts and traveled 18,000 miles. On his return, he reported to the President, who invited him to a White House dinner at which he, the Winston Churchills, and Averell Harriman were the only guests. His trip was the first in a series of trips on the business of the Ordinariate that were to take him around the world six times, cover more than 500,000 miles, bring him to every continent, and enable him to meet literally thousands of people from every level of society. Such trips would have been impossible without the airplane.

Unlike most of his later trips, his first one did not merit or receive much attention from the press. Though hazardous in parts of Alaska, it was a routine visitation carried out entirely within the continental boundaries of the United States and it had no political significance at all. Things were or seemed to many to be different on his second trip, which took him outside the country. The President, who knew of his plans to visit the overseas bases as soon as the military situation made it possible, suggested he prepare to leave early in February 1943. Clearance with the government was necessary because the only available carrier was the United States Air Transport Command which, by the President's order, gave him Priority I rating and facilitated his trips in every way. By his unfailing cooperation in the work of the Military Vicar, Roosevelt set a precedent that was followed by all the presidents with whom Archbishop Spellman had to deal.

When he left New York on February 9, 1943, the Archbishop did not expect to be gone, as he was, until August, nor did he know he would travel 46,000 miles. His original plan to visit China had to be postponed, but he did get to Portugal, Spain, the Vatican, England, Ireland, and Scotland, every country in North Africa, and the Near and Middle East, most of the remaining countries in Africa, and Brazil. In Constantinople, he stayed with an old friend, Archbishop Angelo Giuseppe Roncalli, the future Pope John XXIII, then Apostolic Delegate to Turkey, who was a close friend of Monsignor Borgongini-Duca.

He was fortified by personal letters from the President to the American commanders and diplomats, all of whom received an advance notice of his coming that opened all doors. His schedule could not be arranged fully in advance because of uncertainty about the available transportation, which in turn was dependent on the military situation. Another problem was communication with home. Everywhere he went the wartime censorship was in full force. Still, he managed to keep in touch with New York and even to launch the 1943 Catholic Charities Drive by radio from London.

The Military Vicar's trips developed a pattern of their own. Normally, and depending on local conditions, each included Mass for the Catholic personnel, a bed to bed visitation of the military hospitals, a session with each chaplain, visits with the commanding officers, the American and papal diplomats, the local bishops, the leading public officials, and often the missionaries. Mass was said in all sorts of places ranging from great cathedrals, ancient shrines, parish churches, and military barracks to improvised altars in the desert or the African bush or islands in the Pacific. One additional task which grew to great proportions and was performed very cheerfully was suggested by a wounded soldier in a military hospital. He, apparently aware of the mail situation, asked the Archbishop to notify his parents on his return that he had seen him and found him well. This led to taking names and addresses and ultimately to the sending of literally thousands of letters to people all over the country. This much-appreciated favor was done for all who asked for it.

There were other constants that received less notice. From first to last, the Archbishop paid his own way. He had no claim to, did not want, and would not have accepted transportation at the expense of the government. He preserved his own independence and protected both the Church and the government from criticism by those who are ever on the look-out for violations of the separation of Church and State and ready to warn against a "Roman Raid on the Treasury." He sought no advantage for himself, and was pleased when some who did protest the assistance given to him were told it was available to them on the same terms. With the exception of his last trip in December 1966, when he yielded to his doctors' insistence and took a companion with him, he always traveled alone. In wartime and whenever else the situation suggested it, he took concentrated food and vitamins with him so as not to be a burden to his hosts. He was an excellent traveler, always ready to take the rough with the smooth and to adapt himself cheerfully to circumstances. He was helped by his apparently inexhaustible energy and by the almost total indifference to food and comfort that had been fostered by his student days in Rome.

The part of his trip that first aroused the interest of the American press was his visit to Spain on his way to Rome. Franco's victory in the Spanish Civil War had been a bitter disappointment to all the anti-Catholics here and especially to their Marxist and liberal members. It had also disappointed the Catholic liberals who believed sincerely that the Church could win the goodwill of the liberals in general and that it was of paramount importance that she do so. The liberals and leftists were unable to see any religious reason why the Military Vicar should visit a country where there were no American servicemen, so they concluded he must have a political reason and they could think of no good one. They, who were enchanted by the American-Soviet Alliance and were playing down both Stalin's complicity with Hitler in starting the war and his attacks on Finland and the Baltic states, were upset by the Archbishop's visit to a dictator. Their suspicion of his visit to Madrid was extended quickly to the rest of his trip.

Their views were shared by their peers in Europe, including the No-Popery brigade in England, and as they ignored the facts their imaginations had full rein. They had the Archbishop planning to move the Pope to Brazil, or arranging a Concordat with Stalin, or negotiating peace with Hitler. Three leftwing magazines published in New York City, each of which considered itself the organ of a sophisticated elite, were particularly silly. *The Nation* saw a new Axis being formed and running from Washington to the Vatican through Madrid. *The New Republic* saw Vatican, British and American diplomacy aiming at preserving the "Clerical Fascist" regime in Italy if Mussolini fell. *The Protestant,* an ultra-leftist periodical masquerading as a religious one, described the Archbishop's trip as "the devious flittings of the dainty servant of Vatican intrigue" and wondered by what authority he would negotiate with the enemy. These and other absurdities and the animus they expressed revealed an attitude to the Archbishop and the values he stood for that lasted all his life and surfaced regularly during his subsequent trips.

The real reason for his trip to Spain was that, because of the military and political situation, the road to Rome ran through Madrid, and the Pope had urged him to visit him if at all possible. That had not been on his original itinerary and it was not easy to do. It was his first visit to Rome since September 1932, and his first visit with the Pope since they parted in New York on November 7, 1936. He stayed for ten days, leaving on March 3rd, and spent hours with the Pope, who gave him as a parting gift the chain and cross he himself had worn since his consecration in May 1917. No statements were issued to the press and once again speculation ran wild. He found the Pope well but under a great strain and deeply concerned about the future of Europe.

THE HOLY SEE AND THE WAR

Pius XII made every effort to follow the wartime policy of Benedict XV, with whom he had worked long and closely and who had sent him to Germany, but he had to work in even more difficult circumstances. In the First World War, every major power in Europe except France and Turkey had a Christian government and the war was a two-sided struggle. In the Second World War, the two leading military powers on the continent were led by fiercely anti-Christian, though rival, governments and the war there was basically three-sided, with the Pacific war as a sideshow. Once again the Germans and the Western Powers wished to use the Holy See. Each side, firmly convinced of the justice of its cause and the invincibility of its arms, thought anything less than full approval by the Vatican was tantamount to secret sympathy with the enemy. The Soviet Union, which then had no hope of exerting any influence in Rome, ignored the Vatican and refused to have contact of any kind with it.

In the Vatican's judgment, Russia was a greater long-term menace than Germany, but there was no evidence that the Western Powers were concerned about or even aware of that. If Hitler had won, which by 1943 seemed unlikely to the Vatican, he would have given short shrift to the Church as the Communists did whenever they could, but while the war lasted he had to bide his time. He never forgot that the Catholic and Protestant churches provoked the first and most persistent opposition he encountered in Germany. In 1939, 43 percent of the total population of the Greater German Reich was at least nominally Catholic. Their numbers were swollen so greatly by his conquests that a full scale attack on the Church was deemed inadvisable at the time. The Pope refused firmly to bless Hitler's bogus crusade against Bolshevism or to do anything that would give approval to the oncoming Communist tide.

The problem of atrocities and of how to mitigate the sufferings of the civilian population in the war zones, whose ranks included millions of refugees and deportees of every kind, was a very difficult one that lasted to the end of the war. In the First World War, most of the suffering was incidental to the war effort, but in the Second much of it was due to the deliberate policy of the Germans and, when their chance came, of the Russians. Moreover, as the tide of war turned and control of the skies passed to the Western Powers, their aerial bombardments, heavier and wider than Hitler's, made their own contribution. Many in the West would have welcomed a papal condemnation of the wanton destruction of Coventry and Rotterdam by Hitler but not of the destruction of Dresden by the Allies, not to mention Hiroshima and Nagasaki. The Pope was determined to hold the scales even and, as he told Washington, if he condemned the crimes of Hitler he must do the same for the Russians, which he thought would not please the West.

A point often overlooked by those who were anxious for the Pope to condemn Hitler's atrocities was the effect such a condemnation would have had, not on public opinion in the West but on the people it was intended to help. There was no assurance it would have achieved its purpose. Hitler himself said in April 1942 that, when Pius XI put Alfred Rosenberg's *The Myth of the Twentieth Century* on the Index in 1934, the circulation of that pro-Nazi book increased substantially. Much more importantly, in September 1939 Prince Adam Sapieha, Archbishop of Cracow, and some other Polish bishops implored the Pope to silence the Vatican Radio's protests against persecution in German-occupied Poland. They said each protest was followed by terrible reprisals against which the Poles were completely defenseless. Later in the war, in 1942–1944, the repeated public threats by Roosevelt and Churchill to punish the murderers of the Jews led the Germans to accelerate the pace of the massacres.

Hitler's insane hatred of the Jews and the lengths to which he went in his attempt to exterminate them presented the Holy See with a very special problem. Anti-Semitism was an essential ingredient of National Socialism, but not of Fascism. It had been condemned roundly by Pius XI who said that spiritually we are all Semites. He had also condemned all theories of racial superiority. Taking advantage of the refusal of Pius XII to recognize any territorial changes until the war ended, Hitler refused to receive any papal protests against the persecution of either Catholics or Jews outside the Greater German Reich (Germany and Austria), and he rejected all complaints against conduct within it. This forced the Pope to deal only with the local bishops and, where they had not been expelled, the Nuncios, who could approach the Occupation authorities or the local government directly.

What was possible under the circumstances varied greatly from country to country and the Pope always regretted that he could not have done more. Though in the nature of the case the exact figures can never be known, the overall results were substantial. A Jewish historian of those terrible years has estimated that the area occupied by Hitler contained about eight million Jews, of whom about two million survived. Half of the survivors escaped to the free world and the rest endured the whole of the persecution. The number the Church was instrumental in rescuing was at least 700,000 and probably nearly 860,000. The work was done as inconspicuously as possible in the interest of both sides, each of which was well aware of the German presence. The Jews were concealed in a network of thousands of Catholic institutions and by thousands of Catholic families that hid Jewish children.

The situation was complicated further by the German occupation of Rome, which meant that from September 12, 1943 to June 5, 1944 the Vatican was surrounded by German soldiers, and there was the danger that when they left Rome they would take the Pope with them and paralyze the central administration of the Church. Even then, when he and all the Catholic institutions in Rome were at the mercy of a sudden German move, the Pope did not swerve from his course. On September 27, 1943, the Chief Rabbi of Rome was informed by the German Commander that unless he produced fifty kilograms of gold by the following day the Jewish community in Rome would be "dispersed." That same day, he was informed that whatever was needed to make up the required amount would be supplied by the Vatican. None was needed but the offer was remembered by the Jews. It was one of the reasons why Paul VI could speak later of seeing "those who came with tears in their eyes to thank Pius XII for saving their lives." Characteristically, Pius XII did not allow the war and the imminent danger to Rome and to the Holy See itself to divert him from the fulfillment of his role as chief pastor and teacher of the Church. In 1943 he issued two of the most important of his forty-three encyclicals. The first, *Mystici Corporis* (June 30th), dealt with the Mystical Body. The second, *Divino Afflante Spiritu* (September 10th), was a landmark in Catholic biblical studies.

The German presence also brought the danger that Rome would be bombed by the Allies, as it had been on July 19th and August 13th. Though that danger was averted, the Pope had to mourn the destruction of the great Abbey of Monte Cassino, the cradle of Western Monasticism, which was founded by St. Benedict circa 529. It had been destroyed by the Lombards in 581 and by the Saracens in 883. Now it was the Americans' turn. They demolished it by a massive aerial bombardment on February 15, 1944. Later, General Mark Clark, the United States Commander in Italy, said he thought the destruction of the Abbey was a serious blunder.

The Archbishop could do nothing about many of the Pope's problems, but what could be done was done. He led the unsuccessful effort of the American hierarchy to prevent the bombing of Rome, the only religious capital bombed during the war, and in June 1944 at the Pope's request he broadcast to Hungary to protest the persecution of the Jews. He worked effectively through Roosevelt to bring the Allied Control Commission to a more humane and realistic attitude toward occupied Italy, to which the early stages of

Liberation brought intense suffering. The basic daily ration, for instance, was one-fifth the pre-War average, infant mortality was multiplied by four, and in June 1943 the death rate in Rome was twice what it had been a year earlier.

He was more directly helpful as the Liberation proceeded, and innumerable appeals for help poured into the Vatican from all sides. The problem had been foreseen and the solution was at hand. In 1940 the American bishops set up the Bishops War Emergency and Relief Committee to coordinate and handle all their relief work for refugees and war victims, and in 1941 the first Laetare Sunday Collection had been taken up to help it. In 1943 it became the War Relief Services, and since 1955 has been the Catholic Relief Services (C.R.S.). Its headquarters have been in New York from the start and the Archbishop, who was a prime mover in its establishment, took a very active interest in it. He saw the fruits of its work when he returned to Europe in 1944 (June to October), and again in September 1945 when he visited Rome on his way home from the Far East. In 1944 he visited France and Germany and in August, in recently liberated Paris, said Mass for the American soldiers in Notre Dame at the request of General DeGaulle. In July, while he and King George VI were luncheon guests of General Clark at the American Headquarters on the Italian Front, they narrowly escaped injury when a bomb exploded nearby.

POSTWAR DOUBTS

The mounting successes of the Allies as they approached the total victory they had foreseen from the start found the Archbishop filled with mixed emotions of elation and foreboding. The latter was caused by his gradual loss of confidence in the political wisdom of the President as he came to a clearer understanding of the latter's attitude toward Germany and Russia. As late as February 1943, he said, "Each time I see the President, I am more and more impressed with his stature as a great man, one of the great men of history, and I hope and pray he will lead this country on the road to victory, peace, and prosperity." He had become accustomed to bringing him into every speech, but not every sermon, he delivered.

The first doubts came as he had time and occasion to reflect on the "unconditional surrender" the President announced as a war aim at the Casablanca Conference of January 1943, and to discuss it with some of the military and political leaders he met on his travels. Roosevelt assured him he had in mind Grant's treatment of Lee at Appomattox. There was no calming the fears aroused by a long private conference with the President in September 1944 which reawakened the doubts of the preceding year. In view of subsequent events and of our contemporary relations with Germany and Russia, it is interesting to recall how those relations appeared to the most powerful man in the world in 1944.

The President's plans for Germany were quite clear. It was to be divided, disarmed, de-industrialized, and pauperized. If a strictly pastoral and agricultural economy could not sustain the population, whatever was needed to avoid starvation would be supplied by the United States Army, which would distribute soup three times a day for many, many years. The controls were to be so strict that no German could become a civilian pilot for forty years. The objection that such a program would ruin Germany's neighbors too and lead to the Communization of Europe was dismissed with the observation that that was coming anyway. The President hoped that after twenty years occupation the Western Europeans would make their Russian masters less barbarous.

Roosevelt's views on Russia were just as interesting. Russia, he felt, needed protection from the West. She would be given, and in any case could take—for England and America could not fight her—the Baltic States, part of Poland and the Balkans, and would control Austria, Hungary, Czechoslovakia, Finland, Poland, and even Germany. He was much impressed by the Russian economy which he thought was so strong that except for trucks American aid was negligible. He felt it necessary for America to prove her good faith to Russia and that the Pope was much too worried about Communism. He felt too that he needed, and was sure to receive, Russian cooperation with his plan for the post-war organization of the world. He foresaw four spheres of influence dominated ultimately by the four Great Powers, all of whom would work in perfect harmony. England would dominate western Europe, China the Far East, and America the Pacific. He was sure he could handle Stalin better than Churchill could, because the latter was too much of an idealist while Stalin and he were realists. "Don't worry, I know how to talk to Stalin. He's just another practical man who wants peace and prosperity." The Archbishop answered: "He is not just another anything. He is different. You can't trust him. He will never cooperate."

The Archbishop was unable to reconcile Roosevelt's views with the professed war aims of the Western Allies or with the Pope's repeated appeals for "Peace with Justice." He knew the Vatican hoped for a de-nazified Germany but believed that a strong, prosperous Germany offered the only hope of preventing a Russian conquest of Western Europe. He knew too that while the Vatican viewed the Reformation as a revolt against the Church and the French Revolution as a revolt against Christianity, it regarded Communism as a revolt against God and as the ultimate rejection of religion in any form. He comforted himself with the hope that the President would change his mind and that, since his plans were clearly incompatible with the long-term interests of America, calmer counsels would prevail and they would never be carried out.

At the same time, he recognized that Roosevelt had an alarmingly superficial grasp of the nature and long-term significance of Communism, a fact that could lead to tragedy for the President himself, the country, the world, and the Church. Nonetheless, he welcomed the fourth term, partly because he had no reason to suppose Dewey would handle the existing situation any better, and he was one of the small crowd invited to the inaugural lunch at the White House. Its supporters justified the fourth term on the ground that the country needed an experienced man to win the peace, as they had justified the third term by the need of such a man to keep the peace. He continued to like and admire Roosevelt and to be grateful for the kindness Roosevelt had shown him. He mourned him sincerely and, as at that time it was impossible to have a public Mass for a non-Catholic, he copied what Archbishop Corrigan had done when McKinley died and sang a solemn Pontifical Mass of Intercession for the Country in the Cathedral.

Archbishop Spellman's interest in the Ordinariate and the war did not lead to any neglect of New York. It was a time for planning expansion that could not be undertaken at the time, for reducing debts, and collecting funds for future growth. In the Archbishop's absence, routine affairs were handled mainly by Monsignor McIntyre, who became an auxiliary bishop in January 1941, Vicar General in 1945, and coadjutor without-right-of-succession in July 1946. Before leaving for his first trip as Military Vicar, the Archbishop told him, "You can do everything but sell the Cathedral."

Among the projects that could not be postponed was the restoration of the exterior of the Cathedral. In July 1945 a large block of masonry was dislodged by some blasting in the area. The resultant examination showed a process of deterioration that was arrested only by very extensive and expensive repairs to the Cathedral itself and to the adjoining rectory and Archbishop's house. The cost, over 3 million dollars, was met by a legacy from Major Edward Bowes, a widely known radio personality of the time, who left a substantial part of his fortune to the Archbishop to be used for the Cathedral. Other improvements to the Cathedral that came later included the great rose window, the bronze doors on the Fifth Avenue side, and (less noticeable but much appreciated) an elevator to the choir loft.

THE CARDINALATE

The end of the war brought the long-awaited first consistory of Pius XII. He had refused to hold it sooner because he wanted to have the complete freedom of choice he felt was impossible just before or during the war. In the meantime, vacancies multiplied and by December 23, 1945, the membership of the Sacred College of Cardinals was down to thirty-seven, the lowest it had been in centuries. On that day, the Pope announced the names of thirty-two prelates who would enter it in the consistory of February 18, 1946. It was the largest distribution of red hats in the history of the Church and broke the record set by Leo X in July 1517 when he distributed thirty-one.

The list took into account the changes made by the war. For the first time, every continent was represented. Only seventeen, including four Italians, came from Europe and there the scales were balanced nicely. France, Germany and Spain got three each and England, Holland, Hungary, and Poland one each. There were some famous names on the list. Many of the new Cardinals and especially Von Galen of Munster, Frings of Cologne, Von Preysing of Berlin, Saliège of Toulouse, and Sapieha of Cracow had suffered much from the Nazis. The new Primate of Hungary, Joseph Mindzenty, was to suffer much from the Communists, as was Thomas Tien, the first Chinese Cardinal. South America got six of the hats and North America five, including one Canadian.

Many thought the most obvious sign of a new age in the Church was that four of the hats went to the United States, which raised its number from one to five. No one was surprised by the choice of Archbishop Spellman who had been on every list of possible candidates published since March 2, 1939. The other Americans were John J. Glennon (1862–1946), Archbishop of St. Louis; Edward A. Mooney (1882–1958), Archbishop of Detroit; and Samuel A. Stritch (1887–1958), Archbishop of Chicago.

Archbishop Spellman, who had been notified of his promotion by the Pope himself on September 30th, left for Rome in a chartered plane on February 11th, accompanied by a large party that included Archbishops Glennon and Tien and their companions. After brief stops in Ireland and France, they reached Rome on the eve of the consistory. The city was still occupied by American and British troops and the situation was grave. To avoid overtaxing the available supplies, Archbishop Spellman brought along everything he and all his guests would need. The ceremonies were carried out with traditional splendor and lasted from February 18th to the 22nd. The actual conferral of the hat took place in St. Peter's on February 21st, and on that occasion the forthcoming canonization of Mother Cabrini was announced and set for July 7th. As special marks of favor, the new Cardinal of New York received both the titular church (the ancient basilica of Sts. John and Paul) and the red hat that had belonged to Cardinal Pacelli. After brief stopovers in Spain and Portugal, which provoked further outcries from the left-wing press, the Cardinal arrived in New York on March 5th. The only shadow on the trip was the death of Cardinal Glennon, which occurred in Dublin on March 9th on his way home.

A CHANGING POPULATION

The Spellman administration saw a sharp drop in the rate at which the population of New York City grew. Whereas from 1920 to 1940 the population itself grew by 1,852,947, it grew only 412,765 from 1940 to 1970 and that figure was well below the growth during the depression years. In

1970 the population was larger by only 3,606 than in 1950. Brooklyn and Queens, which had passed the other boroughs by 1930 with 3,589,430 to 3,290,916 continued to widen their lead. In 1940 it was 3,994,919 to 3,459,456 and by 1970 it was 4,575,560 to 3,292,200. Manhattan gained 70,177 between 1940 and 1950, then sank again and in 1970 at 1,524,541 was 365,383 below its 1940 total. Brooklyn peaked in 1950 at 2,738,175 and sank to 2,601,832 by 1970. Staten Island went from 174,441 to 295,443 and the Bronx 1,394,711 to 1,472,216, but the real winner was Queens which went from 1,297,634 to 1,973,708, a gain of 676,074.

Though the three city counties in the Archdiocese lost 166,956 people between 1940 and 1970, the situation was different in the suburbs. The seven counties there gained 774,669 of whom almost half, 323,129, were in Westchester. The growth rate was lowest in the 1940s when wartime restrictions barred much new housing and in that decade, for example, Westchester gained 2,281, Ulster 939 and Sullivan 216. Even so, by 1950, when the great spurt began, the Catholic population of the Archdiocese was back to the level it had reached when Cardinal Farley died.

The changes in the population were not only in numbers and in location in the city. Once again, new people were coming, this time Hispanics and Blacks, chiefly in two great waves of internal migration that have only recently shown signs of tapering off. They were distinguished from their predecessors, whose poverty and low literacy rate they shared, by the fact that most of them were American citizens. The Puerto Ricans, the largest group among the Hispanics, had been citizens since the Jones Act of 1917, and most of the Blacks since the Civil War. Many, but a definite minority of the latter, came from the Caribbean islands.

The official figures indicate that over 600,000 Puerto Ricans came to New York City between 1940 and 1960, as did about 150,000 other Hispanics from Central America and the Caribbean. By 1965 about 700,000 Puerto Ricans had arrived, and 200,000 of them had settled in the Bronx. They were thought to make up about one percent of the population in 1934 when the Casita Maria, a settlement house for them, was opened by Elizabeth Sullivan (who later married Charles H. Ridder, the publisher of *The Catholic News*).

The Hispanics presented the Church in New York and Brooklyn with a new version of an old and serious problem as well as with a great opportunity. They came from areas that for cultural as well as political reasons have always had a woefully inadequate number of vocations to the priesthood and the religious life, and in which the standard of Catholic practice has often been very low. Through no fault of their own, they were generally very poorly instructed and had no awareness of the way in which the Church must be organized and supported here. Like so many who preceded them, they suffered keenly during the sudden transition from a stable rural society to the level of urban life open to them here, and from the religious, cultural, and racial discrimination they experienced here for the first time.

Because of their rapid arrival in such great numbers (they were the chief reason why the Catholic population of the Archdiocese increased by about 80 percent from 1940 to 1970), their poverty, and the lack of religious personnel, no effort was made to organize them in national parishes. If a particular parish or group of parishes became predominantly or wholly Spanish, all well and good. The plant or plants were already there and could be staffed when it was possible by Spanish-speaking personnel, who were recruited widely. In general, an effort was made to integrate them into the existing parishes.

Other steps were also taken. The Spanish Catholic Action Office, now the Spanish Apostolate, was opened in 1952 to coordinate what was done. Spanish replaced Italian as the major modern language in the seminary, and in 1956 the custom of sending half the ordination class away to study Spanish was inaugurated. It was so successful that the number of parishes with Spanish sermons rose from ten in 1953 to seventy-seven in 1967. Many young priests were sent to Puerto Rico not only to learn Spanish but to study the cultural background and pastoral practices their future parishioners were familiar with. The Puerto Ricans were the only immigrant group for whom it was possible to provide such a service. Classes were arranged here for other priests, Brothers, Sisters, and lay people who could help in the ever-growing effort to meet the needs of the new arrivals.

Although the Blacks also made their mark on the city, they presented less of a problem to the Church because of fewer traditional links with them and because the shortage of personnel and resources made it impossible to launch a major program for them. Still, by 1970 there were about 57,000 Black Catholics in the Archdiocese and each of their seven churches had a school. The Church's chief contribution to them was the maintenance and expansion of the Harlem apostolate, the effective banning of segregation in Catholic schools and institutions, the help given to the schools in the Black parishes, several of which had a majority of non-Catholic pupils, and support for the various State or Federal efforts to end or mitigate racial discrimination. Like the Puerto Ricans, the new Black arrivals came from a predominantly rural background. Like all other groups they had to start at the bottom, but both groups arrived when an aroused social conscience had started the steadily expanding social services which eased their lot considerably and were often the magnet that drew them here. The great Black migration to the North started in earnest after 1920 and accelerated sharply after 1940. In 1860, 92 percent of all the Blacks in the United States lived in the South. In 1920, the percentage in the South was 85 but by 1960 it was only 60. In 1900, there were 99,000 Blacks in New York State, in 1940 the number was 571,221, and in 1970 it was 2,168,636. In 1950, the white population was down by 12 percent from 1940, and in 1970 by 9.3 percent from 1960. Between 1950 and 1960 the number of whites who moved out of the State was more than the number that moved in.

The Hispanics and Blacks were not the only immigrants. The very sharp drop in the 1930s was made up for between 1940 and 1970 when, by decades, 1,035,039, 2,515,479, and 2,690,461 foreigners arrived, though they did not all come through New York. The Jewish population remained fairly constant but was redistributed. In 1970, for example, Manhattan, the Bronx, and Staten Island respectively had only 250,000, 395,000 and 11,000 Jews, a total of 656,000, while Brooklyn and Queens had 760,000 and 420,000, a total of 1,180,000. While the city had 1,836,000 Jews, Nassau and Suffolk had 414,000 and Westchester 31,000. The metropolitan area had between a third and a half of the Jewish population of the country. It is hard to be sure of the precise figures for many of the national groups because the Jews were usually included in the figures for the country from which they came, but there were large numbers of other foreign immigrants, too. The percentage of foreign-born had shrunk from 2,228,870 or 29 percent in 1950 to 1,556,663, or 20 percent in 1960. In that year, about half the people in every borough except Staten Island were born abroad or had at least one parent who was. In 1970 the city had 178,000 Orientals.

OTHER CHANGES IN THE CITY

The Second World War confirmed and strengthened New York's position as the financial capital of the world, and as the cultural capital of America. Its position as the most cosmopolitan city in the western hemisphere was enhanced by the decision of the United Nations to establish its permanent headquarters in New York. It is housed in an ultra-modern building on which work was started in 1948, and soon became a major tourist attraction. It is now the center of a foreign colony, numbering about 30,000 and drawn from every country in the world; it makes its own special contribution to the social and cultural life of the city.

As usual, traffic problems received high priority and, also as usual, many were dissatisfied with the progress made. That was so partly because each improvement came to be taken for granted very quickly. Aviation was well served by LaGuardia Airport (1939), which handles domestic flights, and Idlewild (known as John F. Kennedy Airport or J.F.K. since 1963), which opened in 1948 to handle foreign flights. The growth in air traffic, which was interrupted by the war, started in 1939 when Pan American made its first commercial flight to Europe. It compensated New York for the decline in seaborne passengers. The Queens Midtown Tunnel opened in 1940 and the Battery Tunnel in 1950.

Public transportation continued to be a controversial topic. General dissatisfaction with it led to the establishment in 1952 of the Transit Authority from which great things were expected. Meantime, in 1948, the public was shocked when the five-cent subway fare, sacred from the beginning of the system, vanished and was replaced by a ten-cent fare for both subway and bus. A further shock, when the fare went to fifteen cents in 1953, was mitigated by the assurance it would go no higher. The long awaited Second Avenue Subway was postponed and the huge sums raised to pay for it were diverted to other purposes. The West Side Bus Terminal opened in 1950.

CULTURAL DEVELOPMENTS

There were other developments. For better or worse, Modern Architecture came into its own and striking examples of it like Lever House (1952) and the Seagram Building (1958) began the transformation of Park Avenue. The housing situation continued to defy all attempts to solve it by the public authorities on every level and by private industry. Many believed no solution was possible until the issue of rent control was faced squarely but that did not happen. Still, some useful steps were taken. In 1949 the National Housing Act encouraged local authorities to acquire and resell substandard areas at a cost below what private investors would require, and in 1955 the Mitchell-Lama Law was passed by the State to help private middle-income housing. In 1957 the city passed the country's first Fair Housing Practices Act outlawing discrimination. The long planning for the World Trade Center with its huge towers started in 1964; it opened its doors in 1976.

One of the most notable developments was the Lincoln Center of the Performing Arts on which work was in progress from 1959 to 1968. Among its prominent structures are the new Philharmonic Hall (1962) and the Opera House (1965).

Not all the cultural developments were beneficial. One which the Cardinal tried vainly to stop and which brought him much ridicule and abuse was the progressive deterioration of the moral standards of the movies. Some of the leaders of the motion picture industry resented the limits imposed by the various State Boards of Censorship and were anxious for unlimited freedom of expression. On December 12, 1950, a foreign film called "The Miracle," which was described by the Legion of Decency as "a sacrilegious and blasphemous mockery of Christian religious truths," opened in New York. After protests from the Catholics, the New York City Commissioner of Licenses stopped the performance on the ground that it was a "blasphemous affront to a great many of our citizens."

The reaction was immediate and predictable. The *POAU* (Protestants and Other Americans United for the Separation of Church and State) and the *Daily Worker* said the Cardinal was trying to establish a clerical political tyranny in violation of the United States Constitution. They joined the American Civil Liberties Union, the American Jewish Congress, and others in urging the New York State Court of Appeals to revoke the ban. When the

Court upheld the ban, which had previously been approved by the New York Board of Regents, the case was appealed to the United States Supreme Court, which revoked it on the ground that both the First and the Fourteenth Amendments forbade a State to ban anything on the ground that it was sacrilegious.

Sacrilegious movies are less likely to be as numerous and lucrative as sexually explicit ones, so the next question that came up was about immoral movies. What, if anything, can the States do to protect public morals? Once again, the answer came from Washington and it was "not much." In 1956 a movie called "Baby Doll" was condemned by the Legion of Decency as evil in concept and certain to exert corrupting influence on those who saw it. The Supreme Court solved the problem by announcing that movies, formerly regarded as primarily a form of entertainment, were entitled to the full protection of the First Amendment. That in effect killed all local censorship.

While asserting more than once that pornography does not enjoy the protection of the law, the Supreme Court has left its legal standing in such confusion that, in fact, it does enjoy that protection. Most of the press welcomed the Court's decisions, and some of the leading papers assured those who dissented from them that good taste would protect the public interest and curb the greed of the producers. They did not foresee the present condition of the Times Square area or the notoriety New York has earned as one of the chief pornography centers of the world. A survey published in October 1978 estimated that the pornography industry grosses about four billion dollars a year, a sum larger than the combined income of all legitimate forms of entertainment. It is helped by the apparent inability of the courts, the public prosecutors, the police, and the legislatures to devise a policy that would curb it in any meaningful way.

Two transient developments that brought much pleasure to millions were the New York World's Fair of 1939–1940, which was overshadowed by the approaching war, and the World's Fair of 1964–1965. The Vatican had a pavilion at the latter and the Cardinal persuaded Pope Paul VI to lend Michelangelo's *Pietà* to it. It proved to be one of the most popular exhibits, second only to General Motors Futurama. The *Pietà*'s visit gave the Cardinal's critics ammunition they welcomed. There was much talk of reckless endangerment of an irreplaceable treasure, but it came and went without incident or damage and its temporary custodians breathed a sigh of relief when it reached home. The only injury it has ever suffered was inflicted in St. Peter's several years later (1972) by a madman.

PARISHES AND SCHOOLS

The Spellman administration opened fewer new parishes than any since that of Bishop Dubois. The decision to integrate the newly arrived Hispanics into the existing parishes, and (with the single exception of St. Ann's Italian parish in Yonkers) to open no more national parishes relieved it of one of the pressures that had weighed heavily on its predecessors. Of the forty-five new parishes, only thirteen were in the city. In spite of its declining population, Manhattan got five, the Bronx got five and Staten Island, three. In the counties, the new parishes reflected the growth in population. Westchester, Rockland and Orange got respectively twelve, seven and five, Dutchess and Putnam three and two, Sullivan two, and Ulster one.

The growth in the field of education was more obvious, and the papal letter congratulating the Cardinal on his silver jubilee in New York singled out his work for the schools as worthy of special commendation. The years 1940–1965 saw a steady increase in the number of parochial schools here. It reflected the growth in the country at large that continued a national trend in existence since 1920. The ordinary Catholics were anxious for the schools and were prepared to make the sacrifices needed to support and expand them. Contrary to the opinion of some non-Catholic writers, the schools were not forced on a reluctant laity by the clergy and the growth of the system came in response to genuine and substantial popular pressure.

Even during the Depression years of the 1930s when the number of their pupils fell from 2,223,000 to 2,035,000, the number of schools increased from 7,923 to 7,924. The numbers peaked in 1965 with 10,879 schools and 4,492,000 pupils. By 1967 they had fallen to 10,350 and 4,106,000, and were below the 1960 figures of 10,501 and 4,373,000. According to Archbishop John O'Hara of Philadelphia, who made a careful study of Catholic school statistics for many years, from the school years 1944–1945 to 1956–1957 the enrollment in Catholic schools on every level increased by 2,067,162. The elementary and high schools gained 1,885,096, colleges and universities 261,000, and seminaries 7,156. The increase on the elementary level was 80 percent, on the high school level 61 percent, and in the seminaries 71 percent. The colleges and universities, with 57 percent of the Catholic students of college age, had 13.8 percent of the national enrollment. He thought they should have had 23 percent.

The growth in New York got off to a slow start. Of the 295 building projects for elementary schools that were completed in the Spellman years, only nine belong to 1939–1949. The 295 included 105 new buildings, forty-seven replacements, thirty-four complete renovations, and 109 additions. The enrollment rose from 99,641 to 172,927. There were also a few new private schools and a couple in the child-caring institutions. The schools in the three urban counties went from 146 with 77,373 pupils to 183 with 111,312. The seven suburban counties went from seventy-two with 18,414 to 156 with 61,615 pupils. By October 1960 there was one child in a parochial or private school for every two children in the public schools in the city, and 93.3 percent of the children outside the public schools were in parochial schools of all faiths.

The high schools grew from seventy-five to ninety-nine, but their enrollment went from 12,187 to 50,037, a fourfold increase. While several new diocesan high schools were built, the main burden on the secondary level continued to be carried by the religious communities. They expanded their facilities steadily. To help the high schools bear the increased cost of higher education for their faculties, the Archdiocese paid half the tuition of the religious and all the tuition of the diocesan clergy.

In spite of the great progress made in expanding the Catholic school system in New York, the majority of Catholic children were not in it. In 1966 it was estimated that 60 percent of those on the elementary school level were not in it and that 38 percent of them received no religious instruction. Things were worse on the secondary level, on which 71 percent were outside the system and 64 percent received no religious instruction. The situation was due in large part to the changing population. In 1967 the Puerto Ricans were 22.1 percent and the Blacks 30.1 percent of the 1,102,510 children in the public schools. They had risen respectively from 13.5 percent and 18.2 percent in 1957 and became the majority for the first time in 1966.

Cardinal Spellman paid special attention to the Seminary. Besides renovating the original structure, he added a library and a gymnasium and recreation center. The library, which was built to match the main building and was attached to it, was dedicated to Archbishop Corrigan for whom his admiration grew as he became increasingly familiar with his record in New York. Archbishop Corrigan had disposed of all his patrimony before his death and his only remaining asset, a $10,000 insurance policy, was left to the Seminary library. It provided its only income from 1902 to 1939.

Cardinal Spellman's attention was not limited to the fabric. He was pleased when the Seminary was accredited by the Middle Atlantic States Association of Colleges in 1961. He was always anxious that the faculty and candidates for it be as well trained as possible. He accepted wholeheartedly Pius XI's statement that the priest must be as well educated as the well educated laity of his time and place, and have, in addition to the necessary knowledge, a solid, manly, and apostolic spirit. He was a frequent visitor and brought or sent there a succession of distinguished people, including especially the large number of cardinals who were his guests in New York.

The Second World War did for college education what the First War did for secondary education and greatly accelerated a long-term trend. The improvement was made possible by the improvement in the standard of living that made more leisure time available. The G.I. Bill of Rights also helped. A few figures show the difference. In 1900 when the population was 76 million, the number who graduated from regular colleges was 27,410. That number had risen to 48,622 by 1920, when the population was about 105 million. By 1940 there were 186,500 graduates in a population of 132 million. In 1970 there were 827,234 in a population of 203 million. A significant social change is reflected in the number of women graduates: 5,237 in 1900; 16,642 in 1920; 76,954 in 1940; and 343,066 in 1970. There was a corresponding increase in the number of colleges and universities, public and private, Catholic and non-Catholic. In the Archdiocese of New York, the nine colleges and universities of 1940 rose by 1967 to nineteen with 28,599 pupils.

The growth of the public educational system led to an increasing demand for federal aid, a proposal opposed by many who feared the loss of local control. It is an issue with many facets, and there would have been ample room for differences of opinion if it had been considered solely on its merits. Unfortunately, it became entangled in the discussion of the relations of Church and State that became very lively after World War II. The war was not followed by an organized anti-Catholic movement as the Civil War and World War I were, but that did not mean that anti-Catholic feeling had vanished. This time, instead of using the frontal assault of former years, it expressed itself in often sincere and strident warnings against what was perceived as a renewed Catholic threat to the cherished principle of separation of Church and State. The agitation reached a point at which the hierarchy at its annual meeting in November 1948 found it necessary to reaffirm its acceptance of that principle as traditionally understood in this country.

It is not easy to be sure what caused the excitement. It was probably several things, such as the increased prestige of the Holy See, the signs of vigor in the Church in the United States, especially as seen in the rapid expansion of the school system, and even an awareness that the mood of the country was opposed to anything blatant like a revival of the Klan. Like Federal aid, the Church and State issue has many facets, but it soon became apparent that attention was focused on two questions: religion in the State schools, and the attitude of the State to Church-related schools.

Those were quite distinct issues and it was possible for many who supported the first to differ sharply among themselves about the second. A complicating factor was the enhanced role of the Federal courts, which came to exercise supreme authority in these matters and to impose a uniform standard on the entire country. In practice, this meant the Supreme Court, on which Catholics have long been underrepresented and sometimes misrepresented, to which all the test cases went ultimately. In 1948, in the McCollum Case from Illinois, it forbade any form of "release time" for religious instruction in which the instruction was given on government property. In 1952, in the Zorach Case from New York, it allowed release time programs that were not held on government property. In the Everson Case, from New Jersey in 1947, it permitted the use of government funds to transport parochial and other private school pupils to and from school. There were later decisions like the one in 1962 forbidding the recitation of a non-denominational prayer composed by the Regents of the University of the State of New York, and in 1963 forbidding Bible-reading or the recitation of the Lord's Prayer.

All the Supreme Court decisions except the Everson Case concerned only the public schools, and they caused mixed reactions. The Catholics and many, but by no means all, Protestants and some Jews regretted the decision on prayer and the Bible. The Everson Case decision caused a surprising uproar. There was no serious effort to bar pupils in nonprofit private schools from the benefits of the National School Lunch Act in 1946, or from the loan of secular textbooks from the State, or from using the G.I. Bill or State scholarships to pay tuition at Catholic schools, and therefore many Catholics wondered what made busing so special. The decision was condemned with an exceptional bitterness reminiscent of 1928 by many Protestant groups and was depicted by them as a blow to the Constitution. The attacks were prompted in part by the fear that they represented the first step toward what their authors regarded as the ultimate horror, direct government aid to Catholic schools. This decision led to the forming of "Protestants and Other Americans United for the Separation of Church and State" (POAU), an openly anti-Catholic group led for years by G. Bromley Oxnam, the Methodist Bishop of New York.

While the Catholics got some support in their approval of the Everson Decision, they were practically isolated when the question of Catholic schools sharing in Federal aid came up. Moreover, they were divided on Federal aid itself. Many, including some leaders of the hierarchy, were opposed to it on patriotic grounds. They agreed with millions of non-Catholics in regarding it as an unnecessary and unfortunate extension of Federal authority (with the risk of ultimate Federal control) from which much trouble might come. Cardinal Spellman recognized the legitimate division in Catholic ranks but felt very strongly that if Federal aid came it would be wrong to exclude Catholic school pupils from its benefits. He thought, too, with the Administrative Board of the N.C.W.C., that those who opposed all aid to church schools clearly had the Catholic schools as their chief target and that their ultimate aim was to drive religion from education, secularize public education, and then claim for it a total monopoly of education.

Such was the atmosphere in which, in May 1949, Congressman Barden of North Carolina introduced a bill to grant each state fifty dollars a head for the children of primary or secondary school age. The money was to be spent for the current expenses of the public schools and the States were expressly forbidden to spend any of it for transportation. The Catholic resentment at being excluded from the benefits of the Barden Bill was heightened by the way in which the State quota was to be determined. All the Catholic school pupils were included in their State's total and then excluded from the benefits. They noted too that it was supported by, among others, the American Association for the Advancement of Atheism and the American Society of Freethinkers, who urged its passage as a victory over the Catholic Church.

The Cardinal's opposition to the Barden Bill was remembered by many chiefly because it led him into a controversy with Eleanor Roosevelt that was a nine-day wonder at the time. She had carved a special niche for herself in the public life of the country and was justly renowned as a champion of two of the three principal minorities, the Jews and the Blacks. Her political skills and contacts, her adroit use of her newspaper .column and the lecture platform, and her tireless and quite sincere advocacy of liberal and left-wing causes of every kind, had won her a large constituency that made her an important political figure apart from her famous name. She wrote several columns on the Barden Bill, in which in her characteristic style she said she had not read it carefully, was sympathetic to its general thrust, approved of Federal aid to education, disapproved of Federal aid to private schools, and thought the Cardinal was responsible for the controversy surrounding the bill.

None of Mrs. Roosevelt's views on the Barden Bill or any similar topic could have surprised anyone with an elementary knowledge of her general attitude to public questions and of her record. What did surprise even many of her critics was the Cardinal's blunt charge that she was motivated by an anti-Catholic bias. He made it in an unfortunately worded letter in which he accused her of "discrimination unworthy of an American mother," a clause she seized on, fairly enough, and answered by reminding him that "the final judgment, my dear Cardinal Spellman, of the unworthiness of all human beings is in the hands of God."

The wording of his letter was all the more unfortunate because it distracted attention from the basic charge that she was anti-Catholic, which was quite true. Nothing in her early life could have led anyone to expect anything else. By background, training and conviction she was wholly unsympathetic to Catholic values and interests, as she had shown in a number of ways and on many occasions. She offered as proof that she was not anti-Catholic her support of Al Smith in 1928. But if that had been lacking, her husband would not have become Governor of New York and President.

Under our system, she was entirely within her rights in being anti-Catholic and in acting accordingly. What was not recognized as widely was that under the same system the Cardinal was entitled to recognize her attitude for what it was and to express his opinion of it. Many of her admirers were shocked less by her being anti-Catholic than by the fact that she, whom they revered as the high priestess of the Left, was publicly accused of bigotry. The controversy was distressing to many highly placed friends of both parties and strenuous efforts were made to end it. In the event the Barden Bill was beaten, the Cardinal retreated from his demand for a full share in Federal aid, and neither side changed its views.

The latent anti-Catholic feeling aroused by the Church-and-State and the Federal aid issues, and by Cardinal Spellman's pugnacious defense of Catholic interests, brought a considerable amount of criticism of the Cardinal, and he found himself attacked more sharply in some sections of the press than any of his predecessors since Archbishop Hughes. More than a century later, the same issues playing on the same anti-Catholic fears provoked much the same response. It showed how enduring a force in American life those fears are.

The Cardinal had other educational interests that received much less attention. He was a loyal supporter of the Catholic University, and played a major role in the erection of the new North American College in Rome which Pius XII himself dedicated on October 14, 1953. He helped, too, with *The New Catholic Encyclopedia* (1967) and a junior model, *The Catholic Encyclopedia for School and Home* (1965). He gave the Vatican Library a valuable and much appreciated copy of *The Princeton Index of Christian Art.* He himself wrote nine books, the royalties from which went to charity. While Archbishop Corrigan had gathered methodically over a period of years most of what we know of the pioneer priests in New York and New Jersey, and Cardinal Farley wrote a biography of Cardinal McCloskey and a history of St. Patrick's Cathedral, Cardinal Spellman was the first Archbishop of New York to venture into fields of poetry and fiction. In 1966 he opened a closed circuit educational television station for the parochial schools at Dunwoodie.

The Catholic Charities

His work for the Catholic charitable institutions was uncontroversial and, therefore, received less attention than his work for education, but it was a major and long-term contribution to the work of the Church in New York and one in which he took a deep personal interest. On his arrival, he had pledged himself to continue and, where possible and necessary, to expand the work of the Catholic charities. When he died, the effort he had made to fulfill that pledge could be seen from one end of the Archdiocese to the other.

The time was ripe for the expansion of the hospitals, as there was a pent-up demand for better and more abundant facilities. While a few small ones were closed or merged with others, some twenty were enlarged and either renovated or rebuilt entirely. In Manhattan, St. Vincent's was almost doubled in bed capacity and was rebuilt. Several of its new wings or facilities were named after generous benefactors. One, the Alfred E. Smith Pavilion, was a memorial to the late governor who had served on the Board of Trustees for years. Another memorial to him is the annual Alfred E. Smith Dinner, first held in October 1945, which is still an important fund-raising affair for hospitals. Misericordia Hospital was moved to new and larger quarters in the Bronx in September 1958. In the same month the Foundling Hospital moved to new and more commodious quarters across the street from the old one. Columbus Hospital became the Cabrini Medical Center. The counties were not neglected, as can be seen in the new facilities made available in Harrison, Kingston, Port Jervis, Poughkeepsie, Suffern, and White Plains.

The hospitals were not the only institutions that received attention. The growing need for accommodation for senior citizens was met in part by the opening of the Mary Manning Walsh Home (1952) and the Josephine Baird Home (1955), both of which were staffed by the Carmelite Sisters. All the other Homes, including the three run by the Little Sisters of the Poor, were renovated or enlarged. Six new child-caring homes were opened. One of them, the Astor Home in Rhinebeck, was the first Catholic residential psychiatric treatment center for emotionally disturbed children in the country. The Kennedy Child Study Center for mentally retarded pre-school age children met another need. Other developments were an expansion of the Catholic Youth Organization (C.Y.O.) with new camps and programs, seven community centers, the introductions of youth counseling (1944) and opening of the Family Life Bureau (1949).

Every Archbishop of New York has been aware of his deep indebtedness not only to the staffs and supporters of the institutions but also in a special way to the administrators who supplied the necessary dedicated leadership. Three, who in Cardinal Spellman's time rendered outstanding service in quite different circumstances, may be mentioned here and represent all the others.

In 1939, Sister Loretto Bernard Beagan became Administrator of St. Vincent's Hospital, Manhattan. She had been trained carefully in the then relatively new field of professional hospital administration and she brought to her new post both high technical competence and an exceptional capacity to deal with people. St. Vincent's, with which she was thoroughly familiar after six years as Assistant Administrator, was an old and well-established institution with deep roots in the community. She guided it through a period of unparalleled developments, and, when she left, it was one of the largest and best Catholic hospitals in the world. It was not just a matter of bigger and better buildings and a larger staff. The post-war years saw an explosion in medical knowledge and a growth of specialization in many fields that made a major hospital a much more complicated organism than it had ever been before. She left St. Vincent's to become Superior of the Sisters of Charity in New York and then successively Administrator and Treasurer of St. Vincent's, Staten Island, which also expanded notably.

Mother Alice, O.S.F. (Catherine Henry, 1879–1960), the Foundress of St. Clare's Hospital, Manhattan, had a very different task for which her background, personality, and unusual experience equipped her well. She represented a type the post-Conciliar Church in this country is unlikely to see often, if ever. She was born into a poor family in County Sligo, Ireland, emigrated to Boston at seventeen, and worked for five years in a commercial laundry for $2.50 a week before entering the Franciscan Sisters of Allegany. They were in charge of St. Elizabeth's Hospital in Boston, which was the scene of her labors for many years. Much of the heavy work was done by the Sisters and it had to come first, but she became the first Sister in Massachusetts to become a licensed pharmacist. Later she earned her B.S. at Boston College. She became an R.N., too, and often functioned as an anesthetist. Her energy, her competence, her way of handling people (especially the difficult cases in the out-patient clinic) and her unconventional methods marked her as a valuable but sometimes difficult assistant. Her superiors decided she needed more rather than less to do and watched for an opening that would give her talents greater scope.

The opportunity came in 1927 when the Sisters were asked to take over a private hospital in Miami Beach that was in financial difficulties. Sister Alice, henceforth Mother Alice, was made Superior and in October opened St. Francis Hospital. She soon showed her mettle. It was a success and so were St. Anthony's in St. Petersburg, and St. Joseph's, Tampa. She opened all three in the same difficult financial circumstances. There was a lot of anti-Catholic feeling in Florida at that time but it did not interfere with her work. She soon became one of the best known figures in the growing Catholic community and had many friends outside it.

Her success in Florida led to unforeseeable consequences in New York. St. Elizabeth's Hospital, a small institution her community ran in mid-Manhattan, moved to Washington Heights in 1918 and the premises it vacated on West 51st Street became a residence for working women. By 1934 the deterioration of the neighborhood made the site unsuitable for such a purpose and Cardinal Hayes made the surprising suggestion that a hospital be opened instead. While he authorized and encouraged the venture, he made it quite clear the Sisters were on their own. It did not seem to be the right time to open a new hospital because several of the existing ones had whole floors of empty beds, but the Sisters accepted his suggestion because they trusted his judgment in his chosen field and because they had Mother Alice in reserve. Her reputation as a reviver of sinking institutions was well established.

Her talent for that kind of work was tested severely at St. Clare's, but she emerged triumphant and wrote one of the great success stories in the history of the Church in New York. She began with a dilapidated building that had forty-five beds and no patients. She was helped by a small group of Sisters and nurses who answered her S.O.S. to Boston. There was not one doctor on the staff. She notified the local doctors by postcards followed by a personal visit. When she died, St. Clare's, with over five hundred beds and three hundred doctors, was the second largest Catholic hospital in the metropolitan area. It occupied a multimillion dollar modern plant in eight buildings, complete with a nursing school, a residence for graduate nurses, and a research center. It had overcome the initial hostility of many in the neighborhood and was regarded as a credit to the city as well as to Hell's Kitchen. The area provided a suitable outlet for Mother Alice's deep sympathy for the poor of all kinds, deserving and undeserving, and her special apostolate to drunkards of every kind and from every social level.

Mrs. Catherine McParlan (1855–1958) had a narrower range than Sister Loretto Bernard or Mother Alice and she walked a path on which few would have cared to follow her, but just as their names are linked inseparably with those of St. Vincent's and St. Clare's, hers is linked with the House of Calvary and the care of the destitute cancer patients who are so numerous in New York. Nothing in her background or early life gave any indication of the contribution she was to make to the Church in New York, and her opportunity to do so did not come until she was a woman of what was then considered a mature age.

In 1895 she suffered a double blow that a woman of lesser faith might well have found crushing. Her husband, a fireman, was killed in the line of duty and shortly afterwards their only child, a girl of five, died suddenly. Left alone in moderate circumstances and with a strong character and much energy, she rose above the temptation to self-pity. She was not attracted to the religious life but, believing that God never closes one door without opening another, she looked around for a good work to which she could dedicate herself as a laywoman. She found it in 1899 when she joined a newly formed group of Catholic widows, a dozen strong, called the Women of Calvary, who were interested in helping the cancerous poor. They opened the House of Calvary on a modest scale in two houses on Perry Street in Greenwich Village and began to care for as many as possible of the poor who could not afford hospitals or for whom the hospitals could do no more.

From the start, Mrs. McParlan was the only one of the group who could give it full time and after the death of their leader, Mrs. Anne Storrs, in 1906, she was clearly the mainspring of the organization. They had always wanted a hospital of their own and she succeeded in opening one in the Bronx in 1915. It was enlarged several times as the work developed. Though the day-to-day administration passed to younger hands some years before, Mrs. McParlan remained there until her own death.

Though the work of the Catholic hospitals was a major concern of Cardinal Spellman, he did not forget the Catholic patients in the public hospitals. In June 1952 he established the Hospital Apostolate to see that Mass was said and spiritual care provided regularly in as many as possible of the public and private non-Catholic institutions. It was a development of a work started by Monsignor John F. Brady on a limited scale in the early days of the Catholic Charities.

The massive Spellman building program in hospitals cost $500 million, much the greater part of which the Catholics raised themselves. Some of the cost of the new hospitals came from the Federal government under the Hill-Burton Act, and some very generous gifts came from individual non-Catholic donors or from foundations under their control. Large sums were raised on such occasions as the Cardinal's Episcopal Silver Jubilee in 1957, his Silver Jubilee in New York in 1964, and his Golden Jubilee in the priesthood in 1966. In 1960, he had an archdiocesan drive that raised $37 million. There were some large individual gifts from Catholic sources. One of them was the first Mary Manning Walsh Home.

LABOR RELATIONS

The building program brought him into close contact with organized labor with which his relations were generally friendly. He was a strong supporter of the unions and insisted that all Church work in New York be done with union labor. At the same time, he was not a blind partisan and he rejected totally the concept of the class war. In 1948 at the New York State convention of the A.F. of L., he pleaded for full cooperation between labor and management. He stressed his belief in fair collective bargaining and thought a strike should be the last resort. The Taft-Hartley Act had recently been passed over Truman's veto and was being denounced bitterly in the labor circles as a "slave labor law." He reminded them that it was the law of the land and urged them to obey it while it was. The labor leaders remembered gratefully his action in May 1947 when, during a slump in the construction industry, he announced a $25 million building program to help offset it.

His normally friendly relations with labor were strained for awhile by an unpleasant episode that occurred in 1949. It was a strike by the Calvary Cemetery workers. Though he was not legally obliged to do so, the Cardinal had consented willingly to the unionization of the workers in December 1946 and had agreed to the raise in their wages that followed. In two years, they went from ninety-seven cents an hour to $1.23 or $59 for a 48-hour week. At that time, the national average wage was $54.77 for a 40-hour week. The United Cemetery Workers Local 293, to which the Calvary workers belonged, was affiliated with the C.I.O. Food, Tobacco, Agricultural, and Allied Workers Union which the Cardinal suspected was subject to Communist influence.

When the contract expired on December 31, 1948, the Union asked for a 30 percent raise and management offered 8 percent. The Union wanted 48 hours pay for 40 hours work. Management objected to a 40-hour week on the ground that it would prevent Saturday burials and interfere with proper preparation for Monday ones. When neither side would budge, the strike began, on January 13th. By March 3rd, when more than a thousand unburied bodies had piled up, the Cardinal resorted to drastic measures and brought in the seminarians from Dunwoodie to dig graves and break the strike. On March 11th the strike was settled. The workers got a raise of 8.3 percent, the dispute over hours was placed in the hands of mediators, and soon eight hundred members of Local 293 voted to secede from the C.I.O. and join an A.F. of L. unit.

The Cardinal knew that in this country it takes more courage for a Catholic bishop to criticize labor than to praise it, but he was prepared to do so publicly as a candid friend when he thought it helpful or necessary. He did so on December 8, 1957, in a sermon from the Cathedral pulpit in which he denounced various abuses on all levels of organized labor and begged it to clean house. In the same spirit, he criticized John F. Kennedy's too-ready acceptance of the Supreme Court's decision on prayer.

SPECIAL INTERESTS

One of the pleasantest and most useful by-products of his trips as Military Vicar was the chance to see the work of the Catholic missionaries at first hand, to get to know many of them and their problems. It encouraged his long-term interest in the Society for the Propagation of the Faith, which he encouraged in every possible way. From 1942 on, the figures show all the money the missions received from any source in the Archdiocese. That year they got $565,116 and in 1967 $3,107,908. In 1947 the Missionary Cooperative Plan, by which each parish has two annual collections for the Society, one for the missions in general and one for a particular mission field, was introduced. Apart from fund raising, the Cardinal was often able to remove obstacles to mission work. In the Philippine War Claims case, he helped greatly to win recognition of the Church's just claims.

The Spellman years saw great changes in the liturgical and devotional life of the Church that made a deep impact on New York. What started as a stream of changes under Pius XII became a flood and even a tidal wave after Vatican Council II began. At first, the traditional devotions held their own (the Miraculous Medal Novena at Holy Cross Church on West 42nd Street was attended by thousands daily during World War II) but gradually attention shifted to the changes in the liturgy itself. Pius XII allowed the restored Easter Vigil (1951), some English in the administration of Baptism, Extreme Unction and Marriage, and in the prayers at funerals (1954), and the revised order of the Holy Week Services (1956).

One of Pius XII's major changes was the introduction of evening Masses (1953). That would have been impossible without a drastic revision of the laws regulating the Eucharistic fast. Therefore, the fast from midnight was abolished. In its stead, people were bound to abstain from solid food and all forms of alcohol for three hours. Later, in December 1964, even that was judged to be too difficult by Paul VI, and fasting from any kind of food or drink except natural water for one hour became the rule. The evening Masses were introduced slowly in New York. They began in 1957 with one or two on holydays that were not legal holidays. By 1959 permission was given to have them on New Year's Day, but not yet on Sunday or Corpus Christi. The vernacular Mass came in part in Advent 1964, and in greater part in March 1966.

Other events that touched the inner life of the Church in New York were the Archdiocesan Synod of 1950, the canonization of Mother Cabrini (July 7, 1946), and the beatification of Mother Seton (March 7, 1963) and Bishop John Neumann (October 12, 1963). The Synod was the first since Cardinal Farley's time and brought the local legislation up to date. The Cardinal was not inclined to multiply laws. It was held to mark the centennial of the erection of the Archdiocese. It is noteworthy that, while each of the three saints had definite links with New York, no one of them did his or her chief work here, and all three died outside it. St. Patrick received special attention.

It came to light that he had never been officially declared the patron of the diocese, though he had always been considered as such. That oversight was corrected and on June 12, 1962 Rome made him the official patron. Another change, and one of the first he made, was the establishment of a full-time Marriage Tribunal to deal with the increasing number of broken marriages.

Long before Vatican II made collegiality a common term, and even before he entered the Sacred College, Cardinal Spellman took a global view of his responsibilities in the Church and was always willing to help wherever he could. He attended faithfully all the International Eucharistic Congresses held after World War II and was Papal Legate to the first National Eucharistic Congress held in the Philippines (1956) and in Central America (1959). He continued his interest in Catholic Relief Services which spread to every continent and, while meeting the need for immediate relief, was trying to help the local inhabitants tackle the root causes of their poverty and distress.

"SPELLMANISM"

The Taylor Mission to the Vatican had never been acceptable to important segments of American public opinion and, when it ended with Taylor's resignation in January 1950, many thought the post itself should be abolished. Truman, a devout Southern Baptist and an active Free Mason, wanted to maintain relations with the Vatican but had to consider his own constituents. Having, he thought, given ample time for feeling to die down, he announced on October 20, 1951, a few hours before Congress was to adjourn, that he was nominating General Mark Clark as full-time Ambassador to the State of Vatican City. It soon became apparent that he had misread the situation badly. A group of several hundred Protestant ministers meeting in Washington under the auspices of the American Council of Christian Churches told him "he had driven a sword deep in the heart of Protestant America," and they applauded the statement that "Communism is an enemy, we are all against it, but we have another enemy, older, shrewder. It is Roman Catholicism and its bid for world power. In the United States, it is Spellmanism." There were legal obstacles to the Clark appointment, too. He could not accept the Vatican post without leaving the Army, which he did not care to do. Congress could have granted him a waiver but was unwilling to do so. Consequently, the nomination had to be withdrawn and the plan for an envoy to the Vatican was set aside for some years. Later, under President Nixon, the office of special representative was revived quietly and still exists.

A more authentic form of Spellmanism was spotted by some of the Cardinal's Catholic critics as they counted the number of bishops appointed through his influence. Though under all his predecessors only twenty New

York priests became bishops, nineteen were chosen in his time and five non-New Yorkers became auxiliaries of the Military Ordinariate. In addition, Monsignor Fulton J. Sheen was brought to New York from the Catholic University as National Director of the Society for the Propagation of the Faith and made a bishop, as was Monsignor Edward E. Swanstrom of Brooklyn, the director of the War Relief Services. Pius XII had made it easier to obtain an auxiliary because he considered the convenience as well as the needs of the bishop of the diocese. He took into account the case of priests who were considered to have rendered special service and were judged worthy of the episcopate even if, strictly speaking, their appointment could not be considered necessary. As papal honors on every level but the cardinalate multiplied, it was the only way to give such men adequate recognition. Moreover, as customs changed, especially in the larger dioceses, the number of functions at which people expected a bishop to be present increased and more help was welcome. In 1938 the Archdiocese had only one auxiliary bishop, but in 1967 it had ten. The Ordinariate had two, and Catholic Relief Services had one.

All that having been said, the number of bishops from New York was exceptional and it attracted much attention in clerical circles all over the country. It was not just a matter of promotions within the Archdiocese and the Province of New York. The Spellman influence was felt in many areas and none could feel immune. It was clearly through it that Archbishop McIntyre went to Los Angeles and Monsignor Patrick A. O'Boyle of the War Relief Services became Archbishop of Washington in 1948, and that Bishop John O'Hara, who had been sent to Buffalo in 1945, was moved to Philadelphia in 1951.

To many New Yorkers the clearest proof of his great influence in Rome came when, after the death of Archbishop Thomas E. Molloy, Bishop of Brooklyn, the diocese of Rockville Centre was cut out of Brooklyn and it was announced, on April 6, 1957, that both dioceses had been filled by former members of the Spellman staff. Bishop Bryan J. McEntegart went from the rectorship of the Catholic University to Brooklyn, and Bishop Walter P. Kellenberg from Ogdensburg to Rockville Centre. Those appointments settled the long-standing rumor that some day, in a very uneven exchange, New York would reclaim Queens from Brooklyn and give Staten Island in return.

Others paid more attention to the Spellman influence on the choice of cardinals, which was also conspicuous. Pius XII held only two consistories in almost twenty years. The Sacred College was smaller when he died than when he was elected but, in 1953, Archbishop McIntyre was admitted to it. In December 1958, in the first consistory of John XXIII, Archbishops Richard Cushing and John O'Hara were promoted, and in June 1967 Paul VI made Archbishop O'Boyle a cardinal. Before his death, four men who had worked closely with Cardinal Spellman had joined him in the Sacred College.

Three of them had belonged to his staff in New York. The fourth, his old friend Father Richard J. Cushing, was the third most remarkable man the Church in New England has produced. He owed his appointment as auxiliary of Boston in 1939, and as Archbishop there in 1944, largely to his good friend in New York.

Cardinal Spellman took criticism of his activity in that area in stride. He belonged to the Roman Congregation that selects bishops in this country, he was entitled to make recommendations, he felt his candidates were as good as any others, and he knew that his influence, which some of his colleagues resented, was often invoked on behalf of candidates he himself did not select. His intervention was not confined to this country. He did not always win his point, even under Pius XII, but he did so often enough to justify the comment that no English-speaking prelate since Cardinal Wolsey (d. 1530), the great Minister of Henry VIII, had such a voice in the affairs of the Universal Church. The death of Pius XII ended a relationship that could not be duplicated but, though it diminished, it did not end the Spellman influence in Rome. That was so because both John XXIII and Paul VI, whom he had known for many years, valued the services he continued to render the Holy See.

PUBLIC AFFAIRS

His interest in ecclesiastical matters did not blind Cardinal Spellman to the gravity of the problems presented to both the Universal Church and the American government by the way the war had ended in Europe. The rise of the Soviet Union, then the undisputed master of international Communism, to the position of one of the two major powers in the world, opened the prospect of a long-term global struggle between two incompatible systems. His strong and unwavering opposition to Communism was based on his conviction that it was irreconcilably opposed to the Catholic religion and the American system of government. He was convinced, too, that opposition to Communism would dominate American foreign policy for years to come and he took it for granted that Catholic opposition to it would not slacken. He disagreed wholeheartedly with those, Catholic and non-Catholic alike, who felt that time and some concessions by the Church or the United States, would bring the Communists to a happier frame of mind toward either. Though his worst fears had not been realized and the Russians had not entered Paris, as they did in 1815, the situation was bad enough and, in his opinion, much worse than it need have been. Once again, a major war in which American strength was decisive had been fought without any enforceable agreement about the terms of peace. Winning the war had become an end in itself instead of a means to an end.

The policy of unconditional surrender on which Roosevelt had set his heart and which had aroused very little criticism in America was unattainable without massive aid from the Russian Army. To obtain it, America had to make substantial political and territorial concessions that the Russians had hardly dared to hope for, and to obtain which they were quite willing to give assurances, however implausible, that would make it easier for the Americans to give in. When VE Day came on May 7, 1945, the Russians were in possession of 47 percent of prewar Germany, part of Austria, all of Hungary, Czechoslovakia, and Poland, and of the Baltic States they had seized before the war. Communist regimes had been established in Romania, Yugoslavia, and Albania. The prolongation of the war had led to economic prostration in Western Europe and to real danger that the Communists might come to power in France and Italy.

These things made very little impression in America at first. The general reaction to the end of the war was much as it had been in 1918. There was great relief that it was over, a strong desire to get back to normal as rapidly as possible (which included a rush to demobilize the armed forces), and a marked lack of enthusiasm for further foreign entanglements. There was also a general awareness of the great gap between what the war was supposed to accomplish and what it had actually done. The contrast between the situation in Poland and Eastern Europe on the one hand and the Four Freedoms and the Atlantic Charter on the other was obvious to all and distressing to many. Poland, which had been encouraged to resist Hitler, had been handed over lock, stock, and barrel to the Russians for the indefinite future. The Fifth Partition of Poland by Hitler and Stalin had been condemned here, but the Sixth Partition by Roosevelt and Stalin was accepted by much of the press and many of the journals of opinion, which tried to make it look right.

If some reactions here in 1945 were similar to those of 1918, others were significantly different because the political and military situation had been transformed permanently. America emerged from the war as the leading power in the free world. For the first time, that position was occupied by a country that had not sought it and was uncomfortable in it. In 1918, England, France, and Japan were important militarily and were friendly to us, Germany had been disarmed, and Russian military strength was negligible. From 1918 to 1936, when Hitler remilitarized the Rhineland, there was no sign of a substantial military force in Europe that was potentially dangerous to us. In 1945, Russia was the only important military power in Europe and she was unfriendly to America. The fundamental reason for our entry into both wars was the belief that a Europe dominated by a military power hostile to us would be a serious threat to our vital interests. In 1945 Europe was nearer to that position than she had been in 1914 or in 1939.

The gravity of the situation was not grasped here at once because, among other things, of the peace movement. The general yearning for peace had been strengthened by the fear of the unimaginable horrors of an atomic war, in which America would be vulnerable too, and it led people to cling almost desperately to the hope that the United Nations Organization (which was founded in San Francisco in April 1945) would guarantee peace. The wartime propaganda had convinced millions, erroneously, that the failure of the League of Nations to avert World War II was due to America's refusal to join it. It seemed clear to them that we were bound to join the U.N. and that our membership would guarantee its success. The balance of power was thought to be completely outmoded, and those who thought it might still be useful and even necessary were suspected of being opposed to the U.N. The American hierarchy welcomed the establishment of the U.N. as better than nothing, but had reservations, shared emphatically by Cardinal Spellman, about the uses to which it could be put by the non-Christian forces.

If the awakening from the dreams of lasting peace and a return to pre-1941 insulation from world affairs was not immediate, it was rapid enough, and was precipitated by events few could misunderstand. In March 1946, Churchill delivered his famous speech at Fulton, Missouri, in which he warned of Russian designs on Europe and made the term "iron curtain" a household word. In March 1947, Russian pressure on Turkey and open support of the attempted Communist takeover in Greece evoked the Truman Doctrine by which America pledged sufficient military and economic aid to block Russia's plans. In June 1947 the Marshall Plan—to assist the economic recovery of Western Europe on humanitarian grounds and to avert a Communist takeover by peaceful methods—was proposed to Congress. It started in 1948. Strangely enough, the Russians were invited to share the benefits. Stalin could not believe that even the Americans would offer him so much for nothing and he refused to have anything to do with it. In February 1948, the Communists seized total control of Czechoslovakia and on April 1st the Russians begàn the blockade of Berlin that was broken by the Anglo-American airlift. It lasted until September 1, 1949.

Three major developments in 1949 had lasting effects. In March the North Atlantic Treaty Organization (NATO) was formed to protect the western world from the Communists. It became at once and remains the cornerstone of our policy in Europe. Less than four years after VE Day, the balance of power was back in force. The British and Chinese were unable, and the Russians unwilling, to play the roles Roosevelt had in mind for them when the war ended. In September, Truman announced that the Russians had the atomic bomb, and in December the Communists conquered mainland China. The Chinese Communists had long enjoyed (and still have) much support in certain academic circles here, where they were described as agrarian reformers with only a superficial link with Communism that would be broken when their just demands for a better social order were granted.

These developments led to a major change in public opinion here. The people accepted reluctantly the fact, of which they had been given no inkling in 1940–1945, that we were now necessarily involved in a series of permanent military alliances that required maintaining an immense defense establishment with hundreds of overseas bases. These alliances also involved vast expenditures for the economic support of our allies, actual or potential. By 1967, military and economic aid to foreign countries had amounted to more than one hundred billion dollars and, as is still the case, there was no end in sight. That was in addition to the much greater sums spent on our own defenses.

The Communist triumphs in Europe and Asia brought great suffering to the Church. Wherever Communists took power, they started a persecution that is still in progress. It varies from country to country depending chiefly on the number of Catholics, their proportion of the population, the depth of their loyalty to the Church, and the quality of their leaders. The Communists give nothing they can afford to withhold and are uninfluenced by foreign protests. The script is the same everywhere and usually, but not always, involves the trial of the chief bishop on trumped-up charges of treason. In Czechoslovakia, Cardinal Beran and his successor, Cardinal Tomasek; in Yugoslavia, Cardinal Stepinac of Zagreb; and in Hungary Cardinal Mindzenty of Esztergom were imprisoned after patently fraudulent judicial proceedings. In Poland Cardinal Wyszynski of Warsaw was imprisoned without a trial. In China, things went more quietly. Cardinal Tien and his successor, the future Cardinal Yü-Pin, eluded their enemies and escaped to Taiwan, but the persecution on mainland China, described by the Inter-Nuncio, Archbishop Riberi, as "the most subtle and total in history," practically obliterated the Church there.

To their credit, most of the American journalists and many public officials denounced the trials. President Truman called the Mindzenty trial "the infamous proceedings of a kangaroo court," and Secretary of State Dean Acheson called it "wanton persecution." The Beran and Mindzenty trials aroused special interest in New York because both defendants were accused of having conspired, separately, with Cardinal Spellman, whom a Czech paper called "the archenemy of everything that has the least connection with progress." On a later occasion, when he preached an anti-Communist sermon in Munich, he was described by a Soviet paper as "The Archangel of Atomic War."

The awakening of public opinion here to the reality of the Communist menace was not caused solely by events in Europe and Asia. It was helped greatly by the discovery of Communist espionage and subversion here that led to an anti-Communist movement in which the Catholics became deeply involved. During the war, there had been recurrent and unspecified rumors of such activities but nothing came of them, and neither the government nor the press showed much interest in them. After 1945 the gap between the goals and achievements of the war, not to mention subsequent developments, led some who wondered how it came about to ask if it could all have been due to misfortune or honest miscalculation or exceptional incompetence—or if something sinister like espionage and treachery had been added to those parts of the puzzle.

The answer was not long in coming. From 1948 to 1953 the public was treated to a series of revelations of Communist activity, some of which led to the trial and conviction of the accused. It appeared that the secret of the atomic bomb was betrayed to the Russians by the Rosenbergs who were executed in 1953, and that the Russians had their agents among the Anglo-American-Canadian scientists working on atomic energy all through the war. It appeared too that much of the information about Russian activity here had been reported to the government before 1939 and had been ignored.

The most famous episode in the anti-Communist movement activated by these revelations was the trial of Alger Hiss, the president of the Carnegie Endowment for International Peace and a former State Department official, who was imprisoned for perjury in denying that he had given Whittaker Chambers confidential State Department documents for transmission to the Russians. Apart from its great intrinsic importance and its dramatic aspects, the Hiss case stirred up deep feelings that have not yet subsided fully and that made it the most controversial political trial here since the impeachment of President Andrew Johnson. One element in that was the time factor. Though by ordinary American standards the proceedings were relatively swift, the case was before the public eye from August 3, 1948, when Hiss was accused, to March 12, 1951, when his conviction was upheld by the United States Supreme Court. In England it would have taken about six weeks.

One special feature of the Hiss case, which was tried in New York, was the caliber of the people who rallied to his aid. Most of them denied Communist sympathies or affiliations and few of them took any visible interest in the eleven nondescript leaders of the Communist party who were convicted in October 1949 of advocating the overthrow of the American government by force. The Communists made very few converts among the American equivalent of the workers and peasants. Most of their members and sympathizers came from the well-to-do and better-educated classes who had done very well and could hope to do better under the American system. No single explanation of their hatred of it and their admiration for the Soviet system—whose crimes had been well known for years—applies to all of them. Their blind loyalty to the party line justifies Stalin's response when he was urged, in 1936, to moderate his policies lest public opinion in the West be alienated. He said, quite correctly: "Never mind, they'll swallow it."

A practical reason why some were so vehement in denying even the possibility of Hiss's guilt was fear. They were not enrolled Communists and they had refrained from overt actions, but they had gone along with the party line and feared being caught in the popular backlash against it and against all with Communist associations. The least plausible explanation of their conduct, and the one many of them favor, is that they were innocents who were led astray. In fact, they were people who prided themselves on their sophistication and on having special insights denied to their ordinary neighbors.

A new chapter in the anti-Communist movement opened on February 9, 1950 in Wheeling, West Virginia, when Senator Joseph R. McCarthy of

Wisconsin made a speech charging that the State Department was full of subversives. Coming so soon after the conviction of Alger Hiss on January 21, 1950, his speech caused a national sensation and the resultant uproar lasted until 1954. It is hard to know which annoyed his critics more, his extravagant and often mistaken attacks on individuals, or his capacity to reach the ordinary people—a trait in which he excelled all the other anti-Communist speakers of the time.

Since most Americans were anti-Communist, the attempt to make that a Catholic issue fizzled. Nearly all the Catholics were anti-Communist but not all supported Senator McCarthy. Many felt he overstated his case and they joined a new movement called the anti-anti-Communists, an umbrella organization or movement of diverse groups that, with varying degrees of sincerity, professed a desire to curb subversion in any form, but only if it could be done with a scrupulous regard for the civil rights of the accused. The division in Catholic ranks was seen when, on April 4, 1954, Senator McCarthy spoke at the annual Communion Breakfast of the Police Holy Name Society in New York. Cardinal Spellman was present and clearly intended his presence and his brief remarks on Communism to be supportive of the guest speaker. Five days later in Chicago, Bishop Sheil delivered a sharp attack on the Senator in speaking at a UAW-CIO Convention. Archbishop O'Hara of Philadelphia joined the Cardinal and many other bishops in thinking the Senator had rendered a public service in alerting so many to the menace of Communism.

It was a real misfortune for the country that the long overdue investigation of Communist infiltration was not carried out by a bi-partisan panel that put the security of the country first. As it was, it became a partisan issue and both sides share the blame. The Republicans used it to discredit the Democrats and the Democrats hit back by denying the existence of the problem. Much of the blame goes to President Truman. He was wholly unsympathetic to Communism in any form, but he was also a stubborn and intensely partisan man. In his view, any admission of laxity in security would aid the Republicans, and anything that aided the Republicans was bad for the country. When Coolidge succeeded Harding and learned of the Teapot Dome Scandal, he cleaned the rascals out. By so doing, he did himself, the Republican Party, and the country a favor. Truman could not bring himself to do the same. By his stubborn refusal to admit the guilt of Alger Hiss, even after the Supreme Court upheld his conviction, and by his repeated charge that the anti-subversive investigations were a red herring, he lost credit even for the quiet anti-subversive purge he did carry out.

THE KOREAN WAR

One of the immediate results of the fall of China was the Korean War, which broke out on June 25, 1950, and was interpreted as a test of America's will to resist Communist aggression. Although it was nominally a U.N. enterprise, it was mainly an American affair. Before it ended in 1953 in a draw, 1.6 million members of the United States Armed Forces had taken part in it and 24,000 had been killed. It led to an expansion of the armed forces and a corresponding expansion of the Ordinariate. Once again the Military Vicar was looking for chaplains, and once again he was off on his travels. In 1951 he was invited by General Van Fleet to visit the troops in Korea. He did so, and he spent Christmas with them every year from 1951 to 1955, except for 1952 when he went to Greenland. The Korean War was the first one America decided not to win. It did so partly because of pressure from our allies who feared the outbreak of the Third World War. It was also one in which we refused to accept compulsory repatriation, which would have meant sending refugees back to the Communists in North Korea. We had sent thousands back to Stalin after World War II.

Even after the Korean War ended, the Military Vicar's travels continued. From 1951 on, he spent every Christmas with the troops outside the United States. From 1962 to 1966, except for 1963 when he went to the South Pole, he visited Vietnam. In other years, he went to Europe, Asia Minor, Labrador, parts of the Far East other than Korea and Vietnam, and the Arctic. He approved of American intervention in Korea and South Vietnam. In the latter case, he deplored the Kennedy Administration's involvement in the coup that led to the overthrow and murder of President Diem and his brother, and he foresaw that it would lead to very unpleasant consequences for Vietnam, America and the Church.

On his travels as Military Vicar or Archbishop of New York, he was often asked to address groups which, even though friendly, were quite critical of America, and he welcomed the chance to state the American position as he saw it. He never thought things were perfect here in either Church or State. He knew that the leading power is never popular and that some people find it hard to forgive those who have helped them. Just as he did not like to see Catholics treated as second-class citizens here, he did not like to see Americans, Catholic or non-Catholic, treated as barbarians abroad. Many years ago, a Fenian leader observed that England had the ear of the world. After 1945, as an incessant stream of anti-American propaganda, often fed from here, poured through the Western world, he could have said that the Marxists and pro-Marxists with their liberal allies or dupes had the ear of the world.

In October 1953, the Cardinal spoke to a large Catholic Conference in Brussels and, after acknowledging America's debt to Europe and her pleasure in repaying it, dealt with two topics that troubled his hosts. They were the Congressional investigations of subversion here, which he defended, and the allegedly dominant if not exclusive role of materialism in American life, which he denied. It seemed unnecessary to point out that at that very hour Belgium was sheltered happily by NATO and had shared very willingly in the Marshall Plan. The question of materialism here came up again in Brazil after the Eucharistic Congress in Rio in 1955, when Cardinal Spellman was astounded to hear from a Brazilian cardinal that the root of all the social problems confronting the Church in Latin America was the spirit of materialism imported from North America.

A Catholic President

One public event that had a special interest for Cardinal Spellman and all other American Catholics was the election of John F. Kennedy to the presidency of the United States. It was important chiefly because it removed a symbolic obstacle to full participation by Catholics in the political life of the country. The campaign of 1960 was less exciting than that of 1928 because the times and the issues were different and feeling did not run as high in either camp.

The candidates were very different, too. Kennedy, the youngest man ever elected to the presidency, was not the product of a local political machine. He had no administrative experience of any kind and so had escaped the enmities that accrue to all executives. His position as Senator from Massachusetts had enabled him to seek and acquire national recognition. His youth, his Harvard background, his naval service, his social position, and his family's great wealth and fame appealed to many who had opposed Smith in 1928 or would have opposed him in 1960. Some who recalled the earlier campaign noted with amusement that in 1960 all the snobs were on Kennedy's side. One of the meanest tactics in the 1928 election was the false charge that the Smiths were not quite up to the social duties of the White House. That could not be said of the Kennedys, who personified style and glamour for so many and who made even the Beautiful People take a momentary interest in politics.

Though the fires of religious bigotry were banked, they were still burning before the Democratic Convention met in Los Angeles in June. Kennedy faced the issue squarely in the primaries and especially, in May, in West Virginia where the anti-Catholic feeling was very strong. He stressed that he was not the Catholic candidate, that he did not speak for the Church, and that no one in it spoke for him. He stressed, too, his full support of the separation of Church and State and his opposition to State aid for parochial schools. He had powerful opposition in the party. Eleanor Roosevelt urged him to accept the Vice-Presidency so that he could "learn and grow." Truman criticized his youth and, some felt, his religion in a nationally televised speech.

Kennedy was nominated on the first ballot with 806 votes to Lyndon B. Johnson's 409, but it was noted that he got only thirteen votes from the entire South while Johnson, who had been claiming for years that he was not a Southerner, got 307. Recognizing that he could not win the election without the South, he persuaded Johnson to accept the Vice-Presidential nomination, a move that brought both those very different men to the White House. Neither could have reached it without the other. The campaign was strongly influenced by television. The Kennedy-Nixon debates showed that the time available on television made it impossible to discuss any issue in depth, and what mattered and was very important was the general impression left with the audience.

The religious issue worked both ways. The Catholics were not solidly pro-Kennedy, though undoubtedly many voted for him who would not have done so if his religion had not been made such an issue. It is thought that about 20 million pieces of anti-Catholic literature were distributed. Kennedy himself left nothing to chance. In September he made a televised address to the Houston Ministers Association in which he repeated his views on Church and State.

In the end, his victory was a very narrow one, the closest in popular votes in seventy-six years, though there were millions more votes cast than in 1956. The Electoral College vote was 303 to 219. If fewer than 12,000 voters had shifted in Hawaii, Illinois, Missouri, New Mexico, and Nevada, Nixon would have won. The single factor influencing most swing voters was religion. Many Catholics who had voted against Stevenson returned to the Democratic fold and about 4 million Protestants switched to the Republicans. Like every Democrat but Roosevelt in the preceding hundred years, Kennedy received a minority of the votes cast. In his case, it was 49.7 percent. He lost upstate New York by 250,000, but his huge vote in New York City gave him the State by a comfortable margin. Once Nixon had lost, many pointed out that no incumbent Vice-President had been elected President since Van Buren in 1836.

Those who thought the election of a Catholic President would bring the Pope to the White House or subordinate the interests of the American government to those of the Church here or abroad, or that Catholics would dominate the government, soon discovered how baseless their fears were. Kennedy found it easy and expedient to bend over backwards to conciliate such potential critics, and as the Catholics neither sought nor expected favors from him everyone was contented.

His extraordinary posthumous hold on the affections of the people was not due to the achievements of his rather undistinguished administration but to the popular resentment of the manner and timing of his death. He would have been mourned deeply and widely anyway, but the assassination added a special dimension to the general grief and evoked an emotional response both here and abroad unequalled by the death of any American since Lincoln. That one on whom the gods had lavished so many of their gifts should die so early by treachery and violence at the hand of a faceless antisocial misfit seemed to many too much to bear. It was a heavy blow to the cult of youth that is so congenial to the American temperament. The impact was heightened by the uniquely close relationship of the Kennedy family with the press and media. One consequence of it all was the election of Robert F. Kennedy as a United States Senator from New York in November 1964. He was the first Catholic elected to that office by popular vote.

THE SECOND VATICAN COUNCIL

Though he was on the key committees and attended every session, Cardinal Spellman did not attempt to play a major role in the Second Vatican Council (1962–1965), which was easily the most important event in the history of the Church since 1870. He confined his efforts largely to two topics that had a special interest for him. The first was the Declaration on Religious Liberty (Dignitatis Humanae), which was promulgated on December 7, 1965. It was the result of intensive study and much controversy in the Council and was regarded as one of its most notable achievements. It was influenced by Father John Courtney Murray, S.J., the outstanding American scholar in that field, whom the Cardinal took with him as his personal theologian. Father Murray, whose views were suspect in some circles here and in Rome, would not otherwise have had a chance to attend the Council as an expert.

The second topic was the Relation of the Church to non-Christian religions which the Council dealt with in the Declaration (Nostra Aetate) of October 28, 1965. The section dealing with the Jews strongly repudiated anti-Semitism in any form and absolved the Jews of collective guilt of the death of Christ. Though he had good personal relations with the leaders of other religious groups, the Cardinal was not enthusiastic about the Ecumenical Movement from which he thought much more was being expected than it could possibly produce. He had similar reservations about the liturgical reforms and the move to decentralize authority in the Church. In spite of that, he went along with the changes. In October 1966, he established the new office of episcopal vicar in the Archdiocese, a new title for the old office of "dean" in each county. On that occasion, he announced that he had offered his resignation because he was over seventy-five and that it had been refused.

A PAPAL VISIT

If the Second Vatican Council was the most important event in the Cardinal's time in New York, the visit of Pope Paul VI on October 4, 1965 was the most spectacular. It originated with the desire of the Pope, whose pontificate laid such heavy stress on peace, to support the United Nations' efforts in that direction. He chose to do so by a personal visit that would commemorate belatedly the twentieth anniversary of the founding of the

U.N. (April 1945) and provide the occasion for an impassioned plea for peace to a forum representing all mankind. Since the Vatican Council was in session, it was decided that the visit be limited to a single day. How best to divide that day was the subject of much anxious deliberation by the experts on protocol and security. They came up with a schedule that made it one of the busiest days in the Pope's life and one of the most memorable days in the history of New York. It was an extremely gratifying day for the Cardinal, who was the prime mover behind the arrangements.

Though officially the Pope was the guest of the U.N., he had several other important things to consider. His was the first papal visit to the Western Hemisphere, to the United States, to New York State and City, and to two of the major dioceses in the Universal Church, New York and Brooklyn. How were all the inescapable formalities involved in such a visit to be handled in so short a time? The answer was through the courtesy and cooperation of the officials he was expected to meet. He was greeted at the airport by the U.N. officials, Secretary of State Dean Rusk, House Speaker John McCormack, Senators Robert and Edward Kennedy, Governor Nelson Rockefeller, Mayor John Lindsay, and of course, Cardinal Spellman and Bishop Bryan McEntegart. The Pope had brought with him all the other American cardinals, except Cardinal Ritter of St. Louis who was ill.

After the reception at the airport, the papal party set out to meet a very tight schedule. A motorcade through Queens and Spanish Harlem brought him to the Cathedral for the solemn liturgical reception. Then the Pope went to the Waldorf to call, as protocol required, on President Lyndon Johnson, who had most kindly come from Washington for the occasion. After a quiet lunch with his own secretary and Cardinal Spellman, the Pope went to the U.N. where he spoke to a carefully screened audience of about 2,000 of whom he later met about five hundred. In his speech, he paid high tribute to the U.N., which he called "the obligatory path of modern civilization and of world peace" and "the last hope of concord and peace." He then made his famous appeal: "No more war. War never again." He warned against encouraging artificial birth control and urged the U.N. to multiply bread rather than diminish the number of guests at the banquet of life. Later at Holy Family Church on East 47th Street (the Catholic church serving the U.N.), he held a special ecumenical reception for representatives of other faiths.

In the evening, he said Mass for 92,000 people at Yankee Stadium and then visited the Vatican Pavilion at the World's Fair, where he saw the *Pietà*, on his way to the plane. He was thought to have been about the twenty-five-millionth person to have seen it here. The police estimated that almost four million people saw him at some point during the visit. The TV people thought at least 100 million people in this country watched him and more than twice as many elsewhere. The success of his visit, in which there was not a single unpleasant incident, was due to cooperation on every level. Only the weather, which was unseasonably cool, could have been better.

ROUTINE DUTIES

Just as the Cardinal's work as Military Vicar developed a pattern of its own, so did his work as Archbishop of New York. There was only a certain amount of time and energy available and as demands on him increased and he grew older, something had to give. It was not easy because he enjoyed work and he knew the people wanted to see him. Many things, like his dealings with the Holy See and the other bishops, his share in the work of the Ordinariate, his contacts with the government and the meetings of the various charitable corporations he headed, could not be delegated. He felt obliged to attend dedications of new buildings, university and college commencements, parish centennials, religious order jubilees, many civic functions, and similar events.

Still, some of the burden could be shared. From the beginning many, and later most, but never all routine affairs were handled by the Vicars General, especially by Archbishop McIntyre and later by Archbishop John Maguire who became Vicar General in 1953, auxiliary bishop in 1959, and coadjutor without right of succession in 1965. Monsignor Edward R. Gaffney (1898–1952) was Vicar General from 1948 until his untimely death in 1952. He was a competent, self-effacing, and notably understanding man whom the priests as a body held in special affection and respect.

Though very faithful in attendance at the Solemn Mass each Sunday in the Cathedral, the Cardinal preached there fewer than a dozen times. Most of his sermons were on formal occasions such as his installation, his various jubilees, and the arrival of a new Apostolic Delegate. On July 3, 1941, as a gesture of sympathy for Poland and respect for the man, he sang the Mass and gave the English sermon at the funeral of Ignatz Paderewski, the great Polish patriot and musician, who was the first of the three laymen who have been waked in the Cathedral. The other two were Al Smith in October 1944 and Robert F. Kennedy in June 1968. In September 1959, he denounced Khrushchev's visit to this country and ordered a Holy Hour in every parish, with special prayers for the country, on September 14th, the feast of the Exaltation of the Holy Cross.

DEATH OF CARDINAL SPELLMAN

Though it was clear in the last months of 1967 that his health was failing, the Cardinal kept to his regular schedule and was planning another Christmas visit to Vietnam. Because of that, some of the holiday festivities were held early in the hope that he could share in them. On Friday evening, December 1st, after a busy day, he dropped in at the Waldorf at a benefit for the Casita Maria. It was his last public appearance. The following morning, he suffered a massive stroke, was anointed by Bishop Terence Cooke, and was rushed to

St. Vincent's Hospital where he died just before noon. He was fortunate in the manner of his death because, supreme activist that he was, he would have found invalidism of any kind very hard to bear.

The general public condolences and the assemblage of notables at his funeral were a tribute to the special position he had come to occupy in the Church and in public life at home and abroad. The foreign tributes included messages from General DeGaulle of France, Chiang Kai-shek of China, DeValera of Ireland and Salazar of Portugal. The Spanish government mourned the death of "a true friend of Spain." The domestic tributes showed something of the range of his interests, and of the contacts he had established with the leaders of many sectors of American life. Revealing too, though stressed less by the media, was the very large number of ordinary people who filed through the Cathedral by day and night from the arrival of the body on Sunday afternoon to the funeral Thursday morning. Many were thought to be non-Catholic veterans who had met or seen him on his trips as Military Vicar.

The funeral, which was seen by millions on television, was celebrated according to the new liturgy. The concelebrants, led by the Apostolic Delegate, Archbishop Raimondi, included nine cardinals (among whom were those of Armagh, Quebec, and Westminster), Archbishop Maguire, the bishops of the suffragan sees and the Cardinal's nephew, Father John W. Pegnam of Boston. The Cardinal of Mexico was present, too. The mourners were led by President Lyndon Johnson and Vice President Hubert Humphrey, making a rare joint appearance, and included most of the American hierarchy, Governor Rockefeller, Mayor Lindsay, a host of other public officials, some fifty Orthodox, Protestant, and Jewish clergy-men, many other prominent people and an overflowing congregation. The eulogy was given by Father Robert I. Gannon, S.J., the Cardinal's biographer, who described him as a "complex and very positive character, the wrong man to cross when he decided he was right and you were wrong" and as, first and foremost, a faithful and devoted priest. The interment took place in the Cathedral crypt.

Epilogue

The attention paid to the death of Cardinal Spellman led to exceptional interest in the selection of his successor, and a number of possible choices from different parts of the country were discussed at some length in the secular press. In the meantime, the routine affairs of the Archdiocese went on as usual. Archbishop John Maguire was the Administrator. Many of the New York clergy, believing the appointment of Cardinal Spellman had set a precedent, shared the expectation that another extern would be sent here. They shared, too, in the general astonishment when, after the shortest vacancy in the history of the See, it was announced on March 8, 1968, that Bishop Terence Cooke, the youngest of the local auxiliaries, was the new Archbishop. With the exception of Archbishops Hughes and Corrigan, he was the youngest man ever appointed to New York. He had not been on any of the published lists and he had neither the Roman experience and contacts, nor the national or international standing some prophets had judged necessary or desirable.

The Archbishop, whose official appointment was dated March 2, 1968, was installed on April 4th, by the Apostolic Delegate in the presence of six United States cardinals and about fifty other bishops. A number of Orthodox, Protestant and Jewish clergy attended. The public authorities present were headed by President Johnson and included the Governor, the Mayor and many others. The armed forces, of which he became the Military Vicar that day, were represented too. The joy of the day was marred by the murder of Dr. Martin Luther King, Jr., which led to riots in 125 cities in twenty-nine States. On April 28, 1969, the Archbishop entered the Sacred College of Cardinals (which he did more rapidly than any of his predecessors) and he received Cardinal Spellman's titular church of Saints John and Paul. The consistory, in which thirty-three Hats were conferred, was the largest ever and included three other Americans: John J. Carberry (1944–   ), Archbishop of St. Louis; John F. Dearden (1907–   ), Archbishop of Detroit; and John J. Wright (1909–1979), who had been moved from Pittsburgh to the Roman Curia in January 1969.

Terence James Cooke (March 1, 1921–   ) was born on LaSalle Street in Manhattan, and baptized in Corpus Christi Church. He was the youngest of three children, and both his parents were born in County Galway, Ireland. When he was four, his father, who was a chauffeur, moved the family to St. Benedict's parish in the Bronx, which was then in the care of the Benedictine Fathers. Terence attended the parochial school and then went on to Cathedral College and Dunwoodie. He and the other members of the class of 1946 were ordained on December 1, 1945, by Cardinal Spellman because of the accelerated course of studies made necessary by the war.

Father Cooke's first assignment was to studies in education at the University of Chicago. After brief periods as assistant at Saint Athanasius in the Bronx, and as chaplain at St. Agatha's Home, Nanuet, he entered the School of Social Service at the Catholic University. On his return from Washington with a Master's Degree in Social Work, he was assigned, in June 1949, to the Catholic Youth Organization and the Youth Division of Catholic Charities where he remained until he became procurator of the seminary at Dunwoodie in January 1954. During that time, he resided at the Cenacle of Saint Regis and assisted at the new parish of Saint Jude, Manhattan. From 1950 to 1956 he was also an instructor in the Fordham University School of Social Service.

On January 1, 1957 he joined Cardinal Spellman's staff, on which he served in various capacities until December 2, 1967. He was successively a secretary, vice-chancellor, chancellor, and on February 15, 1965, a Vicar General, and he lived in the Cardinal's Residence from May 1958 on. Promotion in office was matched by promotion in rank, and he became a papal chamberlain, a domestic prelate, a protonotary apostolic and, on September 15, 1965, a bishop. His appointment as titular bishop of Summa and an auxiliary of New York was made on the same day on which Bishop Maguire became coadjutor-archbishop without right of succession and Monsignor William J. Moran of San Francisco became the new auxiliary of the Military Ordinariate. His two new auxiliaries were consecrated on December 13, 1965, by Cardinal Spellman, who was assisted by Archbishop Maguire and Archbishop McGucken of San Francisco.

Like Cardinals McCloskey, Farley and Hayes, the three among his nine predecessors who had been ordained for New York, Bishop Cooke came to his high office with an extensive knowledge of the clergy, of the parochial and institutional structure of the Archdiocese, and of the lay societies that he had been acquiring since his student days. He was the first alumnus of either seminary to become the Archbishop. He knew from the inside the central administrative agencies (which had hardly existed in Cardinal McCloskey's time) and the charitable institutions. He knew, too, many of the large number of people, clerical, religious and lay, Catholic and non-Catholic, with whom they deal. His work in the C.Y.O. and as auxiliary bishop had taken him to every county and to most of the parishes.

In turn, many of them had come to see in him some of the qualities that had brought him the patronage of Cardinal Spellman. They noted the capacity for work, the eye for detail, the phenomenal memory, the genuine enjoyment of the routine duties of his office—including by a special grace, meetings and paper work—and the other administrative skills that were evident even before he became Vicar General. By nature inclined to prefer persuasion to command and unlikely to provoke confrontation, he had a firm belief in the possibilities of dialogue and in the presence in every camp of the goodwill it presupposes. His basic optimism and self-confidence, his outgoing personality and his gregarious nature made it easy for him to get on with people on every level—particularly with the clergy and the ordinary people, whom he put at their ease more thoroughly than any of the preceding archbishops had done.

Because Archbishop Cooke was less involved than his predecessor in Roman and international affairs, it was expected that his administration would concentrate on local affairs and in that area would continue the policies and programs of Cardinal Spellman. In fact it has differed greatly from them as it has adjusted to major and unexpected developments in both the Church and the City of New York. Since those developments lie outside the scope of this book, the detailed and extensive treatment they deserve must be reserved for another day. It is enough to say here that the changes made by Vatican II were the most important because they affected the inner life of the Church in New York more than any event in its history. We cannot understand what has happened here unless we place it in the context of the changes in the Universal Church. Vatican II and its effects will be felt, studied and debated for generations and have already produced an abundant literature.

Among the basic elements that did not change for the Catholics of New York was their loyalty to the Holy See. Hence like their coreligionists (and millions of other people) in the Free World, they followed with the closest attention the dramatic events that unfolded in Rome in August through October 1978, in the year of the Three Popes. They were grateful for the extensive, friendly and respectful coverage those events received from the press and especially from television. They shared in the sympathetic farewell to Paul VI, in the joy that greeted the wholly unexpected election of John Paul

I, and in the sorrow evoked by his equally swift and unexpected departure.

The second conclave of 1978 was even more surprising in its results than the first and brought to the papal throne one of the most remarkable ecclesiastics of modern times. Its impact was heightened because, while the great gifts of Karol Cardinal Wojtyla of Cracow were well known to his native Poland, they attracted little attention in the West until he became John Paul II. One of the most interesting things about his election was the instant recognition, here and everywhere else, that he is a man of a most exceptional kind, with a very special capacity for leadership.

First impressions were confirmed by the Pope's visit to the United States in October 1979. Those who shared in it or merely saw it will not soon forget the reception he received. At his formal reception in St. Patrick's Cathedral, he summed up his purpose in coming and the perennial mission of the Church in New York. His purpose was "to confirm you in your holy, Catholic and apostolic faith, to invoke upon you the joy and strength that will sustain you in Christian living." Her mission is, "the expression of her vital and distinctive service to humanity; to direct hearts to God, to keep alive hope in the world. And so we repeat with St. Paul: 'This explains why we work and struggle as we do, our hopes are fixed on the living God.' " (I Tim., 4:10)

Glossary of Terms

Apostolic Delegate—The personal representative of the Pope in a country with which the Holy See does not have formal diplomatic relations. He is sent to the bishops of the country, not the government, and is usually a titular Archbishop.

Bishop, Auxiliary—A bishop who is assigned as an assistant to a residential bishop. He does not enjoy the right to succeed to the diocese when it is vacated. This title is not used for assistant bishops who are titular Archbishops in a given see but do not enjoy the right of succession. They are called coadjutors without right of succession.

Bishop, Residential—A bishop who is in charge of a particular diocese.

Bishop, Titular—A bishop who is not in charge of a particular diocese. Usually he is assigned a diocese that no longer exists, so that its name is perpetuated. These titular sees are assigned to auxiliary bishops, to papal diplomats, to the higher officials of the Roman Court, and often to retired bishops.

Chancellor—A priest who is in charge of the official documents incidental to the administration of a diocese. Frequently he undertakes other secretarial duties at the discretion of the bishop.

Church Councils—Depending on the area covered, these are: A. Ecumenical—includes all the bishops of the world and the heads of the major religious communities of men. It can be summoned and ended only by the Pope. He presides over it either in person or through his representative. Its decrees are not valid until approved and published by him. B. Plenary—includes all the bishops of a country containing more than one ecclesiastical province. C. Provincial—includes all the bishops of a particular province.

Diocese—The territory governed by a bishop. It is the normal unit of government in the Church. The Pope alone can erect, divide, alter, unite or suppress dioceses. A diocese is subdivided into episcopal vicariates or deaneries which in turn are subdivided into parishes.

Faculties—The permission given to a priest to say Mass publicly, to administer the sacraments, and to preach in a given diocese.

Jubilee or Holy Year—A celebration generally held every twenty-five years by the Pope. Special indulgences are granted to pilgrims who visit Rome and perform the prescribed spiritual exercises in designated churches. By custom, it is extended at the end of the year to the Universal Church, for the benefit of those who cannot go to Rome and who perform the spiritual exercises at the time and in the places designated in the letter extending the Jubilee.

Local Ordinary—A cleric with ecclesiastical jurisdiction in the external forum. Jurisdiction is the power to govern the faithful for the supernatural for which the Church was established by Christ.

Military Ordinariate or Diocese—The diocese erected to care for the spiritual needs of the members of the armed forces of a given country and their dependents. It has jurisdiction over them, the chaplains who serve them, and people on the bases the armed forces operate.

Nuncio—The title borne by the Papal Ambassador to any government with which the Holy See has formal diplomatic relations. He is usually a titular archbishop. If he is not the dean of the diplomatic corps, he is called the Pro-Nuncio.

The Pallium—A small vestment worn on the shoulders by the Pope, and by residential archbishops who are metropolitans. Before receiving it from the Pope the latter may not exercise metropolitan jurisdiction on those liturgical functions, e.g., ordinations, that require its liturgical use.

Prefect Apostolic—A priest in charge of a Prefecture Apostolic. Usually he is given the power to confirm, to consecrate chalices, to give or withdraw priestly faculties and a few other things normally reserved to bishops.

Prefecture Apostolic—The first stage in the ecclesiastical organization of a mission area.

Province—A group of dioceses united under an archbishop who is called the Metropolitan of the Province. Usually it has at least three dioceses including the archdiocese. The dioceses other than the archdiocese are called suffragan dioceses or sees and their bishops, suffragan bishops. The Province of New York, coterminous with the State, has eight.

Provincial—In religious orders, the higher superior in a given area who has local superiors under him or her and is in turn under the Superior General of the entire community.

The Roman Curia—The collective name of the various congregations, tribunals, commissions and offices that assist the Pope in the government and administration of the Church.

The Sacred College of Cardinals—These are the highest counselors of the Pope, and their membership is now drawn from all parts of the world and from the highest officials in the Roman Curia. Their chief duty and exclusive right is to elect a Pope when the Holy See is vacated. At present, every Cardinal must be a bishop.

Titular Church—Each Cardinal is the titular pastor of a church in the diocese of Rome and that is the legal basis for his participation in the conclave that elects a Pope. The Pope is elected by the pastors of the principal churches in Rome.

Vicar Apostolic—A titular bishop who is in charge of a vicariate apostolic.

Vicariate Apostolic—A mission area in which the Church is not sufficiently well established to be made a diocese.

Index

334